LEARNING LEGAL RULES

A Student's Guide to Legal Method and Reasoning

Second Edition

James A Holland LLB, PhD

Associate Dean (Academic Studies),
Faculty of Law, University of the West of England, Bristol

Julian S Webb BA, LLM,
Dip Socio-Legal Studies

Principal Lecturer in Law, University of the West of England,
Bristol

BLACKSTONE
PRESS LIMITED

First published in Great Britain 1991 by Blackstone Press Limited,
9-15 Aldine Street, London W12 8AW. Telephone: 081-740 1173

© J. A. Holland and J. S. Webb, 1991

ISBN: 1 85431 263 4

First edition 1991
Reprinted 1991
Reprinted 1992
Second edition 1993
Reprinted 1994

British Library Cataloguing in Publication Data
A CIP cataloguing record for this book is available from the British Library

Typeset by Kerrypress Ltd, Luton, Bedfordshire
Printed by BPC Wheatons Ltd, Exeter

LEARNING LEGAL RULES
A Student's Guide to Legal Method and Reasoning

Contents

This book is dedicated to our respective parents and particularly to the memory of Jim Holland.

Foreword

The Rt Hon Lord Templeman MBE,
Lord of Appeal in Ordinary

This book answers all the questions which a student of the law ought to ask and propounds answers to questions which every lawyer and every judge should ask himself from time to time.

The lawyer is a manipulator of words; this is an assertion and not a criticism. Language is the means of disclosing facts, expressing ideas and applying principles. The ultimate solution of any legal problem is to be found in the application of basic principles to ascertained facts. The difficulties which obstruct the ultimate solution lie in the selection of appropriate principles and the rejection of irrelevant facts. The practice of the law is an art and not a science because the applicability of principle and the analysis of complicated facts depend on the language employed. The judge resembles a conductor of a nineteenth century symphony. The conductor and the judge must establish the main themes, eliminate discordant sounds and present an harmonious whole. Modern litigation, like a twentieth century symphony, suffers from the obscurity of themes and the tyranny of discordant sounds. In this book the authors set out to teach the art of conducting the law.

For the student the first task is to become well acquainted with the instruments of English law and Community law, namely, primary legislation, delegated legislation, judicial authorities and textbooks. The first three chapters introduce all these sources of the law. The fourth chapter deals with the interplay of law, fact and language. The authors illustrate the fact that the flexibility of words affords a danger to logic as well as an effective aid to explanation. Rhetoric and jargon may disguise principle and obscure uncomfortable fact. The fifth and sixth chapters are invaluable guides to the dissection and application of precedents — those themes which enable the lawyer and the judge to determine the presence or absence of compatible variations. The seventh and eighth chapters manfully grapple with the different problems of construing English and Community legislation. The differences are substantial; Articles 30 and 35 of the Treaty of Rome, prohibiting quantitative restrictions on imports and exports, enabled the European Court of Justice to establish a free trade regime which could only have been established by about four English statutes containing 500 sections and 15 Schedules and hundreds of statutory instruments. The interplay of United Kingdom law and Community law is explored, not always in agreement with the House of Lords. Finally, in Chapters nine and ten, the art of reconciling fact, principle and language in English law and in Community law is explained and illustrated.

The book is aimed at law students but is valuable to the citizen who knows no law, the lawyer who has forgotten some law and a judge who fears that a just result may be buried under torrents of oral and written words. The book should enable all its readers to guard against asking a silly question and thus provoking a silly answer. The language of the book is clear and the style interesting and thought-provoking.

The authors make a new contribution to legal literature and, at the same time, illuminate and recognise old controversies.

Templeman
House of Lords

Preface

This second edition has come only two years after original publication. One would have thought that a book on how lawyers reason might be safe for a few more years, but there have been a number of significant changes in the law even in this short time. Consequently, although we have kept to the same general structure as in the first edition, every chapter has been changed to some extent.

We have sought to do four things in this edition. First, we have incorporated some key new decisions affecting English Legal Method and reasoning; notably the House of Lords' decision in *Pepper* v *Hart* concerning the interpretation of statutes. We have also taken this opportunity to update the material on the use of computer databases, to take account of recent changes to the court system, and to extend the book's discussion of fact analysis.

Secondly, we have been extremely grateful for all the comments received on the first edition and have tried to make use of them wherever possible in order to make the text clearer. We have, hopefully, also continued to learn from our own students; it is they who often bear the brunt of our experimentations. As a result, some of our ideas for explaining Legal Method have changed or developed and we have sought to incorporate those changes into the text.

Thirdly, we have attempted to extend and update the European aspects of our work (throughout the text, but especially in Chapter Ten). Our problem here was twofold: making sense of what is happening, and keeping the additions as short as possible. The major additions here are the inclusion of new text on interlingual problems in law (chiefly in Chapter Four) and on the principles governing the direct applicability and effect of Community legislation.

Fourthly, we have altered some of the exercises and added new ones. In particular, we have removed the exercise which originally appeared in the Appendix and inserted a different one, together with two students' answers. Our hope here was that by providing this form of example, rather than supplying an answer ourselves, we could better demonstrate the standard that can be obtained by students in applying Legal Method principles.

The most common comment we received on the first edition was that the book was readable and user-friendly. This had been one of our primary aims in writing *Learning Legal Rules*, and we were delighted to hear that we had succeeded for so many of you. We hope that the second edition achieves a similar response.

Finally (and somewhat ironically in a book concerning language and interpretation), we would like to clarify one point arising out of a few letters we received: although not wishing to tempt fate, can we add that James Holland is still alive and well; the dedication in this book relates to his father who shared the same first name!

James Holland
Julian Webb
5 April 1993

Preface to the First Edition

Why Read a Book on Legal Method?

If you are new to studying law as an undergraduate or postgraduate student, the chances are that you are finding it (or will find it) a distinctly different experience from any previous education you have had; if not a disconcerting one!

This book is intended to help you develop both the learning and reasoning skills appropriate to the study of law. The most common problem a law student faces is not *'what are the rules?'* but rather *'how do I make use of the rules?'*. Our text aims to arm you with the techniques required to support your studies of the substantive law subjects. It is based upon our own experiences as both students and teachers of law, and it particularly reflects a combined total of about 15 years of course development work on LLB courses in England and in Malaysia; on European law programmes and on undergraduate and postgraduate courses for (amongst others) accountants, business executives, computer scientists and social workers.

What this Book is About

This book is not about learning specific laws, it is about learning to study the use and construction of legal rules. Studying law at any level, whether as a specialist lawyer or not, is not just a matter of acquiring legal knowledge about 'substantive' law subjects, such as Contract Law, or Crime. It is also fundamentally about developing 'Legal Method', or what is sometimes called the technique of 'thinking like a lawyer'.

A great deal of mystique has built up around the idea of 'thinking like a lawyer'. We would suggest that, in essence, it is concerned with the way lawyers reason and analyse, and, in particular, the adoption of the rules and principles that they use in legal reasoning.

In law, reasoning is based on three things explored in this book:

First, it is dependent upon an ability to **find** and make sense of a wide variety of legal material including documents such as *statutes, law reports* and textbooks (See Chapters One to Three).

Secondly, it is built upon the **interpretation** of *authorities*; and by the term authorities we mean primarily *statutes* and reported *cases* that can be found in a law library (see Chapters Five to Eight, and Ten).

Thirdly, it is also based upon an ability to **construct** arguments both about the *facts* of a case, and as to *how* and *why* a particular authority should or should not be applied in that case. Inevitably, this overlaps substantially with our second point. As the Oxford jurist (ie, legal philosopher) Ronald Dworkin has said: **'legal reasoning is an exercise in constructive interpretation'** (1986:vii). That is probably as good a definition as any to send us on our way (see Chapters Four, Six, Eight and Nine).

Research, both here and in the United States, has shown that for many students, learning to 'think like a lawyer' is the most important of legal skills; however, many also feel that it is not always sufficiently emphasised in the curriculum (see, eg, Sherr & Webb, 1989:239–40). We have written this book in an attempt to fill the gap which we feel exists for a practical, but critical, introduction to legal method.

Within these pages we therefore hope you will find an attempt to demystify Legal Method; to show that, in fact, it probably is not so very different from (for example) thinking like a doctor, an accountant, or a systems analyst. 'Thinking like a lawyer' largely requires techniques of information-gathering and reasoning that are of general application. Indeed, we would suggest that much of what passes for 'thinking' is in reality a matter of style—of talking and writing like a lawyer.

This book takes a step-by-step approach to the mechanics of reasoning, precedent and interpretation, with the support of practical exercises which are designed to enable the student to gain experience in, as well as knowledge of, the area.

How to Use this Book

This book can be used either to support a course of study in Legal Method, or as a self-teaching guide to the subject. We are aware that more and more people are now studying law by independent or distance-learning methods, and have tried to anticipate their needs, in addition to those of students on traditional full- or part-time courses. We would, however, say that the course of study laid down in this book cannot be wholly followed without access to, at least, a basic library containing some primary sources (law reports and statutes).

Unlike many legal texts, which are made up of largely self-contained chapters, this book adopts a narrative structure, which is intended to build your knowledge sequentially from Chapter One to Chapter Ten. You are advised not to read the later chapters until you have worked through the earlier material. Having said that, there are two chapters which are more heavily theoretical than the rest (Chapters Four and Nine). These may not be appropriate material for all courses at either first degree or postgraduate level, and so we have tried to ensure that the material in them may be disregarded (or taken far more selectively) without destroying the sense of the rest of the text.

In order to make the text easier to follow, we have avoided the use of footnotes. All case references appear in the text. References to books and articles in the text are cited using what is called the Harvard reference system. This gives the name of the author followed by date of publication and (if appropriate) the page number, thus, 'Smith (1986:123)'. The full citation of references is listed at the end of each chapter. Some of those references are marked with an asterisk (*). This indicates a text which we consider particularly suitable for further reading; though you should (where possible) be guided by your teachers with regard to what additional reading is required for your course.

Before we begin, a final word of advice: learning legal rules is *not* like the substantive law subjects you will study as a student. Contract and Crime (etc.) are concerned with the rules and policies which govern specific areas of human behaviour. Legal Method, on the other hand, is about developing skills that you should apply to those substantive topics. It follows that because Legal Method is not a substantive subject, it does not consist of hard and fast rules and cannot be 'learnt' in the same way. Courses on Legal Method do not produce 'notes' that can be memorised. 'Thinking like a lawyer' is a technique that you must develop by practice. It is for that reason that most chapters contain self-testing exercises. We have not removed the answers from the main text, though question and answer are separated by a line, thus:

So if you do not want to know the answer before attempting the question, either do not let your eyes wander, or cover that part of the page!

We also believe that studying law should not be a boring experience, so our final hope is that you find the rest of this book not only useful, but also enjoyable.

Julian Webb
James Holland

REFERENCES

Dworkin, R. (1986) *Law's Empire*, London, Fontana Press.
Sherr, A. & Webb, J. (1989) 'Law Students, the External Market and Socialization' *Journal of Law and Society*, vol. 16, p. 225.

Acknowledgments

This book would not have been possible, let alone have reached a second edition, without the support of many people. In particular, we would like to thank our colleagues at UWE, Bristol: Dr Adrian Chandler, Carol Crowdy, Frances Winch and Tim Angell. Our thanks also go to a number of colleagues elsewhere: Dr Philip Leith of Queen's University, Belfast; Helen Norman at Bristol; Phil Jones at Sheffield; and Nick Wikely at Birmingham Universities; all of whom have provided valuable comments which have influenced the contents of this book. We remain indebted to Dr Geoffrey Samuel of Lancaster University for access to his translations of material from the works of Bergel and Villey, cited in Chapter Nine. We must also acknowledge the unsolicited but much appreciated assistance of those university and college teachers who have shared their experiences of using *Learning Legal Rules* with us. You have helped us greatly in the preparation of this new edition. Finally, we must once again thank everyone at Blackstone Press both for their enthusiasm and friendliness.

A more personal debt is owed to Vicki Webb, without whose support this second edition would have been short of one author, and to Rebecca and Joseph Webb, whose arrival since the first edition meant that it nearly was!

Last but not least, our gratitude also goes out to our students, past and present, who over the years have been the victims of our particular attempts to introduce legal method skills into the law curriculum. Within this group special thanks are due to Fiona Salvin and Jonathan Grant for their assistance with the material for this edition.

We owe a special word of gratitude to The Rt Hon Lord Templeman MBE, Lord of Appeal in Ordinary, for agreeing to write the Foreword to this book; and for the interest he has shown in our approach to the development of legal method.

The authors and publishers also wish to thank the following for permission to reprint copyright material: Butterworth & Co. (Publishers) Ltd for extracts from the *All England Law Reports*; The Controller of Her Majesty's Stationery Office for an extract from *Statutes in Force*.

Table of Cases

Chapter One

What is Law?

A friend who is a shopkeeper has recently received a consignment of camping and other knives, including a small number of flick-knives. She is concerned that the police may take action if she were to display and sell these flick-knives to the public, and asks you for advice.

How can you find out if she would be breaking the law?

Obviously you need to know the law relating to flick-knives, displaying them in shop windows etc. How do you go about this?

It is easy to assume that the 'law' can be found in one book; that somewhere there is a book which will give you the answer to every legal question you might pose. If this were true there would be little need for lawyers! Clearly it is not true. So a fundamental legal skill must be the ability to find the law. It is the purpose of both this and the following chapter to set you on the right road.

Why ask 'What is Law?'

To anyone other than a philosopher, the question 'what is law?' may seem rather strange. In fact, if you are new to studying law it is an extremely important one. The ability to find the law presupposes that we know how to identify it: this leads us back to that fundamental question: 'what is law?' This chapter answers that question by looking at the 'institutional' sources of law. This is the easiest way of beginning to define 'law', and the most practical, though it does not pretend to tackle the philosophical problems attached to the question of defining law in the abstract. We shall present our definition in two stages. First, we shall briefly distinguish law from other (what we call 'social') rules; then we shall explain what we mean by an 'institutional' source, and how that helps us to identify laws.

Legal Rules and Social Rules

Law, in the sense that we are using it, is definable as a system of rules. It guides and directs our activities in much of day to day life: the purchases we make in a shop; our conduct at work and our relationship with the state are all built upon the foundation of legal rules. Of course, any society is governed by a mass of other rules which are not laws in the formal sense, but merely social conventions—perceptions of 'proper' behaviour. In reality, these are also means of controlling social conduct, but the different mechanisms employed to enforce these rules reflect different social values regarding the behaviour in question. Thus, while most of us would accept that anyone stealing the possessions of another should be liable to a penalty under the criminal law, we might be rightly surprised to see someone in court for eating peas off their knife! Regulating the latter is not really so important to our society as to require the force of law.

Why some rules should be given the force of law and others not is another of those philosophical questions to which we do not have a full answer. Law certainly is not the same everywhere; it will reflect different values in different cultures and different epochs. Take laws governing adultery for example; in modern English law, a person who has a sexual relationship with another's spouse will incur no legal penalty (though he or she may end up being cited in a divorce case if the other found out). In Islamic Law, the *Qur'an* prohibits adultery by making it a crime, and subjects the parties to the *hudud* punishment of flogging or stoning (though the evidential requirements are so stringent that, unless the adultery is confessed, it is unusual for the full punishment to be handed out); in Ancient Greece, to give an historical example, a man who seduced another man's wife could face a claim for compensation, since he had violated the 'property' rights of his lover's husband. In a more deterrent mode, the seducer risked other physical penalties—the most widely used of which involved pushing radishes up his backside, or pulling out his pubic hair!

Thus, the different laws on adultery could be said to exist as a reflection of different religious or moral standpoints taken by the law; perhaps they also reflect diverse views of human sexuality, or the different status of men and women in a society. This cultural dimension of law can be quite important in developing our understanding of why particular legal rules have developed, or why different legal traditions have evolved in different countries.

The Institutional Sources of Law

Generally, laws are identifiable by the fact that they take a form which distinguishes them from those social conventions. Their form tells us that they are derived from an 'institutional' source that is socially recognised as having the power to create law. Only laws so created can be said to be legally *binding* upon the individual, or even upon the state itself. Thus our first step in finding the law governing the sale of flick-knives would be to discover whether any of the legal institutions have had anything to say on the matter.

In English law there are three main institutional sources which we shall consider: Parliament, the Courts, and the European Community. By taking them as our starting point, we are defining legal material by concentrating on the 'law-makers'. This is, perhaps, a slightly narrow basis. It does, however, emphasise the importance of what are often called the 'primary' sources, and distinguishes them from the 'secondary' or literary sources of law that provide only a commentary on or analysis of the rules (see Chapter Two).

Parliament

Parliament is significant for three reasons. First, it is the originator of what is probably the single most important modern source of law—that is, **statute law**. Secondly, through its legislative powers, Parliament is able to give law-making powers to other bodies, such as local councils and Government departments. This results in a form of law that is referred to as **delegated**, or **secondary legislation**. Thirdly, Parliament's delegatory powers are being increasingly used to create sets of **informal rules** which operate within the framework of formal rules created by statute.

Statute Law

A statute is a document which contains laws made by Parliament. Each statute usually deals with a separate topic such as, eg, the Theft Act 1968, or the Sale of Goods Act 1979. Statutes are now found in virtually all fields of law and regulate all sorts of activities. Some Acts affect our lives without us even knowing about them. For instance, how is the date of Easter calculated? For the answer to that one has to turn to a strange Act of 1750—The Calendar (New Style) Act. This Act determined many calendar calculations, including leap years and Easter. The strangest provision, however, came with the calendar itself. In 1750 Britain used the old Julian calendar. Many other countries had switched to the Gregorian calendar. There was a difference of eleven days between these calendars. When it was the end of September here, it was October elsewhere. The Julian calendar was wrong and a change had to be made. The question was, how? The Act provided the answer by stating that September 2nd 1752 was followed by September 14th 1752. Eleven days were thus simply deemed not to exist! This led to riots in the streets; not least because some people were not getting birthdays in September 1752, and everyone was suddenly eleven days older!

Statutes are created directly by Parliament, following procedures laid down in both the House of Commons and the House of Lords. The details of that process belong more properly within a course on Constitutional Law, but it should be noted that a statute (also called an *Act of Parliament)* only becomes law after it has been introduced into Parliament as a Bill, been approved by Parliament and has satisfied the formality of obtaining the Royal Assent. Once an Act has been passed it is unimpeachable, so far as English law is concerned. As Lord Campbell put it in *Edinburgh & Dalkeith Railway* v *Wauchope* [1842] 8 Cl & F 710: 'no Court of Justice can inquire into the mode in which it was introduced into Parliament, nor into what was done previous to its introduction, or what passed in Parliament during its progress.'

This rule is reflective of a wider principle which is referred to as the *Sovereignty of Parliament*. This is a rather legalistic way of describing Parliamentary dominance within the legal system. An Act of Parliament is the supreme form of English law; indeed until comparatively recently it could also be supreme for many other countries which were dependent territories of the British Crown, so that the Westminster Parliament has been significant in shaping much of the law of what is still described as the 'Common Law' world. The fact of supremacy is particularly important in Legal Method, since it is used to impose major limitations on the law-making powers of the judges, who will be reluctant to do anything that might be construed as usurping the law-making function of Parliament. The United Kingdom's membership of the European Community has almost certainly had an impact on the relationship between the Courts and Parliament, particularly following the decision of the House of Lords in *R* v *Secretary of State ex parte Factortame (No. 2)* [1991] 1 AC 603; [1991] 1 All ER 70. We shall discuss this case further below, and in Chapter Ten.

The growth of legislation has been a key feature of the English legal system over the last hundred or so years. It reflects the extent to which government has extended its control over our activities. This is particularly true of the legal developments that followed the emergence of the Welfare State in the 1940s. As a result, many important fields, such as employment, child care, and social security law owe their modern existence almost exclusively to statute. This has, of course, meant that there has been significant growth in the volume of legislation actually in force. This does not necessarily mean that there are more Acts of Parliament in force now than, say, thirty years ago, because Parliament is also active in removing redundant or unwanted legislation from the statute books, but there is evidence that the number of Acts being passed is increasing—by 20 per cent in the decade between 1964 and 1974 for example (Miers, 1986). If we take into account the length of legislation, that too suggests that there is an expanding statute book. Miers (1989) has also shown that the volume of legislation by this measure has risen steadily from an average of 745 pages per session in the 1950s to 1525 pages in the 1980s.

Against this background there would therefore seem a fair chance that there is legislation somewhere governing the display and sale of flick knives.

Acts of Parliament are not only a major source of law in their own right, they provide a legitimate means whereby Parliament can pass on, or delegate, its law-making powers to another body or person. Parliament's power of delegation has in fact been widely used for many years, but because its exercise is much less visible than the act of legislating, it is easy to lose sight of the importance of delegated legislation.

Delegated Legislation

Most delegated legislation is published as **statutory instruments**, these are also sometimes referred to as *Regulations.* The volume of statutory instruments is considerable. Taking the important category of general instruments (that is, those that affect the general law, rather than some local or private interest) it is possible to say that, as a rough average, they have been passed at a rate of about 2,000 per year, thereby exceeding the number of Public Acts by a ratio approaching 20:1. Statutory instruments are not just quantitatively important. It is worth remembering that, in practice, the operation of whole areas of law, such as social security and immigration, is dependent upon a network of regulations, which will be of greater day-to-day significance than statute. For instance, the important rules governing employees' rights on the sale of a business are covered in the Transfer of Undertakings (Protection of Employment) Regulations 1981, a statutory instrument rather than an Act.

Delegation always requires the express authority of an Act of Parliament, which, in respect of any delegated legislation created under its authority, will be referred to as the *parent Act.* The parent Act will not only give authority to the process of delegation, but also will set the parameters of the delegated power. Sometimes these will be extremely wide and generalised, for example, where an Act provides that 'the Secretary of State may make such regulations as he sees fit', but equally they can be highly detailed and specific. For example, s. 5(1) of the Social Security Administration Act 1992 requires 18 paragraphs and six sub-paragraphs to specify the powers available to regulate claims and payments of benefit. Practically, the ability to delegate carries great advantages, as delegated legislation can take effect more quickly, and deal more easily with technical detail than statute law; however, Parliament does not maintain the same level of supervision over delegated legislation, so there is concern that those advantages are bought at some cost to the Constitution.

Informal Rules

Informal rules are mostly created by ministerial powers granted under the authority of statute. They go under a wide variety of names, such as Directions, Guidance, Circulars and Codes of Practice. They are called informal because they can be contrasted with the formalities necessary to create an Act or statutory instrument, and because their structure and operation is also often less formalised. The bulk of this book is concerned with the formal rules, so we shall deal with informal rules in some detail here.

Do not let the term 'informal' lead you into thinking that these rules are unimportant. They play a significant part in the regulation of a wide variety of public bodies. Although it may seem rather odd that we should have such different types of rules, it can be argued that the difference in form is reflective of a genuine difference in function. The chief function of informal rules is to regulate official discretion. By discretion we mean, to quote Professor Galligan (1986:1):

the extent to which officials . . . make decisions in the absence of previously fixed, relatively clear, and binding legal standards.

Discretion is of considerable importance in legal contexts. As we shall see, it is both difficult and often undesirable to make a legal rule so precise that there is only one way that an official could apply the rule. Few rules are so clear that they can be used like an on-off switch. The person using the rule cannot always say with certainty 'yes, it applies' or 'it does not apply here'. This means that officials must often resort to their own judgment in deciding whether a rule applies. Informal rules are instrumental in guiding officials in the use of their discretion, and can actually impose significant restraints upon it. At the same time, however, there is concern that the increasing use of such rules reduces the ability of Parliament and the courts to maintain a check on the activities of state bureaucracies.

To an even greater extent than delegated legislation, informal rules are a modern development in the English Legal System. The range of operation of such rules is almost as varied as the names they are called. Social workers, police officers and social security officials, amongst others, all operate within a framework of such rules. Baldwin & Houghton (1986:239) have suggested that informal rules will fall into one or other of three categories:

Procedural rules: Many bodies lay down procedures for outsiders to follow—eg, procedures for making a claim for social security benefit. Informal rules often play an important part in establishing these procedures, although, in practice, they are often the result of an amalgam of statute, statutory instrument and informal rules.

Interpretative guides: These are 'official statements of departmental policy . . . expressions of criteria to be followed, standards to be enforced or considerations to be taken into account' (Baldwin & Houghton, 1986:241) which may be made available to citizens to inform them of their rights, etc. An example of such a guide is the guidance issued by the Inland Revenue to taxpayers.

Instructions to officials: Although akin to interpretative guides, these are often intended purely to give guidance to officials, not to citizens. This may mean that they operate as secret codes, though this is not always the case. For example, the *Adjudication Officers' Guide* used by social security officials is published and thus would seem to fall between our two categories.

It is intended primarily as official guidance, but can also provide useful information to the citizen on how the rules will be applied.

Informal rules do not apply to the public at large (so they would not be of immediate relevance to the problem we posed at the beginning of the chapter). Some are not published, while others are available publicly. Many will not be legally enforceable, but even here there is considerable variation. Consider, for example, the Codes of Practice created by the Home Office under powers in the Police and Criminal Evidence Act 1984. A particularly important one is Code of Practice 'C' governing the detention and questioning of persons held at a police station. It is not directly enforceable in the courts, by virtue of s. 67 of the 1984 Act. This means that breaches of the Code are not themselves breaches of law; however, the Act does enable them to be used by a court to justify excluding any item of evidence that has been improperly obtained by the police (see, eg, *R* v *Samuel* [1988] QB 615; [1988] 2 All ER 135).

In form, such rules will also vary considerably; often their structure is not so very different from the formal rules they support, but equally they may lack the detailed language of Acts and Regulations, and particularly the emphasis on internal definition often found in the latter. A particularly interesting example of the types of informal rule that exist is provided by the *Social Fund Manual*. This contains a two-tiered system of informal rules which are provided to officers of the Department of Social Security to assist in determining applications made by social security claimants, for grants or loans for special needs. The distinction is made between 'Directions' and 'Guidance' in the scheme. The former, as the name suggests have to be strictly applied by the officers, while the latter is intended only to be indicative, leaving the officer with some degree of choice in applying it to the claim at hand. As you can see from the following, the style of the two types of rule is quite distinctive (we would advise you to concentrate on the style and form of the language, rather than the content, which is difficult to understand when taken out of its technical context). You might also like to contrast these examples with the form and language of statutes (a number of examples of which appear in Chapter Three).

Directions:

2. *A social fund payment may be awarded to assist an eligible person to meet important intermittent expenses (except those excluded by these directions) for which it may be difficult to budget.*
. . .
8. *A person is eligible for a budgeting loan if, at the date of the award, the following conditions are satisfied–*
    (a) he is in receipt of income support, either for:
        (i) each week of the last 26 weeks; or
        (ii) each week of the last 26 weeks, less a single period of not more than 14 days; . . .

Guidance:

> *1016 . . . S.F.O's [Social Fund Officers] must use their discretion to arrive at a decision which is reasonable in all the circumstances, but they should:*
>
> > *(a) be aware of the possibility that either national guidelines or local priorities may not apply in a particular case; . . .*
>
> *. . .*
>
> *6377. A C.C.G. [Community Care Grant] [for minor structural repairs to property] up to a suggested maximum (see Annex 4) may be awarded, but only when . . . there are no other readily available means to meet the cost, eg help from the L.A. Housing Department, relatives or charities.*

Differences in form, function and language between rule-types are not merely a matter of esoteric interest, because those differences can affect decisions about the legitimacy of the rules. Thus, to take our example of the *Social Fund Manual*, we can see that the Directions, which are binding on officials, are couched in more detailed, imperative language, and possess a structure which is hardly distinguishable from conventional secondary legislation. The Guidance is less closely structured, less formal, and less peremptory in its language, reflecting its function of merely *guiding* officials in the exercise of their discretion. It is not surprising that the courts have used this difference in function and form to help determine the legality of such rules. When the Secretary of State published Guidance which used the mandatory language of the Directions, he was held to be acting in excess of his statutory powers—see *R v Social Fund Inspector and Secretary of State for Social Security ex parte Roberts, The Times*, 23 February 1990. To put it simply, guidance which directs officials to do something is no longer guidance.

Although legislation is extremely important, it cannot operate in isolation. Legislation requires implementation. On a day-to-day basis, that is the function of a wide variety of officials, whose job is either to carry out Parliament's commands, or else to make sure that other organisations or private individuals are doing so. In this process, questions may be raised about the effect of a particular piece of legislation. Often these will involve technical questions of *interpretation*. On a day-to-day basis officials are constantly engaged in interpreting both primary or secondary legislation, but sometimes we require a more authoritative statement of what the law means. That process of interpretation is usually undertaken by the courts.

The Courts

The courts are not only important as interpreters of legislation, they are also the second major source of English law in their own right, through the development of the **Common Law**, a term which we first need to define.

The Meaning of 'Common Law'

This term is used in two ways:

To distinguish Common Law from statute: 'Common Law' is used to describe all those rules of law that have evolved through court cases (as opposed to those which have emerged from Parliament) over the past 800 years. Despite the growth of statute, English law is still generally understood in Common Law terms. By this we mean that the way in which we think about law, and categorise laws, is still heavily influenced by the old Common Law *forms of action* which determine what types of problem we now call 'contract', 'tort', etc.

To distinguish between 'legal families': Comparative lawyers use the term 'legal families' to group together legal systems which share certain common features. In the Western legal tradition, there are two dominant 'families' which we call Civil and Common Law systems, though there are a number of legal systems, such as the Scottish, which reflect elements of both traditions.
    The term Common Law is thus used as a means of defining all those legal systems in the world whose laws are derived from the English system. We use the term English rather than British with good cause. For reasons of history, not only Scotland, but also Northern Ireland and even the Isle of Man and Channel Islands have evolved as separate legal systems from England and Wales. Although much of the legislation passed by the Westminster Parliament now governs the whole United Kingdom, there remain substantial differences in law and the legal processes that apply in the different jurisdictions that make up the British Isles.
    The Common Law world remains extensive; it includes the Federal laws of the United States of America, and most existing or former members of the British Commonwealth, such as Australia, Canada, Hong Kong and Singapore, though in many such systems the English influence may co-exist with elements of local customary law or even with other legal traditions, such as Islamic Law.
    The term Civil Law describes those systems which have developed out of the Romano-Germanic legal tradition of continental Europe. It is the Civil Law tradition which dominates within the present European Community. Of the 12 member States, only two, the Republic of Ireland and the United Kingdom (subject to the *caveat* already noted), belong to the Common Law world. As large sections of this book will be concerned with comparative issues between English and 'European' Law, it is worth taking a brief excursion at this point to highlight some of the features of these two legal traditions.
    Underlying a number of practical variations there is, ultimately, a rather different way of thinking about law within each tradition. In Civilian systems (as they are called) one can conventionally identify a higher level of conceptualisation, reflected in a theoretically complex 'institutional basis'

of Civil Law (see, eg, Stein 1984). This is sometimes said to create a more 'scientific' or rational legal system than the highly pragmatic tradition of the Common Law (cf. Chapter Nine of this book). This has a number of practical implications.

First, it can be said that our dependence upon descriptive factual categories (the forms of action) may actually hold back new developments in English Law, because we do not have the conceptual apparatus to incorporate change easily. This is sometimes seen as the key difference between the English and Roman traditions (eg, Samuel, 1990).

Secondly, the modern Civil Law tradition is chiefly based upon principles of *codified* law. The modern process of codification in Europe is one that can be traced back to about the eighteenth century, though the structure of most Western European legal codes owes a major debt to the thinking of the ancient Roman lawyers, and particularly to the *Corpus Iuris Civilis* (meaning literally, 'the body of civil law') of the Emperor Justinian, who ruled from 527 to 565 AD. The assumption underlying a codified legal system is that it is possible to create a set of texts containing an authoritative statement of the law, usually in the form of Civil and Criminal 'Codes', or sub-divisions thereof. Although English lawyers also talk about 'codifying' legislation, the term is used to mean rather different things in Common as opposed to Civil Law systems.

In the Common Law, a codifying Act is primarily a tidying-up operation It is a piece of legislation which brings together all the existing law on a topic, both statute and case law, and converts it into a single entity— the codifying Act. An oft-cited example is the original Sale of Goods Act of 1893. The aim of tidying-up is one which codifying Acts share with the continental codes. However, by contrast with the continent, codification in England has been used as a limited means of imposing legislative coherence on a particularly problematic area of law, such as the sale of goods, or the law relating to theft. What English codifications have not done is to produce a complete restatement of the whole of, say, Commercial or Criminal Law in a statutory form. Yet it is precisely the latter approach that has been adopted in the majority of Civilian systems. Though the codification of the English Criminal Law has now been proposed by the Law Commission in its Reports of 1985 and 1989, the Commission's approach, as exemplified by its latest paper on the subject (Law Commission, 1992) has been to propose a far more gradual and particularistic codification process than originally envisaged (see generally de Búrca & Gardner, 1990; Gardner, 1992). This would seem to suggest that we still have a long way to go before English lawyers are prepared to use codification as anything other than a discrete solution to a specific problem. For the English, codification has never been the key mechanism for organising and conceptualising the rules of law that go to make up a legal system.

Thirdly, it follows that, in theory, codification reduces the role of the Civil Law courts to simply interpreting and applying the law of the Code. Common Law lawyers have traditionally argued that Civilian judges have not had the dual roles of their Common Law counterparts; that is, being both interpreters of legislation, *and* custodians of a distinct body of case law. In truth, that difference has probably been over-emphasised, so that we are in danger of missing the significance of case law in continental Europe. In many European states, the law (or part of it) is not fully codified— German Administrative Law, is one such example—and most countries have their own systems of precedent, some of which are not so far removed from English practice. Paradoxically, perhaps, the way in which the Codes tend to be structured leaves European judges with far more discretion in interpretation than their English counterparts are supposed to have! We shall come back to this point in Chapters Seven and Eight; but, for now, let us return to considering the details of that English system.

The Court Structure

In looking at the English courts as a source of law, it is important to draw two basic distinctions. One is the distinction between *trial* and *appellate* courts; the other is between *civil* and *criminal* courts.

The function of trial courts, such as the county court, is to hear cases 'at first instance'; that is, to make a ruling on the issues of fact and law (this is a distinction that we shall discuss in detail in Chapters Three and Four) that arise in the case. This distinguishes them from appellate courts, whose function it is to reconsider the application of legal principles to a case that has already been heard by a lower court. Some appeal courts also have jurisdiction to reconsider disputed issues of fact—ie, disputes about the events leading to the legal action. Thus, any one case may well be heard by more than one court before the issues are finally resolved. Rights of appeal can be a complex subject in their own right, governed by a whole set of procedural rules; the detail of these fall outside the scope of this book, and we shall only outline the general principles that apply.

Trial and appellate functions are often combined within one court; the system is not simple enough for us to say that court X is solely a trial court, while court Y is purely appellate.

Civil and criminal law are significantly different in their aims, and employ different legal procedures. This latter point is particularly true of rules of evidence, for example. 'Evidence' describes the legal rules which control what facts may be proved, and the manner of their proving, before the courts. If you were to study the Law of Evidence, you would soon be struck by the greater evidential restrictions governing criminal as opposed to civil cases.

The term civil law (as opposed to 'Civil Law' as already considered) is used to describe all those areas of law which govern the relationship between legal persons—ie individuals and corporations—such as contract, employment, or tort (itself an umbrella term used to describe a whole variety of specific wrongs such as negligence, libel, trespass).

Criminal law, by contrast, describes those wrongs which are sufficiently important for society, usually through the intervention of the state, to outlaw as crimes, and to impose special penalties on the wrongdoer (such as a fine or term of imprisonment). By and large there is a fairly clear distinction between those courts having civil and those having criminal law responsibilities (what lawyers call *jurisdiction*). The following diagram provides a basic guide to the structure of the English court system.

Let us now briefly consider the role of each of these courts. The full details of the courts' respective jurisdictions can be found in textbooks on the English Legal System (eg, Ingman, 1992).

THE COURT STRUCTURE

```
            THE
           HOUSE
         OF LORDS
```

```
            THE COURT OF APPEAL

      CIVIL DIVISION        CRIMINAL DIVISION
```

```
    THE HIGH COURT                        THE CROWN
                                            COURT
  QUEEN'S BENCH   FAMILY   CHANCERY
```

```
  THE COUNTY COURT          THE MAGISTRATES' COURT
```

The House of Lords: The House of Lords is at the top of the hierarchy of English courts. It deals only with appeals, usually from the Court of Appeal, but, by a special procedure, it may also hear appeals direct from the High Court. Cases are normally heard by five judges, or, exceptionally, by as many as seven judges if the case is felt to raise issues of extreme importance—see, eg, *Pepper* v *Hart* [1992] 3 WLR 1032, [1993] 1 All ER 42. These judges are known formally as Lords of Appeal in Ordinary, or less formally as the 'Law Lords'. The Lords have final jurisdiction over both civil and criminal appeals, but hear few cases by comparison with other courts—usually some 90 to 100 cases a year. This is primarily for two reasons. First, the House of Lords will only allow appeals in respect of cases which raise points of law of 'general public importance'—that means that there must be some significant area of doubt regarding the operation of a rule of law before the Lords will hear the case. Such cases are relatively few. Secondly, the cost of taking a case as far as the House of Lords is extremely high, and this may deter people from exercising the rights of appeal that they may have, unless their claims are financially assisted by the state.

The Court of Appeal: The Court of Appeal is divided into two Divisions, Civil and Criminal. The Civil Division will hear appeals from the High Court and county court. Cases will normally be heard by a minimum of two, but normally three judges called Lords Justices of Appeal (the title 'Lord Justice' is used regardless of whether the judge is male or female; it is written as 'LJ' following the judge's name—hence 'Smith LJ'). The Civil Division is headed by a senior judge known as the Master of the Rolls. He (as yet there has never been a female Master of the Rolls) is referred to by whatever title is appropriate with the suffix 'MR'. The present incumbent is thus Sir Thomas Bingham MR.

The Criminal Division will hear criminal appeals against either conviction or sentence from the Crown Court. Criminal cases will normally be heard by at least two or three judges drawn from among the Lord Chief Justice (head of the Criminal Division), the Lords Justices of Appeal and the Judges of the High Court.

The High Court: This is the most complex of the courts to understand. The best way to grasp how it operates is to consider the trial functions of the various elements.

The Court is first sub-divided into three divisions, each of which has a separate jurisdiction to hear cases at first instance. These divisions are the Queen's Bench—which deals with the main areas of common law, such as contract and tort; Family, which deals with matrimonial cases and the wardship and adoption of children, and the Chancery Division, which deals chiefly with certain property, corporate and tax matters.

In addition to the first instance jurisdictions, each division has appellate functions performed by a 'Divisional Court'. The Divisional Courts of the Chancery and Family Divisions have jurisdiction over certain appeals from the county and magistrates' courts. The main function of the Divisional Court of the Queen's Bench Division is to exercise what is called the 'supervisory jurisdiction' of the High Court; that is, the power to oversee the quality and legality of decision-making in inferior courts and tribunals, though it also (occasionally) hears criminal appeals 'by way of case stated' on points of law from the magistrates' courts.

A Divisional Court will normally be presided over by two or three judges. At first instance cases are heard by usually a single Puisne (pronounced 'puny') Judge, referred to as 'Mr Justice . . . ' and written as, eg, 'Brown J' (plural—'JJ'). There are at present four women judges in the High Court, and two of these were appointed only in 1992. They are referred to as 'Mrs Justice', an appellation which seems to apply regardless of marital status—we do not have a 'Miss', let alone 'Ms. Justice'!

The Crown Court: This court deals almost exclusively with criminal trials and appeals. Most of its case load involves the trial at first instance of the more serious criminal offences, such as homicides, serious physical and sexual assaults, and property offences involving loss or damage of a 'high value' — see *Practice Note (Mode of Trial Guidelines)* [1990] 1 WLR 1439. It is in this context that the Crown Court remains the only court in the English system in which a judge regularly sits with a jury. The function of the judge is to advise the jury on the law; the jury, however, remains the sole tribunal of fact, and it is for the jury alone to decide whether an accused is guilty or innocent as charged.

The Crown Court has an appellate function whereby it also hears appeals from the magistrates' courts on issues of fact or law.

The Magistrates' Courts: Magistrates' Courts are purely courts of first instance. The bulk of their caseload involves the trial of less serious criminal offences (in fact over 90 per cent of all criminal cases are tried by magistrates), though the Courts also have a civil jurisdiction over liquor licensing, community charge and tax arrears, and some matrimonial matters. The Court is unique in that the great majority of cases are heard before Justices of the Peace—lay persons with little formalised legal training, though they are advised on the legal issues by a legally qualified Justices' Clerk.

The County Courts: County courts have always had some overlap of jurisdiction with the High Court in respect of civil matters. For over a century the jurisdiction of the two courts was determined by assigning a series of upper limits on the business of the county court. These limits varied between different forms of action (eg, as between actions in contract and actions concerning land). The jurisdictional rules have now been significantly amended by s. 1 of the Courts and Legal Services Act 1990, which gives the Lord Chancellor the power to make orders distributing the business of the High Court and the county courts as he thinks fit. The present rules governing allocation of business are contained in the High Court and County Court Jurisdiction Order 1991 (SI 1991 No. 724).

As a result, with effect from 1 July 1991, there are now two basic principles governing civil actions:

(a) If the value of the claim is less than £50,000, proceedings normally will be issued from the county court. Only actions where the value of the claim is £50,000 plus will commence *automatically* in the High Court.

(b) For an action of which the value is less than £25,000, the trial must generally take place in the county court. Above £50,000 trial will take place in the High Court.

Actions falling between the £25,000 and £50,000 limits potentially can be tried in either court, though it is presumed that the majority will be tried in the county court (where proceedings were issued), unless the case raises sufficiently complex points of law to make the High Court the most appropriate forum. In such cases proceedings can be transferred to the High Court at the instigation of the county court.

The effect of this is to transfer a large volume of work from the High Court into the county courts, with the intention of making the county courts the main forum for civil trials at first instance. The one major reservation has been in respect of the supervisory jurisdiction of the Queen's Bench Division, which remains unchanged.

Other courts and tribunals: There are a number of other local or special courts in existence, which are rather too specialised to merit discussion here. Exceptionally, however, some mention should be made of the **Privy Council**. The Judicial Committee of the Privy Council has a number of rather esoteric functions in the English Legal System, relating to matters such as Admiralty cases. However, as a relic of the British imperial past, it has held the function of a final court of appeal for cases from a number of jurisdictions within, for example, Malaysia and the West Indies. Virtually that entire caseload has been taken away from the Privy Council now (Malaysia having been one of the last to remove rights of appeal to London). Singapore remains one of the few Commonwealth states to preserve appeals to the Privy Council, and then only with the consent of the parties to the litigation. In that context, its role will be further discussed later in this book. Cases before the Privy Council are normally heard by the Law Lords (though judges from other Commonwealth states are entitled to preside, that right has been rarely exercised). Given the status of the judges, Privy Council decisions may carry some considerable weight within the English Legal System.

In addition to the formal courts, there is a plethora of **administrative tribunals**, many of which have only been created since the Second World War (though some, like the Commissioners of the Inland Revenue, are far older). They control a vast range of activities from the issuing of passenger licences to airlines, through employment disputes, to social security entitlement. Most of these tribunals have their own rules of procedure, and are regulated by specific statutory controls. No tribunals have ever been created by the Common Law. The majority have relatively little contact with the traditional courts, though rights of appeal from some important tribunals exist, either to the High Court or to the Court of Appeal.

One thing procedurally that virtually all civil and criminal courts (it is much less true of tribunals) have in common is the assumption of what is commonly called an *adversarial process*. This was described by Justice (1974:18) as:

> . . . a fight, a pitting of strengths and wits against each other, a display
> of aggression mitigated only by the ritual of a complex set of rules and
> conventions

This notion of 'trial by battle' is deeply embedded, both historically and
psychologically, within English law. It has created a system in which it
is the parties themselves who make the running in any case; it is they,
not the judge, who select the facts and the legal issues upon which a case
is to be fought. The role of the judge is thus essentially reduced to one
of a passive umpire, overseeing proceedings, and ensuring that the trial
is pursued according to the rules of the legal game. Of course, this does
not mean that the judge is a silent bystander; he is quite at liberty to
interject, for example, either to test the quality of the legal arguments being
put forward, to seek clarification of some point of fact or law, or to prevent
an improper line of questioning. Even so, it is sometimes said that the
system is of rather limited efficacy; that court cases are not about discovering
the truth behind a case, but about ensuring procedural fairness. Defenders
of the system argue that this way the law is doing the best it can. In *Air
Canada* v *Secretary of State for Trade (No. 2)* [1983] 1 All ER 910, Lord
Wilberforce put it in these terms (at p. 919):

> In a contest purely between one litigant and another, such as the present,
> the task of the court is to do . . . justice between the parties . . . There
> is no higher or additional duty to ascertain some independent truth.
> It often happens, from the imperfection of evidence, or the withholding
> of it, sometimes by the party in whose favour it would tell if presented,
> that an adjudication has to be made which is not and is known not
> to be, the whole truth of the matter; yet if the decision has been in
> accordance with the available evidence, and with the law, justice will
> have been fairly done.

However, this notion of the legal process differs somewhat from the
inquisitorial procedure in the majority of Civil Law systems.

The inquisitorial process is typified by a far more pro-active judicial
role. The difference is most marked in civil cases. In criminal cases, there
remains, as in France, for example, considerable emphasis on the spectacle
of the trial, with its stress upon the examination of oral testimony presented
to a full court in a public process, though in the case of serious crimes
the role of the trial is diminished by extensive pre-trial judicial investigations.
The emphasis on public testimony is much less in Civilian as opposed to
Common Law civil proceedings (this is one reason why Civilian civil
procedure is often described as 'bureaucratic' in style). Typically, it is the
judge who makes most of the running. For example, he or she will be
responsible for questioning witnesses and compiling a dossier of evidence;
he or she will also be largely responsible for identifying the legal issues
prior to the final trial. Thus, in France, for example, these functions will

be performed by an 'investigating magistrate' known as the *juge de la mise en état* who has no precise equivalent in the Common Law.

The perception of the legal process is accordingly rather different. There is not an assumption, in Civilian systems, that the court's function is to vindicate the winner, to establish that one party has a legal right. Rather there is a more open and free-ranging search for 'truth'. This difference in perception affects the substantive procedures used. Because there is no perceived battle between two sides, there is less need to control inquisitorial proceedings by restrictive procedural and evidential rules (a point we shall explore in more detail in Chapter Four). It is common to draw quite a stark contrast between these two types of process, though in reality that is rather artificial. There are legal institutions in Common Law countries (including England) which adopt a form of inquisitorial process. Equally, there are Civilian legal systems (such as Italy) where adversarial procedure is much in evidence. A fuller comparison of forms of legal procedure in the EC can be found in Sheridan and Cameron (1992). There are in any event many specific procedures which have their parallel counterparts in both systems. Nevertheless, the emphasis upon an adversarial structure explains many of the specific concepts within, and reasoning processes governing, the English Legal System, as we shall see throughout this book.

Precedent and the Common Law

The Common Law has not, as a system of rules, evolved from the totality of case law. It would be physically impossible to maintain records of and develop principles from every decision of every court that has ever heard a case. Rather, the origins of the Common Law can be traced back to the practice which developed in mediaeval England, whereby records of arguments used in the Royal courts were kept and circulated, at first unofficially, among the judges and practitioners. This practice gradually hardened into an officially sanctioned system of *precedent*, whereby important cases were recorded and subsequently used as authority for specific rules of law. As a reflection of that original practice, precedent is still only created by the superior courts—the High Court, Court of Appeal and House of Lords, though some of the major tribunals have separately created their own internal systems of precedent, and where rights of appeal to the courts exist, they will also be bound to follow the precedents set. Precedent is, in theory, binding on all inferior courts (and tribunals). These include, chiefly, the Crown Court, magistrates' courts and county courts; the details of our system of precedent will be discussed at much greater length in Chapters Five and Six.

So, in advising our friend we would almost certainly have to take some account of case law, either because the legal rules concerned are actually a creation of the Common Law, or because the courts have considered the operation and effect of some relevant statutory provision. In advising her, we would not only have to know what cases (if any) existed, but also, by reference to the doctrine of precedent, assess what impact those cases might have on any future proceedings against her. Let us close this chapter by now looking at an important, and relatively new dimension of English Law.

English Law and The European Community

The United Kingdom has been a member of the European Community (EC) since 1972. For nearly two decades there has been a gradual, and perhaps irreversible mingling of European and English concepts within the legal system. The days are thus gone when anyone studying Law in this country could afford to concentrate only on English Law and the English Legal System. To this end we have dedicated the final chapter of this book to the European influence and 'European Legal Method', though we have also sought to make some specific comparisons with Civil Law practices and institutions in each chapter. We have also, as here, tried to incorporate specific references to European Community institutions and legal method, where we have thought it helpful in appreciating the context in which our law now operates.

As a general point, our leaving the 'European Community dimension' until the last chapter should not be seen as relegating the topic to an afterthought. The European influence is now too important for that. EC Law is now widely taught as a subject in its own right, and has its own established principles and procedures. However, it is also of much wider significance to the English Legal System, because of the constitutional relationship that now exists between the Community and Britain. It is not like studying, say, Contract Law where you might decide in your examination revision to ignore Chapter 8 on 'Illegality'. Experience has shown us, however, that a student (on whatever course and at whatever level) who is new to legal studies needs to become accustomed to and comfortable with English Legal System and Method before investigating other systems too deeply. In this chapter we shall simply introduce you to some basic EC concepts which will be developed more fully in the final chapter.

The Legal Foundations of the EC

The EC is an international organisation created by treaty in 1957 (the so-called 'Treaty of Rome' or 'EEC Treaty'). This Treaty, as amended (notably by the Single European Act of 1986, which commits member States to completing the so-called Internal Market) remains the foundation of the Community. In legal terms, the Treaty is significant in two ways.

First, it created the institutions which enable the Community to function. These are the Commission; the Council of Ministers; the European Parliament, and the two Community courts. The Commission and Council wield both political and legal (ie, law-making) power; the European Parliament, to date, has only a political, advisory function, and so is a very different body from the Westminster Parliament. The two courts are the Court of Justice of the European Communities (CJEC), and the newly established Court of First Instance.

The Treaty gave to the Court of Justice powers to rule on matters of European Community Law brought before it by the Commission, or by a reference from a court within one of the Member states (this latter process is generally referred to as a reference for a preliminary ruling under Article 177—that being the provision in the EEC Treaty creating the power). Private individuals also have rights to bring actions before the Court, but these are strictly controlled by the terms of the Treaty. The Court of First Instance (CFI) has been in operation since September 1989. It was created under Art. 11 of the Single European Act, which, despite its name, is a Community treaty not a statute of any Member state. The CFI was created to take-up some of the caseload of the CJEC. However, it presently has a restricted jurisdiction, concerned with competition law, staff cases, and certain cases arising from the European Coal and Steel Community Treaty of 1951. The CFI is of lower standing than the CJEC, and certain rights of appeal exist from its decisions to the Court of Justice.

Secondly, the Treaty is unusual in that it contains a number of provisions which give individuals (as opposed to nation states) substantive legal rights. A particularly important and well known example is Article 119, which lays down a general principle that men and women are entitled to equal pay for work of equal value. This has been used in the UK to give rights to equal pay to women who have fallen outside the protection of our own sex discrimination laws (*Garland* v *British Rail Engineering Ltd* [1983] 2 AC 751, [1982] 2 All ER 402).

EC Legislation

Apart from the substantive provisions of the Treaty, there are three types of laws emanating from the EC Commission or Council of Ministers:

Regulations: These are directly applicable in each Member state and take precedence over any conflicting provisions of domestic (ie national) law.

Directives: These are binding upon each Member state 'as to result', but not as regards methods of 'implementation'. What this means in plain English is that each state is obliged to pass such laws as are necessary to give effect to a particular Directive, and then usually within a specified period of time. The Commission may commence proceedings against a state for failure to implement within the required period, but generally a Directive may not be enforced by or against private organisations or citizens *before* it is implemented as, say, an Act of Parliament or statutory instrument.

Decisions: These are only binding upon the Member state(s) or individual(s) to whom they are addressed; they thus tend to have a much narrower field of application than either Regulations or Directives. They take effect from the date at which they are notified to the addressee. You should be careful not to get caught up in some terminological confusion. Decisions as referred to here are a species of legislation; they should not be mistaken for the decisions of the Court of Justice, which have a distinct legal status.

The European Dimension of English Law

The EC is not unusual in owing its existence to an international agreement. Many multi-national organisations of states are created in this way. What makes the EC unique is that the Treaty itself creates rights and obligations which are enforceable within not only the institutions of the EC (as just considered), but before the national courts of each member State.

In English law the enforceability of the EEC Treaty and of legislation emanating from the EC Institutions is guaranteed by the European Communities Act 1972—an Act of the Westminster Parliament. Although the effects of that Act are still widely debated by EC and British constitutional lawyers, it seems increasingly to be accepted that by passing the Act, Parliament has, to a limited extent, ceded some of its sovereign power to the EC. How much power is probably impossible to quantify, but we seem presently to be upon the threshold of an important new stage in the legal relationship. In July 1990, following a reference to the CJEC, the House of Lords prevented the Secretary of State for Trade from implementing provisions of the Merchant Shipping Act 1988; see *R v Secretary of State for Transport ex parte Factortame (No. 2)* (C–213/89) [1991] 1 AC 603, [1991] 1 All ER 70.

The House of Lords, in delivering the reasons for its decision, concentrated upon the issues of granting 'interim relief' until the question finally came to court. By so doing their Lordships avoided the necessity of discussing the implications of their decision to disapply the Act. This case is undoubtedly of constitutional significance. Prior to the decision in *Factortame (No. 2)* no English court, in modern times, had accepted that it had the power to disapply an Act of Parliament. Indeed, in the original *Factortame* case the House of Lords had expressly denied that such power existed—see [1990] 2 AC 85, [1989] 2 All ER 692. Although the issue in the *Factortame* cases was a rather technical, preliminary point regarding the powers of the court to grant 'interim relief' (that is, to give a provisional remedy to a plaintiff to protect his interests until the case is heard on the substantive issue), the effect of *Factortame (No. 2)* is far more general. It now seems uncontestable that, in cases where there is a conflict between principles of directly enforceable Community law and national law, Community law must prevail, regardless of the source of that domestic law. To EC lawyers, this is hardly a shock, since it reflects one of the founding principles of the Community legal order — the principle of supremacy of EC law. As Lord Bridge explained in *Factortame (No. 2)* ([1991] 1 All ER 70 at 108):

[the principle of supremacy] was certainly well established in the jurisprudence of the Court of Justice long before the United Kingdom joined the Community. Thus whatever limitation of its sovereignty Parliament accepted when it enacted the European Communities Act 1972 was entirely voluntary. Under the terms of the 1972 Act it has always been clear that it was the duty of a United Kingdom court, when delivering final judgment, to override any rule of national law found to be in conflict with any directly enforceable rule of Community law . . . Thus there is nothing in any way novel in according supremacy to rules of Community law in those areas to which they apply and to insist that, in the protection of rights under Community law, national courts must not be inhibited by rules of national law from granting interim relief in appropriate cases is no more than a logical recognition of that supremacy.

The *Factortame* case is one illustration of how English and European case law is developing in response to the new legal order established by the EC. But it is important to remember that that legal order is also capable of undergoing change. The scope of Community law today is significantly greater than 20 years ago, when the UK joined the Community. It is more than likely that, in another 20 years, we shall see a legal order that is significantly different from that which exists today. Indeed, as we write, the Member states of the EC are (in various degrees) attempting to implement legal reforms based on two important Treaties: the Community Charter of Fundamental Social Rights (1989) and the Maastricht Treaty on European Union, signed on 7 February 1992. These will do much to determine the course of the Community's future (see further Chapter Ten). They both signal a widening of focus beyond the Community's original, *economic*, concerns (such as agriculture, competition, the free movement of goods and workers) to incorporate greater responsibility for social policy and other governmental functions.

One implication of this is that, for the lawyer, it is becoming increasingly difficult to identify clear points of demarcation between national and Community law, and to find areas of national law which are wholly unaffected by EC law. We are already seeing examples of this trend. One graphic, and highly emotive, illustration that comes to mind relates to the Irish laws on abortion.

The Irish Constitution contains a specific provision protecting the life of the unborn child. The effect of this is to make abortions illegal within the Republic, except in cases where policy dictates that the risks to the life of the mother justify the termination. On the face of it, it is hard to see what connection could exist between such constitutional rights and EC law. However, in 1992, the Irish High and Supreme Courts were asked to rule on the Constitutional legality of Irish citizens travelling to England, where abortion operations are lawfully available on less restrictive grounds than in Ireland—see *Attorney General* v *X* [1992] 2 CMLR 277. The case concerned a 14-year-old girl who had become pregnant after being raped. Relying on the Irish Constitution, the Irish Attorney General sought an order preventing her and her family from travelling to England in order to have the pregnancy terminated. In the High Court, the applicant relied in part on the decision of the Court of Justice of the European Communities in Case C-159/90 *Society for the Protection of the Unborn Child* v *Grogan* [1991] 3 CMLR 849 and argued that, if it did prevent travel in this way, the Constitution was contrary to EC law, as contained in Article 60 of the Treaty of Rome and Directive 73/148 (on access to services across the Community). The High Court rejected this argument, but *not* on the basis that EC law did not apply to the issue. Rather, the Court relied on Article 8 of the Directive, which allows Member states to restrict travel in cases where public policy so dictates.

Attorney General v *X* was ultimately determined in the applicant's favour on other grounds by the Supreme Court, which did not rule on the point of EC law. That left the High Court's decision as precedent on this point. But the story does not quite end there. In a further Irish High Court case, *SPUC* v *Grogan* [1993] 1 CMLR 197, the applicant sought to overturn *Attorney General* v *X* in the light of a further Community law development. When the Maastricht Treaty was signed, it contained a specific Protocol guaranteeing freedom to travel to obtain abortion services within the EC. The applicant in *Grogan (No. 2)* thus argued that, as the Irish Government was a signatory to the Protocol, the policy arguments relied on in *Attorney General* v *X* could no longer apply. This argument was also rejected by the High Court. The applicant could not rely on the Maastricht Protocol itself, as it had yet to be implemented by national law. Once Maastricht is law, the Irish courts will then, presumably, be obliged to reassess the scope of their constitutional protection of the fetus.

Thus we have a clear example of an area of law, concerning what most people would regard, first and foremost as a high *moral*, rather than *economic*, issue in which EC law is not only becoming increasingly significant, but will ultimately override contrary domestic rules of law. Whether the EC should become so involved in determining the fundamental rights and freedoms of citizens remains a moot point, and one which much of the literature on Community law has left underdeveloped.

Nevertheless, to return to our flick-knife example, if our concern was whether there are any controls on the importation of flick-knives, then we might have to consider Community law; but the question as raised would be unlikely to require consideration of EC law.

Conclusions

In summary, therefore, in solving any legal problem, including the one set at the beginning of this chapter, we need to be aware of the many dimensions of English law. Any advice we give must take into account the kind of issue with which we are dealing. Is it a question of criminal or civil law? Have we considered all relevant Acts (if any), and checked on the existence of any secondary legislation? What about case law? Have the courts said anything about the matter, either in interpreting a relevant statute, or in applying rules of Common Law? Does the problem have an EC dimension? It is only by appreciating this context that we can, ultimately, find the relevant law to solve our problem. In practice, of course, you quickly overcome the need to run through the kind of checklist we have just presented. Your knowledge and understanding of substantive areas of law will help to make the job of researching legal issues much simpler. Even so, no one can retain sufficient detailed knowledge to make legal research redundant. The next chapter is intended to help you develop the basic research skills necessary to find the law on any basic legal problem.

REFERENCES

Baldwin, R. & Houghton, J. (1986) 'Circular Arguments: The Status and Legitimacy of Administrative Rules' *Public Law*, p. 239.

de Búrca, G. & Gardner, S. (1990) 'The Codification of the Criminal Law' *Oxford Journal of Legal Studies*, vol. 10, p. 559.

Galligan, D. (1986) *Discretionary Powers: A Legal Study of Official Discretion*, Oxford: Clarendon Press.

Gardner, S. (1992) 'Reiterating the Criminal Code' *Modern Law Review*, vol. 55, p. 839.

Ingman, T. (1992) *The English Legal Process*, 4th Edition, London: Blackstone Press.

Justice, (1974) *Going to Law: A Critique of English Civil Procedure*, London: Stevens.

Law Commission (1985) *Codification of the Criminal Law*, Law Comm. No. 143, London: HMSO.

— (1989) *A Criminal Code for England and Wales*, Law Comm. No. 177, London: HMSO.

— (1992) *Legislating the Criminal Code—Offences Against the Person and General Principles*, Law Comm. No. 122, London: HMSO.

Miers, D. (1986) 'Legislation, Linguistic Adequacy and Public Policy' *Statute Law Review*, p. 90.

— (1989) 'Legislation and the Legislative Process: A Case for Reform?' *Statute Law Review*, p. 26.

Samuel, G. (1990) 'La notion d'intérêt en droit anglais' in Gérard, Ost & van de Kerchove, *Droit et Intérêt*, vol. 3, Brussells: Facultés universitaires Saint-Louis.

Sheridan, M. & Cameron, J. (1992) *EC Legal Systems: An Introductory Guide*, London: Butterworths.

Stein, P. (1984) *Legal Institutions: The Development of Dispute Settlement*, London: Butterworths.

Chapter Two

Finding the Law

Let us begin by considering again the problem of the shopkeeper, which we introduced in Chapter One. We now know that the answer to her question lies somewhere in either existing legislation, or in case law, or perhaps a combination of the two. We also know that there is a vast amount of that primary material to be searched.

How do we go about finding the law on a particular issue? That is a question of developing the appropriate skills to do the job—what we would call library and research skills. Law is above all else a library-based subject. You must be prepared to spend a substantial amount of time doing library-based research. This chapter is intended to provide an introduction to such skills. It is by no means complete, as lack of space prevents us from considering a number of sources—notably British Government publications, and sources of International Law. You may therefore find the more detailed account of research sources provided by Dane & Thomas (1987) or by Clinch (1992) of assistance with specific problems. Most law libraries keep reference copies of these works.

Getting Started

The starting point of any research depends upon a number of variables. It depends, of course, upon the level of your existing knowledge of law. Once you have mastered the basic principles of a subject, research becomes a little easier, in so far as the parameters of your research will become much more clearly defined—there are possibilities that you will be able to exclude from the outset, for example.

To be an effective researcher, you need to develop some sense of how lawyers think about legal issues (eg, the terminology they use, and so on). It is a question of becoming familiar with the way in which we structure and classify information. This does mean that, to start with, legal research can be sometimes slow and frustrating as you try to find your way around the material. Persevere, it becomes easier with experience.

The context may also define the level of research you need to undertake. Are you reading to fill in the background of a subject; to enhance your own understanding, or to provide a detailed study of some issue or point of law? Each of these exercises may require rather different research strategies (we develop this further in Chapter Three), and may influence your choice of sources. Lawyers have essentially two types of library sources: what we call **literary** and **primary** sources. These may be further sub-divided. Accordingly, we have split the discussion into three constituent parts, covering:

(a) literary sources
(b) case law
(c) legislation.

We have then separately considered the special issues governing the use of:

(d) EC law
(e) information retrieval systems.

Literary Sources

In practice, the simplest way to begin researching a problem is to find a book about it. The term 'literary sources' is used to describe books about law, as opposed to books of law, which contain 'official' copies of legislation or case reports. Literary sources are sometimes also referred to as *secondary* sources, to distinguish them from books of law, which are *primary* sources. Be careful that you do not confuse the term secondary meaning literary, with other uses of the term, particularly in relation to secondary legislation. We shall discuss the use of literary sources under two headings: legal encyclopedias, and textbooks and journals.

Legal Encyclopedias

Encyclopedias are usually designed to provide a reasonably complete statement of the law in a concise form. They come in a variety of shapes and sizes. Many of them are subject specific—so, for example there are encyclopedias on Consumer Protection, Social Welfare Law, Employment Law, and so on. Most of these are large looseleaf volumes designed mainly for legal practitioners.

One of the most valuable starting points, particularly if you are researching a topic about which you have little or no existing knowledge, is the legal encyclopedia called *Halsbury's Laws of England*. The current edition (the fourth) was completed in 1986, though some of its 56 volumes have already been revised and reissued since then. The whole work is regularly updated by a loose-leaf *Current Service* volume. *Halsbury's Laws* covers all areas of English Law, by summarising the present state of the law with references to the relevant case law and statutes. The quality of its coverage is generally good, but it is not exhaustive! Searching *Halsbury* involves using four distinct elements.

The index: To use *Halsbury's Laws*, you must begin by looking through the index, which takes up two separate volumes by itself. Like any index, it operates by identifying and referencing what we might call *key words*, so the first step has to be to think of the kind of terms that the index might use to identify the problem we are interested in. Once you hit on the right key word (which often involves a process of elimination) the index will give you a set of references to another volume within the series. Thus, if we were interested in problems related to arsenic poisoning contracted at work, we could look up 'arsenic' in the index; we would find:

ARSENIC
    control, **18**, 1111
    importation in food, **18**, 1181
    poisoning, factory in, notification of, **20**, 514

Each of these references gives us an indication of the context in which arsenic is being discussed, followed by (in **bold**) the number of the volume in which it appears, and then the paragraph—not page—number. Often, the paragraph number will be followed by a little 'n', which indicates that the reference is to a footnote to that paragraph.

Sometimes you will not find a reference to the subject you are looking for. Be careful that you do not assume that there is, therefore, no legal material on that point, it may be that you are not using the correct research strategy. For example, the reference to arsenic says nothing about its use in homicide cases. Obviously, it would be silly to assume that it is perfectly lawful to kill someone by arsenic poisoning—so the answer must be that you are not looking for the right thing. In a homicide case, the fact that the murder was committed by poisoning is not of itself likely to be legally significant, so you would need to consider what it is about that particular method of committing the crime that is important. For example, it might be important because the person accused has previously been convicted of offences involving arsenic poisoning; so what you really want to know is whether, as a matter of procedure, you can use that information in court. In short, you must have a clear idea of what you are looking for and why.

The main volumes: From the index of *Halsbury*, you can go direct to the main volume which is relevant, and make a note of what appears there. Rarely you may find that, particularly if a volume has been reissued, paragraph numbers will have changed, or perhaps for some other reason the main index seems to be wrong. In that case, it is worth checking the index which appears in the back of the main volume, as that may give you a different paragraph number. From the main volume, you must go first to the *Cumulative Supplement*, and then to the *Current Service* to update your search.

The Cumulative Supplement: This is searched by looking for the relevant reference to the main volume. Any updates will appear under the same paragraph number. The *Supplements* are published annually and contain all updates to the main volume, up to their own date of publication. It is therefore only necessary to use the latest *Supplement*. Thus, if you followed up the arsenic reference to Vol. 20, para. 514, you would find that, at the time of writing, the latest (1992) *Supplement* refers to a variety of amendments effecting the notification of industrial diseases, passed between 1981 and 1985.

The Current Service: This provides an update on everything that has happened since the publication of the last *Supplement,* in the form of 'Monthly Reviews' and a 'Noter-Up' section. The *Current Service* is searched by using the *Key* which appears at the front of that volume. This is another kind of index. Again, we must look up the original volume and paragraph reference—say the reference to arsenic poisoning (**20**, 514). If it appears, there will be separate references opposite to the relevant Monthly Review and/or the Noter-Up which are filed in the *Current Service* volume.

So, *Halsbury* might well be a good starting point for researching our friend's problem. But you must remember that the first step is to think about how lawyers would describe it. We know that she is concerned about her liability for offering those knives for sale, so what are the likely key words? We would suggest that there might be a number of possibilities. 'Sale of knives' might be too specific, but perhaps there may be something under 'Knife', or even 'Weapon' or possibly under the general concept of 'Sale of Goods'? Those are all possible key words that might be worth exploring. Can you think of any others?

Books and Journals

In terms simply of quantity, textbooks are the main literary source of law. We conventionally make a distinction between academic and practitioner texts. That distinction is a bit arbitrary, as many books may be as useful to the practitioner as to the academic lawyer, but, to generalise, academic texts tend to be less concerned with matters of procedure, and to offer a more critical perspective on the law than practitioner texts. Many academic texts now take a specifically *contextual approach* to law; that is, an approach which attempts to place law in a social, political or economic perspective, rather than just concentrate on what we call the *black-letter* law—ie, the rules themselves. Accordingly, the answers you find may well reflect the function of the text, and the perspective of the author on the subject.

Law journals also take a wide variety of forms. Some, such as the *Law*

Society's Gazette are primarily practitioner journals, which will contain articles of interest to legal practitioners on matters of substantive law or practice management; they will also normally maintain an element of updating, with short casenotes, and information about recent or planned legislation. Many of the more 'heavyweight' journals appeal to both practitioner and academic audiences, such as the *Law Quarterly Review,* for example. Of these, the majority have some kind of specialist focus— hence we have titles like the *Journal of Business Law, Industrial Law Journal* and *Journal of Social Welfare and Family Law.* Others such as the *Modern Law Review, Cambridge Law Journal* and *Journal of Law and Society* have a broad coverage of subject matter, but a primarily academic outlook. Most of the main journals have adopted a similar format, with each containing a number of leading articles, plus shorter articles on cases or new legislation, and book reviews.

Finding Literary Sources

As a starting point in your studies you will almost certainly be given guidance as to what texts are required for the course, though for most purposes you will be expected to read more widely than just the required or recommended text. So, sooner rather than later, you will be required to look for other sources (both textbooks and journal articles) from which to work. There are a number of ways of going about this.

In relation to textbooks, start with a library catalogue. All libraries have a catalogue of their collections, either as a card index or in a computerised form. It will be normal for such catalogues to be indexed by subject, as well as by author. A search of the subject catalogue for 'Criminal Law', for example, should quickly guide you to the main books on the subject. However, this is a fairly crude technique that is just a means of getting started. Catalogues contain only general search terms, so you could not use one to find, for example, any law books containing references to flick-knives!

A more thorough way of checking on what has been written on a subject is to use one of the commercially produced indexes of law books published. The most widely used is entitled *Law Books in Print* and gives details of all British and American law books currently in print. Books found this way, if not held by your library, can usually be obtained through an inter-library loans scheme. However, this is usually only worthwhile if you are doing a sustained piece of research, say for a project or dissertation, as such loans can take several weeks to arrive.

Searching for journal articles is not so straightforward. Most libraries will have a catalogue of periodicals and journals; but this will only tell you which journals the library carries, without giving any indication of their specific contents. There are, however, a number of published indexes to help you; these are:

The Legal Journals Index: This only commenced publishing in 1986, but it contains full details of all the legal journals published in the United Kingdom, and so provides an extremely valuable research resource. It is indexed according to both subject matter (with a brief summary) and name of author. Cases and Acts of Parliament which have been the subject of a commentary are also indexed under their title. The *Index* is issued monthly, though some libraries take only the quarterly and annual cumulative issues. It is also available as a computerised database.

Current Law: This is published monthly, and most libraries carry bound volumes (called the *Current Law Year Book*) back to its commencement in 1947. Recent articles can be found under each subject heading, and the *Year Book* contains a separate index thereto. The range of journals covered is not exhaustive, so this is less useful than the *Legal Journals Index.* It does, however, provide some assistance in tracing articles before 1986.

Index to Legal Periodicals and *Index to Foreign Legal Periodicals:* These are both American publications. The former is an index to all American journals, plus a selection from Britain, the Republic of Ireland and the Commonwealth; the latter indexes articles on international and comparative law, and on the municipal law of all countries which do not appear in the *Index to Legal Periodicals.* (See Dane & Thomas, 1987:60–1).

Other social science indexes: There are a number of specialist indexes which can be used to discover law-related material written from the perspective of other academic disciplines. In particular, the *British Humanities Index* and *Social Sciences Index* are useful in this respect.

Often textbooks and articles will also make reference to other journal publications, and these can often be valuable in researching a particular topic. In this context particularly, though it applies more generally as well, you should note that certain standard abbreviations are used in the citation of journal articles. Thus, for example, an article in the *Modern Law Review*, volume 53, beginning at page 116 would be cited as (1990) 53 MLR 116. Another in *Public Law* would be cited as [1990] PL 183. Each citation depends on the form adopted by the particular journal, so it takes a while to get used to the different citations. Do be precise in their use. This is not just a matter of pedantry, it is a way of ensuring that we are all 'speaking the same language' and that references can be easily traced. A guide to legal abbreviations has been written by Donald Raistrick (1981), and a list of the main abbreviations in use is also contained in Appendix 1 of Dane & Thomas.

How Authoritative are Literary Sources?

Literary sources do not really contain 'the law'; they contain the author's interpretation of it. This is reflected in the way the courts use them. By and large, the courts have been rather reluctant to place reliance on secondary sources in coming to decisions—though exceptionally, *Halsbury's Laws* have long been cited before the courts. Indeed, at one time, it was the practice that no living author could be cited in court—a rather curious rule which seemed to suggest that death gives an author authority which he or she never had while alive! There is some evidence that this restriction has fallen into disuse, and some well established texts are now quite widely cited.

It is even more unusual to see journal articles cited as being influential on the court's decision, but even here, there is evidence that the courts will consider such sources occasionally—though there are no clear guidelines as to when or why. A couple of examples of the latter practice can be seen from the House of Lords decisions in *R* v *Shivpuri* [1987] AC 1, [1986] 2 All ER 334, where the House acknowledged the influence of Professor Glanville Williams's criticism (in [1986] CLJ 33) of their earlier decision on the law of attempts in *Anderton* v *Ryan* [1985] AC 567, [1985] 2 All ER 355, and in *Morris* v *Beardmore* [1981] AC 446, [1980] 2 All ER 753, where Lord Edmund Davies quoted with approval a casenote by Geoffrey Samuel in (1980) 96 LQR 12.

Even though the courts show some reluctance to rely on literary sources they can still provide assistance for legal research, as we shall see in Chapter Three.

Finding Cases

The operation of our system of precedent is dependent upon us being able to find out what the courts have said about any given question. This means that we are dependent upon having a record of the courts' decisions. These records are referred to as 'law reports'.

Whenever possible you are recommended to look at actual reports of cases rather than just to accept the interpretation given in textbooks. This section is intended to give you some guidance to the English system of law reporting, and then to help you find and update specific cases.

Law Reporting

The tradition of law reporting is very ancient in the English Legal System, though many of these early reports are now regarded as highly unreliable. In essence the law reports can be divided into two historical phases, pre- and post-1865.

Before 1865, there were two main sources of case reports:

Year books: Established about 1285, these continued in existence until 1535. They were probably derived from the notes of cases taken by student advocates. Consequently they are not consistently reliable: would you want to rely on your notes as law reports? They are often difficult to read and make relatively little sense to anyone except a legal historian.

Private reports: Sometimes called 'Nominate Reports' because each series is named after the counsel who compiled them. Hundreds of reports appeared in this era. The same case could be reported by a range of reporters, and in such cases it is not unusual for the contents, even the decision, to vary as between reports! The advantage of these reports, however, lay in the evolution of more precise methods of recording judgments, eg Burrow's Reports introduced the idea of a 'Headnote' (a summary of the facts, decision and reasoning—a device which is used in every report today) in about 1765. Some were good, eg Coke's Reports [1600–1658]; some were not so, eg Espinasse's Reports [1793–1807], of whom it was said: he was deaf; he heard only half of what went on in court, and reported the other half. These reports are now collected together in *The English Reports*. These require a search technique all of their own, and you are advised to read Dane & Thomas before you attempt to search for a case in the English Reports. Cases from the nominate reports are still cited, though increasingly rarely. Some of the most important have also been reprinted in a series called the All England Law Reports Reprint (cited as All ER Rep), which contains a selection of cases from between 1558 and 1935.

Even after 1865, there remains no single 'official'(ie state sponsored) source of law reports in the English Legal System. This is yet another respect in which our system differs from much of continental Europe. For example, in France there are separate criminal and civil series of the *Bulletin des arrets de la Cour de Cassation* (the final court of appeal in most civil matters) dating back to 1798, while in Germany there are about 12 current sets of official law reports; these tend to be published separately by reference to the particular court in which the cases were heard. Thus, eg, the Supreme Court (*Bundesgerichtshof*) and Constitutional Court (*Bundesverfassungsgericht*) reports constitute separate series.

In England, in 1865, a body called the Incorporated Council of Law Reporting introduced what is now recognised as the main source of law reports. The Council is still responsible for these today, though there are a number of other organisations which publish various law reports, as well as a body of case law that is never published. We shall consider each of these in turn.

The Law Reports and alternatives: The so-called 'Law Reports' consist of Queen's Bench Reports (abbreviated to QB), Chancery (Ch), Family (Fam) and Appeal Cases (AC). This broadly reflects the division of work between the superior courts, as Queen's Bench, Chancery, and Family Reports will contain reports of both High Court and Court of Appeal decisions. Appeal Cases contain chiefly House of Lords and Privy Council cases.The Council also publishes the Weekly Law Reports (WLR), which are relied upon by many practitioners.

There are other reputable reports not published by the Council. The All England Law Reports (All ER), published by Butterworths, is a prime example. These are probably the most widely used alternative. Indeed, many smaller law libraries in the UK and abroad rely purely on the All England

Law Reports. For this reason, we have cited both the Law Reports and the All England Reports wherever possible. Both the Weekly Law Reports and the All England Reports are published in weekly parts as well as annual bound volumes.

The Times, The Guardian, the *Financial Times* and *The Independent* newspapers all publish case reports within their papers, though the comprehensiveness of reporting varies from paper to paper. *The Times* provides the most regular coverage, and its reports are also available in a looseleaf compilation volume. Although *The Times* reports are the longest established and best known of these, all these newspapers' reports are capable of citation. These can be a useful means of keeping abreast of current developments. Cases published in these newspapers are all indexed in a volume called the *Daily Law Reports Index* (as well as in *Current Law),* which is published along similar lines to the *Legal Journals Index.*

Even though, technically, they do not have any special status the Law Reports are generally preferred to other reports in the case of any conflict. This is because judgments in the Law Reports are revised either by the judges themselves, or with their co-operation. This should ensure that they are a more reliable source of what was said. However, the opportunity for correction enables a judge sometimes to introduce changes to the text which may reflect what he meant to say, rather than what he said. This is, perhaps a rather more controversial practice, though in some cases it has enabled judges to amend or clarify their reasoning in the light of criticisms directed at the unreported transcript—see, eg, Lord Denning's judgment in *Ghani* v *Jones* [1970] 1 QB 693; and Jackson (1970:3).

Conflicts between the various law reports are comparatively rare, but not wholly unknown. For an example you might like to look at the reports of *Davies* v *Swan Motor Co. (Swansea) Ltd* [1949] 2 KB 291 at 319, [1949] 1 All ER 620 at 629, where there is a small but confusing discrepancy in the reporting of the judgment of Evershed LJ.

Specialist reports: More particularly, there are many and varied specialist reports such as the Criminal Appeal Reports, Reports of Patents Cases and Industrial Cases Reports. These are of considerable assistance to subject specialists. A list of the majority of such reports can be found in Dane & Thomas.

Unreported cases: The reporting of cases is still largely a matter of choice by the editor of the particular series of reports. There are still many cases, even in the higher courts, which go unreported. This does not mean that they are wholly irrelevant. Transcripts of unreported Court of Appeal cases are available to judges and practising lawyers, and unreported cases can quite properly be cited to a court.

Occasionally the editors of the law reports get it badly wrong by excluding a case which subsequently proves to be important. This happened in 1973, for example, with the case of *Mesher* v *Mesher,* which introduced a new kind of 'property adjustment order' for use in divorce cases. Initially the case had only been picked up by *The Times,* (a point that seems to have been forgotten as the case is widely cited as unreported). Even so, the Mesher Order (as it was called) became very popular with the divorce courts for a time, with the result that the case was belatedly reported in the All England Law Reports in 1980 (see *Mesher v Mesher and Hall (Note)* [1980] 1 All ER 126).

The advent of information technology in the form of data-retrieval systems has created additional access to unreported cases, and with it created a number of new problems, which we shall discuss below.

How to Find a Case

In attempting to find cases there are a number of different strategies which may be adopted depending on the information you have.

First, a case can most easily be found by its name and the reference to its location in the law reports. Taken together, these provide a means of identification as unique as a fingerprint. The name of any case in English law is normally based upon the parties involved—hence some of the case names we have already seen, such as *Mesher v Mesher* or *R v Shivpuri*. The case reference is more properly called its **citation**. The most common form of citation of any case will be made up of the following elements:

	YEAR	VOLUME (if any)	REPORT	PAGE
Thus				
	[1989]	2	QB	123

tells us that the case is to be found in volume 2 of the Queen's Bench Law Reports for 1989, beginning at page 123. There is one significant variation on that, which affects the style of citing dates and volume numbers. Some series of law reports in the last century, and a few modern sets, have consecutively numbered volumes, year by year—eg, the case of *Bowker v Rose* which is reported only in (1978) 122 Sol Jo 147. Theoretically, the date there is not significant—we could find that case merely by knowing that it is in volume 122 of the *Solicitors Journal.* For that reason, where the set of reports is consecutively numbered, the date is cited in round brackets. If the date is in square brackets, it is vital to the finding of that case, because any subsequent volume number will only refer to volumes *within that particular year.*

The style of citing cases is, as with journal citations, rigidly adhered to. You may find the system rather complex and confusing at first, but it will soon become familiar. We have already indicated the main reports, with their abbreviations, above. If you need help, fuller lists of specialist, and of American and Commonwealth reports, with their abbreviations, can be found in Raistrick and in Dane & Thomas.

Cases can be found, within reason, even if you only know the name. This can be done by finding the citation in the *Current Law Case Citators*. There are two bound volumes; the first covers cases reported from 1947–76, the second, from 1977–88. Supplements have been published covering the years from 1989. Note also that, since the 1991 issue, the citator has been rearranged into two parts. Part I contains English cases, while Part II contains those cases formerly digested in the Scottish section of the citator. All reported cases are listed in the citator in alphabetical order, based upon the first-named party to the case. The citator will then give a list of all citations of that case, and a reference to a summary of the case in the relevant annual volume of *Current Law*. There are limits to this strategy. It is sometimes possible to find a case this way even if you only know the first-named party—so long as it is not a particularly common name, like Smith! It is not practicable to find cases where you only know the second-named party, as these are not separately identified. It may also prove difficult to find cases if you are unaware of the spelling—if possible do try to keep an accurate note of case names handy when undertaking research—some, such as *Spettabile Consorzio Veneziano* v *Northern Ireland Shipbuilding Co.* (1919) are likely to tax any but the most exceptional memory. The criteria for naming cases are more fully discussed in Chapter Three.

Updating Cases

Once you have found your case, it will be necessary to check if it is still relevant, unless it is exceptionally recent. As we shall see in later chapters, cases are not immutable. They may be rejected by higher courts, distinguished in other cases, or otherwise discussed in some way that may be relevant to your research.

To find out what has happened to a particular case, it is best to turn again to the *Current Law Case Citators*. In addition to the citations of the case named, the citator also charts its subsequent history. If a case predates 1977, it is still worth checking the later citators, as they will tell you when the case has been most recently considered. If it appears, it will still be necessary to go back to the earlier citator, as the whole history will not be given in the latest entry. The form of reference in the citators is broadly the same so, to give a *fictitious* example, the citators may have the following entry:

in the 1947–76 edition:

Balderdash v *Ballyhooley* [1966] QB 201; [1966] 2 WLR 32; 130 JP 789; [1966] 1 All ER 468, CA . . .*Digested* 66/571: *Approved* 76/552.

and, in the 1977–88 edition:
Balderdash v *Ballyhooley* [1966] . . . .*Distinguished* 87/579.

This tells us that the case of *Balderdash* v *Ballyhooley* appears in the *Current Law Year Book* of 1966 at para. 571; that it was approved of by a later case, which is digested in the 1976 *Year Book* at para. 552, and that it was distinguished in 1987, by the case digested at para. 579 (note that in the later citator you do not get the original case reference—this should help to remind you to look it up in the earlier citator, if you have not already done so). By looking up those references it would be possible to get the names and citations of all those cases, and, if necessary, to trace their history using the citators.

For very recent cases, it is normally sufficient to use the monthly parts of *Current Law*, by searching through either the abbreviated case citator, to be found near the centre of each monthly issue (if you know the case name), or the relevant subject headings. These subject headings also form the basis of a more detailed index which can be found at the back of each bound volume of the *Current Law Year Book*.

Finding and Updating Legislation

Legislation, you will recall, can be divided chiefly into Acts of Parliament and Statutory Instruments. The publication of each of these is a separate activity, so separate search techniques are required.

Acts of Parliament: The Sources

Before we begin, one important thing you need to know about an Act is the way in which it is cited. Like cases, Acts of Parliament have a unique signature. This is not based solely upon their name (or **short title** to use the technical term), however. Many different Acts share a common name—for example, there are presently five statutes in force bearing the title 'Criminal Justice Act', the last having been passed in 1991. This means that the year in which the Act became law will be crucial in identifying it. Additionally, every Act passed has a 'chapter number' which may also be used in its identification. In practice, it is quite possible to find legislation by reference to the year and chapter number alone. The citation of an Act as '1988 c. 33', for example, could only refer to the Criminal Justice Act 1988.

Until comparatively modern times, Acts were not formally given short titles (though such titles were quite widely used on an informal basis) so that all legislation was identified by chapter number and **regnal year** (that is, a number assigned to the year in which it was passed, counting it from the first year of that monarch's reign). Hence, the famous Poor Law Amendment Act passed in 1834 was properly cited as '4 & 5 Will. IV c. 76'. This indicates that it was the 76th statute passed in the Parliamentary session which overlapped the fourth and fifth years of William IV's reign.

The tradition of citing regnal years gradually declined after World War II, and the system was formally dropped in 1963. Since there are numerous older Acts of Parliament still in force, the old system of citation cannot be wholly disregarded. However, do remember that when writing about any statutes it is conventional now to refer to them, wherever possible, by their short title and date only.

Acts of Parliament are published in a variety of series. The initial responsibility for publication lies with Her Majesty's Stationery Office (HMSO), which is required to publish individual copies of all statutes as they are passed. These are ultimately brought together in the annual bound editions of the *Public General Acts and Measures.* HMSO is also responsible for publishing a collection of all legislation currently in operation, called *Statutes in Force.* This should be a useful collection as it is published in both microfiche and loose-leaf formats and is therefore easily and quickly updated when new legislation comes into effect. Material within the collection is organised under subject headings, but these are not always well indexed, so that *Statutes in Force* can be rather difficult to use unless you have a very good idea of what you are looking for. The value of *Statutes in Force* is that all the legislation it contains is kept fully revised. This means that any changes made by later legislation will be included within the *amended* Act. This saves you the tedious and sometimes complicated job of comparing different pieces of legislation in order to work out what has happened. An example of an Act from *Statutes in Force* appears in Chapter Three.

In addition to the various official collections, there are a number of unofficial series which are worth knowing about. The most widely available of these are the *Law Reports: Statutes; Halsbury's Statutes,* and *Current Law Statutes Annotated.*

Law Reports: Statutes: This rather incongruously named collection is also published by the Incorporated Council of Law Reporting—hence the title. The contents are not annotated or revised, and so they do not provide anything different from the HMSO copies.

Halsbury's Statutes of England: This provides a partner series to *Halsbury's Laws,* containing an annotated version of all legislation presently in force, organised by subject. It is therefore the main resource for discovering whether legislation exists on any topic.

The search strategy here explained works on the assumption that you have access to a complete set of fourth edition titles. If you do not, you are advised to consult Dane & Thomas (pp. 112–3). Search techniques are similar to those employed in respect of *Halsbury's Laws.* If you begin with the *General Index,* this gives you a wide range of key words, each of which will refer you to a volume and paragraph within the main collection. If you are looking for a specific statute by title, you can take a short-cut by referring instead to the Alphabetical List of Statutes at the beginning of the *Table of Statutes and General Index.* Any revisions which post-date the publication of the relevant main volume will be traceable to the *Cumulative Supplement* and for recent changes, to the *Noter-up* binder. The text of very recent legislation will appear, alphabetically by subject, in one of the five binders of the *Current Statutes Service*; it can be found by reference to the alphabetical list of statutes at the front of the *Service*.

Current Law Statutes Annotated: All Acts are published in a loose-leaf format soon after coming into force. Of these, those which the editors judge to be sufficiently important are annotated by someone who is a specialist in that area of law. The annotations are not part of the Act, and do not, of course, have any legal effect, though they can be very useful in explaining the background, scope, and operation of the Act. During the course of each year, bound volumes of the *Current Law Statutes Annotated* are published; they are printed in order, according to the chapter numbers of the Acts.

Statute Law Search Techniques

Current Law is of some basic assistance in finding out what has happened, as it will contain a brief description, under the relevant subject heading, of any legislation passed during the year. It is not sufficiently detailed to be of substantive help, but it can make you aware of legislation which you would not otherwise have known about. Sweet & Maxwell also publish the *Current Law Statute Citators*. There are three of these, containing information on all legislation passed in 1947-71, 1972-88 and 1989-91 respectively. These provide a valuable means of updating statutes. Each citator is organised chronologically by year and chapter number (it also gives the title). Any changes to an Act are then listed *section by section*. This is important; it means that to use the citator most effectively you need to know not only the short title and chapter number, but also the specific parts, or *sections,* of the Act that you wish to trace.

Suppose, for example, you wish to discover what has happened to s.1 of the Criminal Evidence Act 1898 (c.36). The latest changes will be contained in the 1972-88 and 1989-91 Citators, and subsequent *Year Books.* The 1972-88 Citator has the following entry:

s. 1, amended: 1979, c. 16, s. 1; repealed in part: 1982, c. 48, sch. 16; 1984, c. 60, s. 80, sch. 7.

This shows that part of the section is no longer in force *(repealed),* and that other elements of the wording have been amended. To work out the detailed effect of those amendments, you would, of course, have to compare the various texts. The titles of those later Acts can either be found elsewhere in the Citator, or you could go direct to the relevant volumes of the *Public General Acts,* or *Current Law Statutes Annotated.*

As we suggested in Chapter One, legislation does not stand alone, but is explained and applied through case law. One question, therefore, might be whether we can discover what case law exists on a particular statutory provision, if we only know the details of the Act. In this respect, *Halsbury's Laws* may be a valuable starting point, as this will usually refer to both statute and case law underlying any legal proposition. The *Current Law Legislation Citator* also lists important cases under the relevant sections of each Act. Thus, to take the example of the 1898 Act, the 1989/91 citator shows no further textual amendments, but gives references to a number of court decisions where s. 1 has been applied. These citations can be followed up in the manner suggested above. In the later Citators cases appear by name, though in the 1947–71 volume cases are identified only by their reference in the *Current Law Yearbooks*. The reference comprises two elements, the year and paragraph number, in the form '60/766'. This is sufficient to enable you to trace it to the relevant passage in a Yearbook, where you will find the full citation.

Statutory Instruments

Statutory instruments are also published by HMSO, both separately and in the annual bound volumes of *Statutory Instruments* (entitled, until 1948, *Statutory Rules and Orders*).

The main alternative source for statutory instruments is *Halsbury's Statutory Instruments*, a multiple volume set organised by subject, with a Current Service containing instruments passed since the publication of the bound volumes. *Halsbury's* contains information on all instruments in force, though not necessarily in a full-text form. Summaries may also be found under the appropriate subject headings in *Current Law* and the *Current Law Year Books*.

Note that statutory instruments also have their own mode of citation, which is made up of their title, the year in which they were passed, and the instrument number.

So, for example, the Income Support (General) Amendment Regulations of 1988 are cited as SI 1988/663.

Finding EC Law

Because the EC has separate law-making institutions from the United Kingdom, it is hardly surprising that much Community law is found in locations distinct from those we have so far discussed.

However, elements of Community law can often be found in the kind of sources we have already considered. Both *Halsbury's Laws* and *Halsbury's Statutes* have volumes specifically on European Community law, while a looseleaf *Encyclopedia of European Community Law* has been published since 1973. A rather less daunting encyclopedia is *Croner's Europe*. This has been designed to provide a legal and business reference work for managers in the run-up to the Single Market in 1992, and beyond. In so doing, it provides an accessible guide to the European institutions, and to much substantive Community law, and can thus be a useful point of first reference.

In addition to occasional articles in the journals already considered, there are now quite a number of journals which specialise in EC law matters. These include the *European Law Review, Common Market Law Review* and

Legal Issues of European Integration. Articles on the Community may also be found in the main journals of International Law, such as *The International and Comparative Law Quarterly.* These all appear in the *Legal Journals Index.*

The various English law reports increasingly contain cases concerned with EC law—where the English courts are either considering the application of Community law *ab initio,* or in response to a preliminary ruling of the Court of Justice of the European Communities (CJEC). Furthermore, it is becoming more common to find decisions of the CJEC (particularly, though not exclusively, those involving the UK) reported in the usual English law reports—eg case 171/88 *Rinner-Kühn* v *FWW Spezial Gebäudereiningung GmbH and Co. KG* [1989] IRLR 493 which we shall consider in detail in Chapter Ten.

Despite this, there are a number of specific sources of EC law with which you ought to be familiar.

European Court Reports: The European Court Reports (cited as ECR) are the official reports published by the CJEC. The Reports are available in all the Community languages, including English, but the demands of producing multiple translations of every case does mean that there are substantial delays between the court handing down its decision, and that case being reported.

Common Market Law Reports: The CMLR are an 'unofficial' series published weekly in English by the European Law Centre. They cover cases before the Court of Justice and the Couit of First Instance, and before national courts within the EC. Although unofficial, the relative speed of publication makes them largely preferable to the ECR, though they do not report every case before the CJEC or CFI.

Both series are indexed by subject and case name or number. The case number is an important feature of CJEC decisions. The proper mode of citation is to give the case *number* first, followed by its name, and then the citation of any report. Thus for example, one of the leading cases on the impact of EC membership on national sovereignty, is properly cited as case 6/64 *Costa* v *Ente Nazionale per l'Energia Elettrica (ENEL)* [1964] ECR 585. The case number, it can be seen, contains two elements: the actual number at which the case was listed (here, no. 6) and the year in which the application or reference was made (64—indicating 1964). Since the creation of the Court of First Instance, a new element has been introduced into the citation of cases. Now all cases have the prefix 'C-' or 'T-'. This indicates that the case was listed, respectively, either before the CJEC or the CFI.

Note also that the year contained in the case number is not necessarily the same year that judgment was given, or that the case was reported. For example, the reference for a preliminary ruling in *R* v *Secretary of State ex parte Factortame Ltd* was made in 1989. The case therefore received the number C-213/89. Judgment by the CJEC, however, was not handed down until June 1990. So, you must be careful when searching for cases. If you do not have the case number, you should not automatically assume it will be for the same year that the judgment was given. You should also be aware that some English textbooks do not adopt the full European mode of citation, and either disregard the case number, or place it after the names of the parties.

The Official Journal: The *Official Journal* (OJ) is the primary organ of legal information within the Community. Mastering the OJ is also one of the major challenges of researching Community Law. It is made up of several sections, of which the most important are referred to as the *L* and *C Series.*

The *L Series* contains a record of all Community legislation. This covers the text of all the treaties, their protocols and amendments, and also other legislative measures. In respect of the latter, it is published and indexed in two parallel sequences, one containing Regulations, which, under Article 191 of the EEC Treaty, must be published in the *Journal*, the other contains all other (non-obligatory) legislation. Though there is no legal requirement that this be published, it is accepted practice that all Directives appear, as do some Decisions. Each piece of legislation will have its own identifiers. Like cases, each Regulation, etc, has an 'act number', so, for example, the important Equal Treatment Directive of 1976 (on sex discrimination) is cited as 'Directive 76/207' (ie number 207 of 1976). The same format applies to Decisions. That numerical sequence is reversed in respect of Regulations, hence we speak of 'Regulation 1408/71', not 71/1408. Full references should also indicate the institutional source of the legislation (Commission or Council) and the Treaty of its origin (EEC, ECSC or EURATOM—see further Chapter Ten). *Journal* references to legislation are usually cited by series, issue number, page and date. For example, the 1985 Product Liability Directive is found at OJ L210, p. 29, 7.8.85,— meaning *L Series,* issue number 210, of 7th August 1985 (note that the date of the citation is to the OJ reference, not the date that the act was passed).

The *C Series* covers a wide range of information generally falling under the heading of 'Communications'. In particular, it includes the text of legislation proposed by the Commission (but not yet law, such as Draft Directives), and both the listings of cases to appear before the CJEC, and brief summaries of decisions handed down by the Court. The OJ is quite a useful source of basic information on Court decisions, as the summaries may appear in advance of any full reports. Cases reported in the *Journal* are usually cited in the same form, thus, OJ C146, p. 9, 15.6.90 refers to case C–70/88 *European Parliament* v *Council of the European Community.*

The chief difficulties in using the *Journal* are twofold. First, it is published almost on a daily basis, which makes for a vast amount of information accruing over a relatively short space of time. It is not re-issued in a bound form, so that physically locating specific copies of the OJ can be a time-consuming business. Secondly, searching for information in the OJ is made more difficult by the limitations of the index. The index is issued monthly, and consolidated into annual parts. It is divided into two separate sections, an Alphabetical Index and the Methodological Table.

The Alphabetical Index is a subject-based index for use where you do not have a full reference (or any reference) to a legislative act or case. The limitation of the Index is that it does sometimes adopt a rather odd choice of key words, so that some terms you would expect to find simply do not appear. In an attempt to overcome the difficulties of getting to grips with the appropriate 'Eurospeak', there is a further volume, which contains the rather Orwellian-sounding 'Eurovoc Thesaurus' (properly called the *Official Journal: Annex to the Index: Eurovoc Alphabetical Thesaurus*). This lists most conceivable search terms, and then gives the actual key word that you should look up in the Alphabetical Index.

References in the Alphabetical Index take the following form:

Document No.   OJ Reference   Legal Form

The document number refers to the case or act number. You do not need to know the legal form to find a document in the *Journal*, but this will tell what the reference is to, eg, that it is a Commission Directive, or a decision of the Court of Justice. The OJ reference in this Index is listed in the form 'C1/212/10'; indicating, in order, the series, issue number and page.

The Methodological Table is far simpler to use, provided you have full references. Acts and cases are indexed separately. All legislative acts are listed in numerical order, and all cases by the year in which the application was made, and then the case number. The Table separately records cases in one of three categories; those listed before the court; those in which judgment has been given, and those which have been withdrawn before a hearing.

Other legislative sources: In addition to publication in the OJ, the Community has published a consolidated volume of the Treaties, entitled *Treaties establishing the European Communities* (1987). There is no official equivalent in respect of other Community legislation, though there are a number of student texts which contain selections of source documents, for example, Rudden & Wyatt's *Basic Community Laws*, and Nigel Foster's *EEC Legislation.*

Using Computerised Information Retrieval Systems

The basic problem facing any legal researcher is that the law library only expands, it never contracts. Payne (1983) put it more graphically:

The Ten Commandments consist of 120 words, the Magna Carta 63 Clauses and the American Declaration of Independence 500 words. The

Common Market regulations concerning duck eggs run to no fewer than
120,000 words!

Since the 1970s, the availability of computerised legal information retrieval
(IR) systems has been presented as a possible solution to the problems
created by this glut of information. The advantages of such systems are
fairly obvious. They have the potential to store, with relative ease, large
quantities of information in electronic form, as a *database*. This information
can also be searched thoroughly and accessed far more quickly than by
traditional means.

There are three main legal IR systems; these are called LEXIS; JUSTIS
and LAWTEL.

Each system has its own user manual, and it is advisable to be familiar
with that if possible, though this does not match the value of formalised
training from an experienced user. Space prevents us from giving more
than an overview of each of these.

LEXIS

The LEXIS database is probably the most extensive. It includes full text
case reports of most cases reported in England and Wales since 1945; all
public general Acts and statutory instruments in force; Scottish, Irish,
Australian and New Zealand law reports; decisions of the CJEC; some
French cases and legislation (in French) and extensive American materials.
Since January 1991, LEXIS has also incorporated the Celex database of
EC secondary legislation in its INTLAW library. For more manageable
searching this material is broken down into two tiers of segments. At the
first level, these are called libraries. Each library is then sub-divided into
a set of files. It is only possible to search one file of one library at a
time. Thus to search the English case database it is necessary to enter
first the 'ENGGEN' library and then the CASES file. The system prompts
you with on-screen commands, so accessing files is not difficult. Searches
are then performed by typing key words onto the screen and transmitting
them as a 'search request'.

The database is searched by a technique called 'on-line' searching, either
through a special LEXIS terminal, or through a networked personal
computer (PC) with the necessary software. To use the system efficiently,
it is important to become familiar with the special LEXIS keyboard
commands, and to plan your search strategy in advance—do not sit in
front of the screen and hope for inspiration! Documents found as the result
of a search can be browsed on-screen, and printed off either in full or
as extracts. Documents can be browsed either in their full text form, or
by using the **KWIC** key ('KeyWords In Context') the system will display
the search term together with a few lines immediately surrounding it. The
negative aspects of the system are that, in computing terms, material is
accessed from the database quite slowly, and the communications link cannot
always be relied upon.

JUSTIS

The JUSTIS software was developed in the late 1980s to run Context's series of databases either on-line or using the relatively new CD-ROM technology. CD-ROM (Compact Disk—Read Only Memory) uses essentially the same technology as the music CDs with which most of us are familiar. It is a major advance in legal database technology, since it has a far greater storage capacity than conventional software—the equivalent of about 250,000 typed A4 pages of text can be stored on one disk. CD is faster than on-line searching, and since it does not require a modem, can be rather more portable. In the early days of CD-ROM, cost prevented regular updating, but this is becoming less of a problem, with most systems now offering quarterly updates. This does mean, however, that CD databases still tend to be less up-to-date than on-line systems. In addition to the various JUSTIS systems, the *Current Law Yearbooks* have been published by Sweet & Maxwell on CD-ROM. The first disk was published in 1991, and contained the text of the *Yearbooks* from 1986 to 1990; updates maintain that basic database and will incorporate each *Yearbook* after 1990.

The Context databases are: JUSTIS (on-line); JUSTIS WL-CD; JUSTIS-CELEX and SCAD+CD.

JUSTIS   contains a full text version of cases reported in the *Weekly Law Reports* after December 1984 and the indexes of the *Law Reports* (1981 to 1986) and the Criminal Appeal Office list of judgments (from 1982 to the present). It also has all cases reported in *The Times* and *The Independent* newspapers (from December 1989 and October 1987 respectively).

JUSTIS WL-CD   is a CD database containing both the full text of the *Weekly Law Reports* from January 1986 to date and the *Law Reports Index.*

JUSTIS-CELEX   contains an English-language version of the EC's Celex database. It contains the full text of the *Official Journal*, which is sub-divided into four sections: Treaties, Proposals, Legislation and Cases. JUSTIS-CELEX is available in both on-line and CD-ROM forms, and search procedures vary slightly between them (see Clinch, 1992:183).

SCAD+CD   is based on the EC's official bibliographic database. It contains abstracts of over 100,000 Community information sources. It is a multilingual database in which all documents are stored in their language of publication. The system operates through keyword searching, with all keywords translated into (and therefore searchable in) Dutch, English, French, German and Italian.

Search Techniques

Both LEXIS and JUSTIS require some care in respect of developing a search strategy appropriate to the database structure. Neither database is structured other than in the crudest sense of being divided into libraries and files or databases. In particular, the material is not (unlike LAWTEL) organised with reference to any subject indexing. You cannot therefore, to give a crude example, use 'Contract Law' as a search term and hope to find all the cases concerned with Contract. Instead, searching these systems involves what is technically described (for reasons we cannot go into here) as 'boolean searching' (see Leith, 1991). This involves fairly simple word matching techniques, so that, for example, if you search for cases containing the word 'knife', that is precisely what you will get—all cases in which the word knife appears, regardless of its legal significance. This is probably the greatest practical limitation of such systems, as it means they are not very effective if you are trying to research concepts, particularly concepts which are difficult to define.

An example of such is 'good faith' which is an important concept relating to Contract Law (see further Chapter Ten). However, it is extremely difficult to define; is not always identified by name, and arises in a range of legal contexts, as well as being a term that may be used colloquially. As a result it is almost impossible to construct an effective LEXIS search related to that concept.

Against this, these systems do have the advantage of being *interactive*. It is not necessary to get one's search terms exactly right first time; it is quite possible to modify a search request in response to the information that one has received from the system already. In developing search terms, it is important to note that various systems use particular words to enable you to structure your request with some degree of precession. These special words are normally referred to as *connectors, or logical operators*. This means that those particular terms will not actually be searched for, but will tell the system how your search terms relate to each other. The main connectors can be described diagrammatically as shown below.

LOGICAL OPERATORS

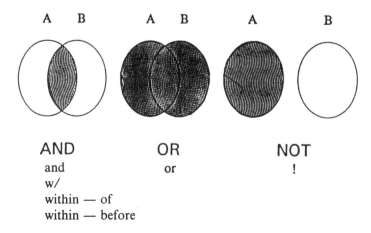

A B	A B	A B
AND	**OR**	**NOT**
and	or	!
w/		
within — of		
within — before		

As you can see there are essentially three ways in which search terms can be connected; we have identified them by the most commonly used connectors as AND, OR and NOT:

AND will search documents for terms A and B, and will only retrieve those where *both* terms are discovered (here represented by the shaded area in the two circles. Both LEXIS and JUSTIS use **and** as a logical operator. The terms w/ (LEXIS: meaning 'within') and the JUSTIS 'within' options have a similar function, except that they enable you to prescribe the *degree* of proximity between terms. So, the LEXIS command 'negligence w/20 building' would retrieve any documents where your second term is within 20 words of the first one.

OR will retrieve all documents containing *either or both* search terms A and B. It is used by both LEXIS and JUSTIS.

NOT enables you to search for term A, but *excludes* documents which also contain word B. LEXIS does not have a **not** connector. In JUSTIS it is symbolised by an — !, or the term 'not' may be used.

LAWTEL

LAWTEL is different from LEXIS and JUSTIS in that searching the system is far more structured. It works on the same principles as PRESTEL, upon which it is based. This means that you start by keying-in the relevant page number to take you to one of the LAWTEL indexes (the numbers should be available wherever your PRESTEL terminal is located—provided the machine is registered as a LAWTEL user—otherwise access will be denied). The Main Index has a set of further numbers linked to the various features of the system, such as the Daily Update, which highlights the main developments of the last 24 hours. Pressing the relevant number will take you to the selected feature. Movement between pages within a feature is very simple. If you key '9' you will move forward one page; key '8' and you will go back one. The main index can always be accessed by keying '0' until you get back to it. In addition to the main index, there are three separate local indexes within the system. These are the Subjects Index, which gives a generalised list of the main legal subjects covered by the database; the list is duplicated in the Lawtel Users' Guide. The other two indexes are a Table of Cases and Statute Citator. The former enables you to search for cases by name. The latter also refers to cases, but by the statute(s) cited therein.

The database itself contains a wide range of material, much of which is not available on LEXIS, including the progress of Bills through Parliament; decisions of Social Security Commissioners, and White and Green Papers. This is in addition to the 'normal' fare of leading cases, and primary and secondary legislation. The limitation of the system, is that the material is summarised, rather than full-text, which rather restricts LAWTEL to an updating or initial research function. The system, however, is generally well indexed, cross-referenced and quite easy to use. More detailed explanations of LAWTEL can be found in Payne and in Dane & Thomas.

Unreported Cases and IR Systems

Now, through systems such as LEXIS, which carries a high percentage of unreported material, one can retrieve all manner of hitherto unknown authorities. Dearth of authority is thus potentially replaced by excess.

In 1983 Lord Diplock, in *Roberts Petroleum Ltd* v *Bernard Kenney Ltd* [1983] AC 192; [1983] 1 All ER 564 sought to restrict severely the use of unreported authorities made available by computer transcripts, even though they are verbatim reports of the official record. His lordship's complaint was that the relative ease of accessing such cases by computer had led lawyers increasingly to cite cases which established no new or important principle. This extra material was seen to cause a greater waste of time.

Clearly, there is some merit to the core of his lordship's argument, to the effect that lawyers should only cite cases that actually lay down or explain a principle of law. However, there are plenty of reported cases that, at best, provide only a gloss on established principles, so the problem does not apply solely to unreported cases. Furthermore, if we were to take Lord Diplock's argument to its logical extreme, then, even more than now, we would be creating a situation where the law reporter, not the court, becomes arbiter of what is law. To that extent, his lordship's suggestion is of doubtful assistance.

However, perhaps our concern with the use of legal IR systems should be directed at a more fundamental issue which might explain some of Lord Diplock's unease.

A number of authors (see, eg, Leith, 1990 and 1991) argue that, regardless of the form of the cases accessed, the problem is that the medium can become the message. In other words, that the use of legal IR systems could actively distort the legal process by, for example, disadvantaging lawyers unable to afford access to a system, or more fundamentally distorting the stability of the doctrine of precedent, by, as Lord Diplock feared, overloading the courts with information, and perhaps thereby restricting judicial creativity. From this perspective, despite its advantages as a research tool, there are lawyers and computer scientists who doubt that legal IR in its present rather unsophisticated form is an unqualified good. The development of systems that are better capable of handling concepts might be an improvement, and that might enhance systems' capability to extract that which is really relevant; though such developments would still not overcome any concerns about access.

Even so, it seems pretty certain that legal IR systems are here to stay. The range of information available seems to be almost constantly expanding through increasing access to or the creation of new databases. The availability of relatively cheap telecommunications has meant that access to databases outside the UK has certainly increased. Satellite communications to existing

European Community databases, for example, are already being exploited by educational institutions such as our own. As an example of the expansion of information, the Council of Europe has recently completed a feasibility study favourable to the creation of a public database on Human Rights research in Europe. In a slightly different context, many of the larger law firms have access to their own internal databases for document precedents, etc, as well as links to external IR systems such as LEXIS. These may not only be available 'locally', but also across 'wide area networks' which are capable of linking offices in, say, London, Brussels and Hong Kong. There is thus considerable potential to use new technology in legal research, if future generations of lawyers are willing and able to exploit it.

Finally, before moving on to Chapter Three, you will find a couple of exercises based upon some of the material in this chapter, and intended to help you test your research skills.

Exercise 1: Flick-knives for sale

If you were wondering whether you would ever find the answer to the problem we have used to develop the themes of this book, now is *your* chance to find out. See if you can find answers to the following questions. If you can, you will have the basic material to advise our fictitious friend.

(a)   Using the index and main volumes to *Halsbury's Laws,* find the volume number and paragraph containing information on criminal liability for the display and sale of flick-knives.

(b)   Using any appropriate research strategy, what is the current **statutory** provision governing that liability?

(c)   Can you find any **cases** on the interpretation of that provision?

(d)   Using your research, what is your advice?

Here are the answers:

(a)   There are in fact two alternative references to flick-knives. One reference, indexed under *'Offensive weapons, flick knives, making or selling'* refers you to vol. 11, para. 854. However, vol. 11 was re-issued in 1990, and the reference is incorrect! Using the index to vol. 11, you will find that the correct paragraph is no. 174. Alternatively, the index also lists *Knife, flick, prohibition on.* This refers you to a separate source in vol. 47, para. 379.

(b)   Either volume 11 or 47 of *Halsbury* refer you to the Restriction of Offensive Weapons Act 1959 s. 1(1), as amended. In vol. 11, the latest amendment noted refers to the Criminal Justice Act 1988. This does not appear in the older vol. 47, but if you look up vol. 47 para. 379 in the 1992 *Cumulative Supplement,* the 1988 Act is mentioned there. At the time of writing, no further updates appear in the *Noter-Up.* Searches could also be made using the title of the 1959 Act in either the *Current Law Statute*

Citator, or *Halsbury's Statutes*, though the latter would be a rather more long-winded process.

(c)   Volume 11 mentions no cases; that is misleading, they do exist! Volume 47 mentions *Fisher v Bell* [1961] 1 QB 394, [1960] 3 All ER 731; this is a case that led to the amendment of the Act, but it is not necessarily the only case—though it may be a leading one. The *Current Law Statute Citators* are more helpful. The 1989–91 citator lists no cases. The 1972–88 citator mentions two cases in 1983: *Gibson v Wales* and *R v Simpson*. The 1947–71 citator again only lists *Fisher v Bell*. These could be followed up (if required) in outline using the *Current Law Yearbooks*, or in full through the various law reports.

(d)   Your advice should take into account that, though initially it was not an offence to offer a flick-knife for sale *(Fisher v Bell)*, the Act has been amended. As a result it is now an offence not only to sell, but also to have on display, or in one's possession, a flick-knife for sale.

Exercise 2: (Un)equal treatment?

Imagine you are working in a law firm. Your principal is in a hurry, and has asked you to do some research for her. She is concerned with a problem on equal pay, and recalls that there was a case listed before the CJEC sometime in 1989, in which the European Commission was seeking to question the compatibility of the UK Sex Discrimination Act 1975 with EC law. She cannot remember the case number, nor when the Court actually delivered its judgment. Can you:

(a)   find it in the *Official Journal?*
(b)   give her the case name and number?
(c)   find out what has happened to it since?

Answers:

(a)   As you do not know the case number and may be uncertain of the name, it would be best to use the OJ's Alphabetical Index. You should have started with the Annual Edition for 1989. There are a number of search terms you might have tried, such as equal pay, or sex discrimination, but neither of those would have helped. In fact the case fitting that description is listed twice, under 'equal rights for men and women' and under 'equal treatment'. These refer to OJ C1/192/13: ie *C Series*, No. 192, p. 13.

(b)   If you follow-up that reference in Issue 192 of 1989, you will find it refers to case 202/89 *European Commission v United Kingdom*.

(c)   The reference you have looked up tells you only that the case has been presented; it is silent as to any judgment. To find a reference to the judgment, you need to use the Annual Edition for 1990. As you have the case number now, it would be easier to search the Methodological Table (though you could use the Alphabetical Table, it is rather more long-winded). This will tell you whether the case has been decided or withdrawn. In fact, the case was withdrawn on 28 December 1990—see OJ C1/326/18.

REFERENCES

Clinch, P. (1992) *Using A Law Library*, London: Blackstone Press.

Dane, J. & Thomas, P. (1987) *How to Use a Law Library*, 2nd Edition, London: Sweet & Maxwell.

Jackson, R. (1970) 'Police Search—Law Reports—Law Reform by Precedent' *Cambridge Law Journal*, p. 1.

Leith, P. (1990) *Formalism in AI and Computer Science*, Chichester: Ellis Horwood.

— (1991) *The Computerised Lawyer*, London: Springer-Verlag.

Payne, R. (1983) 'Lawtel: a Prestel based legal retrieval service' in *The Progress in Legal Information Systems in Europe*, Strasbourg: Council of Europe.

Raistrick, D. (1981) *Index to Legal Citations and Abbreviations*, Abingdon: Professional Books.

Chapter Three

Reading the Law

One of the key factors which distinguishes law from the social rules we considered in Chapter One is its nature as written text. Law derives at least some of its authority and power from the status that this confers (for a critical development of this argument see Goodrich, 1986:21 4).

Much of this book is concerned with principles of interpretation—both of statutes and of cases. At its heart, any process of interpretation is one of reading. Reading is an activity that can be carried on at different levels— if you have ever studied English Literature you will be familiar with the idea of reading as a search for layers of meaning. On this basis, for example, one does not just find in Dickens' *Hard Times* the story of the characters involved, but also a powerful critique of mid-Victorian social values, and a particular attack on the doctrine of Utilitarianism which dominated that age.

Legal texts can similarly be seen as displaying layers of meaning. These layers broadly correspond to the three questions that we might ask about a legal text, what we call the *What, How & Why* of law, that is:

(a) *What* kind of law is it?
(b) *How* does it affect existing law?
(c) *Why* was it made?

At the first level (*what*), the form of the document itself tells us something about it. If, for example, it takes the form of an Act of Parliament, we know that it takes precedence over case law.

At another level (*how*) we must work out what it is actually about; this is a matter of constructing meaning from the text, though, again, the way in which legal documents are put together can sometimes help us in this task.

At a third level, legal texts contain a deeper meaning, which may help us to answer the question *why* the law has developed in such a way. Legislation has a history which may reflect particular economic, political or social values. Court decisions may also reflect a variety of underlying influences, for example: the values which the legal system has traditionally served; the prejudices of a particular judge; or the perceived internal logic of the case law system. Asking *why* may involve an element of historical analysis (eg, to see how a law has developed over the years—though note that, traditionally, reading the law has been treated as a largely ahistorical process), or a consideration of governmental or judicial policy making. This will help us to understand the reasoning behind the court's decision in a case, or why an Act with those particular provisions was passed at that particular time.

In this chapter, we shall consider primarily the questions *what* and *why*. In looking at the structure of legal rules, we may occasionally trespass on the territory of *how*, though that will generally be left to Chapters Six, Eight and Nine. In so doing, we have broken this chapter down into four sections: reading statutes; reading cases; reading literary sources, and, lastly, we shall take the step from reading to writing about law.

Reading Statutes

Once a bill has received the Royal Assent it becomes an Act of Parliament. An Act is a public document and must be published by Her Majesty's Stationery Office; it will also, as we have seen, be published in a variety of other sources, including *Statutes in Force*. A copy of such an Act is reproduced below.

Any modern Act of Parliament will take the following form (each number here corresponds to that on the illustration):

(1) Short Title
(2) Citation
(3) Long Title
(4) Date of Royal Assent
(5) Sections
(6) Marginal Note

In addition to these, copies of the statutes may also contain:

(a) Enacting formula
(b) Textual amendments and annotations
(c) Date of Commencement
(d) Schedules and Tables

We shall now consider each of these in the order in which they appear in the Act. The numbers or letters in bold text after each heading refer to the illustration.

(2)
(1) PUBLIC LAVATORIES (TURNSTILES) ACT 1963 (c. 32)

Ss. 1,2

(3)   An Act to make it the duty of local authorities to
        abolish turnstiles in public lavatories and sanitary
        conveniences.   [31st July 1963]   (4)

1.—(1) Every turnstile in any part of a public lavatory or public   Abolition of
sanitary convenience controlled or managed by a local authority,   turnstiles.   (6)
or in any entrance or exit of such a public lavatory or convenience,
shall be removed not later than six months after the passing of
this Act; and after the passing of this Act no turnstile shall be
(5)   installed in, or in any entrance or exit of, any such public lavatory
or convenience.

(2) It shall be the duty of local authorities to ensure that the
provisions of this Act are complied with notwithstanding anything
in any other Act, whether public or local.

(3) If any local authority in England and Wales fail to discharge
a duty imposed on them by the foregoing provisions of this section,
that duty shall be enforceable, on the application of [¹the Secretary
of State], by mandamus.

(4) There shall be paid out of moneys provided by Parliament
any increase attributable to this Act in the sums of payable by
way of Rate-deficiency Grant or Exchequer Equalisation Grant
under the enactments relating to local government in England and
Wales or in Scotland.

(5) In this section the expression "local authority" means, in
England and Wales, a local authority within the meaning of [²the   1972 c. 70.
Local Government Act 1972], a local authority within the meaning   1939 c. 40.   (b)
of the London Government Act 1939 or the Common Council
of the City of London and, in Scotland, the council of a county,
the town council of a burgh or a district council.

2.—(1) This Act may be cited as the Public Lavatories (Turnstiles)   Short title and
Act 1963.   extent.

(2) This Act shall not extend to Northern Ireland.

---

¹ Words substituted by virtue of (W.) S.I. 1965/319, arts. 2(1), 10(1)(a), Sch. 1
    Pt. 1 and (E.) 1970/1681, arts. 2(1), 6(3)
2 Words substituted by virtue of Local Government Act 1972 (c. 70), s. 272(2)

(b)

Long and short titles **(3)** & **(1)**: Older Acts contain a *Preamble* which introduces the legislation, often in some detail, and usually explaining why it had been passed. This device is not used in modern statutes.

Modern Acts will have both a **long** and **short title**. The long title describes the general scope of the Act. The short title is for convenience of citation. As neither provide more than the most general indication of what the Act is about they are of very little help in deducing the scope or meaning of legislation. By contrast, the Preambles of the older Acts are used as an aid to interpreting those particular Acts (see Chapter Eight). This difference may seem rather odd; why should a preamble be of use when the long title is not? The answer lies in the fact that they serve diverse functions.

Consider, for example, an Act you may meet in the Law of Contract: the Unfair Contract Terms Act 1977 (referred to here as UCTA). The short title does not tell you, in fact, that the Act is concerned with exclusion clauses in contracts. The long title is not much more help. It states:

An Act to impose further limits on the extent to which under the Law of England and Wales and Northern Ireland civil liability for breach of contract, or for negligence or other breach of duty, can be avoided by means of contract terms or otherwise, and under the Law of Scotland civil liability can be avoided by means of contract terms.

In this way, they are perhaps analogous to the label on a jam jar. If you look at a jar, you will usually find the title in large letters on the front—STRAWBERRY JAM—but that does not really tell you what is in the jar. It does no more than broadly identify the product to us. You need to look much more closely to find that the jar does not just contain strawberries and sugar, but also, say, pectin, citric acid and sodium citrate, and often a collection of 'E numbers' as well. So it is with an Act, to find out what it is really about you need to look at the contents (ie the operative sections) in detail. By comparison, preambles served to give the courts some notice of Parliamentary intent, though even then, this was often in rather vague terms.

This does not mean that the long title is wholly useless; it will give you a general indication of the scope of the Act, and, together with the contents list which sometimes precedes it (headed *Arrangement of Sections*) it can be helpful in establishing a sense of the Act's contents and structure when *skim reading* (see below).

Citation **(2)**: Statutes obviously have their short title and the year of their creation cited, but, as we explained in the previous chapter, they also have what is known as a **Chapter number**. If a Statute was the 50th to be passed in 1977 then it will have that number. This is a means of reference only.

Royal Assent **(4)**: No Statute is law until assented to by the Monarch. The date of assent is given in the Statute—in UCTA it is 26th October 1977. Frequently this is the date on which the Act becomes law. However, the Act may state that all or part of it will come into effect at a later date (in UCTA's case this was 1st February 1978) or at a date to be appointed by the appropriate minister. Different parts of the Act can thus come into effect at different times. Obviously this may have important practical consequences for the advice lawyers give. Inevitably it can make life very complicated, where you need to know which rules have been superseded already, which have not, and which are going to be, and when!

Enacting formula (a): Although not always reproduced in *Statutes in Force* (they are missing from our example), these are introductory words which appear in every Act stating that both Houses of Parliament and the Monarch have passed the Act. The form of words used is identical in every case, and is of long historical standing. They are of little practical legal significance, though the publication of the Act, with these words, is taken as conclusive evidence that the Act has been passed and is good law.

Sections (5): All Acts are divided into sections—these are usually cited in an abbreviated form as s. 1 or s. 2, or (in the plural) ss. 2 and 3. Sometimes it may be possible to perceive a logical development of concepts as the sections progress, but this is not always the case, so you may, in resolving a single problem find yourself starting at s. 1, which is qualified by something in s. 3, which contains terms defined in s. 45 and repeals part of an earlier enactment listed in Sch. 3! The way in which statutes are internally structured has long been a matter of some contention (see also Chapter Seven), and though it was criticised by the Report of the Renton Committee (1975:30–1) little seems to have changed.

Each section will often be divided into **subsections**—cited as s. 1(1) or s. 1(4). After subsections we can have **paragraphs**—cited as s. 1(1)(a) or s. 1(2)(g); and even **sub-paragraphs** as in s.1(1)(a)(i). Section 3 of UCTA has such a division. If you have ever tried to draft the rules of a committee or a game you will appreciate that this device can be used to split up ideas or clarify particular points. Thus, each separate section of an Act might deal with a separate issue (though these sections may often remain closely related), and each sub-section (etc.) within a section may express a different aspect of that issue. For example, if you have a definition section, it may be that the phrase to be defined has more than one statutory meaning, in which case you could use a different sub-section for each meaning.

Often, you will also find that groups of sections dealing with the same point have *headings* and that very large groupings are divided into *parts*. These titles are of little significance; they are essentially a form of indexing. At best they will indicate some general thematic coherence among the sections under that heading, but they have virtually no value as an aid to interpretation.

Marginal notes (6): Most Acts display marginal notes as a kind of quick reference mechanism, to help you find the section you want. They are generally, like headings, thought to have little legal significance; though there is judicial disagreement over whether, as a last resort, both marginal notes and headings may be used as indicative of the general purpose of the section(s) to which they refer (cf *Chandler* v *DPP* [1964] AC 736, [1962] 3 All ER 142 and *DPP* v *Schildkamp* [1971] AC 1, [1969] 3 All ER 1640). In any event, it is an issue which seldom arises.

Amendments and annotations **(b)**: In *Statutes in Force*, it is normal for any amendments to an Act made subsequent to its passing to be incorporated into the text. As in the illustrated Act, the amendments are shown within square brackets. These amendments are cited as being part of the Act, and have the full force of law. Any footnotes or commentary annotated to an Act (as eg in *Current Law Statutes Annotated*) do not form part of the Act and, of course, have no direct legal effect.

Date of commencement **(c)**: Acts will normally have a specific commencement section near to the end of the statute. It may either state that the Act, or parts of the Act will come into force on a specific date or dates, or that it comes into force on a date to be fixed by the relevant government minister. On the latter occasions the normal form of words runs more or less as follows:

> . . . *this Act shall come into force on such day as the Secretary of State may by order appoint; and different days may be so appointed for different provisions or different purposes of the same provision* . . .

This gives the minister *carte blanche* in deciding what comes into force and when.

Schedules **(d)**: Schedules (the term may be abbreviated to 'sched.' or 'sch.') can be found at the end of most Acts of Parliament. Schedules are parts of an Act that provide more detail regarding sections or groups of sections. Sometimes they give examples of how to calculate things contained in the Act, such as pensions, tax assessments, and so on; sometimes they simply expand upon phrases; sometimes they define phrases; or sometimes they contain detailed amendments of earlier legislation. As such, they may be quite detailed, perhaps even exceeding the length of the rest of the Act. Each provision within a schedule is called a **paragraph**, and there may also be **sub-paragraphs**. So, a provision is properly cited in the form 'sch.1 para. 3(a)'.

A schedule, normally the last, tells you which earlier Acts the present Act repeals. This is important because, generally speaking, once an Act is passed it remains in force until repealed by another Act. This is why vestiges of the Witchcraft Acts were still in force as late as 1951 and why other such anachronisms remain 'on the Statute book'. By an odd quirk it also meant that, in English Law, the USA did not gain its independence until 1963!

Note, here, that though lawyers sometimes talk of Acts being 'obsolete', there is no formal basis upon which an Act could be disapplied by the courts simply because it has become old or out-of-date. At most it can be argued that a statute should not apply to a novel situation, because that situation was not within the original legislative intent; this reflects what is sometimes called the *principle of contemporary exposition*: see *Aerated Bread Co.* v *Gregg* [1873] LR 8 QB 355. In this case Blackburn J refused to apply provisions of the Bread Act 1836 regarding 'fancy bread' to the plaintiff's product, because at the time the Act was passed, the term had a very specific meaning, which could not be applied to the disputed product some 36 years later.

Some obsolete legislation is periodically repealed by the passing of Statute Law Revision Acts, which are purely administrative measures intended to tidy-up the statute book.

Reading Cases

Like statutes, modern English law reports tend to follow a standard format, similar to the illustration (see the following page) from *Finnegan* v *Clowney Youth Training Programme Ltd* [1990] 2 All ER 546. Running down the pages, you will find:

    (1)   The name of the case.
    (2)   The court in which it was heard.
    (3)   The names of the judge(s) presiding.
    (4)   The hearing date(s).
    (5)   The headnote.
    (6)   Notes of cross-references to *Halsbury*.
    (7)   A list of cases referred to.
    (8)   Details of the appeal.
    (9)   The names of counsel appearing in the case.
   (10)   The judgment(s) [not shown].
   (11)   Letters in the margin.

Some of these are quite self-explanatory, so we will be selective in the points we discuss.

The name of the case **(1)**: It was said in Chapter Two that English case names follow the names of the parties involved. In this respect, Common Law case citations tend to differ from the forms adopted in many Civilian systems, which often adopt a more anonymous, administrative title, based usually on the court, and a case number or date, though this is not always so. The French, for example, use both styles. Cases before the *Cour de Cassation* are cited by giving an abbreviated version of the division concerned *(civile, criminelle, sociale, commerciale)*, the date of the decision and its location in the relevant reports, *les recueils généraux*, known as the *Recueil Dalloz, Recueil Sirey* and the *Juris-Classeur Périodique*.

Finnegan v Clowney Youth Training Programme Ltd

(1)

a

HOUSE OF LORDS (2)
LORD BRIDGE OF HARWICH, LORD GRIFFITHS, LORD ACKNER, LORD OLIVER OF AYLMERTON AND
LORD LOWRY

(3)

2 APRIL, 17 MAY 1990
(4)

b

Northern Ireland – Employment – Discrimination against a woman – Provision in relation to retirement – Female employees required to retire at 60 whereas men retiring at 65 – Northern Ireland and English legislation identical – English legislation passed before adoption of EEC equal treatment directive whereas Northern Ireland legislation passed subsequent to directive – Whether Northern Ireland provision passed to implement directive – Whether Northern Ireland ***c*** *provision to be construed differently from English provision – Whether unlawful discrimination for women to be required to retire earlier than men – Whether necessary to refer question to European Court – Sex Discrimination (Northern Ireland) Order 1976, art 8(2)(4) – Council Directive (EEC) 76/207, art 5(1).*

European Economic Community – National legislation – Construction – Construction of legislation ***d*** *relating to death or retirement – Determination of case not dependent on question of Community law – Whether court should make reference to European Court.*

In February 1986 the employee, who was employed by the employer as a supervisor, was told that she would be required to retire on 1 April 1986 following her sixtieth birthday on 22 March. Her request to be allowed to continue working beyond her sixtieth ***e*** birthday was refused and her employment was duly terminated on 1 April. The employee made a complaint to an industrial tribunal alleging that she had been unlawfully discriminated against by the employer on the grounds of sex, contrary to art 8(2)*ᵃ* of the Sex Discrimination (Northern Ireland) Order 1976, in that she had been forced to retire at the age of 60 whereas male employees retired at 65. The employer relied on art 8(4)*ᵇ* of the 1976 order, which ***f*** provided that art 8(2) did not apply to provisions relating to death or retirement. The tribunal upheld the complaint and awarded the employee compensation, on the ground that art 8(2) and (4) had to be construed consistently with art 5(1)*ᶜ* of Council Directive (EEC) 76/207 (the equal treatment directive), which prohibited discrimination in working conditions, including conditions governing dismissal, on grounds of sex. The employer appealed to the ***g*** Court of Appeal in Northern Ireland, which allowed the appeal on the ground, inter alia, that art 8(2) of the 1976 order was to be given the same meaning as identical legislation in England which had been construed as permitting discrimination in retirement ages. The employee appealed to the House of Lords, contending, inter alia, that the English legislation was distinguishable since it had been passed before the equal treatment directive was adopted whereas the 1976 order had not been made until after the adoption of the directive, so that the order had to be construed in the light of the directive. The employee also requested ***h*** the court to seek a preliminary ruling from the Court of Justice of the European Communities (11) under art 177 of the EEC Treaty on the question which arose on the appeal.

Held — (1) Since art 8(4) of the 1976 order was in identical terms and in an identical context to the English legislation it must have been intended to have identical effect and should not be presumed to have been made for the purpose of implementing the equal

a   Article 8(2), so far as material, provides: 'It is unlawful for a person, in the case of a woman employed by him at an establishment in Northern Ireland, to discriminate against her . . . (*b*) by dismissing her, or subjecting her to any other detriment.'

b   Article 8(4) provides: 'Paragraphs . . . (2) do not apply to provision in relation to death or retirement.'

c   Article 5(1) is set out at p 548 *h*, post

a treatment directive, notwithstanding that the order was made subsequently to that directive. It followed that although the employee's compulsory retirement at the age of 60 was a contravention of art 8(2) of the 1976 order, since it discriminated against her on the grounds of sex, it was a provision in relation to death or retirement which fell within the exception permitted by art 8(4) and therefore did not constitute unlawful discrimination. The employee's dismissal therefore did not contravene art 8(2). The appeal would accordingly be dismissed
b (see pp 551 *a b d* to *f h* to p 552 *b*, post); *Duke v GEC Reliance Ltd* [1988] 1 All ER 626 applied; *Marshall v Southampton and South West Hampshire Area Health Authority (Teaching)* Case 152/84 [1986] 2 All ER 584 considered.

(2) Since it was for the United Kingdom courts to interpret the 1976 order and since the equal treatment directive did not have direct effect between citizens the determination of the appeal did not depend on any question of Community law. Accordingly, a reference
c to the European Court under art 177 was not necessary (see p 551 *h* to p 552 *b*, post).

Notes
For discrimination against employees, see 16 Halsbury's Laws (4th edn) paras 771·2, 771·5, and for cases on the subject, see 20 Digest (Reissue) 588-593, *4495-4515*.
For Community provisions on equal treatment of employees, see 52 Halsbury's Laws (4th
d edn) paras 21·13, 21·17.   (6)
For references to the Court of Justice of the European Communities for a preliminary ruling, see 51 ibid paras 3·79-3·81.
For the EEC Treaty, art 177, see 50 Halsbury's Statutes (4th edn) 325.
Article 8 of the Sex Discrimination (Northern Ireland) Order 1976 corresponds to s 6 of the Sex Discrimination Act 1975. For s 6 of the 1975 Act, see 6 ibid 702.
e
Cases referred to in opinions
Burton v British Railways Board Case 19/81 [1982] 3 All ER 537, [1982] QB 1080, [1982] 3 WLR 387, [1982] ECR 555, CJEC.
Duke v GEC Reliance Ltd [1988]1 All ER 626, [1988] AC 618, [1988] 2 WLR 359, HL.
f Litster v Forth Dry Dock and Engineering Co Ltd [1989] 1 All ER 1134, [1990] AC 546, [1989] 2 WLR 634, HL.   (7)
Marshall v Southampton and South West Hampshire Area Health Authority (Teaching) Case 152/84 [1986] 2 All ER 584, [1986] QB 401, [1986] 2 WLR 780, [1986] ECR 723, CJEC.
Note [1966] 3 All ER 77, [1966] 1 WLR 1234, HL.
g Pickstone v Freemans plc [1988] 2 All ER 803, [1989] AC 66, [1989] 2 WLR 634, HL.
von Colson and Kamann v Land Nordrhein-Westfalen Case 14/83 [1984] ECR 1891.

Appeal
Frances Finnegan (the employee) appealed with leave of the Court of Appeal in Northern Ireland against the decision of that court (Hutton LCJ and Mac Dermott LJ) on 28 November
h 1988 allowing the appeal of the respondent, Clowney Youth Training Programme Ltd (the employer), by way of case stated by an industrial tribunal (J E Maguire chairman) sitting at Belfast on 23 November 1987 in respect of its decision that the employer had unlawfully discriminated against the employee on grounds of sex, contrary to the provisions of art 8 of the Sex Discrimination (Northern Ireland) Order 1976, SI 1976/1042, in compulsorily (8)
j retiring the employee at 60 when comparable male employees were allowed to work until the age of 65. The facts are set out in the opinion of Lord Bridge.

Patrick Coghlin QC and *Seamus Treacy* (both of the Northern Ireland Bar) for the employee. (9)
Patrick Markey QC and *Brian Kennedy* (both of the Northern Ireland Bar) for the employer.

Their Lordships took time for consideration.

Conversely, decisions of the *Conseil d'État* are cited by a case name. By comparison, the English system sounds simple, but as is so often the case, that impression is misleading; there is a wide array of forms that the case name can take. These forms can themselves tell us quite a lot about the nature of the case.

In *civil* cases the normal mode of citation is the name of the person bringing the case or appeal (**plaintiff** or **appellant**) first followed by the name of the **defendant** (or **respondent** in an appeal): thus, 'Smith v Jones'. The v means *versus*, that is 'against' (reflecting the adversarial nature of the process); it is usually spoken as 'and', hence 'Smith and Jones'—spoken citations can thus sound confusing if there are more than two parties, as you will have a multiplicity of 'ands', one of which is a 'v'!); if Jones were to lose his case and appeal, the form of citation should switch to 'Jones v Smith'. For an apparently unfathomable reason this does not always happen. Four other forms of civil citations crop-up with some regularity.

First, in shipping cases (a number of which come up in contract and commercial law), it is a convention to abbreviate the case name to that of the ship involved, so for example, the case of *Compania Financiera Soleada S.A., Netherlands Antilles Ships Management Corp. and Dammers and van der Heide's Shipping and Trading Co.* v *Hamoor Tanker Corp. Inc.* (1981) is mercifully known as *The Borag*. That abbreviation will be sufficient to find the case in most books or citators.

Secondly, cases may appear in the form 'Re Smith' (where *Re* roughly means 'concerning'). This form arises in some property cases, particularly those relating to trusts, or the estates of deceased persons. It is also used in cases where the court is considering its wardship jurisdiction (where the court effectively takes ultimate control over the affairs of a child). In the latter cases the name of the child will not normally be disclosed, and the case citation will appear as 'Re M', for example. They are usually indexed under the name referred to, not under *Re*. (There are also some other situations where the court will not disclose the names of the parties, so that cases are identified by an initial letter, in the form of 'A v B').

Thirdly, you may come across cases cited as 'In B' or 'In E'. These cases arise in the law relating to wills and estates. In B stands for *In Bonis* (in the goods of). In E stands for *In the Estate of*. The distinction arose because, prior to the 1897 Land Transfer Act, personal representatives could only deal with a deceased's goods, not their land. The citations reflect this. All such modern cases can now be referred to as *Re*.

Lastly, another form appears where the High Court has exercised its public law jurisdiction judicially to review the administration, or an inferior court. These cases are invariably cited in the form 'R v Bloggs *ex parte* Smith'. This is the only context when the Crown ('R') is commonly cited in civil proceedings. It reflects the fact that technically the action has been taken by the Crown, on the application of some other party, under what are, historically, the *prerogative* powers of the Crown. The term *ex parte* properly denotes someone who is outside the proceedings. In this situation it seems rather peculiar, though strictly correct, as it identifies the person who made the application for judicial review.

Criminal cases are normally cited as 'R v Smith'. The 'R' stands for *Rex* or *Regina* (Latin for king and queen) denoting the state's role as **prosecutor**; the accused is normally cited as the **defendant**. The oral form of the citation is 'the Crown against Smith'.

Once again, there is a variety of alternative forms. Some criminal prosecutions can only be commenced with the approval of one of the government's law officers—the Attorney-General (A-G) or the Director of Public Prosecutions (DPP). In such cases that official's title will appear instead of the Crown as prosecutor. Some cases, notably those which commenced in the magistrates' courts before the Crown Prosecution Service was set up in 1985, bore the name of the (police) prosecutor (see, eg *Albert* v *Lavin* [1982] AC 546, [1981] 3 All ER 878). This principle still applies in those very rare cases where a member of the public brings a private prosecution.

The court and presiding judge(s) **(2)** and **(3)**: These are perhaps of greater significance than you might at first think. Given that our system of precedent depends upon a ranking of courts, we need to know whereabouts in the 'batting-order' this particular case is placed. Furthermore, in cases before the House of Lords, Court of Appeal and a Divisional Court of the High Court, it will be normal to have more than one judge presiding. Sometimes the number, and even the status of the judges presiding will influence the weight of that decision.

The headnote **(5)**: This does three things. First, it provides a brief statement of the **material facts** of the case. By facts we are talking about the description of events leading up to the case (see further Chapters Four and Six); the term *material* denotes those facts which the judge considered important in deciding the case (we discuss the concept of materiality in detail in Chapter Six). Secondly, it will normally indicate the legal issues (usually called the **questions of law**) to be considered by the court. Thirdly, the headnote contains a summary of the court's decision on the issues of fact and law (as appropriate), including details of any *dissenting* judgment (where one or more judges disagree with the majority view).

It will also frequently give some indication of the effect of this decision on existing case law. This is indicated by the use of the following terms in conjunction with the citation of the relevant case.

Affirmed: this indicates that the court has agreed with the decision of a lower court in respect of the *same* case.

Applied: this means that a court has regarded itself as bound by an earlier decision, and has therefore employed the same reasoning in the instant case. The alternative would have been to *distinguish* the earlier case (below).

Approved: this is used where a higher court states that another case before a lower court was correctly decided.

Considered: this seems to be something of a residual category. If the court has discussed a reported case (particularly one decided by a court of equal status) but not reached any dramatic conclusion about its application, then it will probably appear as 'considered'.

Distinguished: an earlier case will be distinguished where a court has no power (or no wish) to overrule it, but does not want to apply it either. The court will therefore find some ground for saying it is different, and should not be followed *in this particular case*.

Overruled: this is used to show where a court has rejected and invalidated an earlier decision of a court of lower (or sometimes equal) status to itself.

Reversed: this is the opposite of affirmed. It means that the higher court has decided that the lower court in the *same* case came to the wrong decision.

Although the headnote is intended as a summary of the whole case, it is not authority for anything within the case. It is simply a *résumé* provided by the publishers of the report. Though they are usually fairly reliable, mistakes are sometimes made. For example, in *O'Grady* v *Saper* [1940] 3 All ER 527, which concerned an appeal from an action originally brought against an employer in respect of unpaid wages during the employee's absence for sickness, the headnote reads:

> *Held,* the facts proved showed by implication that there was no agreement that the respondent should be paid wages while absent through illness and he was not entitled to recover.

This significantly distorts the contractual point which was made in that case. What the court actually said was that the respondent (the employee) could not recover because there was an implied contractual term that he was *not* to be paid wages during any sick leave. So be careful in relying upon the headnote of a case—it certainly should not be used as a substitute for reading the judgments.

List of cases (7): Most law reports will contain two separate lists. The first is a list of cases cited by the judge(s) in the judgment. That list is useful if you are trying to discover how the courts have subsequently used a particular decision. In other words, it provides a list of possible precedents used in that case. The second list (if there is one) will refer to additional cases cited in argument by counsel. Since the judge has not cited them, they are obviously of much less significance, but they can sometimes be worth considering if you are undertaking detailed research into the rationale of a decision, as they may show up points that the judge has apparently ignored or rejected, but without formal consideration of the case in the written judgment.

Details of the appeal **(8)**: Here the report gives a short history of the case, stating the parties, the previous hearing(s) of the case, and usually the legal findings which form the basis of the appeal.

There are a number of basic points regarding appeal terminology that we can deal with here. In most cases, the case will refer simply to an 'appeal', which may be an appeal on a point of law, or fact, or both depending upon the jurisdiction of the court. However, there are three particular procedures that you may confront quite frequently, which require a little more explanation.

(a)   Appeal by way of case stated: this most commonly arises in appeals from the magistrates court to the High Court, either where the applicant believes the magistrates have made an error of law (eg misinterpreted a statute) or acted outside their jurisdiction. The magistrates state a case by submitting to the High Court a statement of facts found by the justices, together with the question(s) of law or jurisdiction on which guidance is sought. The High Court may then come to its own decision on the issue, or refer the case back to the magistrates for reconsideration in the light of the High Court's opinion. Further rights of appeal exist on a case stated. These lie directly to the House of Lords in criminal cases. A good example of the whole appeal process is provided by the case of *Albert* v *Lavin*, already mentioned. The law report includes the form of words used by the magistrates to state a case concerning police powers of arrest for a breach of the peace. In civil cases the appeal is normally to the Court of Appeal. In *Finnegan* v *Clowney Youth Training Programme Ltd* the appeal shows that a case was stated by an industrial tribunal to the Court of Appeal in Northern Ireland. This particular procedure is unique to the Northern Irish system, though there are a number of contexts in which an English civil case can be stated for the High Court, these tend to be rare.

(b)   Interlocutory application: in civil proceedings an interlocutory application is an application to the court for some kind of temporary order, that will take effect until the case comes to a full trial at a later date. Such applications most commonly arise as requests for an *injunction* (an order requiring the other party to do, or stop doing, something). They are thus meant to preserve the *status quo* until the trial. Interlocutory applications will normally be heard by a single judge in the High Court, with a right of appeal to the Court of Appeal.

(c)   'Leapfrog appeal': under Part II of the Administration of Justice Act 1969, a civil case may exceptionally move from the High Court direct to the House of Lords. This is colloquially referred to as a 'leapfrog appeal'. It may only be used where the case involves a point of law of general public importance relating to a matter of interpretation of primary or secondary legislation, and it is a point where the High Court is bound on that point by a precedent from the Court of Appeal or House of Lords. The procedure seems to be used in few cases (see Drewry, 1973).

The names of counsel **(9)**: historically, the only lawyers entitled to appear before the High Court and above were barristers. Changes to the rules are contained in the Courts and Legal Services Act 1990, s. 27, which came into force in January 1991. This extends rights of audience to solicitors who have undergone additional advocacy training.

In the majority of cases before the higher courts, each side will be represented by two barristers, a leader and a junior counsel. Until late 1977, this was a formal requirement where the leader was a 'QC' (Queen's Counsel). Now a QC may appear alone, though she or he can decline to do so. The change in rules seems to have made comparatively little difference in practice.

The judgments **(10)**   The judgments are the most important part of any case, and as we shall in Chapters Five and Six, they are crucial to the operation of the English doctrine of precedent. It is normally the practice that, where there is more than one judge sitting, each is entitled to deliver his own opinion on the case. The first judgment given tends to be that of the senior judge. The judges following may then either give a full judgment of their own, either supporting or dissenting from the decision of one or more of the other speakers, or give a brief *concurring* judgment, which may be no more than 'I agree'. The chief exception to this practice is the Privy Council, where a unanimous or majority opinion is presented by one judge alone, and only dissenting voices from that have a separate right to be heard.

So far as the formalities of judgments are concerned, there appear to be none of any real significance, though there are many points of style, particularly in respect of forms of address. Titles are always given—a matter of style which is normally followed in academic writing, though the judges are also strong on ritual courtesy. A fellow judge is seldom anything less than 'learned'—even where the discussion of his judgment strongly suggests that the speaker considers him to have the reasoning powers of a codfish. In deference to their exalted position, Law Lords can usually expect to be both 'noble and learned'.

The style of judgments tends to be quite individual. Some judges adopt a clear narrative pattern; Lord Denning was a prime, in his later decisions one might say an extreme, example of this style, whereby the facts and the law are woven into a continuous 'story'. Others have a far more formal style, which can produce some very dense prose indeed. A fairly recent innovation by some judges is to break up the text with headings and sub-headings, which can much improve the clarity of the argument contained therein.

One final feature of English cases, which differentiates our process from that of most other countries, is the high proportion of *extempore,* or 'off the cuff' judgments. It is common practice in the High Court, though less common in the Court of Appeal, for judgment to be given either immediately after the conclusion of argument, or following a brief adjournment. Judges in these courts have the power to **reserve** judgment, that is, to go away, think about the issues, and present a full written judgment at a later date. The House of Lords will always reserve its decisions. In the former courts it is for the judges to decide. A number of factors, including the judge's self-confidence, or views of the complexity of the case, and particularly the pressures of his or her caseload, will influence that decision. Despite some judicial and academic doubts as to the quality of unreserved as compared with reserved judgments, it would seem that the practice of giving unreserved judgments is set to continue for the foreseeable future.

Where a judgment in the law reports has been reserved, that is usually indicated, at a point just preceding the judgment(s), by the abbreviation *'Cur. adv. vult.'* This is short for *Curia advisari vult,* meaning 'the court wishes to be advised'. Judgments in the Lords are preceded by the more mundane: 'Their Lordships took time for consideration'. Presumably it would be inappropriate for the House of Lords even to pretend to take advice on the law!

Letters in the margin **(11)** are a useful addendum to the page number, which may be cited in the form 'p. 123a'. (Note also that, conventionally the 'p.' denoting the page can be dropped when citing pages of the law reports). Taken together they can be used to locate more accurately a piece of text which is being referred to in court, in the headnote to a law report, or in an essay, and so on.

Reading Books and Articles

Reading of secondary sources may be undertaken in a number of ways. First, you may only want an *overview* of the contents; second, you may be after *detail* on some specific point or area of law, or, thirdly, you may be seeking a *critical* perspective on certain concepts or values. It is in this latter context that some texts can be of particular assistance in discovering the *why* of a legal rule.

Reading for an Overview, or in Detail

It is always helpful to start by obtaining an overview of any material. If it is a book, look to the contents list first. Consider how the text (either of the book as a whole or a specific chapter) is broken down. Similarly, many articles are divided into different sections, each with a heading and sometimes sub-headings. These should give you some idea of what the text is about, and how useful it will be. Virtually all books will have a short preface, or introduction, telling you something about the contents which can also help to identify the nature of the work. Some journals publish a brief *abstract* of an article at its beginning, which outlines the argument it contains. Both of these may be of similar assistance. Often it will then be sufficient to skim (see below under 'note-taking') that material.

If you are after specific detail, it is still advisable (unless or until you are familiar with a work) to obtain an overview first. Do not 'dive in' unprepared. A first reading will give you a sense of how the writer structures the material. Having a good idea of what is there before you start making detailed notes helps to ensure that those notes are coherent and reflect what the author actually said, not what you may have taken totally out of context.

Critical Reading

If your purpose is critical, in that, for example, you are attempting to analyse or challenge the ideas presented by a particular author, your reading must be directed to that purpose. In that case you must consider how the author has developed his argument, has he:

(a)   made any unsupported or unrecognised assumptions?
(b)   reached conclusions unsupported by his argument?
(c)   ignored counter-arguments that exist?

Often, a comparison of different texts can help you sort out the range of arguments and counter-arguments which exist. Do not fall into the trap of being dependent upon a single book or article when constructing any kind of critical analysis. Literary sources may also be of assistance if you are attempting some critical analysis of a case or statutory provision.

The idea that texts can be read critically should also warn us that literary sources are subject to limitations. There are two which are particularly important.

The question of authority: It is wrong to treat books and articles as wholly authoritative. We have already said the courts do not place that much weight on secondary sources, and ultimately that is because texts are not the law itself. The author may be, consciously or unconsciously, advancing one argument over another which could in fact be equally valid. Though so long as you are aware of this, it can be used positively if you are trying to offer a critical analysis of the way the law has developed on a specific point. You should also remember that writers and editors are fallible, and, however much care is taken, substantive mistakes do sometimes appear in books and articles. They do not, and cannot, replace the primary sources.

This does not just apply to your normal studying. It is also relevant to exam preparation. Remember that if you revise from the notes you have made on a textbook's commentary about a case, your answer will be two stages removed from its original source. Obviously you cannot read *every* case and section of a statute cited during the year, but at least make sure you are acquainted with the most important primary sources in your subject.

The question of accuracy: It is something of a truism to say that law books (including this one!) are already out of date on the day they are published. Law is a constantly developing subject. Details can change quite frequently, which is why established textbooks are updated by the publication of new editions. Even so, there is always a risk that, before a new edition comes out, the law on your particular point has changed. This means that in using textbooks two things must be remembered. First, always use the latest edition of any text. Secondly, even when using the latest edition, be prepared to search your primary sources for any updating that needs to be done. The problem with journal articles is even more acute, as those are not updated in the way that books are. Current notes and articles can themselves be a useful way of keeping up to date, but once they become a few years old, they may have to be treated with caution, though, of course, there is no general rule that can tell us when any piece of legal writing is past its 'sell by' date.

From Reading to Writing

Reading is only the first stage in the learning process. Ultimately, your reading of any legal materials can serve one or more of a number of functions: it can supplement your lecture notes or other course material; it can form the basis of seminar preparation, or it can provide source material for an essay or problem question. Reading by itself is not an effective mechanism for remembering, so you need to convert your reading into a more appropriate—written—form. This means that there are essentially two writing skills you need to develop. Firstly, the ability to make worthwhile notes from your reading and, secondly, the technique of constructing an answer to an essay or problem question. We shall consider each of these in turn.

Note-taking Technique

Whether you are reading primary or literary material, your first stage must be to make notes. In taking notes, we would suggest the following steps could be followed:

Make sure you know why you are reading: Whenever you read legal materials, you should have some purpose in mind; for example, a search for judicial statements supporting a specific argument. If your reading lacks purpose, your notes will lack coherence and structure, and will be of limited value.

If it is useful, note the reference: Make sure you keep a note of the reference to the material so that you can, if necessary, cite it, or find the material again. It is generally adequate to keep a note of the reference with your other notes, though some people like to maintain a separate card index of all their references. The latter can certainly be useful if you are engaged in a substantial piece of work, like an extended essay or dissertation, where you might gather quite a large number of references. Do not forget to make a note of any other primary or literary sources cited by your material, if they appear at all relevant.

Start by 'skim' reading the material: Once you have worked out what you are looking for, quickly scan the material to see if it is of assistance. This is certainly necessary where you have relied on summaries in, say, *Current Law*, or footnotes to a book or article, as you will often find that these do not really contain enough detail to tell whether the case, etc. referred to is the one you need. Skim reading can save you time which might otherwise be wasted making notes on something that is ultimately irrelevant. During this first reading, it often helps to note down initial impressions of the content or structure of the article, and specifically to identify any sections of the text which you think will be of further assistance. Please do not make notes in any books other than those you own. Such notes can be a serious distraction to other readers; any such notes you find are best ignored. Following another's comments can sometimes mean you are simply copying their mistakes.

Now start to take detailed notes: On your second reading, you can start making fuller notes. If you think that there are sections you might want to quote *verbatim*, then by all means copy them directly. But be careful: copying large sections of text is slow and tedious, and lengthy quotes may be better photocopied (though you should be aware that copyright restrictions limit the amount of text you may legally copy, even for private study). It is a far better practice to put the material into your own words. To do that, you actually have to think about what has been said, and what it *means!* Converting someone else's ideas into your own words is a major step towards understanding those ideas. For this reason simply photocopying material, and going through it with a coloured pen or highlighter, is a poor substitute for proper note-taking.

Writing Essays

Writing essays is essentially about two things.

First, it is about conveying *information.* Any essay you are asked to write will require you to tell the reader what you know about the subject under discussion. In conveying that information there are three cardinal rules:

Be accurate.   Try to be as precise as possible in the information you put down. Vagueness is a sure sign of a lack of understanding or insufficient thought. If it is not possible to give an accurate statement of the principles involved (perhaps because the law is in a muddle), then say that there is no single answer and *clearly distinguish any alternatives that seem to exist.*

Accuracy is also about clarity of meaning. Style is important because a good style enhances the clarity of your exposition; in the end your arguments can only be as good as your ability to express them. Do not ignore the fact that language has its own rhythm, and this can often guide you to sentences or phrases which do not work. Some people find that reading work aloud helps in this, because if a phrase sounds wrong, it probably is wrong. This is not recommended practice in a library!

It is equally important to avoid jargon or words you do not understand. Do not be like the famous Mrs Malaprop, with her 'nice derangement of epitaphs'. If in doubt use a dictionary, or a thesaurus if you want to bring in alternative vocabulary. A good guide to a simple writing style remains Sir Ernest Gowers' *The Complete Plain Words*, which was originally written for the Civil Service. One can only assume it has fallen into some disuse among its original audience, but if you are worried that you write like a (bad) civil servant, it is recommended reading.

Be relevant. Do not introduce something you know to be irrelevant into an answer. There is a great temptation to throw every possible bit of information you have at the question, and hope that some of it is right (what many teachers call a 'shotgun' approach). This does not look impressive, as it again suggests a lack of forethought. Keeping to what is relevant is not magic; it is simply a question of familiarity with and understanding of your material. If you have taken the time to analyse the question, and thought out what is expected of you there should be no need to adopt such an approach.

Be concise. In our experience, teachers do not award marks on the basis of the number of pages filled. It is obviously impossible for us to state what the 'average' acceptable length of an essay is, as criteria vary from course to course and year to year. You should always be guided by your tutors as to what is required. If you are given an indication of the appropriate length, then any significant shortfall would normally indicate that something is missing.

Brevity is not, ultimately, just about the number of words you use; it is about how you use them. Again, it is a matter of clarity. Clarity is best achieved by short sentences and the proper use of paragraphs. Remember that a sentence should always make sense, and that each separate issue you discuss deserves its own paragraph. Sentences full of long words do not impress unless they convey a meaning not otherwise possible. Lawyers, perhaps more than any other profession, have a reputation for pomposity. It is a reputation that is not wholly undeserved. Formal legal writing is still perceived to be very different from everyday English. Indeed, there are those who suspect that its connections with the English language are little more than coincidental! This is because, at its worst, it not only uses technical terms outside of the general language, but also uses forms of language and phrasing that are archaic, and often redundant—documents full of jargon interspersed with the occasional 'whatsoever', 'wheresoever', 'heretofore' and 'hereafter'. In a brilliant parody, James D. Gordon III (1991:1689) offers a classic example of such 'legaleze'; a lawyers's translation of the phrase, 'I give you this orange':

Know all men by these presents that I hereby give, grant, bargain, sell, release, convey, transfer, and quitclaim all my right, title, interest, benefit and use whatever in, of, and concerning this chattel, otherwise known as an orange, or citrus orantium, together with all the appurtenances thereto of skin, pulp, pip, rind, seeds and juice, to have and to hold the said orange together with its skin, pulp, pip, rind, seeds and juice for his own use and behoof, to himself and his heirs in fee simple forever, free from all leins, encumbrances, easements, limitations, restraints or conditions whatsoever, and all prior deeds, tranfers or other documents whatsoever, now or anywhere made to the contrary notwithstanding, with full power to bite, cut, suck or otherwise eat the said orange or to give away the same, with or without its skin, pulp, pip, rind, seeds or juice.

Fortunately, this kind of 'supernatural incantation' (to borrow Gordon's phrase) is becoming far less common in legal practice, where there is a growing tendency to simplify documents and to move towards a system of 'plain English' drafting (see Adler, 1990). Although mastery of technical legal language is a requisite for both the study and practice of law, jargon used for its own sake has no place in the law school. Do not let your choice of words turn your work into a parody of legal language.

Secondly, essay writing is about constructing an *argument* based on the information you have acquired. Essay questions inevitably ask you to structure your material in one way or another. The clue usually lies in the first or last words of the question . . . 'Consider critically'; 'Discuss'; 'Evaluate', and so on. The greatest failing of all is to miss the significance of those words and simply 'write all you know' about a topic without bringing any critical faculty into play.

The key thing to remember about argument in academic writing is that there are certain conventional rules about what constitutes a 'good argument'. If you have had little or no previous experience of this type of writing, it is something you will certainly need to think about, and practise. The Open University (1985) has published a guide to study skills, which includes a section on the techniques of argument. It can be found in many academic libraries, and gives a more detailed discussion than we can provide here. We can briefly summarise the techniques, however:

(a) A good argument requires authority: it is insufficient to rely on your own value judgments or 'commonsense'. Any arguments you advance must be supported by authority from primary or literary sources. Your own value judgments do not constitute evidence of how things work. Value judgments also personalise the debate so that your arguments lack a sense of objectivity. You may bring an element of value judgment into play in

1. *Criminal Law*

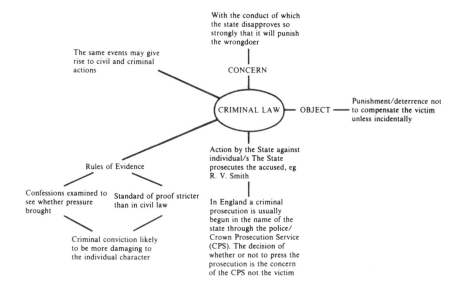

With the conduct of which
the state disapproves so
strongly that it will punish
the wrongdoer

The same events may give
rise to civil and criminal
actions

CONCERN

CRIMINAL LAW — OBJECT —

Punishment/deterrence not
to compensate the victim
unless incidentally

Rules of Evidence

Action by the State against
individual/s The State
prosecutes the accused, eg
R. V. Smith

Confessions examined to
see whether pressure
brought

Standard of proof stricter
than in civil law

Criminal conviction likely
to be more damaging to
the individual character

In England a criminal
prosecution is usually
begun in the name of the
state through the police/
Crown Prosecution Service
(CPS). The decision of
whether or not to press the
prosecution is the concern
of the CPS not the victim

2. *Civil Law*

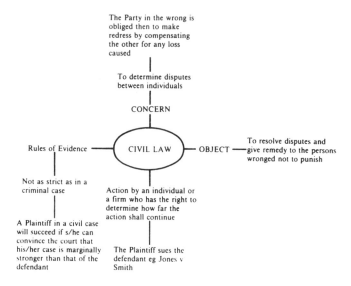

The Party in the wrong is
obliged then to make
redress by compensating
the other for any loss
caused

To determine disputes
between individuals

CONCERN

Rules of Evidence — CIVIL LAW — OBJECT —

To resolve disputes and
give remedy to the persons
wronged not to punish

Not as strict as in a
criminal case

Action by an individual or
a firm who has the right to
determine how far the
action shall continue

A Plaintiff in a civil case
will succeed if s/he can
convince the court that
his/her case is marginally
stronger than that of the
defendant

The Plaintiff sues the
defendant eg Jones v
Smith

a conclusion, for example, where you have to choose between two established alternative arguments, but even then you should indicate *why* one argument is to be preferred. Your preference should be supportable on rational grounds, not just on the basis that 'I think it is the better answer'. Commonsense is of no more worth than one person's value judgment. An argument is not necessarily true because the proponent believes most other people would support it.

(b)   A good argument is built up carefully: in developing an argument it is important to have a plan of where you are going. Arguments need to be developed gradually. A good essay comprises three elements: INTRODUCTION—DISCUSSION—CONCLUSION.

Your introduction should explain what you are setting out to do. Your discussion should display the relevant information, derived from the appropriate sources, and show clearly on what side of the argument each piece falls. The conclusion should sum up the main points you have made and make clear your conclusion regarding the question asked. Keep these separate functions clearly in mind. Do not fall into the trap of presenting a lengthy ramble through the detail of the law, followed by a final paragraph containing a number of disparate critical remarks. That does not constitute an argument!

(c)   You may find it helpful when planning an answer to reduce your plan to a diagrammatic form. You may already have your own preference, but one technique which is quite widely used involves the construction of what are sometimes called 'mind maps'. This technique was first developed by Tony Buzan (1989) and his book is recommended as the primary source and guide.

'Mind maps' are intended to harness 'natural' patterns of thinking to studying and writing. To draw a mind map is quite simple. You should always start at the centre of a (preferably) blank sheet of paper. At the centre, place the question, or concept, you are seeking to analyse. From the centre, move out to your first stage of development, and jot down the overall themes you wish to develop. From each of those themes, you may then radiate outwards, noting specific arguments and examples that you need to develop in respect of those themes.

Suppose, for example, you wish to make notes on the distinctions between civil and criminal proceedings, or that you have been asked to present a simple descriptive essay requiring you to 'describe the different consequences of defining an act as a criminal or civil wrong'. In either situation you could use the 'mind map' technique to display the basic information you need to have. We have included a possible outline on the facing page.

A final word of warning: good planning and good writing technique can never wholly disguise a lack of content. It can, however, enable you to use your knowledge to its best effect. Failure to abide by the basic rules can be met with the kind of indignity once meted out to an attorney by the United States' Supreme Court. The Court returned a brief with the instruction that a whole new set of papers be filed in a form that was 'logically arranged . . . concise and free from burdensome, irrelevant and immaterial matter . . . ' (*Gilchrist* v *Interborough Rapid Transit Co.* (1929) 279 US 159). We hope that none of your work receives a similar epitaph!

Answering Problems

In studying law you will encounter what law teachers call 'problem questions' for the first time. The basic techniques of introduction and discussion which we have already considered apply to problems as much as essays, but you must be aware of the fact that you are dealing with a different kind of question.

The essence of any problem question is that it requires you to analyse some fictitious fact-situation and consider questions of legal liability that it creates. The precise scope of your answer will depend on what you are asked to do. The facts will normally be followed by some such request as 'Discuss'; 'Advise Ann' or 'Advise Ken of his liability to Lee'. Do not ignore this; questions of standpoint and objective are as important to the student as the practitioner; so, in dealing with problems always remember who you are advising, and what you are trying to do. For example, it may be that the problem concerning Ken and Lee also involves a third party, Mary. But if you have not been asked about Mary's rights or liabilities, it would be a serious error to discuss them.

Problem questions are usually constructed on a number of levels. Chiefly, this enables teachers to differentiate more clearly between the various qualities of answer. Most will therefore have one or two major issues, plus a number of less obvious legal points, or 'twists' to the facts which, for example, could distinguish the events from an earlier case which you might cite as a precedent. Particularly in examinations, it can be difficult to sort out the factual material and assess its legal implications in the time available. There is no instant solution to this. The answer lies in having a good working knowledge of the relevant law (this helps you to identify those facts which will have legal significance), and in adopting a systematic approach to the question.

By 'systematic' we mean that you must learn to use the question to help construct an answer. Let us explain. Most problems involve a sequence of events, so that x happens, followed by y, then z. Often x, y and z have separate legal consequences, so by following the facts as laid down, you can explore the consequences of each event, as it 'happens'. This should help ensure that you do not miss elements of the question completely. Sometimes, of course, one fact only becomes relevant when linked with something else which appears later in the question. So long as you make the right links, and do not lose sight of them, the same technique can apply. Again, you may find using 'mind maps' helps you to keep track of facts and the legal issues they raise. Above all else, developing a good problem-solving technique takes practice; do not miss out because of a lack of it! To help you we have included a specimen problem and outline answer as Exercise 15 in Chapter Eight.

Finally, whatever you are writing, remember two cardinal principles. First, there is one vital ingredient in any writing—WILL POWER! Unfortunately, essays do not write themselves, and a tutor's patience is rarely infinite. The hardest part of any piece of writing is actually to sit down at your desk and begin. It is much easier to go and make the tenth cup of coffee that evening, or to sit down and read that fascinating article on law reporting in thirteenth century Outer Mongolia. Such delaying tactics can reflect a whole variety of difficulties—from a lack of confidence to total boredom with the subject matter; though normal human inertia is probably the most common cause. We cannot pretend to have a magic cure, but would offer the following advice:

(a) Find a period in which you can work reasonably undisturbed. Time to think and plan is normally vital to producing good written work, particularly as careful planning can remove much of the apprehension that surrounds the writing process. Also try to ensure that you have a relatively long period in which to compose the actual essay. It is not advisable to try and cram writing into odd half-hours scattered through the day.

(b) The hardest parts to write are often the introduction and/or the conclusion, so leave these until last. Draft the various points of your argument first, then come back to the finishing touches. Probably the worst thing you can do is to try and finalise your opening sentence before anything else has been written.

(c) Pace yourself. Many of us justify leaving things to the last minute on the basis that we 'work better under pressure'. That is nearly always a myth. Perhaps some of us *only* work under pressure; but it is rarely the best that we can do. Instead it is usually hurried and full of half-developed ideas that sound fine at 2.00 am, but are much less convincing in the cold light of day.

Secondly, you should never miss an opportunity to check your work before submitting it. Many minor errors can be found this way. It also gives you an opportunity to review your own writing critically, and make sure that it does make sense. A student who begins an essay on the cost of litigation with the sentence 'Litigation is expensive, particularly if the defendant contests the case' will probably be given the benefit of the doubt; but repeat that sort of error too often in one piece of work, and the marker will inevitably question your understanding of the subject.

Conclusion

There is perhaps a danger at this stage of having replaced the myth that the law can be found in one book, with another, more sophisticated version, which says that law is simply about constructing a solution from a variety of written sources. Provided your research is adequate, and you understand how to go about reading what you have found, you will come up with the answer. To an extent there is some truth in that, but the reality is rather more uncertain.

In practice, the process of reading the law does not operate in a vacuum; it is not an arid activity, but one that is applied in real legal disputes. Going to law is not simply a case of lawyers dusting down the appropriate statutes and cases, and reading them (though that will inevitably be part of it); it is, at its heart, a process of re-constructing disputed events ('the facts') and proposing a legal solution to them. The implications of this reality on *our* reading of the law is the subject of the next chapter.

Exercise 3: Attempting the impossible

Before attempting this exercise you are advised to read and make notes on:

(a)   the case of *R* v *Shivpuri* [1986] 2 All ER 334—an important case in both Criminal Law and Legal Method. You are advised to use the All England report, as the answers make specific reference to that version.
(b)   the introductory parts and s.1 of the Criminal Attempts Act 1981.

Make sure that you understand the basic context of the dispute—ie what the case was about; why it was before the particular court hearing the case, what that court decided and why. Once you have done so, you should be ready to test your comprehension against the following questions.

(1)   Starting with the Criminal Attempts Act, let us check your basic information:

(a)   What is its full citation?
(b)   When did it receive the Royal Assent?
(c)   What is the subject of Part I of the Act?

(2)   Is the short title (Answer YES or NO to each):

(a)   an accurate statement of what the Act is about?
(b)   capable of assisting our interpretation of the Act?

(3)   Answer TRUE or FALSE to each of the following.
Section 1 of the Act:
(a)   makes it a statutory offence to attempt to commit an indictable offence;
(b)   seeks to exclude from criminal attempts any significant steps towards a crime where the offence is in fact impossible to complete;
(c)   includes within the definition of an attempt any acts of an accused which he believes would involve the commission of a crime, but which, if completed, would not, in reality, be criminal.

(4) Turning to *R* v *Shivpuri:*

(a) Which court's decision appears in the report cited?
(b) In which court(s) had the case appeared previously?

(5) Which of the following statements contain(s) a material (ie important) fact (there may be more than one):

(a) The accused believed he was carrying heroin or cannabis?
(b) The substance in the suitcase was not a prohibited drug?
(c) The full offence of 'dealing' could not be committed?

(6) Which of the following statements reflects the legal issue(s) at the root of the appeal? Again, there *may* be more than one right answer:

(a) Whether a merely 'preparatory' action constitutes an attempt in English law.
(b) Whether it is possible to be convicted of attempting to commit an offence where the facts make its actual commission impossible.
(c) Whether the requirement that the accused acted 'knowingly' means that the prosecution must prove that the accused *knew* it was a particular controlled drug.

(7) Do the judges all agree on the outcome of the case (YES or NO)?

(8) Was that outcome:

(a) that the appeal was upheld on the question of attempting the impossible?
(b) that the appeal was dismissed because the judge had wrongly advised (*misdirected*) the jury?
(c) that the appeal was dismissed on the question of attempting the impossible?
(d) that the appeal was dismissed on *both* issues (ie attempting the impossible and on the misdirection of the jury)?

(9) What was *Shivpuri's* impact on the standing of the earlier decision in *Anderton* v *Ryan?* Did it:
(a) Overrule *Anderton* v *Ryan?*
(b) Apply it?
(c) Distinguish it?

Answers:
(1) (a) It is cited as the Criminal Attempts Act 1981, c.(ie *chapter)* 47.

(b)   It received the Royal Assent on 27 July 1981 (the date given just below the long title).

(c)   Simply 'Attempts etc'! This is to distinguish it from the repeal of the so-called 'sus' laws created under the Vagrancy Act 1824, which form the subject of Part II (see the 'Arrangement of Sections' and long title).

(2)   (a)   is correct; it is a brief but accurate description.

(b)   does not correctly state the principle: if you got this wrong, think back to the 'Strawberry Jam' analogy used earlier in this chapter.

(3)   (a)   TRUE: this is the combined effect of ss.(1) and (4)—the latter restricts liability only to *indictable* (ie serious) criminal offences.

(b)   FALSE: this statement actually reverses the effect of ss.(2) which deals with cases of 'factual impossibility'—eg, the situation where A attempts to poison B with a substance which is, in fact, harmless.

(c)   TRUE: this is the most difficult to work out. Subsection (3) is concerned with the intention of the accused. So long as the accused intends to commit the offence, it does not matter that, because of some mistake on his part about the law, what he does is not a crime. A widely cited example is the situation where A has sexual intercourse with B, believing her to be under the legal age of consent. Technically, A has committed the offence of attempting unlawful sexual intercourse, even though B is not in fact 'under age'.

(4)   (a)   The House of Lords.

(b)   The Crown Court and Court of Appeal—see p.335i.

(5)   This comes close to being a trick question! All three of (a), (b) and (c) would have been material questions of fact. That this is the case with (a) and (b) should be reasonably evident. The accused's belief and the nature of the substance are both material to the question of attempting the impossible; they are both matters which are proved by evidence. Item (c) is rather more difficult. The *definition* of an offence is a matter of law; but that is not the point here. Here the issue is one of *proving* that the accused could not commit the offence. That, we suggest, is a matter of fact.

(6)   (b) & (c) are both correct.

(b) is probably the more obvious answer, but the issue identified by (c) also arises, eg at p.339b *per* Lord Bridge. (a) is incorrect; though this point has arisen in a number of cases, it was not critical here—see eg Lord Bridge at p.342g.

(7)   Yes is the right answer, though they do not necessarily arrive at the same outcome for the same reasons. If you got this one wrong it is

probably because you have confused the *result* of the appeal with the *reasoning* used by the judges to come to their decision (see further the answer to Qu. 9). They should always be kept separate in your mind.

(8) (d) is the correct answer. The misdirection point is less obviously a ground of the appeal, but it is raised by the defence and discussed by the House of Lords. They held that though there had been a technical misdirection, it had caused no miscarriage of justice, and so could be disregarded under their lordships' statutory powers—see Lord Bridge at approximately p.341d–h.

(9) The correct answer is (a). The decision of the House was unanimous in this respect, though Lords Hailsham and MacKay state that they would have been content to distinguish *Anderton* v *Ryan* (see pp.337b & 345h), but they do not actually dissent from the judgment given by Lord Bridge.

REFERENCES

Alder, M. (1990) *Clarity for Lawyers*, London: The Law Society.

Buzan, T. (1989) *Use Your Head*, Revised Edition, London: BBC Books.

Drewry, G. (1973) 'Leapfrogging—And a Lord Justice's Eye View of the Final Appeal' *Law Quarterly Review*, vol. 89, p. 260.

Goodrich, P. (1986) *Reading the Law*, Oxford: Blackwell.

Gordon, J. (1991) 'How not to Succeed in Law School' *Yale Law Journal*, vol. 100, p. 1679.

Open University (1985) *Preparing for the Social Sciences Foundation Course*, Milton Keynes: Open University Press.

Renton Committee (1975) *The Preparation of Legislation*, Cmnd. 6053, London: HMSO.

Chapter Four

Law, Fact and Language

In any legal argument that gets to court someone wins and someone loses. So why are people prepared to go to court when statistically they only have a 50 per cent chance of success? There may be many more or less rational reasons, but usually a litigant will only go to court if advised that he or she has an arguable case. So what is it about legal disputes which means that *both* parties can be sufficiently certain of the 'truth' of their claim, and the legal merits of their case to go to court, even though only one of them can win? Surely their lawyers read the same law?

The answer to this conundrum lies in the difference between the law in books and the law in practice. In practice, legal disputes are often affected by a range of variables that are not wholly predictable. In this chapter we shall explore some of these variables through two key factors. These tell us much about how legal disputes are actually *constructed* in court. The factors we consider are the relationship between:

(a) law and fact, and
(b) law and language.

We shall close the chapter by attempting to pull those two strands together in a discussion of how these elements combine to give the judges a high degree of flexibility in deciding cases.

In exploring these issues, it is important to bear in mind that the range of problems discussed probably do not affect all cases, and certainly do not affect them to the same degree. The greatest difficulties arise in those cases which are conventionally described as 'hard cases', that is, cases for which there is no recognised legal solution.

Law and Fact

Law does not operate in a vacuum. Obviously, legal disputes only arise out of factual situations—eg, a boundary dispute between neighbours, or an assault by one person on another. This means that such disputes will always involve a mixture of law and fact—eg to prove in negligence that X has acted in breach of his or her duty of care, requires us to establish as a matter of *law* that there is a duty of care governing X, and that on the *facts* X has broken that duty.

We can define 'questions of fact' as all questions which attempt to prove what happened. They are established by various types of evidence, eg, oral witness statements, forensic evidence etc. 'Questions of law' arise in connection with legal principles that may be argued in a case (eg, what is the definition of 'theft'), together with any procedural matters (eg, the jurisdiction of a particular court). We can explore the practical importance of this a little more deeply.

Using the Law/Fact Distinction

Our experience with both undergraduate and postgraduate students shows that it can be very difficult to grasp the implications of the law/fact distinction.

The difference between questions of law and of fact is used in three ways:

To define the function of judge and jury: In many courts it is lay people who act as assessors of fact (notably as a jury in some criminal trials, and in tribunals) whilst judges deal with the legal problems. One needs to be sure which issue is decided by which person(s).

However, in many criminal and virtually all civil cases, the function of the jury as **tribunal of fact** (as it is called) has been taken over by judges. They will be responsible for ruling on both law and fact in the case before them. They are legally obliged to keep those functions separate within their own minds. This may seem an odd requirement, and in reality it probably requires the kind of mental gymnastics that even experienced judges can find difficult to maintain! However, it does reflect that the determination of the issues of fact is separate from the ultimate issues of law before the court.

To establish rights of appeal: This applies particularly to the higher courts, where appeals on issues of fact are commonly outside the jurisdiction of the appellate court.

To establish the boundaries of precedent: As we shall see in Chapter Six, only a decision on a point of law is capable of creating a binding precedent for use in later cases.

The Limits of the Law/Fact Distinction

Although it is easy enough to provide an abstract definition of fact and law, they can be difficult concepts to apply on a case by case basis. Given its significance, the difficulty we have in distinguishing between law and fact may seem rather surprising. We would argue that, at its root, it is difficult because English lawyers have traditionally treated the question 'what is fact rather than law?' as context-specific. In other words, different approaches have been applied in different situations. This may enhance the flexibility of the courts' response to that question, but it can make it difficult for anyone actually learning the law. As a guide, but nothing more, we would suggest that the following broad principles need to be considered:

Normally, the question is resolved by the substantive law: The statutory or common law rules governing a particular issue may well make explicit that a certain matter is a question of fact, rather than law, or *vice versa.* Again, the issue is complicated by a lack of consistency. Thus, for example, for many purposes the issue of 'reasonableness' is treated as a matter of fact—as in the uses of the 'reasonable man test' in both civil and criminal law (see, eg, *Qualcast (Wolverhampton) Ltd* v *Haynes* [1959] AC 743, [1959] 2 All ER 38). Conversely, on a criminal charge of malicious prosecution, the question whether the accused had 'reasonable cause' to bring the prosecution is a question of law for the judge.

Similarly, further complexity can be caused by the courts' recognition that many issues may raise mixed questions of fact and law. For example, in cases of defamation it is necessary for a plaintiff to establish that the words used by the defendant had a defamatory meaning, and that they were defamatory to the plaintiff. The issue of defamatory meaning is a question of law, while the requirement of actual defamation of the plaintiff is one of fact. Again, there are no general guidelines to recognising where an issue raises such mixed questions—it is purely a matter where we have to be guided by the substantive law.

Special principles govern questions of interpretation of words: The meaning of words can be a question of fact or law. It is now well established that the *ordinary* meaning of words is a matter of fact. In *Brutus* v *Cozens* [1973] AC 854, [1972] 2 All ER 1297, the House of Lords had to decide whether an accused, who had disrupted a tennis match at Wimbledon as a protest against the presence of a South African player at the tournament, had been properly convicted of using 'insulting behaviour' likely to occasion a breach of the peace, contrary to s. 5 of the Public Order Act 1936 (now repealed). Their Lordships noted that the Act did not define the word 'insulting', nor was there anything to suggest that the word was to be given any special or technical meaning. Therefore, they held that 'insulting' was to be given its ordinary meaning (which they did not attempt to explain) and that the question of whether behaviour was insulting was a question of fact to be determined by the magistrates.

One final point, which may be causing you some confusion, needs to be considered. In establishing this principle of interpretation, the courts have arguably extended the concept of 'fact' beyond its most obvious legal usage, which reflects the norm of facts as events which may be proved by evidence from 'eye-' or 'ear-witnesses'. This principle will often have the effect of excluding debates about statutory meaning from the process of appeal, or, in public law matters, the process of judicial review. This must be contrasted with those situations where the courts will, as a matter of *law*, find some *implied meaning* within the words of a statute or other document. Thus, in a famous American case, *Riggs* v *Palmer* (1889) 115 NY 506, the question was whether the beneficiary under a will was entitled to take his bequest, despite the fact that he had murdered the testator. The local wills legislation was silent on the issue, but the Ohio Supreme Court disqualified the beneficiary by applying the long-established principle that a wrongdoer should not benefit by his own wrong. This, the court said, should be implied into the legislation. (A similar principle has been established in English Law: see *Re Sigsworth* (1935), discussed in Chapter Eight.)

So, given these principles, the next logical question is, how do we actually establish the facts in a case?

Proving the Facts

The first job of the court must be to establish the existence of the facts alleged within a given case. That does not mean that all the possible issues of fact will actually be considered. A feature of the adversarial process is that the legal contest is managed by the two sides involved. It is therefore common practice for the parties to sort out in advance the scope of their dispute. This applies as much to questions of fact as it does to questions of law, so that it is not uncommon for certain facts to be agreed or admitted before a case comes to trial. For this reason we conventionally talk of 'material facts' as a way of denoting those facts which remain at issue and which will subsequently form the basis of the judge's decision. Assessing the materiality of facts is chiefly dependent upon the legal issues involved in each case. A knowledge of substantive law is always required, because the substantive law will tell us what facts the parties are required to establish to win their case. What appears to be material to a client is often immaterial to the lawyer, and *vice versa*. This does not always help the lawyer-client relationship!

Let's now try to illustrate the issue of materiality by way of a simple exercise:

Exercise 4: 'On your bike', or the case of the missing bicycle

Andrea has a bright red bicycle which she rides to school every day and leaves unsecured in the bike shed. One afternoon, after classes have ended

at 4 pm, she discovers that her bicycle is missing. She reports this fact
to the headmistress. By 4.30 pm the bike has mysteriously been found
outside Andrea's home. Ben tells Andrea that he saw her friend Caroline
riding a red bike at about 4.15 pm.

*Which of these facts would you consider important in assessing whether
Caroline had attempted to steal the bicycle?*

There are probably only two sets of material facts:

(a)   that the bike has been taken from Andrea, apparently without her
knowledge, and

(b)   Caroline was seen riding a red bike at a time consistent with the
theft.

Others might, of course, be relevant in assessing the veracity of Andrea
or Ben as witnesses, though that is a slightly different issue.

Are these sufficient to support the conclusion that Caroline is a thief?

Certainly not, though that is a possibility, there is still relatively little to
connect Caroline to the theft. If Caroline was unable to explain Ben's
evidence, then our hypothesis that Caroline is the thief would be
strengthened. If she merely denied the allegation we would be little further
forward. There is at present insufficient evidence to say 'beyond reasonable
doubt' that Caroline took the bike.

There are a number of other explanations, some more plausible than
others, that need to be explored, eg:

(a)   Andrea had forgotten that she had not gone to school by bike that
day.

(b)   Caroline has a red bike of her own, and was seen riding that.

(c)   Ben had mistakenly identified Caroline.

(d)   Ben had taken the bike, and blamed Caroline to hide his own guilt,
and so on . . .

The facts we have are therefore far from conclusive (see further the section
on the burden of proof, below).

This example enables us to expand upon some of the points made so far.
It highlights that the facts in any given case are unlikely to be of equal
importance, and that their significance will often depend on their
interrelationship with other facts in the case. Assessing what facts are
material will depend in part on our ability to create an overall picture
of events. For example, the statement that Andrea rides her bike to school
every day does not appear to be particularly relevant to the legal issues—

unless our inquiries lead us to discover that force of habit had caused her to forget that today her mother had driven her to school. Do not forget that experience and knowledge of the law will also play a part in establishing what facts are relevant and material. Thus, in the bicycle case above, once we know that the legal definition of theft requires that the thief has an intention to deprive the owner of that property permanently, Caroline's intentions regarding the future of the bike (assuming she took it) acquire a whole new significance—did she mean to keep it, or was she just borrowing it? This also illustrates an important point about the relationship between law and facts, which is that their dependence works *both ways.* We need a good knowledge of the facts to create a viable legal argument, but at the same time, we need knowledge of the law to sort out the legally relevant facts from the mass of information that will surround a case. We shall return to the relationship between law and fact later in Chapter Nine.

The process whereby the material facts are established is referred to as one of **proof.** There exists within any legal system a variety of procedural rules governing what facts may be proved. Such rules vary from system to system in their restrictiveness. English rules of proof are widely regarded as amongst the more restrictive, though the rules regarding proof in civil cases tend to be less strict than in criminal procedure. Put briefly, the basic evidentiary requirements for proof of a fact are that it is *relevant and admissible,* and that the evidence is sufficiently strong to satisfy the *burden of proof.* We shall consider these points separately.

Relevance and admissibility: A fact will be **relevant** if it enables the court to reach a conclusion on any of the issues before it. In practice facts are often like the pieces of a jigsaw, where you cannot make out the picture until it is nearly complete; so it may be difficult for the court to see where the proof of a single fact is leading. This means that counsel may legitimately be asked to justify why a particular fact should be admitted.

Admissibility is a technical rule. It provides the courts with a means of excluding evidence that is relevant, but for some reason is inherently so unreliable that the court should refuse to be swayed by it. The best example of this is probably the rule in criminal evidence excluding a concocted confession under s. 76 of the Police and Criminal Evidence Act 1984.

Admissibility in English law is complicated by the fact that it operates by means of a mass of exclusionary rules and exceptions thereto—incidentally, it is in this respect that the rule is frequently contrasted with the less restrictive systems operating in most of continental Europe. There, though the question of relevance remains fundamental, admissibility operates more on an assumption of 'freedom of proof'. 'Freedom of proof' requires a wide judicial discretion to admit or exclude evidence as the case demands, rather than the adherence to strict rules of evidence.

Questions of relevance and admissibility will depend, in part, upon the standpoint and objectives of the person using the information. To put it simply: what facts are important may well depend upon whether you are acting for a plaintiff or defendant; in either case you will seek to emphasise those facts which support your case, and play down, discredit, or even seek to exclude those which support your opponent. In that respect facts do not represent an objective truth, but sometimes an accurate, or sometimes a crude, estimate of the most convincing version of events.

The burden of proof: The emphasis in law on notions of proof and probability, is also a way of acknowledging that facts are not as concrete as they may seem. All cases, whether Criminal or Civil, are decided according to the **burden of proof**. This too is a complex subject, and too intricate for full discussion here, though some basic points can be made. The burden of proof places the responsibility for establishing a particular fact on its proponent, so that if A claims that B injured her by his negligent driving, it is up to A to make out a case. The requirement of proof means that facts must be established to the satisfaction of the court, but this does not mean absolute certainty. As Lord Guthrie has said: 'Outside the region of mathematics, proof is never anything more than probability' (*Nobel's Explosives Co.* v *British Dominions General Insurance Co.* [1918] 1 SLT 205 at 206). It will be relatively unusual for facts in a case to be *conclusive*.

The term **conclusive** is one which needs to be used with great caution. Technically, evidence is only conclusive where, by virtue of a rule of law, it cannot be contradicted—a widely cited example is the rule of law treating a child under the age of 10 as incapable of committing a crime. This technical meaning is thus different from the popular sense of the term, where it is used to describe evidence that effectively clinches the case. In reality, what is popularly called 'conclusive' is no more than evidence which carries a very high degree of probability. Thus, in coming to a conclusion on the evidence, the court is normally saying no more than: 'on the facts before us, we are as sure as we feel we need to be'.

The courts have attempted to define the burden of proof in terms of levels of probability; thus in civil cases we conventionally talk of proof 'on a balance of probabilities' and in criminal cases of a 'higher standard' of 'proof beyond reasonable doubt'. What these abstract concepts come to mean in individual cases remains open to question. It is widely accepted that such standards of proof are incapable of precise definition, a point to which we shall return later in this chapter. At the same time the use of terms such as 'proof beyond reasonable doubt' may often work to disguise the extent to which conclusions about the facts of a case are subjective. Put simply, it is not easy to draw the boundaries between doubts which are reasonable, and those which are not.

For example, criminal cases in particular may turn on questions of identification. Witness A may say that the person she saw looked like the accused X, whereas witness B may have given a different description. Identification is a question of fact, but do not let the terminology fool you; in establishing whether X is the guilty person the court will be working in part from a whole range of conscious and unconscious perceptions regarding the person of the accused and the veracity of the witnesses, only some of which are reducible to rules of law, in an attempt to establish 'the facts'. Let us now consider how problems of establishing the facts may have disturbed the verdict in a real case.

The Case of William Wallace

At the time our story begins, in 1931, William Wallace was a 52-year-old insurance collector living in Anfield, Liverpool, with his wife Julia. They had been married for about 17 years. They were known as a quiet, rather formal couple, with relatively few social acquaintances. Wallace was an unremarkable man, except in respect of his beliefs. He was a follower of Stoicism, a virtually dead philosophy based upon the *Meditations* of the Roman general, Marcus Aurelius; as Wallace wrote in his diary: 'For forty years I have drilled myself in iron control and prided myself on never displaying an emotion outwardly in public.'

Wallace was a regular chess player at a club in the city. On the evening of Monday 19 January 1931, the captain of the club took a telephone message for Wallace from 'R.M. Qualtrough', leaving an address and a request for Wallace to visit at 7.30 the following evening. When Wallace arrived at the club half an hour later, he said that he had not heard of Qualtrough, but took a note of the address, assuming the call was in connection with his insurance business.

The following evening, Wallace left home sometime between 6.30 and 6.50 pm, caught a tram at 7.06 to his supposed destination, where he spent over half an hour looking for Qualtrough's address. It did not exist. He caught the tram home, where he was seen by his neighbours at 8.45, trying to enter the house. He explained that, unusually, both back and front door were locked, and he could get no reply from Julia. On trying the back door again, it opened. Inside was Julia's body; she had been beaten to death with an iron bar. The front bedroom of the house had been ransacked and £4 removed from the cash-box in which Wallace kept the monies he collected (though this was subsequently discovered inexplicably stuffed into a vase in the upstairs of the house).

An immediate search of lodging houses, the railway, cafes and clubs in the area revealed no one who might be the murderer. Furthermore, the fact that there was no evidence of a forced entry to the house, or of a struggle between killer and victim, suggested either that Julia was taken wholly by surprise, or that she knew her murderer. The police felt that they were left with two possible suspects.

The first was Gordon Parry, a former colleague of Wallace's, who had a record of petty theft and a reputation as a womaniser. Rightly or wrongly, this was sufficient to make him an initial suspect. He knew Julia; the layout of the Wallace's house, and that normally, on a Tuesday night, the cash-box would have contained over £100—the sum of Wallace's weekly collection. He might also have held a grudge against Wallace, who had caught Parry helping himself to insurance money that he was supposed to be collecting. However, Parry had an alibi. His girlfriend had told the police that they had been together the whole evening. He was dropped from the police enquiries.

The second suspect was Wallace himself. The police had by now heard rumours that the relationship between the Wallaces was far from happy, though this Wallace strenuously denied. There remained no clear motive for the killing. However, Wallace also seemed abnormally calm; he was observed, while being questioned by the police on the night of the killing, casually leaning over Julia's body to flick cigarette ash into an ash tray. This behaviour almost certainly aroused some suspicions. Did the police have a cold, calculating killer in their midst?

But didn't Wallace, like Parry, have an alibi? In a sense he did. Several witnesses, including a police officer, had spoken with Wallace in his search for Mr Qualtrough. However, there was no reliable assessment of the time of Julia's death. One pathologist put it at about 6 pm; another at 8 pm. It was not inconceivable that he had killed his wife before leaving for his appointment with the fictitious Qualtrough. Indeed, Qualtrough could have been a creation of Wallace's own plans. The phone call to the chess club, which created the whole alibi had been traced to a telephone box only some 400 yards from the Wallace's house. Even so, how could the police deal with the fact that no blood was found on Wallace after such a ferocious killing? They surmised that he had worn only a macintosh, found partially burnt under the dead woman's body, to commit the killing. As traces of blood were found in the bathroom, this seemed to suggest that whoever had killed Julia had stopped in the house long enough to try to wash the blood off.

On 2 February Wallace was charged with his wife's murder. He was committed for trial before the Liverpool assize in April 1931. At the trial, the Crown pressed its case in a manner that was later described as 'oppressive'. Counsel claimed that Wallace had planned the entire thing, to the extent of faking his own alibi; witnesses were called attacking Wallace's demeanour; to all this he listened, impassively. The defence countered by emphasising the circumstantial nature of the evidence; the limited time Wallace would have had to commit the crime, clean himself up and leave for his appointment, and the fact that the macintosh could as easily have been burnt by the gas fire in the room as by some deliberate act of the killer—this view, it was argued, was supported by the fact that Julia's skirt had been partially burned by coming into contact with the fire, presumably as she fell. On the fourth day of the trial, the jury retired to consider its verdict.

Obviously it is impossible to recreate accurately the atmosphere and arguments of a capital trial in a few short lines, but from the outline here, what would you expect that verdict to be? Innocent or guilty?

For Wallace, the answer came quickly. After retiring for an hour, the jury returned a verdict of guilty. He was sentenced to death. The day after his trial he was told that he was due to be hanged on 12 May. His lawyers immediately entered an appeal against his conviction. His appeal was heard on 18 and 19 May (sentence having been postponed) by the Court of Criminal Appeal. After what must have been a mercifully short judgment for Wallace (who was present at his appeal), the Court handed down its decision—see *R* v *Wallace* (1932) 23 Cr App Rep 32. The conviction was quashed on the basis that it was unsupported by the evidence. He was free to go.

So, how was it that the trial court had convicted Wallace? The Court of Criminal Appeal (*per* Lord Hewart CJ at 35) made it clear that no fault lay with the judge; the problem was evidential. This was a case of considerable difficulty and doubt, where much of the evidence was consistent with both innocence and guilt. In the end, the jury had (in the eyes of the appeal court) simply got it wrong.

The conviction was thrown out on the basis that the prosecution had not satisfied the burden of proof. They had failed to exclude the possibility that someone else had committed the murder. The reasons behind Wallace's conviction by the jury are difficult to ascribe, and of course, we shall never know the real answer, but it is submitted that there are a number of likely possibilities. Taken together these may help account for what was, with hindsight, a perverse verdict.

First, the jury itself lost sight of the differences between fact and speculation. A court is not concerned, as Lord Hewart said in *Wallace* 'with suspicion, however grave, or with theories, however ingenious.' The prosecution case was full of ingenious theorising—for example the assertion that Wallace had worn the coat found under Julia's body to commit the murder and then sought to burn it—but little of these hypotheses could finally be substantiated.

Secondly, contemporary accounts indicate that there was a powerfully *presented,* aggressive, case by the prosecution. This, ironically, was probably aided by Wallace's own stoicism. His air of detachment in the courtroom probably did little to gain him sympathy, and may have helped foster the image of a cold and calculating killer. The defence also alleged that the police had been unduly obstructive to the preparation of their case (though this view was not supported by the Court of Criminal Appeal, more recent research suggests that it may have had greater foundation than was then realised—see Wilkes (1984)). Taken together these might have served to distort the perceived strength of the prosecution case. The significance of questions of presentation and style will be further considered under the heading 'law and language' (below).

Thirdly, there is also evidence that the defence miscalculated badly in the presentation of its case, by failing to apply to the judge to have the prosecution case rejected for a lack of evidence. This point illustrates rather graphically how much can depend on the forensic skills of the lawyer rather than upon either the actual facts or law in a case. A great deal, perhaps too much, in the adversarial process can depend upon tactics and techniques of argument.

Law and Language

The legal process is intrinsically bound up with language. The popular image of law is one that emphasises the oral element of legal tradition, that is, the process of argumentation before a court. Even the reality, which for most practising lawyers is rather more prosaic than television would have us believe, is still a world in which legal documents fill up much of the day. Words thus dominate the legal landscape; this is hardly surprising, because without language there could be no law. As Bernhard Grossfeld argues: 'Law certainly uses language, but language is the stronger' (1990:99). In the context of legal methods and techniques, there are two issues that need to be addressed; one essentially theoretical, the other more practical. These are the relationship between language and power, and the problem of the flexibility of language.

Law, Language and Power

It is widely recognised that there is a substantial gap between legal and 'everyday' language. In some respects, that gap is narrowing as lawyers are coming to use more naturalistic language, but the continued relevance of old statutes and precedents means that what are really archaic forms of language are still in legal use, though it has to be said that lawyers are not wholly innocent in the perpetuation of this gap. The law has always tended to be a conservative institution, and the traditional usage of legal jargon has often been presented as part of the attraction or mystique of law. Some terms still in use, such as *autrefois convict* or *mandamus*, reflect law's origins in the language of the mediaeval aristocracy or the church; others illustrate specialist usage of quite ordinary words—eg the meaning given to the term 'consideration' in Contract Law. This specialist language has to be learned. There is no escape.

However, the existence of a distinct 'legal language' has wider social effects than just making the law student's life rather difficult. Here we shall discuss two important examples of those wider effects:

Law as camouflage: The extent to which law relies upon its own language is a very basic indication of the closed nature of legal argument. The term 'mystification' is used as a description of the way in which the language of the law defines who can participate in legal argument. The need to develop the 'special' skills of a lawyer has the effect of excluding non-lawyers from entering into legal discourse, with, it is argued, consequent limits upon the ability of citizens to gain access to justice. The special use of certain forms of language also serves to disguise rather than enhance our understanding of the legal system. This reflects what Grossfeld describes as 'law as camouflage' (1990:47). He gives a simple example of this from the United States Constitution which, until amended after the American Civil War, contained rights to slave ownership. Despite this, the term slavery was constantly avoided in the legal terminology; instead slavery was always called the 'particular institution'.

In practice, the process of disguise may often be far more sophisticated. In the early Common Law, for example we talk of the way in which actions could be based on 'legal fictions'—fictional pleadings which did not reflect the true dispute but were used to overcome technicalities and give a suitor access to the courts. A more modern analogy would be the way in which proof of marriage breakdown (particularly 'unreasonable behaviour') will be (to some extent) artificially constructed in divorce proceedings. Here it is employed to put an end to a marriage which, in reality, both parties wish to escape from, but without the restriction of separating and waiting for two years to obtain a divorce by consent. The use of the term 'unreasonable behaviour' thus camouflages the true workings of one aspect of the law of divorce.

This facet of language not only creates difficulties for the lay person, but also for lawyers outside the system. Getting past the camouflage is one of the major problems lawyers face in reaching an accurate understanding of a foreign legal system. Hence legal language is both an important symbol of the power of law itself to define, deliberately or otherwise, who may exercise legal rights, and to disguise the uses of law by those within the system from those outside. We would suggest that there are also other, more immediate ways, in which use of language involves a significant exercise of power. This also enables us to posit formally the links between law, fact and language in the title of this chapter.

Facts, power and the legal process: We have already shown that facts are not plucked out of the air, ready-made. They need to be described—a process which, of course, requires language. Hanson (1959) makes the fundamental point that language and fact are dependent upon each other. This leads us to the conclusion that the way in which facts are described, not surprisingly, governs our perception of the nature of that fact. Linguistic differences thus can be said to effect the 'reality' created. Consider the example of the Eskimo language which contains many different words to describe types of snowfall. We could imagine a situation where a witness is asked to describe the weather conditions at a particular time. The picture of the facts painted by an English-speaking witness saying 'it was snowing hard' would then be very different from the presumably more graphic image created by an Eskimo witness speaking his or her own language.

In the legal environment, the ability of a witness to communicate what she or he has seen will be of great importance, because it is that act of communication which creates the facts of the case. Of course, not all witnesses share the same degree of linguistic competence, least of all in a pressured, artificial, setting such as a court. Stories are often presented in a broken, fragmentary way; narrative patterns can become distorted by lawyers' attempts to discredit testimony. Witnesses can become confused and uncertain.

Variations in presentation can have a dramatic effect on the court's perception of witnesses' credibility, and thence of the court's structuring of the facts. In a study in the early eighties, O'Barr and his colleagues (1982) analysed the way in which different language styles emerged in court.

They identified in particular a difference between 'powerful' and 'powerless' speech. Powerless speech, they found, was typified by the use of more qualified statements; deferential speech styles, hesitation, and other factors which did not affect the nature of the facts contained in testimony, but changed its presentation. In one experiment in particular, the researchers recorded the same information on tape, changing only the language style and the gender of the speaker. The witnesses giving information in a powerful style were rated by subjects as significantly more convincing, trustworthy and competent than those whose linguistic style was 'powerless'. Subjects also tended to rate women speakers generally as being less powerful than men—even on the basis of identical material. Clearly, therefore, the medium can be as significant as the message itself.

The Flexibility of Language

The English language has over the last two or three hundred years become virtually the first global language. It is spoken in some form by, some estimates would suggest, nearly one billion people around the world. Influenced by many different cultures, it has become one of the richest and most complex languages in the world. The current *Oxford English Dictionary* lists some 500,000 words in recognised use (though many may be highly obscure). This represents probably the most extensive vocabulary of any modern language. Buried somewhere within its midst are the many terms that constitute what might be called 'legal English'; but lawyers do not operate exclusively in a linguistically closed environment. Legal discourse must involve large numbers of 'ordinary' English words as well. Given the apparently huge range to choose from, one would have thought that a high degree of precision should be attainable. Unfortunately, this is not always the case.

It is said that legal rules suffer from a problem of indeterminacy, meaning that it is often difficult to predict the scope of those rules. Neither the judges nor Parliament will necessarily provide you with exhaustive explanations of what they mean to say, and much of the indeterminacy of laws is traceable to the flexibility of legal language. Some of that indeterminacy can be avoided by precision—the *correct* use of language (so far as is possible) is vital to the work of a lawyer. At times it is easy to be overly cynical on this matter: to say that lawyers are simply playing with language. But, trite though it sounds, words are all that a lawyer has at his or her disposal. Though whether changes to legal forms of language could reduce the scope for ambiguity, or whether our problems are inherent in the generally flexible and imprecise nature of language remains a hotly debated question.

Problems in establishing meaning affect two stages of the legal process. Meaning must be considered at the point of drafting any legal document, and also subsequently at the stage of interpreting that document. The essence of the problem is that the law has tended to assume that meaning can only be safely ascertained from the document itself. In many situations we have little alternative. If a court is interpreting the contents of a will, for example, it may have little choice in the matter. The document might have been drafted twenty or thirty years ago; the person whose wishes it contains (called the testator) will be dead, and the memories of others involved at the time (if they can be found) might be unreliable. In practice, in such situations, the courts may resort to oral evidence or other documentary evidence that could shed light on the testator's intentions, but that tends to be a last resort. As we shall explain in Chapter Eight, special rules govern statutes as opposed to other documents, but the starting point is essentially the same.

There is, however, an element of artificiality in this approach. The belief that we can establish the meaning of a document purely from the words used seems to assume that we can overcome two discrete problems: first, the difficulty of ascribing meaning to individual words; and, secondly, the problems created by the need to interpret more complex syntactic structures.

The meaning of words: To understand the problems of meaning we need, once again, to think about the relationship between legal and everyday language. We have already said that legal discourse involves the use of both specialist and general language. Knapp (1991:10) suggests that the relationship can be described diagrammatically as follows:

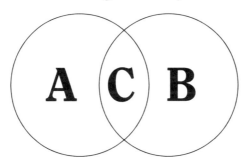

These two circles represent three linguistic subsets. Group A represents words used only in the general language; group B contains words used in legal language only, and group C represents words which are common to both legal and general English. On this basis, group (B + C) represents the sum of the legal language. These sets and subsets are open; their boundaries will change over time. New words will be developed to reflect technological and other changes in society. Words may actually move across the dividing line beteen the general and the legal language (as an example of the latter, Knapp cites the phrase 'corrective measures'—a general expression which had acquired a specific legal meaning in some of the former socialist states). We shall see in Chapter Eight, in the context of statutory interpretation, that major difficulties can arise in ascribing a meaning to the words used in an Act of Parliament or in delegated legislation. We shall also see how the courts have developed principles of interpretation in an attempt to deal with this. Without anticipating too much of that discussion, it can be said that primarily the courts start from the assumption that words should be given their ordinary, everyday, meaning unless the context suggests a special or technical meaning is intended. It is an approach that has wider applications than just statutory interpretation. Courts are regularly engaged in thinking about the meaning of words in interpreting contracts and other written documents, and in applying rules of common law to specific cases. In such situations, lawyers face three major problems in respect of the meaning of words. These are:

(a)   Dealing with semantic ambiguity: to say that words should be given their ordinary commonsense meaning is not always as simple as it sounds. Many words have more than one meaning, and it can be difficult to resolve which of a number of shades of meaning is intended in a particular legal document.

This problem may be especially acute in respect of words in subsets A and C, above. A feature of terms used only in legal language (subset B) is their tendency to be used in a manner that is unequivocal. By and large, legal language can convey very precise meanings—at least to other skilled users of legal language.

By contrast, where words exist in both legal and general usage (ie words in Knapp's subset C), there may be quite distinct ordinary meanings; that is, an ordinary everyday meaning and an ordinary legal meaning—like the term 'consideration' for example. In some instances such a range of meanings may be a cause of confusion. It may be difficult to determine which of the meanings is intended. Though the problem of meaning often can be resolved by looking at the linguistic context (for example, if a written contract contains the phrase '. . . in consideration whereof Jane Smith pays Alan Brown £200', it is pretty obvious that the legal meaning of consideration is the one intended), there are times when such a simple resolution is not possible. With words in subset A (the general language), the difficulties can be profound. The richness of our language means that many words have a multiplicity of meanings which are in general usage, or a range of meanings, some of which are general, others technical. The general language also lacks the common interpretative community which gives (much) legal English its precision. So, how do we resolve problems of interpreting the general language?

It may be argued that these problems can be resolved if we can accept that most ambiguous words have a core meaning that would be widely accepted as the most ordinary meaning of the word. However, to do that we have to accept the idea that a particular word does have a distinguishable core or standard meaning, and this itself may be highly debatable in some specific cases. Consider the following as an example of the problem:

Let us suppose that in leafing through the statutes, we come upon the following enactment: 'It shall be a misdemeanour, punishable by a fine of five dollars, to sleep in any railway station.' . . . Suppose I am a judge, and that two men are brought before me for violating this statute. The first is a passenger who was waiting at 3 am for a delayed train. When he was arrested he was sitting upright in an orderly fashion, but was heard by the arresting officer to be gently snoring. The second is a man who had brought a blanket and pillow to the station and had obviously settled himself down for the night. He was arrested, however, before he had a chance to go to sleep.

(Fuller, 1958:664)

The word 'sleep' in this example is clearly ambiguous. It can denote both the actual state of being asleep, and the action of spending the night in some place in order to sleep. Which is the core meaning? The words themselves are of comparatively little assistance to us in such cases, and it will normally be necessary to look to the context in which the language is used in order to construct some kind of settled meaning for the word being used. Often, it will be sufficient to consider other parts of the same document, which may make it clear, either expressly or by implication, what meaning is intended.

In Professor Fuller's example, it would not be too difficult to argue that such legislation would really be aimed at sleeping in the second sense we have identified. The Act would thus catch tramps and others entering the railway station with the intention of using it as a shelter for the night, without making genuine passengers who 'nod off' waiting for a train guilty of an offence. But, just as we have created an argument in support of the second meaning, could not another lawyer create an argument supporting the first? It is quite possible for lawyers to construct contradictory but equally viable arguments as to why one or other meaning or inference should be applied. In cases of true ambiguity, it is almost impossible to say that there is a particular right answer. Fortunately such instances are comparatively rare.

(b)   Attempting to explain meaning: where problems with interpretation of a word arise, it is easy to assume that such problems can be resolved by simply explaining that word in different terms. In fact, that process is not always easy, and may create a new and unexpected set of difficulties.

One way of trying to define a word is to use a **synonym** for it. Synonyms are not ambiguous in themselves, but they often arise out of attempts to avoid ambiguity. A synonym is one word which has the same meaning as another. Sometimes it is tempting to use a synonym in the hope that it will carry a clearer sense of what is intended than the original word. Thus, in *Brutus* v *Cozens,* counsel sought to define 'insult' by reference to its dictionary definition and by the substitution (per Lord Kilbrandon at p. 1304) of terms such as 'insolence' or 'affront'.

In using synonyms two difficulties can arise. First, given the flexibility of language, it can be dangerous to assume synonymous meanings exist, particularly if one is dealing with technical legal concepts. Take the term 'fraud' for example; this is widely used in both civil and criminal law. The ordinary meaning connotes, according to the *Shorter Oxford English*

Dictionary: 'Criminal deception; the using of false representations to obtain an unjust advantage . . . ' Thus, in ordinary usage fraud could be considered synonymous with deception. In law the terms are not synonymous, however. Buckley J distinguished fraud and deception in the case of *Re London and Globe Finance Corporation Ltd* [1903] 1 Ch 728 at 733:

> . . . to deceive is by falsehood to induce a state of mind; to defraud is by deceit to induce a course of action.

So, a person may be deceived, without being defrauded in the eyes of the law. Secondly, even if the word is a good synonym for the one which it replaces, it will rarely advance our understanding—as Lord Kilbrandon pointed out in respect of our earlier examples from *Brutus* v *Cozens*, such words are all equally 'as much, or as little, in need of interpretation.' In short, synonyms are not really of great value as aids to understanding.

If synonyms are unhelpful, should we seek to explain concepts by the use of some alternative formulation? This may be a superficially attractive way for us to deal with uncertainty of meaning, particularly where ordinary words carry within them complex notions of probability or desirability. But it is an approach that carries a real risk of increasing misunderstanding, as research has shown.

Exercise 5: The uncertainty of uncertainty

The following ten expressions are all used as verbal measures expressing some degree of uncertainty. They are not ordered in any deliberate ranking:

Probable
Quite Certain
Unlikely
Hoped
Possible
Not unreasonable that
Expected
Doubtful
Not certain
Likely

Now place these in rank order from 1–10, starting with the term that is MOST UNcertain and descending to the LEAST UNcertain. If you can, do this as a group exercise, so that each of you compiles his or her own list WITHOUT DISCUSSION; then compare your list with those of other members of the group. What do you find?

There is not, of course, a set of right answers. Do not be surprised if you find considerable disagreement. When this same exercise was attempted by a group of 40 executives on general management courses at a business school, it was found that there was a high level of overlapping between ranks, and hence considerable inconsistency between respondents. Thus, for example, the term 'expected' was on average placed the second most uncertain term in the list; its position for individual respondents nevertheless ranged from first to sixth. 'Unlikely' came bottom of the average rankings, but its range of ranks varied from third to tenth! In fact, the variation was such that only three out of the 40 respondents produced identical lists (Moore & Thomas, 1988:127–8).

In case you are wondering, this does have important implications for legal decision-making. If, in a legal environment, we attempt to define a word or phrase by using some alternative formulation, there is no guarantee that our audience will give our words the same meaning as we intended. This has, in fact, been borne out by research into jury trials (LSE Jury Project, 1973), where 'jurors' have been asked to respond to what lawyers perceive to be equivalent ways of expressing the burden of proof. Needless to say, the subjects of the research did not always agree that the alternatives were equivalent at all!

(c)   Interlingual ambiguity: as law becomes an increasingly international and therefore interlingual phenomenon, it is to be expected that a new crop of linguistic problems will arise. These difficulties tend to take a number of forms, but share a common basis in our (in)capacity to translate legal concepts from one jurisdiction to another. We shall focus on two specific issues here: interlingual synonymy and homonymy.

We have already considered problems of synonymy within a legal language. Between different languages, problems of synonymy arise where terms that appear to be synonymous in fact are not. In the most extreme cases, terms may have direct linguistic equivalents in another language, but in fact mean very different things. Knapp (1991:14) uses the example of the term *lichnaya sobstvennost* in Soviet law. This could be translated literally into English as 'personal property', but the English and Soviet legal notions of personal property are, as Knapp puts it, 'mutually incomparable'. Our translation would therefore be highly misleading. A rather less extreme, but not less difficult, problem arises where there is only a partial overlap of meaning. For example, English law uses the term 'easement' to describe certain rights that one person may acquire over another's land—such as a right of way. French law recognises the similar concept of *servitude*—but although there is some common ground between the concepts these terms denote, they are not identical. Easement would not provide a precise translation of the term *servitude* and vice versa.

A similar problem arises with legal homonyms (a homonym is a term which is either phonetically or in written form more or less identical to a word in another language). Again, these may convey very different ideas through the same term. Knapp (1991:15) uses the example of the term 'magistrate' and its homonyms. In English, 'magistrate' refers to a very particular kind of judge, sitting in the Magistrates' Court. In French, *magistrat* refers more generally to the professional judiciary, and as Weston (1991:109–10) shows, the term is extremely difficult to translate accurately into English, though at least the English and French terms do have judging in common! By contrast, the Czech term *magistrát* has nothing to do with the judiciary. It refers to a city administration—a kind of city council. Of course, just to increase the confusion, what is a misleading homonym for some comparisons is not necessarily so for others. Thus, to develop Knapp's example, the French *magistrats* and Italian *magistrati* are essentially members of the same institutions!

Although this all sounds very academic, such interlingual problems are of practical significance. In multilingual legal communities such as the European Community, problems of translation and of linguistic and conceptual equivalence arise at the stages of drafting and interpreting legislation (see respectively Chapters Seven and Ten of this book where the EC context is developed more fully). These difficulties can occur both at national and supra-national levels. Interlingualism may also need to be addressed in domestic courts when dealing with matters established by international treaty, or when applying conflicts of law rules—eg, in dealing with international trade matters, or with the recognition of foreign divorces.

Interpreting syntax: In law, a second level of difficulty emerges out of syntax, by which is meant the grammatical use of words. Lawyers do not just have to work out the meaning of individual words; words are, of course the constituent parts of more complex linguistic structures, such as phrases and sentences, and in reality these can create separate problems from those which arise in the interpretation of a single word. The primary difficulty is that which has been called **syntactic ambiguity**. This phrase is used to describe the alternative constructions that are created by the use of qualifying phrases and dependent clauses within a sentence or paragraph. Bryan Niblett (1980:10–11) explores this problem by drawing a comparison between the syntax of a legal proposition and that of a computer program. Both constructs can suffer from what computer programmers call the 'dangling else' ambiguity. Niblett presents us with the following expression to illustrate this:

if (condition 1) then if (condition 2) then
(statement 1) else (statement 2)

If we consider this expression it does not take long to work out how the ambiguity arises. If conditions 1 and 2 are satisfied, there is no problem, since statement 1 obviously applies; but what if neither condition is satisfied, or only condition 1? When does statement 2 come into play? The ambiguity is there because we do not know from this expression to which *then* the *else* is an alternative. The ambiguity thus does not depend upon the words used but upon the way the expression is structured. Syntactic ambiguity is a particular problem of statute or delegated legislation. In practice, such instances of ambiguity have to be resolved by the courts choosing one of a number of competing interpretations, or sometimes by Parliament amending the ambiguous construction.

This can be seen from another of Niblett's examples, taken this time from a real statute, namely, the Guard Dogs Act 1975. Section 1(1) of the Act provides:

> *A person shall not use or permit the use of a guard dog at any premises unless a person ('the handler') who is capable of controlling the dog is present on the premises and the dog is under the control of the handler at all times while it is being so used* **except while it is secured so that it is not at liberty to go freely about the premises** (emphasis added).

The phrase in bold type in that section is a classic example of the 'dangling else'. Does it qualify the whole of the foregoing section, or does it just qualify the requirement that 'the dog is under the control of the handler at all times . . .'? Just by looking at the words themselves, either answer is acceptable. The Divisional Court in *Hobson* v *Gledhill* [1978] 1 WLR 215, [1978] 1 All ER 945 was faced with exactly that conundrum. The accused used three Alsatian dogs to guard his premises. There was no handler present on the premises, but the dogs were secured and could not move freely about the property. If our first interpretation was correct, then no offence had been committed; the dogs were secured, so no handler was required. But if the second construction was correct, the accused would be guilty of an offence under the Act. Even if the dogs were secured, it was necessary to have a handler on the premises. The court decided the case by taking the first interpretation, a process which it justified by reference to one of the principles of statutory interpretation which we shall consider below.

More complex forms of ambiguity may arise, particularly within lengthy legal documents, where there is a contradiction between provisions. This is not, strictly speaking, a problem of syntax, just inconsistent drafting. However, it will raise difficult questions about which of the two conflicting provisions should prevail.

Fact, Language and the Judicial Construction of Cases

In the next four chapters of this book we shall be looking at the rules or principles that have been developed, chiefly by the courts, to assist in the interpretation and use of existing statutory and common law authorities. The purpose of this chapter has been to get you to consider the background against which such principles operate. This is not simply a question of setting the scene. Many of those principles exist precisely because of the linguistic difficulties we have discussed in this chapter, and are there to provide guidance to the courts in overcoming such difficulties.

At the same time, however, it would be wrong to assume that such principles create a highly structured body of rules which can dictate with a high degree of certainty how issues, and hence legal cases will be resolved. Cases are ultimately constructed in the courtroom. In *Hobson*, for example, the court was able to justify its decision by reference to a principle of statutory interpretation, which requires ambiguity in a statute imposing criminal liability to be construed in favour of the accused. However, as we shall see, the majority of these principles are not hard and fast rules of law which the judge can only apply one way. The principles are mostly broad and leave much to the wisdom of the particular judge in each case. This means that judges have a considerable degree of discretion in choosing the principles they apply, and hence the meanings they give to statutes and other legal documents.

Similarly, though true semantic ambiguity can be a major problem, flexibility in assigning meaning to words provides another source for the exercise of discretion. This has both positive and negative effects on the development of English law. On the one hand, problems of precision in definition may be such that judges and draftsmen become reluctant to define a word at all, or else avoid the issue by taking the 'ordinary meaning' approach of cases such as *Brutus v Cozens*. On the other hand, the lack of a precise definition may be equally indicative of a positive decision not to impose what might be an unduly restrictive definition on a particular concept. Whether this is desirable is ultimately a political rather than legal question, but it does have a legal cost in that a lack of formalised definitions can sometimes allow the law to develop without the internal coherence and consistency that we might expect. So what, ultimately, dictates how a judge's discretion is applied?

In answer to that question we would suggest that the 'judicial style' of the judge may well be the single most important variable. This can be explained by reference to two cases on the tort of negligence.

In negligence, it is necessary for the plaintiff to show that the injuries suffered are 'reasonably foreseeable' if the claim is to succeed. Let us contrast two cases which shed a rather contradictory light on that question.

In *Bradford v Robinson Rentals Ltd* [1967] 1 WLR 337, [1967] 1 All ER 267, the High Court had to deal with an unusual claim. In this case, the plaintiff was claiming in respect of frostbite suffered as a result of driving his employer's unheated van during an exceptionally harsh winter. On these facts, the plaintiff succeeded in his claim; the employer was negligent in allowing the plaintiff out in such a vehicle, and the plaintiff's injuries were a reasonably foreseeable consequence of that action, despite the fact that the precise kind of injury suffered was uncommon in England.

In *Tremain v Pike* [1969] 1 WLR 1556, [1969] 3 All ER 1303, the plaintiff, a farmworker, contracted a rare disease called Weil's disease which is caused by the sufferer being infected by an organism found in rats' urine. His claim was that his employer had been negligent by allowing the rat population on the farm to grow to such an extent as to place his health at risk. The court did not deny that such behaviour was negligent, but it refused the plaintiff's claim on the basis that the *type* of injury, was not foreseeable. What was foreseeable was a more obvious kind of 'rat injury' such as a bite. In effect, the court held that you cannot foresee a rare disease.

Is the latter decision inconsistent with the former? If the approach in *Bradford* had been followed in *Tremain* there would certainly be grounds to suggest that contracting Weil's Disease is no less foreseeable than contracting frostbite. The difference lies not in the actual tests used; both judges applied the reasonable foresight test, but there is a different attitude to the test displayed by the two courts. In the second case, the judge took a very restrictive view, requiring that the precise *type* of injury should be reasonably foreseeable. In *Bradford,* the judicial view was more relaxed. It was foreseeable that some kind of injury would follow from being thus exposed to the extreme cold, and that was taken to be sufficient. It was not necessary that the precise nature of the injury should be foreseen. This question of 'judicial style' will be significant in determining how a judge handles a case, including the way in which he or she uses precedent— see Llewellyn (1960)—or principles of statutory interpretation (a point to which we shall return in Chapter Eight).

Judicial style may also affect the way in which facts are used. We have already confronted the idea that facts in law are not a wholly objective truth. They are constructed within the courtroom and may be affected by a whole variety of highly subjective factors; for example, the presentation by counsel, the language and appearance of witnesses or the ability of the jury (or judge?) to comprehend the issues. We have also noted that the judge is, in many cases, the arbiter of fact. We would suggest that questions of judicial style might thus also influence the reception of those facts.

In two recent works, by Jackson (1988) and Twining (1990), the judgment of Lord Denning in *Miller v Jackson* [1977] QB 966, [1977] 3 All ER 338 has been considered. Although the two authors adopt different standpoints, they have both used *Miller* critically, as an example of how judges may manipulate a case through the statement of facts. We have used an extract from that judgment as the basis for the final exercise in this chapter.

Exercise 6: It's just not cricket!

Consider the following passage taken from his lordship's judgment (pp. 340–1):

> In summer time village cricket is the delight of everyone. Nearly every village has its own cricket field where the young men play and the old men watch. In the village of Lintz in County Durham they have their own ground, where they have played these last 70 years . . . The village team play there on Saturdays and Sundays. They belong to a league,

competing with the neighbouring villages. On other evenings after work they practise while the light lasts. Yet now after these 70 years a judge of the High Court has ordered that they must not play there any more. He has issued an injunction to stop them. He has done it at the instance of a newcomer who is no lover of cricket. This newcomer built, or has had built for him, a house on the edge of the cricket ground which four years ago was a field where cattle grazed. The animals did not mind the cricket. But now this adjoining field has been turned into a housing estate. The newcomer bought one of the houses on the edge of the cricket ground. No doubt the open space was a selling point. Now he complains that, when a batsman hits a six, the ball has been known to land in his garden or on or near his house. His wife has got so upset about it that they always go out at weekends. They do not go into the garden when cricket is being played. They say that this is intolerable . . . And the judge, much against his will, has felt that he must order the cricket to be stopped; with the consequences, I suppose, that the Lintz Cricket Club will disappear. The cricket ground will be turned to some other use. I expect for more houses or a factory. The young men will turn to other things instead of cricket. The whole village will be much the poorer. And all this because of a newcomer who has just bought a house there next to the cricket ground.

From this statement can you:

(a)   predict Lord Denning's decision on the law: did he find in favour of the cricket club, or of the Millers?
(b)   distinguish fact from supposition within that case.

Answers: The answer to (a) will probably come as little surprise. Lord Denning found in favour of the cricket club. He held that there was no actionable nuisance by the club, and discharged the injunction. His lordship was not, in the end, wholly successful in carrying the rest of the Court of Appeal with him. The other two judges found that there was an actionable nuisance; however, only one of them felt that it was such that an injunction (a discretionary remedy) should be granted, so that Lord Denning was in a majority in favour of dismissing the injunction granted by the High Court.

Is it not rather odd that we can guess the final decision from what is supposed to be a statement of facts? Yes—if one assumes that the facts are supposed to be a fairly objective part of the process. Lord Denning's comments illustrate, as Twining notes, the way in which facts can be formulated so as to advance a particular argument, albeit that, here, Lord Denning's formulation is far more explicitly biased than one would normally expect from a judge. Jackson argues that his technique is strongly rhetorical. It builds an image of a rural community bound together by its love of cricket; it is an idyll that is threatened by an outsider who can destroy that traditional way of life. The effect is to create a narrative framework 'laden with disapproval' (p. 96).

In respect of (b), the construction of a narrative built upon both fact and supposition is another aspect of Lord Denning's attempt to carry us along to his conclusion. He thus creates a picture of socially undesirable consequences that might flow from the continued injunction: the replacement of the cricket ground with houses or a factory; the fear that young men will turn 'to other things' which, though remaining unspoken, are clearly undesirable. These are, of course suppositions, without evidence; they should not impinge on the case, and yet they do.

In saying that judicial style is a central determinant of cases, we are not suggesting that judges have, in effect, a free rein to decide cases as they think fit. Judges operate within an accepted judicial culture which creates limits on what is acceptable practice. One reason why Lord Denning's judgment in *Miller* v *Jackson* is so often seen as rather shocking is because it breaks down the role-perception we have of the judge as impartial umpire. The framework of rules and principles within which judges operate does impose some constraints on them. But in looking at those guiding principles of precedent and interpretation (which make up much of this book), it is worth considering the extent to which these constraints are self-imposed, and therefore capable of revision from within the judiciary itself. As Llewellyn (1960:53) pointed out: a sense of legal tradition may guide lawyers, but it is the lawyers who may reshape and mould it for the future.

REFERENCES

Fuller, L. (1958) 'Positivism and Fidelity to Law—A Reply to Professor Hart' *Harvard Law Review,* vol. 71, p. 630.

Grossfeld, B. (1990) *The Strength and Weakness of Comparative Law* (trans. T. Weir), Oxford: Clarendon Press.

* Hanson, N. (1959) *Patterns of Discovery: an inquiry into the conceptual foundations of science,* Cambridge: Cambridge University Press.

Jackson, B. (1988) *Law, Fact and Narrative Coherence,* Roby: Deborah Charles Publ.

* Knapp, V. (1991) 'Some Problems of Legal Language' *Ratio Juris,* vol. 4, p. 1.

Llewellyn, K. (1960) *The Common Law Tradition,* Boston: Little Brown.

* Lloyd-Bostock, S. (1988) *Law in Practice,* London: British Psychological Society/Routledge.

LSE Jury Project, (1973) 'Juries and the Rules of Evidence' *Criminal Law Review,* p. 208.

Niblett, B. (1980) 'Computer Science and Law: An Introductory Discussion' in Niblett (ed.) *Computer Science and Law: an advanced course,* Cambridge: Cambridge University Press.

O'Barr, W. *et al* (1982) *Linguistic Evidence: Language, Power and Strategy in the Courtroom,* New York: Academic Press.

Twining, W. (1990) *Rethinking Evidence: Exploratory Essays,* Oxford: Basil Blackwell.

Weston, M. (1991) *An English Reader's Guide to the French Legal System,* New York/Oxford: Berg.

Wilkes, R. (1984) *Wallace: The Final Verdict,* London: Grafton.

Chapter Five

The Doctrine of Judicial Precedent

In this chapter we begin to deal with case law in depth. In the study and practice of law we seek to analyse legal principles; and the 'principles' in English law are derived from pure case law or from case law dealing with statutes. Indeed, it is often said to be a strength of English law that it is built upon the concrete examples of case law rather than hypothetical models. This contrast with the European approach, which does depend upon 'models', will be drawn and expanded upon later. As regards the Common Law fixation with a case-by-case development of the law, it is worth noting the observations of Lord MacMillan that, unlike the Civil Law lawyer, the Englishman,

> has found that life is unconformable to any fixed theory and that principles always fail because they never seem to fit the case in hand, and so prefers to leave theory and principle alone. (1937:81)

We shall explore the significance of this statement over the next two chapters.

The doctrine of judicial precedent is concerned with the importance of case law in our system. It is really the lawyer's term for legal experience. We all tend to repeat things we have done before: law is essentially no different. If one case has decided a point of law then it is logical that that solution will be looked at in the future. The American judge, Oliver Wendell Holmes Jnr once said that 'The life of the Law has not been logic; it has been experience'. Miles Kington put it another way in *Punch:* judicial precedent means, 'A trick which has been tried before, successfully.'

But if judicial precedent is simply experience in legal jargon, why does it deserve our attention? Why can we say that, during your training in law and afterwards, you will have to possess a clear understanding of the intricacies of judicial precedent? The answer lies in the fact that the term 'experience' only begins to describe the situation.

First, even when a layman uses the term 'precedent' there is an implication that what was done before should be done again—that a starting point in trying to solve a problem is to see what examples exist where this (or similar) problems have been tackled before. The example—the precedent— is at least a good guide and probably will be followed. This achieves consistency, if nothing else. And the corollary is that people making decisions are often afraid to do something in case 'it creates a precedent'. As MacCormick states:

> To understand case-law . . . is to understand how it is that particular decisions by particular judges concerning particular parties to particular cases can be used in the construction of general rules applying to the actions and transactions of persons at large. (1987:155)

In other words, combining the remarks of Lord MacMillan and MacCormick, the principles of English law are derived from observing the development of a line of particular cases on a particular topic. This is a key factor in English law. Because English lawyers are so avidly fixed on case law, principles do not develop unless plaintiffs bring cases. Academics and practitioners may speculate on the development of legal principles, but it takes real-life cases to settle them. And the judges in each case, to a greater or lesser extent, draw upon the principles established in those earlier cases in reaching their decision. For instance: imagine that a case in 1920 decided that any person selling parrots was under an implied contractual duty to ensure that the parrot could talk. Lawyers could then speculate on a number of different points:

(a)   Would this principle still apply if the pet shop owner clearly told the customer that the parrot could not talk?
(b)   Does the same principle apply to related birds such as budgerigars?
(c)   Should the principle apply to other birds?
(d)   Wider still, is there a general principle to be found in the case which might mean that a similar duty (say as to standards of health) might apply to other animals?

Thus, as MacCormick indicates, the particular case concerning parrots may consequently be seen as giving birth to a more general principle on the duties owed by pet shop owners to their customers, eg that they owed a duty always to deal in good faith. It is not beyond speculation that the same principle might one day then be applied to sellers of other types of goods such as televisions or cars. Eventually a textbook writer will sum up the case law in one general statement on the duties owed by vendors of goods. Looking back at the history of the cases, we might find that one case concerning a mute parrot is now applied to all cases on defective merchandise.

However, to this we need to add one further ingredient. It is this: an important and distinctive element of English law is that the reasoning and decisions found in preceding cases are not simply considered with respect or as a good guide, but can be **BINDING** on later courts. This is known as the principle of *stare rationibus decidendis;* usually referred to as *stare decisis*. It translates simply as 'Let the decision stand'. *Stare rationibus decidendi* is the more accurate statement because, as we shall see, it is the reasoning *(rationibus)* that is the vital binding element in judicial precedent. However, nobody actually refers to it this way.

What *stare decisis* means in practice is that when a court makes a decision in a case then any courts which are of equal or lower status to that court **must** follow that previous decision if the case before them is similar to that earlier case. So, once one court has decided a matter other inferior courts are bound to follow that decision.

You must be careful here: the 'decision' of a case can mean a number of different things. At its simplest, the 'decision' is that X won and Y lost. Thus X and Y are (subject to any appeal) bound by that decision; this is referred to as *res judicata*. But when we use the word 'decision' in the context of legal analysis we are referring to something much wider. We are referring to the whole reasoning process that went into deciding that X won—we are referring to *why* X won; and we shall explore how we set about this below.

So first, you must be aware right at the start that legal reasoning is not simply a process of matching one case against another; it is not merely a question of drawing analogies. There will always be differences in the facts of the two cases, if nothing else. As precedent is founded on comparing cases a primary question is: how significant are the differences? Just because the facts of two cases are apparently similar does not mean they should be decided in the same way. You would not, for instance, say that if a Tabby cat called Henry cannot miaow, that every other Tabby cat called Henry will not be able to miaow.

We can translate this into something more realistic and legally orientated:

Exercise 7: Zebras on the North Circular

Let us say that in *case (1)* a man driving a Ford Escort runs over an old lady who was lawfully using a zebra crossing.

The man is found guilty of reckless driving.

Let us say that in *case (2)* a woman driving a BMW runs over an old man who was crossing the road.

Should she be found guilty, too, or do you need to ask some further questions?

If there are other questions, what might they be?

We do not present a formalised answer to this, because we wish to explore the ramifications of the issues it raises; but you may check your ideas against the comments which follow.

We have seen in earlier exercises that a proper assessment and analysis of factual detail is essential to the application of rules. You might wish to know, for instance, what were the weather conditions in each case; were either of the drivers speeding; was the old man crossing the road at a safe point?

This leads us to ask: what differences in the facts might be significant here? Are the cases, for instance:

(a)   sufficiently different that the decision of case (1) should not be applied (never mind be considered binding) in case (2)? or,

(b)   are the factual differences of minimal significance? or,

(c)   are the facts different, but the principle underlying the decisions in the cases similar? Here you need to be sure what was the principle that was established in the first case: does the 'why?' in the first case apply to the second?

If the answer is the last point, should we apply the principle even though the facts are different? For that matter: how different can the facts be before the principle has no application?

The doctrine of judicial precedent is not simply a mechanical process of matching similarities and differences. It is not merely a science of comparisons for it embodies the art of interpretation; the art of propounding the principle to be derived from each case. It also involves the lifeblood of a lawyer—argument. We will deal with this aspect of precedent in depth in the next chapter. However, by way of introduction, here is an example of what we mean—cases appearing to be similar at first glance, without necessarily proving to be so:

In *Household Fire Insurance Co.* v *Grant* (1879) 4 Ex D 216 Grant made an application in writing to the company for shares. A deposit was paid, the remainder to be paid within twelve months. The company allotted shares to Grant and posted the allotment to him. The letter never arrived. The company later went into liquidation and the liquidator sought the balance of Grant's application which was still outstanding. Grant maintained he had no contract with the company because his offer had not been accepted. No contract would mean no liability to pay. The company maintained that the offer had been accepted when their letter of acceptance had been posted even though it never arrived.

In case you have not studied Contract Law yet (or are not going to) we should explain that a contract is formed when there is an offer which is accepted, without the addition of new terms, by the other party. A person making an offer is termed the *offeror;* the person receiving the offer is the *offeree.* The general rule is that acceptance has to be communicated. There is no contract simply because, in his or her own mind, the offeree is willing to accept. However, a major problem arises when the parties are not face to face. If they communicate by post, when does the acceptance take place? When the letter of acceptance is posted, or only when it arrives with the offeror?

By the end of the nineteenth century there existed a number of authorities on what is now termed the 'postal rules' of acceptance in contract. These stretched back to *Adams* v *Lindsell* (1818) 1 B & A 681, but the key case under scrutiny was to be the House of Lords' case of *Dunlop* v *Higgins* (1848) 1 HLC 381; 9 ER 805. In this case Dunlop wrote to Higgins offering to sell some iron; reply to be by return of post. The offer was accepted by Higgins in a letter but bad weather delayed the post. In the meantime there had been an increase in the price of iron. Dunlop maintained there was no contract—which would allow them to sell to other customers at the new price. The House of Lords decided that a contract existed when the letter of acceptance was posted.

In *Household Fire Insurance* v *Grant* all three judges in the Court of Appeal analysed whether *Dunlop* v *Higgins* applied to the case before them. Thesiger LJ said that the decision in *Dunlop* v *Higgins* rested 'upon a principle which embraces and governs the present case'. To say that the acceptance takes place when the letter is posted and arrives late (as with *Dunlop* v *Higgins)* but not if it never arrives (as with *Household Fire)* would be illogical. The principle was, therefore, that once the letter of acceptance was posted the parties were bound.

Bagallay LJ looked at *Dunlop* v *Higgins* and concluded (at 227,8):

I think that the principle established by that case is limited in its application to cases in which by reason of general usage, or of the relations between the parties . . . or of the terms in which the offer is made, the acceptance of such offer by a letter through the post is expressly or impliedly authorised.

Thus the principle in *Dunlop* v *Higgins* was seen as being more limited than Thesiger LJ's approach; but on the facts Bagallay LJ decided that the present case fell within the rule.

Bramwell LJ dissented. He thought there was no contract because the letter never arrived. He argued that *Dunlop* v *Higgins* had been completely misinterpreted; at best it was authority for the rule that acceptance takes place on posting only where the letter arrives (albeit late and within a reasonable time).

So the same authority was used by two Lords Justices to find for the company; but they had quite different interpretations as to what *Dunlop* v *Higgins* really decided. The same case was also used by Bramwell LJ to argue a completely different conclusion—showing at least that simply knowing about the existence of a case is not enough; you must be able to argue its relevance or irrelevance to the case in hand.

In this chapter we shall concentrate on the position where the facts are sufficiently similar that the cases are 'alike'. How will the doctrine of *stare decisis* affect our analysis?

In answering this question it becomes important that we should look at the mechanical side of precedent. The courts stand in a defined hierarchy: which courts are **bound** to follow the decisions of which other courts? This is not usually perceived as the most stimulating part of legal studies, but understanding the workings of *stare decisis* depends upon having a sound grasp of the court structure. In turn, an efficient system of precedent depends upon dependable law reporting. You should familiarise yourself with the court structure and know how to use a law library. You will find these matters explained earlier in this book and detailed in any text on the English Legal System. These are hardly the thing examination questions are made of, but a lawyer who cannot describe the structure in which the law operates, or find the law, will lose credibility fast!

The system of precedent itself involves a fair degree of detail, but the basic principle to keep in mind is that the precedents created by superior courts bind lower courts and, generally, courts of equal status.

One other idea you need to bear in mind is that not all precedents are binding. For if some precedents are binding there must be others which are not. These we call **persuasive** precedents.

Persuasive precedents arise out of a number of contexts:

(a)   Decisions of *lower* courts cannot bind. They may be persuasive.

(b)   Decisions of the High Court at first instance are persuasive authority for later cases in the High Court.

(c)   Decisions of the Judicial Committee of the Privy Council (see below)

(d)   Decisions of the Scottish and Northern Irish courts.

(e)   Decisions of other courts within the Common Law world: see eg the use of the Australian case of *Sutherland Shire Council* v *Heyman* (1985) 60 ALR 1 in *Murphy* v *Brentwood DC* (1990), detailed below.

The House of Lords

The decisions of the House of Lords bind all lower courts. There has been a long debate as to whether decisions of the House of Lords should bind a future House of Lords. For some hundred years the Law Lords considered themselves bound. This was changed by the *Practice Statement (Judicial Precedent)* [1966] 1 WLR 1234 where it was said that though the doctrine of being bound had many commendable points: 'too rigid adherence to precedent may lead to injustice in a particular case and also unduly restrict the proper development of the law'.

Thus the Lords can depart from their own previous decisions; but they will only do so in rare circumstances. Remember that the House of Lords is the highest court in the land (save, in a quite different way, on European Community law matters). Its pronouncements (only about 100 a year) must be seen as creating an air of certainty in business dealings, in criminal law, in land law and so on. Changing its mind may do 'justice' to a particular case, but at a cost. For instance, if you are conducting complicated contractual negotiations based on a decision of the House of Lords, it is somewhat annoying to find that, having concluded the deal, the law relating to that contract has suddenly been changed by a new House of Lords' decision. One of the authors can bear testimony to this.

However, despite this, the Law Lords will change their minds. Such occasions are rare, but here are a few cases which show this in action.

(a) *British Railways Board* v *Herrington* [1972] AC 877, [1972] 1 All ER 749:

The Lords faced a number of nineteenth century and early twentieth century decisions wherein they had held that there was only a limited duty of care in negligence owed to children who trespassed onto property. This duty was that the occupier should not act recklessly with regard to children whom he knew to be there; and public policy dictated that there was no duty at all to keep out such children or to make the premises safe for them. Since then changes in perceptions of public policy and the development of the law of negligence had altered the approach to the whole topic of responsibility for negligent actions. Thus their Lordships felt able to ignore the earlier decisions and impose on British Railways a duty of care in keeping railway line fences repaired.

(b) *Miliangos* v *George Frank (Textiles) Ltd* [1976] AC 443, [1975] 3 All ER 801:

The House of Lords had previously decided that all awards of damages in an English court had to be made in sterling. In this case, however, because of changes in international trade and the status of sterling they felt the time had come not to adhere to their previous decisions.

(c) *R* v *Shivpuri* [1987] AC 1, [1986] 2 All ER 334:

The case concerned the law as to criminal attempts. A decision of the House of Lords one year earlier (*Anderton* v *Ryan* [1985] AC 567, [1985] 2 All ER 355) had received great criticism. In *R* v *Shivpuri* the House of Lords changed its mind. This is a rare example of the House of Lords overturning its own decisions **simply because it felt the earlier decision was wrong**. Usually the Lords look for wider policy considerations.

In *Food Corp. of India* v *Antclizo Shipping Co.* [1988] 1 WLR 603, [1988] 2 All ER 513, Lord Goff (on behalf of the court) stated that their Lordships would not depart from a previous House of Lords' decision unless:

(1) it felt free to depart from *both* the reasoning and decision of the earlier case; *and*
(2) such a review would affect the resolution of the actual case before them and not be of mere academic interest.

At first sight this is an extremely limiting pronouncement. Point (2) means that the House of Lords will not be prepared to overrule one of their previous decisions, even if they think it wrong, unless by doing so this would affect the case before them. It is not their job to write textbooks on Law, but to decide real cases before them. Their Lordships will, in these circumstances, refuse to overrule their decision because that point is only of academic interest. This is what happened in *Antclizo,* and is in keeping with the spirit of the 1966 Statement. However, it is worth noting that in *Shivpuri* and a later case named *R v Howe* [1987] AC 417, [1987] 1 All ER 771 the overruling took place even though some of their Lordships thought the cases under review could be distinguished on their facts.

Point (1) involves the court in a detailed scrutiny of the earlier case in question. What the Law Lords appear to be saying is that not only must the decision be judged to be incorrect; so too must the reasoning. The problem here is that Lord Goff seems to be saying that if the Lords found the decision to be wrong but the reasoning correct they will not interfere with the case. This then means that they will be agreeing with a case where the final conclusion does not match the analysis. It is rather like a maths exam where an answer, 2 + 2 = 5, is marked correct because the reasoning (though clearly not the result) is sound. This seems puzzling. For further discussion, see Harris (1990:135).

But the *Antclizo* case does allow us to say one further thing, to which we shall return. That is, when a case first appears, stating a principle of law, one can never really be sure as to the impact the case will have. At the instant it appears, when there are no other cases which have attempted to apply it, one can only speculate as to its impact. One famous example is a case called *Junior Books v Veitchi* [1983] AC 520, [1982] 3 All ER 201. When this case was decided many lawyers believed it had cleared the way for major changes in legal thought. A decade later the case has all but fallen into oblivion.

There is thus no one principle by which the House of Lords sets about overturning its precedents. In *Murphy v Brentwood District Council* [1990] 3 WLR 414, [1990] 2 All ER 908, for instance their Lordships were again prepared to overturn one of their previous decisions: *Anns v Merton London Borough Council* [1978] AC 728, [1977] 2 All ER 492. There are various reasons given by their Lordships as to why they were prepared to make this decision. Lord Mackay, the Lord Chancellor, felt that the earlier case was taken as a preliminary issue of law so that the facts had not been considered in detail. The case may have worked in theory but did not relate to real facts. Lord Keith looked at *Sutherland Shire Council v Heyman* (1985), an Australian case which had rejected *Anns*, as well as US cases which had analysed the cases on which *Anns* itself was based and proved these to be faulty. Thus, departure from *Anns* could be justified on the grounds that the case was 'unsatisfactory'. Lord Oliver also noted academic criticism of the decision in *Anns*. *Antclizo* is not mentioned in the case.

Indeed, *Antclizo* itself appears to have become one of the 'lost' cases along with *Junior Books v Veitchi.* It has only been cited in seven cases and, even then, without extensive comment. The case, for instance, makes no appearance in *Pepper (Inspector of Taxes) v Hart* [1992] 3 WLR 1032, [1993] 1 All ER 42 in which the House of Lords overturned a long-established principle on the sources that could be referred to in interpreting a statute. For the moment at least *Antclizo* appears to have gone to ground.

The Court of Appeal

The importance of this court, both because of its place in the hierarchy and because of its heavy workload means that you need to be aware of how it deals with precedent. Most of the important cases you will deal with in your studies were reached by this court or its predecessors such as the Court of Exchequer Chamber.

There are two important questions concerning the Court of Appeal and the notion of *stare decisis.*

To what Extent is the Court of Appeal Bound to Follow Decisions of the House of Lords?

Strictly speaking the answer is always. But there have been campaigns in the Court of Appeal to overcome the principle. The principal crusader was Lord Denning MR. His departure seems to have signalled a halt to the conflict.

The per incuriam campaign: In his major attack Lord Denning advocated that if a House of Lords' decision had been made *per incuriam* it need not be followed. *Per incuriam* means that a court failed to take into account all the relevant and vital statutes or case authorities and that this had a major effect on the decision. The analogy might be made with the writing of a scientific paper. Let us say a famous scientist produces a theory and that a few years later it is discovered that his research was faulty—he had not read two of the leading papers. Would you say there are grounds for arguing that the theory should be open to scrutiny or even doubt?

The *per incuriam* rule is a well established technical rule; but you must be careful here. *Per incuriam* does not simply mean the earlier court got things wrong. It only means there was an oversight. As we shall see soon not only must there have been a failure to take account of relevant authorities; that fault must also have been such a major defect that it seriously affected the reasoning in the case. So, with the example of the scientist, if it is now discovered that had he read the two leading papers this would have had no effect on his theory the fault is a technical one of methodology and does not affect the conclusions drawn.

Lord Denning MR tried this form of reasoning in *Broome* v *Cassell* [1971] 2 QB 354, [1971] 2 All ER 187. Lord Denning persuaded the other members of the Court of Appeal to reach a decision which was contrary to that of an earlier House of Lords' decision, *Rookes* v *Barnard* [1964] AC 1129, [1964] 1 All ER 367. Lord Denning pointed out that *Rookes* v *Barnard* was a decision made *per incuriam* because it had failed to consider even earlier House of Lords' authorities.

However, when *Broome* v *Cassell* went to the House of Lords, the Law

Lords rebuked Lord Denning for adopting such a rule because they believed he had plainly looked for an excuse not to adhere to *stare decisis*. As Lord Hailsham, the then Lord Chancellor, said,

> I am driven to the conclusion that when the Court of Appeal described the decision in *Rookes* v *Barnard* as decided 'per incuriam' or 'unworkable' they really only meant that they did not agree with it . . . (I)n the hierarchical system of courts which exists in this country, it is necessary for each lower tier, including the Court of Appeal, to accept loyally the decisions of the higher tiers. [1972] AC 1027, 1054

So though we have a system which is dependent upon the sound use of existing legal authorities, a House of Lords' decision made *per incuriam* must nevertheless be followed by a lower court.

The 'lapsed rule' campaign: Let us say that the House of Lords reached a decision some years ago based upon a particular rule or set of facts, eg that damages in English courts can only be given in sterling because of the stability of the currency and established forms of procedure. Now let us say that the reason for the rule has disappeared: the forms have changed and sterling has lost its stability. Should the precedent created by the House of Lords be followed even though the whole basis of this precedent has disappeared?

This was the question considered by the Court of Appeal, led by Lord Denning, in *Schorsch Meier GmbH* v *Hennin* [1975] QB 416, [1975] 1 All ER 152. Like so many things in law, a Latin maxim describes the rule thus: *cessante ratione legis, cessat ipsa lex* (with the reason for the rule ceasing, the law itself no longer exists). On this occasion the Court of Appeal was split. Lord Denning and Foster J agreed that a 1961 decision of the House of Lords had run its course. That earlier case, *Re United Railways of Havana and Regla Warehouses* [1961] AC 1007, [1960] 2 All ER 332 is referred to as the *Havana* case. In fact, the rule that damages should be awarded only in Sterling seems to have existed for over 300 years. Lord Justice Lawton, however, did not recognise that the Court of Appeal had such power and found himself bound to follow the House of Lords.

This case did not go on appeal to the House of Lords. However, as we shall see below, the House of Lords soon had opportunity to comment on this issue in a case named *Miliangos* v *George Frank (Textiles) Ltd*; and once again disapproved Lord Denning's attempts to vary the notion of *stare decisis*. As you will have noted above, however, their Lordships did overrule their own previous decisions on the same grounds proposed by Lord Denning, ie the 'lapsed rule' idea.

Thus one is forced to say that (especially with Lord Denning's retirement) the campaigns failed. It is for the House of Lords to change their minds; not for the Court of Appeal to decide the issue for them. On the positive side, this helps to create certainty. Equally, such strict adherence to *stare decisis* may increase costs (because of the need for further appeals), as well as appearing to invite the veneration of rules whatever the logic or perceived justice.

To what Extent is the Court of Appeal Bound by its Own Previous Decisions?

The basic rule is that it is bound. Some exceptions were given in *Young v Bristol Aeroplane Co. Ltd* [1944] KB 718, 723 by Lord Greene MR Thus:

The Court of Appeal can choose between its own conflicting decisions: Such conflict arises because the Court of Appeal does not hear one case at a time; different Lords Justices may be sitting hearing different cases at more or less the same time. It is also possible that some earlier cases might not have been reported.

What Lord Greene MR did not explore is *which* of the conflicting decisions should be followed and neither academic nor judicial debate has resolved this finally. The court is probably free to decide which authority it should follow, with the result that the one not chosen is overruled. For a full debate see Cross (1991:144).

It is worth noting that Lord Denning led another attack on what he clearly perceived to be the fetter of *stare decisis* in the case of *Davis v Johnson* [1979] AC 264, [1978] 1 All ER 1132 (HL); [1978] 2 WLR 182, [1978] 1 All ER 841 (CA). This was not an instance of cleverly adopting rules to excuse departure from precedents. Here, Lord Denning sought to apply the 1966 Practice Statement to the Court of Appeal as well as the House of Lords on the grounds of wasted time and costs of further appeals. Once again, however, the attempt failed.

If its own previous decision has been overruled expressly or impliedly by the House of Lords it need not be followed: Thus if the order of cases ran:

Court of Appeal's *decision 1*
House of Lords' decision   (disapproving the Court of Appeal's decision in case 1)
Court of Appeal's *decision 2*

then the Court of Appeal in case 2 must follow the House of Lords and not the Court of Appeal's decision in case 1.

But this does not answer the question which path should be chosen where the order of cases is:

House of Lords' decision
Court of Appeal's *decision 1*   (which is contrary to the earlier House of Lords' decision)
Court of Appeal's *decision 2*

Now the Court of Appeal is caught between two rules—one saying it is bound to follow its own previous decisions; the other that it is bound to follow the House of Lords.

This situation arose in *Miliangos* v *George Frank (Textiles) Ltd.* Only a year after the Court of Appeal had decided to award judgment in a currency other than sterling, in the *Schorsch Meier* case, the same issue came before the Court of Appeal again. Should it follow its decision in *Schorsch Meier* or follow the decision of the House of Lords which had been by-passed in *Schorsch Meier?* You may wish to speculate as to which answer, which strand of *stare decisis,* you think should be the most appropriate.

The Court of Appeal in *Miliangos* (ie *decision 2)* chose to follow its own previous decision (ie *decision 1),* and not the House of Lords. When the case went before the House of Lords their Lordships agreed that judgment could be given in a currency other than sterling, thereby overruling their own previous decision; but took the opportunity to criticise Lord Denning's approach in the *Schorsch Meier* case for ignoring the doctrine of *stare decisis.* However, to add to the confusion, whereas Lord Simon in the House of Lords agreed that the Court of Appeal in *decision 2* should follow its own precedent created in *decision 1,* Lord Cross felt that the Court of Appeal in *decision 2* should have ignored its own precedent in *decision 1* because *decision 1* conflicted with the earlier House of Lords' decision! So the short answer is: nobody really knows.

As a side point, it is interesting to note that Lord Greene's statement in *Young* v *BAC*—that the Court of Appeal is bound by its own decisions—actually conflicts with some earlier Court of Appeal decisions which stated that the Court of Appeal was *not* bound by its own previous decisions. The sort of conflict that this can send a student into should be avoided; Lord Greene's words reflected the history of the Court of Appeal since its creation and are generally taken as gospel today.

The court is not bound by its own decisions found to have been made per incuriam: We have discussed the *per incuriam* rule to some extent already. For some reason this rule appeals to students and it tends to be used on many occasions. It is worth repeating, therefore, that it does not mean that the court made a mistake. The mere fact that the case being examined had weaknesses in argument, or in the judgment, does not make the decision *per incuriam.* Thus in *Morelle* v *Wakeling* [1955] 2 QB 379, [1955] 1 All ER 708, Lord Evershed MR limited the use of the *per incuriam* rule to cases where

(a)   there was ignorance of authority which would have been binding on the court; and
(b)   that ignorance led to faulty reasoning.

To this the Court of Appeal has added that the rule can only be applied where, had the court reviewed these authorities, the court *would* (not just might) have reached a different decision. Thus in *Williams* v *Fawcett* [1986] QB 604, [1985] 1 All ER 787 and *Duke* v *Reliance Systems* [1987] ICR 491, [1987] 2 All ER 858 the Court of Appeal has shown itself ready to use the *per incuriam* rule regarding its own decisions, but with reservations.

More recently, in the case of *Rakhit* v *Carty* [1990] 2 WLR 1107, [1990] 2 All ER 202, the Court of Appeal was faced with the situation where a Court of Appeal decision *(decision 1)* was plainly *per incuriam* as it had missed some vital statutory provisions. *Decision 1* had been followed without question in another Court of Appeal case *(decision 2)*. Could the present Court of Appeal still declare *decision 1 per incuriam* and therefore *decision 2* of no binding effect? Lord Donaldson MR said (at p. 208):

> If, therefore, that court *(in decision 2)*, having all the relevant authorities before it, had concluded that *(decision 1)* was rightly decided, I would have felt bound to follow it, leaving it to the House of Lords to rectify the error.

As this was not the case, the Court of Appeal in *Rakhit* v *Carty* declared *decision 1* to have been reached *per incuriam,* thereby invalidating both *decision 1* and *decision 2* as precedents.

Are There Any Other Exceptions to the Application of Stare Decisis to the Court of Appeal that have Emerged Since 1944?

(a)   The Criminal Division of the Court is traditionally more relaxed on *stare decisis*, especially where an individual's liberty is at stake. This seems a little strange, given that the House of Lords usually espouses the view that it should rarely change its mind on criminal law matters in order to promote certainty! See, for instance, its reluctance to change its mind in *R* v *Shivpuri.* But then, in the hands of the House of Lords rests the final appeal; which is the very issue that caused all the controversy discussed above.

For further explanation on this topic, see *R* v *Spencer* [1985] 1 All ER 673 and note Pattenden (1984:592). More recently, the Court of Appeal has again addressed this issue in *R* v *Parole Board* [1992] 2 WLR 707, [1992] 2 All ER 576. The case concerned the right to see documents submitted to a parole board. The Court applied the principle that, where liberty is at stake and injustice might occur, *stare decisis* was not applicable. However, the Court of Appeal found the earlier precedents distinguishable in any case so that the comments on *stare decisis* were not strictly necessary.

(b)   If, in exceptional cases, the House of Lords cannot review a decision of the Court of Appeal then the Court of Appeal can choose not to follow its own precedent: *Rickards* v *Rickards* [1989] 3 WLR 748, [1989] 3 All ER 193.

(c)   Where a previous decision has been disapproved by the Judicial Committee of the Privy Council then (though Privy Council decisions are not part of the court structure) the Court of Appeal may depart from its own decisions. This has occurred on a few occasions, most notably in *Doughty* v *Turner Manufacturing Co. Ltd* [1964] 1 QB 518, [1964] 1 All ER 98, where the Court of Appeal chose to follow a Privy Council decision (*The Wagon Mound*) rather than its own previous ruling on the same matter in *Re Polemis.*

(d)   Where the previous decision was on an interlocutory matter and heard by only two judges this will not bind a full Court of Appeal (ie three or more judges sitting): *Boys* v *Chaplin* [1968] 2 QB 1, [1968] 1 All ER 283. An interlocutory decision concerns pre-trial matters. For instance, if there is a dispute as to procedure this will be an interlocutory matter. Some issues depend on interlocutory matters and the main case never actually comes to court. One example is where an employer points to a clause in an employment contract which seeks to stop an ex-employee working for another in the same business once that employee leaves the company. This is known as 'restraint of trade'. If the employer had to wait for a full hearing it would be pointless because the restraint usually lasts for about a year and the case could take longer than this to come to court. The employer will therefore seek an injunction, which (if granted) will prevent the employee from working for the other company until the full case can be heard. The reality is, however, that if the employer obtains the injunction the full case rarely gets heard.

Connected with the idea of interlocutory appeals is an issue which is only just being explored. Two-judge Courts of Appeal have become more common in recent years, mainly for administrative reasons. On the whole they tend to hear mainly appeals from interlocutory decisions as before, plus appeals from county courts. However, cases have arisen which were not interlocutory matters but proved to be important decisions (eg *National Westminster Bank* v *Morgan,* [1983] 3 All ER 85, *Harris* v *Wyre Forest District Council* [1988] QB 835, [1988] 1 All ER 691 and *Interfoto Picture Library* v *Stiletto Visual Programmes Ltd* [1988] 2 WLR 615, [1988] 1 All ER 348). The *Interfoto* case, as we shall see, had the added complication of judges agreeing on the decision but disagreeing on the reasoning. In the first edition of this book we asked what would be the status of a two-judge Court of Appeal. The answer was delivered in *Langley* v *North West Water Authority* [1991] 1 WLR 697, [1991] 3 All ER 610, which accorded the same powers of binding precedent to two judges as to the full court.

We have not yet had a case where a two-member Court of Appeal has failed to agree as to the decision. If this happens one presumes the court will apply the old maxim used by the House of Lords: *semper praesumitur pro negante.* This means that the presumption is always in favour of the negative, which means that the appeal fails. A fascinating example of this arose in *Charter* v *Charter* (1874) LR 7 HL 364 where four of their Lordships were divided evenly as to the outcome and the remaining member died without leaving an opinion.

Does Every Case Have to be Heard by the Court of Appeal Before it Can Proceed to the House of Lords?

Fortunately the answer is no. If the Court of Appeal is bound by the House of Lords and itself then a system which demanded it hear every case anyway would be ludicrous. Thus a civil case may be allowed to go on appeal from the High Court to the House of Lords, by-passing the Court of Appeal. This is known as the 'leap-frogging' procedure. However, if the case began life in the county court then an appeal from that court lies to the Court of Appeal, not the High Court; thus the 'leap-frogging' procedure would be irrelevant

Finally, it is only fair to say that however much writers and judges try to explain the system on a rational basis, there will always be some uncertainty and some cases that simply break the rules. For one thing we have yet to consider in depth how one case can be distinguished from another so that the precedent in question (and therefore the application of *stare decisis)* is sidestepped. For another, judges occasionally surprise everyone with an admission that they were wrong in an earlier case (see Lord Denning in *Dixon* v *BBC* [1979] QB 546, [1979] 2 All ER 112, discussing his earlier judgment on the same issue in *BBC* v *Ioannou* [1975] ICR 267, [1975] 2 All ER 999). This is reassuring when considered in the context of human frailty, but likely to set a practising lawyer's teeth on edge; and is little consolation to the party in the overruled case who originally lost (and probably paid costs). Even more surprising, perhaps, was Lord Denning's admission in one case that his own reasoning in an earlier case (which he now wished to avoid) was not legally correct, but that he had reached that earlier decision to do justice—'It was not really (a case which fell within the definition of dismissal) . . . but we had to stretch it a bit', he commented. The comment occurred in *Western Excavating* v *Sharp* [1978] ICR 221, 227, [1978] 1 All ER 713, 718 in relation to *Marriott* v *Oxford and District Co-operative Society Ltd (No. 2)* [1970] 1 QB 186, [1969] 3 All ER 1126.

A question often posed by students is whether the aggrieved party in the case which has been overruled can now revive the case with the cry, 'There you are, I was right all along'. The answer is no. Parties to a case have to lodge an appeal within time limits. If these have expired it is unfortunately too late to do anything about it.

Other Courts

Trial Courts

All courts which are lower in status than the Court of Appeal (such as the High Court, Crown Court, Magistrates' Court, county court, and the various tribunals) are bound by *stare decisis* in the normal way. It should be noted, however, that the important tribunals also have their own appellate tribunals (eg, the Employment Appeal Tribunal for industrial tribunals) which often incorporate their own variations on the rules of right to appeal and the binding nature of precedent within that system. These courts are trial courts, dealing for the most part with fact and evidence rather than questions of high legal analysis. They do not, therefore, create precedent. There is, however, some attempt to follow the reasoning employed in courts of the same level, eg as between divisions of the High Court. In *Colchester Estates (Cardiff)* v *Carlton Industries plc* [1984] 3 WLR 693, [1984] 2 All ER 601 it was stated that the latest decision should be preferred provided it was reached after full consideration of the earlier decisions. An example of this in operation arose from a decision of Butler-Sloss J (as she then was) in *Re Cherrington* [1984] 1 WLR 772, [1984] 2 All ER 285 which was not followed in a case on exactly the same point *(Re Sinclair* [1984] 3 All ER 362) because there had not been a full discussion of all the issues in *Re Cherrington.*

Divisional Courts

For mainly historical reasons the High Court has a supervisory and limited appellate jurisdiction over the trial courts (sometimes called 'courts of first instance'). Each division of the High Court—Queen's Bench, Family and Chancery—has what is termed a 'Divisional Court'. Thus:

(a)   The Divisional Court of the Chancery Division can hear appeals from a county court in bankruptcy cases.

(b)   The Family Division may hear appeals on guardianship matters from either the magistrates' courts or county courts.

(c)   The most common appellate function relates to the Queen's Bench Division. Say a party to a criminal case in a magistrates' court wishes to appeal on a question of law from the magistrates' decision. This is done by asking the magistrates to state their case, ie to set out their legal reasoning, and the issue goes before the Divisional Court of the Queen's Bench Division. This is therefore known as an 'appeal by way of case stated'. A full re-hearing (eg an appeal against the conviction relating to fact rather than law) of the case would go to the Crown Court. An appeal by way of case stated can also lie, in limited circumstances, from the Crown Court to the High Court

These Divisional Courts are bound by *stare decisis* in the usual way. Whether they bind themselves is a matter of debate at the moment.

Judicial Committee of the Privy Council

At one time this was the final court of appeal for the courts of the British Empire. Its decisions were therefore treated with great respect, even though technically they have never created precedents under English law for English cases. However, for the most part the majority in the court has been (and is) made up of the Law Lords. Consequently, if the Judicial Committee of the Privy Council reached a decision on a point of law (relating, say, to Australia) which was similar to English law, their reasoning would be very persuasive (see, for instance, *Doughty* v *Turner Manufacturing Co. Ltd*, mentioned above, where the Court of Appeal followed a Privy Council decision rather than its own authority). The jurisdiction of this court is now very limited indeed, but you should watch out for decisions made earlier this century.

The Court of Justice of the European Communities

Though Chapter Ten deals extensively with the European influence and 'European Legal Method', specific reference to European Community institutions and legal method is needed here to explain the context in which our law now operates. As we said in Chapter One, leaving the 'European dimension' until the last chapter should not be seen as relegating the topic to some form of afterthought.

Throughout this book you will see that both the 'European' way of dealing with cases (the procedure) and the technique of analysing cases (the legal method) are quite different from our approach. This is because the system used by the Court of Justice was created by countries (eg France and Germany) which rely on the Civil (or Roman) Law system. For various reasons our Common Law system developed separately from the Civil Law system used on the Continent. As Britain did not join the Community until 1973 there is minimal (but perhaps growing) Common Law influence to be seen in the Court of Justice.

The final court to note then (one of increasing importance) is the Court of Justice of the European Communities (CJEC). Today we tend to think only of the European Economic Community (the EEC), but prior to the EEC there existed the European Coal and Steel Community (ECSC), founded under the Treaty of Paris 1951. The Court of Justice began life as the Court for the ECSC and therefore pre-dates the European Economic Community. The Court of Justice became part of the European Economic Community when that Community was founded under the Treaty of Rome 1957. It remained the Court of Justice for the ECSC and became the court for the Community created at the same time as the Economic Community *viz* the European Atomic Energy Community (Euratom).

There are four major institutions which are common to all the European Communities: the Court of Justice, the Parliament, the Commission, and the Council. We will deal with the institutions in depth in Chapter Ten. Note that the Court of Justice is commonly referred to as the 'European Court of Justice' or the 'European Court'. We have used the more accurate title (the Court of Justice of the European Communities) to emphasise three things:

(a)   that the court deals only with Community law; and
(b)   that the word 'Communities' is important because the use of the

plural emphasises that the court has jurisdiction over the ECSC and Euratom too; and

(c)   this is the way the court refers to itself.

For simplicity, throughout this book the working of the Court of Justice will be discussed in relation to the European Economic Community only.

We have listed below a few general points on the Court of Justice which you should bear in mind when reading about the legal method used in English law. For a more detailed description of the Communites and the Court of Justice we recommend reference be made to Steiner (1992) and Brown (1989).

Most of the law you will deal with in your studies will be 'pure' English law; but this will become less true over the years: see Lord Denning MR's famous statement in *HP Bulmer Ltd* v *Bollinger SA* [1974] Ch 401, 418, [1974] 2 All ER 1226, that 'when we come to matters with a European element, the Treaty is like an incoming tide . . . It cannot be held back'. Remember here, however, that we are dealing with the Court of Justice, not the way individual countries' legal systems work.

What is the jurisdiction of the CJEC? The Court of Justice exists to ensure that in the interpretation and application of the Treaty of Rome the law is observed. It is therefore the supreme authority on the interpretation of the law relating to the European Community. It deals only with the interpretation and validity of Community-generated law. Therefore, unless the law in question was generated by the European Community (and there are various ways this can occur), the Court of Justice has no jurisdiction. Many criminal law matters, for instance, are questions of domestic law and have nothing to do with the European Community.

However, as seen in Chapter One, the impact of Community law is growing. As well as dealing with general agricultural matters, administrative law, company law etc, its effect can now be seen in everyday life such as employment rights and social law. Thus an increasing number of matters fall within the jurisdiction of the Court of Justice.

How does a case come before the CJEC? Actions may be brought against individuals, Member states, or the institutions of the Community. We will concentrate in this book on the most common way that a case will come before the Court of Justice—a reference to the court for a *preliminary ruling* under Article 177 of the Treaty of Rome.

Under Article 177 any country's domestic courts or tribunals can ask the Court of Justice for a ruling on Community law; but it is that domestic court or tribunal which implements the decision.

It is for the court to decide whether it wishes to refer a matter to the Court of Justice and there are various rules relating to this which we shall explore later. The national court is only asking for an authoritative interpretation of that particular part of Community law. It does this by posing questions in the abstract; it does not ask for the solution to the particular case before it.

Article 177(3) states that a court or tribunal *shall* refer the matter where, as against that court's decision, there is no judicial remedy under national law. So, any court has a discretionary power to refer a case to the Court of Justice and if a court is the final appeal court it *must* refer the matter. Thus the House of Lords should be bound to refer all cases to the Court of Justice which involve a problem of Community law. The House of Lords does not, however, refer all relevant cases to the Court of Justice. This is because it is only required to do so if it considers that such a referral is 'necessary'. What 'necessary' means we will have to leave until Chapter Ten. Suffice it to say here that for a national court to decide that it is not 'necessary' to refer the matter basically requires that the provision has already been interpreted by the Court of Justice or the correct application is obvious to the national court.

A key point to note here, however, is that Article 177 **is not an appeals procedure**. The Court of Justice does not decide the case, it merely gives its interpretation on Community law. Most importantly, however, the Court of Justice is the *only* court that can authoritatively interpret Community law. The domestic court has then to apply the ruling as it sees fit to the case in hand.

Does the CJEC use a system of judicial precedent? A major distinction between how European lawyers (and courts) reason and the reasoning of Common Law lawyers is the use of *stare decisis*. European lawyers are, traditionally, merely persuaded by precedent. The same is true of the Court of Justice.

Obviously, as Stein has said, 'Every legal system has case law in the sense that the scope of the rules is illustrated by their application to a set of facts' (1984:85), but this is not the same thing as holding to a doctrine of precedent. Further, any legal system seeks to avoid inconsistencies; but, as we have seen, this is certainly not the same as holding to a strict doctrine of *stare decisis*. For whereas the Common Law relies on declaring law only when the occasion requires it (ie through litigants bringing cases), the Civil Law system relies heavily on Codes: written, logical, reasoned, and systematic statements of principles of law. As Lord MacMillan observed:

> From these principles the whole law [can] be deduced, and with the aid of these principles the law [can] be methodised and arranged. It is the conception of order, logic and reason in the regulation by law of human affairs. (1937:79)

Cases, in simple terms, become examples of applications of the Code; hardly the stuff of which *stare decisis* is made.

The Codes vary in form and technicality of language. The language employed in the French Code is aimed more at the layman than is the case with the German Code, for instance. Now, the Civil Law lawyer bases his argument on the explicit or implicit statements in the written law (the

Codes and academic writing), not overtly on the opinions given in earlier cases. Developing this point, reliance on the Codes and the principles stated therein drives the Civil lawyer away from an obsessive interest in the facts of earlier cases. It is the issue that matters. The Common Law lawyer, on the other hand (as we shall explore in the next chapter), holds tightly to the concept of 'material facts', and the importance of individual cases.

Indeed, the predominance of issue over fact has to be the pattern of thought employed by the Court of Justice because the function of the court is to *interpret* Community law. As the court is only required to answer abstract questions from the national court and does not make decisions in a particular case, so the facts of a case (which are so important to the English law lawyer in distinguishing one case from another) take on less significance. This does not mean the facts are ignored, because it is almost impossible to answer a legal question without some reference to the context in which it has arisen. But it does mean that our system of *stare decisis* cannot apply to the Court of Justice. Further, the court is the final court on these questions and the only thing that can alter such a decision (other than the court changing its mind at a later date) is an alteration made to the Treaty itself. As annual minor alterations to the Treaty are an impossibility—major or complete revisions for political reasons are the only likely source of alterations—the court has to favour flexibility over certainty.

However, it is worth noting here the point we made above that the Court of Justice, in trying to define when it is 'necessary' for a domestic court to refer a matter to the Court of Justice, has stated that it would not be necessary if (amongst other things) the provision in question has already been interpreted by the Court of Justice. This at least shows the value of precedent in any system; but it does not mean that the Court of Justice is moving towards our system of *stare decisis*.

The European Court of Human Rights

The United Kingdom is a signatory to the European Convention of Human Rights. This Convention, however, is not part of English law. If there is a conflict between English law and the Convention, therefore, the Convention must lose out. Nevertheless, any case brought before the European Court of Human Rights may well have some effect, for political reasons if nothing else. There is, however, no line of appeal from a decision in an English court to the European Court of Human Rights. Cases are referred to the court by the Commission for Human Rights or by states disagreeing with decisions of the Commission.

The Convention takes a form which you will recognise in the discussion of Community law above: that of general statements as to human rights, eg *Article 3* states that 'No one shall be subjected to torture or to inhuman or degrading treatment or punishment'. As you will see when we turn to the method of interpreting statutes, this bears little relation to the style of drafting legislation in the United Kingdom.

The United Kingdom has appeared before the court on a number of occasions on issues such as the 'closed shop' and *The Sunday Times* thalidomide case. For an interesting discussion on the applicability of the Convention through more indirect routes we would recommend you read the cases of *Brind* v *Secretary of State for the Home Office* [1991] 1 AC 696 at 761, [1991] 1 All ER 720 at 734 and *Derbyshire County Council* v *Times Newspapers Ltd* [1992] 1 QB 770, [1992] 3 All ER 65.

Conclusion

Both the Common Law and the Civil Law traditions utilise the concept of precedent. No case has a meaning by itself; each case stands in a relationship to other cases. Like tracing one's ancestors, therefore, it is at least theoretically possible to go backwards in time, step by step, to see how a complicated principle emerged from perhaps a single case. It is not uncommon to find gross inconsistencies or jumps in logic. Inevitably one will face the same problem as with the 'Big Bang' theory of how the Universe began: what came before the original case?

Sometimes the answer is that the seminal case derived its principle from a mixture of other cases on related (often barely related) principles: see, for instance *Rylands* v *Fletcher* (1868) LR 3 HL 330. On other occasions the principle may be derived from ancient Roman, Greek or Biblical laws. Or the source might lie in a perception of fundmental rights and wrongs, such as laws prohibiting murder. Often the answer lies in works written by eminent scholars centuries ago—their views on the law being accepted by judges in later cases and then set as legal doctrine by the mechanisms of judicial precedent. The fact that these initial cases or scholarly writings were illogical, have exceeded their 'best before' date, or have been misinterpreted does not mean that they can be easily upset.

Much of this reification of (sometimes) archaic principles is due to the fact that there is a world of difference between merely recognising the source and value of precedent, and the concept of *stare decisis*. The great value of the doctrine of *stare decisis* is that it provides certainty. On the other hand, there are dangers: first, that in order to avoid the conclusions of *stare decisis* courts are sometimes forced to find hair-splitting distinctions between cases; secondly, the doctrine limits flexibility and can make unassailable some principles which should have been abandoned long ago.

A rare example of a long-established legal concept being overturned can be found in *R* v *R* [1991] 3 WLR 767, [1991] 4 All ER 481. In *R* v *R*, public policy, together with historical and social considerations, came under review. This case concerned 'marital rape' and posed the question whether a husband could be criminally liable for raping his wife if he had sexual intercourse with her without her consent. The idea that a man would not be guilty in these circumstances could be traced back to Sir Matthew Hale in his *History of the Pleas of the Crown* written in 1736. Texts and cases since that time had taken this proposition as an accurate expression of the law (which it probably was in 1736). In *R* v *R*, however, the House of Lords took the opportunity to restate the law concerning marital rape and declared that the husband could be guilty of rape in these circumstances. As Lord Keith said: 'The common law is . . . capable of evolving in the light of changing social, economic and cultural developments'.

You might, however, ask yourself one final simple question: why should we stand out from the rest of the legal world with our fixation that once a superior court has decided a matter an inferior court *must* follow it?

REFERENCES

* Brown, L.N. (1989) *The Court of Justice of the European Communities,* London: Sweet and Maxwell.
* Cross, R. (1991) *Precedent in English Law,* 4th Edition, Oxford: Clarendon Press.
Harris, J.W. (1990) 'Towards Principles of Overruling—When Should a Final Court of Appeal Second Guess?' *Oxford Journal of Legal Studies,* vol. 10, p. 135.
MacCormick, N. (1987) 'Why Cases have *Rationes* and What These Are', in L. Goldstein (ed) *Precedent in Law*, Oxford: Clarendon Press.
MacMillan, Lord (1937) *Law and Other Things*, Cambridge: Cambridge University Press.
Pattenden, R. (1984) 'The Power of the Criminal Division of the Court of Appeal to Depart from its Own Precedents' *Criminal Law Review,* p. 592.
Stein, P. (1984) *Legal Institutions: The Development of Dispute Settlement*, London: Butterworths
* Steiner, J. (1992) *Textbook on EEC Law,* 3rd Edition, London: Blackstone Press.

Chapter Six

How Precedent Operates

Ratio Decidendi and *Obiter Dictum*

The concept of *stare decisis* provides us only with the ground rules of precedent. It tells us that one court must follow the decision of a superior court when dealing with similar cases. It describes the environment in which our system of precedent operates. What it cannot tell us is **when** two cases are sufficiently similar that the doctrine should be applied.

If the facts of cases were identical we would have no problem. But the facts change from case to case; sometimes in an obviously major way; other times in an apparently insignificant way. Clearly we are not looking only for **identical cases**. What we must be trying to prove is that two (or more) cases are sufficiently similar that they illustrate the same principle and so the doctrine of precedent can be applied. A comparison of facts will obviously help us achieve this. But we must also, and more importantly, try to see if the *reasoning* in the earlier case can be applied to the new set of facts in our case. It is worth remembering that lawyers cite cases in order to give authority to their argument. The question raised by the practitioner or academic is therefore: what is the principle of law for which that case is authority; and how does it relate to the case in hand? Or, to put it the other way: is there a case which is authority for the point I wish to make? This is the way that a busy practitioner is more likely to pose the question.

In the previous chapter we presented an exercise on fact-comparison:

In *case (1)* a man driving a Ford Escort runs over an old lady who was lawfully using a zebra crossing. The man is found guilty of reckless driving.

In *case (2)* a woman driving a BMW runs over an old man who was crossing the road. Should she be found guilty too?

We asked whether you might examine the facts more closely, or ask more questions, before deciding on the answer. Students new to legal studies (and others who should know better) tend to say that the woman in *case 2* is guilty. If asked why this is so, the poor student tends to say: 'It's obvious'. Such students may have a shorter or less successful career in Law than they anticipated. Slightly better students say: 'The woman is guilty because *case 2* is the same as *case 1*.' Actually, this is not quite true—these students tend to announce just the name of *case 1*—usually just that; no explanation; everything is apparently clarified in this one utterance. Still better students say: 'The woman may not be guilty because the old lady in *case 1* was on a zebra crossing, but that is not so in *case 2*'. The best student will ask: 'Why was the man guilty in *case 1*? Before I know that I cannot really say whether *case 2* will follow *case 1*.' For all we know there may be a law against driving Ford Escorts.

Reading this you probably think this is a trite statement of the obvious. Don't! These examples of analysis (on a variety of facts) have all surfaced in seminars and tutorials, in different institutions, spoken by LL.B. undergraduates, undergraduates in other degrees who study Law, and even post-graduates. Karl Llewellyn offered these words of advice (or admonition) in 1930 to American Law students:

> Now the first thing you are to do with [a case] is to read it. Does this sound commonplace? Does this amuse you? There is no reason why it should amuse you. You have already read past seventeen [legal] expressions of whose meaning you have no conception . . . The next thing is to get clear the actual decision, the judgment rendered . . . You can now turn to what you want peculiarly to know . . . what has the case decided, and what can you derive from it as to what will be decided later? (1960:41)

Any law lecturer will echo these words, but it is easy to forget as an academic or practitioner just how daunting reading cases for the first time can be. From the student perspective things look a little different, but the point we are making is still the same. To show you that you are not alone in the minefield of case law, consider these words written by Scott Turow (1988:28) detailing his experiences as a law postgraduate student at Harvard:

> OK. It was nine o'clock when I started reading. The case is four pages long and at 10:35 I finally finished. It was something like stirring concrete with my eyelashes. I had no idea what the words meant. I must have opened *Black's Law Dictionary* twenty-five times and I still can't understand many of the definitions.

The aim of this chapter is to emphasise that legal analysis is not just a question of comparing facts; of using a set of balancing-scales to see if the facts weigh about the same. The game is more complicated, more stimulating, and more enjoyable than that.

Take a look at the following exercise. It sets out the facts of two well-known cases together with the result in each case. Ask yourself *why* the second case should be decided in the same way as the first.

Exercise 8: Dead snails and exploding underpants

CASE 1: *Donoghue v Stevenson* [1932] AC 562

BARE FACTS: Mrs Donoghue and a friend went into a cafe in Paisley. The friend ordered ice-cream and ginger-beer for both of them. The shopkeeper poured out some of the ginger-beer over the ice-cream. Mrs Donoghue consumed some of the mixture. Her friend poured out the remainder of the ginger-beer for Mrs Donoghue and a decomposed snail fell out of the bottle. The bottle was of dark opaque glass so that the contents could not have been detected.
WHAT WAS THE CLAIM?: The claim was against the manufacturer of the ginger-beer (Stevenson) for negligently causing Mrs Donoghue to suffer gastro-enteritis and nervous shock; the negligence arising from the manufacture of the product. As you will see in the Contract Law course Mrs Donoghue could not claim against the cafe owner because she had no contract with him; nor had he been negligent.
WHAT WAS THE DECISION?: Mrs Donoghue succeeded in her claim; the House of Lords holding Stevenson liable by a majority of 3:2. Lord Atkin, in the majority, said that a manufacturer of products will be liable for want of reasonable care if he sells them in a form which shows they are meant to reach the ultimate consumer in the same form as when they were manufactured (with no reasonable possibility of intermediate examination) and if he knows that the absence of reasonable care will cause injury.

CASE 2: *Grant v Australian Knitting Mills* [1936] AC 85 (Privy Council)

BARE FACTS: Grant purchased two pairs of underpants from a retailer in Australia. He contracted severe dermatitis (mainly around the ankles—they were 'long johns') owing to an excess of sulphites in the garments which should have been removed by the manufacturing process. He was ill for a year!
WHAT WAS THE CLAIM? He sued the retailer for breach of contract; and brought a negligence action against the Australian Knitting Mills. This demonstrates that more than one claim can arise from one set of events. However, Grant would not be able to get damages twice: if Grant was successful then one claim would be off-set against the other.
WHAT WAS THE DECISION? Grant won the breach of contract action and the claim for negligence was also successful, following the principles laid down in *Donoghue v Stevenson*.

Questions

(a)   Why do you think Grant was successful? Why should *Donoghue* v *Stevenson* apply to his case?

(b)   What arguments would you have used if you had been representing the Australian Knitting Mills?

Answer: (a) 'Exploding underpants' and dead snails are not the same thing. If you have thought carefully about the cases you will have experienced some problems in assessing why *Donoghue* v *Stevenson* was applied in *Grant* v *Australian Knitting Mills*. But remember, both sides in *Grant* thought they had convincing reasons why they should win. Neither side could simply say 'dead snails equal (or do not equal) underpants'. The Privy Council assessed the principle of *Donoghue* v *Stevenson* by quoting Lord Atkin:

> A manufacturer of products, which he sells in such a form as to show that he intends them to reach the ultimate consumer in the form in which they left him with no reasonable possibility of intermediate examination, and with the knowledge that the absence of reasonable care in the preparation or putting up of the products will result in an injury to the consumer's life or property, owes a duty to the consumer to take that reasonable care.

The Privy Council stated that *Donoghue* could only be applied where the defect is hidden and unknown to the consumer; but that in *Grant* the chemical in the underpants represented a latent defect equivalent to the snail in the opaque bottle.

(b)   Australian Knitting Mills raised a number of arguments. Amongst these were that: *Donoghue* v *Stevenson* only applied, at its widest, to cases of food and drink—that when Lord Atkin referred to 'products' he could only refer to the product in the case; the decision was not unanimous, especially as regards the interpetation of earlier cases; there had been no possibility of anyone tampering with the bottle, but the underpants were loosely packed (it was not alleged there had been any tampering); and that Grant should have washed the underpants before wearing them (which would have removed the danger).

So, however we try to compare the facts, we cannot answer the question whether the woman in our example should be guilty of reckless driving without first understanding *WHY* the man was guilty in case (1). What were the issues on which the first case turned? Was it important that the old lady was using a pedestrian crossing? Was it important that she was an old lady? The question as to *WHY* guilt was found is all-important, and a point often ignored by students who presume that if they have discovered two cases which are similar on their facts, then that is enough.

However, two cases may look similar but produce different results because of a different perception of the apparently similar facts or because of a vital distinction in the reasoning employed by the judges. In other words, cases may be *distinguished* on the material facts or the reasoning employed.

And if we are asking *why* the court decided one way we must equally be aware that cases do not exist in isolation—there is a whole history behind the issues involved in a case. All these previous cases will have affected the language used by the judges and the decisions they reached. The way that a word was legally defined in, say, 1850, might have an enormous impact on the reasoning of a judge in 1990.

Thus when we talk of a judge being bound by a precedent we mean something more than matching the facts of cases—we say that a judge is bound to follow the *ratio decidendi* (the reason for deciding—usually referred to as the *ratio*) of the earlier higher authority. The judge only has to follow the *ratio*. It is not only the facts of the earlier case which are important, but also how the judge expressed the law in relation to those facts—how the judge justified the decision in law. For as long as you study Law the *ratio* of any case will be vital to your investigations.

Difficulties still lie ahead, however. Various judges and academics have tried to define what we mean by *ratio decidendi*. It is a surprisingly difficult problem. One complication is that a judgment may last for two, ten or fifty pages. Somewhere in there is an account of the facts as found, a discussion of legal principles, a comparison with earlier cases, and a decision on the facts as to who won. A judge might apparently formulate a *ratio* only to continue with his judgment and formulate the *ratio* again; this time with different words, with different emphasis. This can prove galling. It happens. And nowhere will you find a sentence saying: 'Here comes the *ratio*'. Yet another complication is that a judge in a later case may perceive the principle that is to be derived from the earlier case as something different from that which the original judge intended.

A question frequently posed by students at this stage is: 'So, how do I spot the *ratio*?' The question is a fair one. If there is an answer, it is the rather unsatisfactory one that, for both the practitioner and academic, this is a matter of skill and interpretation built on experience. After years of reading cases one instinctively formulates an opinion on what a case means (the basic theories of legal method having long been forgotten). The word we wish to stress here, though, is 'opinion'; and opinions can always be wrong or at least open to argument. Further, saying that experience aids one's understanding does not provide any help to someone new to the study of law. Thus in the text below we have attempted to take a practical line by trying to find the most understandable and useful starting point for analysing the *ratio* of a case.

There are a number of excellent articles and books which take this academic debate to its limits: see eg MacCormick (1987); Montrose (1957); Goodhart (1959). However, our experience is that at the outset of legal studies such in-depth analysis tends to produce confusion rather than comfort. We are in some agreement with Twining and Miers that the intricacies of the debate can (at least with regard to students beginning their legal studies) be a 'long and rather sterile' one. Nevertheless, as you encounter a greater range of cases and gain in confidence you may then wish to explore the problem of defining *ratio* in more depth.

There is no set single test for defining what is meant by *ratio* or for establishing the *ratio* of a particular case. As Cross stated: 'It is impossible to devise formulae for determining the *ratio decidendi* of a case'. But before you lose heart altogether, Cross also stated that 'this does not mean it is impossible to give a tolerably accurate description of what lawyers mean when they use the expression'. (1991:72) Like so many things in law this problem of identification is not unique to legal studies. Think of the plot to a book or a film. The facts are clear, the storyline can be described; but if a group of people were asked to say what the film etc. was *about* then opinions would vary. Some might see the film as nothing more than, say, an adventure film; others might see a social or political message in it; others might think the director was clearly paying tribute to an earlier famous director. And even if the writer or director was asked to spell out the meaning, the purpose, of the film (equivalent to reading the judgment of a case) the onlooker's reply could still be: 'You may have meant that, but you produced something different'.

Thus, to the student who asks 'how do I spot the *ratio?*' Twining and Miers would respond:

> Talk of *finding* the *ratio decidendi* of a case obscures the fact that the process of interpreting cases is not like a hunt for buried treasure, but typically involves an element of choice from a range of possibilities.' (1991:313)

It is unwise, therefore, to presume that there is one and only one *ratio* to a case. There are many cases, usually older cases dealing with fundamental principles in a particular area, where lawyers have accepted a general formulation of the *ratio*. For instance, textbooks will normally say more or less the same thing about the nineteenth-century 'offer and acceptance' cases in contract, but reading a case is an exercise in interpretation; an exercise in exploring the range of possibilities. This is why we stressed the word 'opinion' above. Consequently, there is nothing wrong in reading a case and thinking: 'That case is not really authority for the proposition stated in the textbook; or even that stated by a judge.' All you have to do then is prove you are right; but it is surprising how many times the cases cited in footnotes as authority for a legal proposition turn out to be nothing of the sort!

Now, one of the classic ways of 'defining' what *ratio* means is to say that it is the material facts of the case, plus the decision made in relation to those facts. We will discuss what is meant by 'material facts' below. For the moment we will take the term as meaning those facts which were important in the judge's formulation of his decision; and so, the formulation of a rule which proceeds an inch beyond the facts is suspect. This approach was taken by Goodhart (1931:25). It has been criticised mainly on the ground that Goodhart focused on the way in which the original judge formulated the *ratio;* and this fails to recognise sufficiently the role played by later judges in interpreting and applying the earlier case. We can agree with this point but it does not weaken the proposition that there is advantage to be gained in concentrating on what facts were material in a case; provided that one does not lose sight of the fact that a case does not stand in splendid isolation. How the case in question relates to other cases plays an important part in assessing its implications.

The points raised in the last few paragraphs frequently cause students problems. It is not illogical when first studying law to believe that, if cases form the basis for legal propositions you should be able to read a case and say what authority it stands for. After all, if you look at a maths equation you would expect to apply it time and time again in the same way. Why should the same not apply to legal cases?

Before looking at a short exercise on this idea of 'interpreting the ratio', we can summarise the points made above:

(a)   Many cases do not give rise to much argument as to what they mean, what the *ratio* was.

(b)   Every case is, however, open to some reinterpretation.

(c)   The earlier cases will have dealt with specific facts. Later cases will deal with different specific facts.

(d)   The need to interpret the *ratio* of these earlier cases arises when you try to apply that case to the new set of facts in front of you.

(e)   The judge's formulation of the *ratio* in any particular case is not always clear.

(f)   Whether it is clear or not, later judges have the right to interpret these words, to add an emphasis which the earlier judge may not have intended, or which the earlier judge would have intended had he or she been faced with the new set of facts in question.

(g)   Every time a case is decided in a particular area it may:

(i)   apply
(ii)   confirm
(iii)   extend
(iv)   reinterpret
(v)   distinguish
(vi)   criticise
(vii)   narrow
(viii) modify
(ix)   limit
(x)   weaken
(xi)   obliterate
(xii)   ignore

the principles established by the earlier cases.

Exercise 9: Things likely to do mischief

The case of *Rylands* v *Fletcher* (1868) LR 3 HL 330 is one of the more famous tort cases in English law. It was heavily criticised when it first appeared because many perceived the judges as having invented a legal principle not previously found in the case law (perhaps reflected in the fact that the form of liability derived from the case is simply known as the tort of *Rylands* v *Fletcher*). Nevertheless the case has stood the test of time.

In *Rylands* v *Fletcher*, the House of Lords had to consider whether Fletcher could recover damages against Rylands when a reservoir constructed by Rylands burst through some disused mine shafts on his land and flooded the mines of Fletcher, who was Rylands' neighbour. On the facts, Rylands had not been negligent in constructing the reserviour. In holding that Rylands was nevertheless liable for the damage caused, Lord Cairns cited the judgment of Blackburn J in the court below:

We think that the true rule of law is, that the person who, for his own purposes, brings on his land and collects and keeps there anything likely to do mischief if it escapes, must keep it in at his peril; and if he does not do so, is *prima facie* answerable for all the damage which is the natural consequence of its escape.

Questions

(a)   Do you think that this expresses a clear legal proposition which you could apply to other cases?

(b)   Earlier in Lord Cairns's speech he referred to the 'non-natural' use of land. Should this be read in to the statement given above?

(c)   Do you foresee difficulties with the words used? What do you think was meant by 'for his own purposes', 'brings on', 'escape', 'likely to do mischief'?

(d)   Do you think a later judge might say that the principle was expressed wider than was necessary to decide the actual case?

(e)   Would later judges be justified in applying or not applying the words used to situations with very different facts? For instance, how would you use the principle where a visitor to a munitions factory is injured by the explosion of a shell which is being manufactured in the factory (see *Read* v *J. Lyons & Co. Ltd* [1947] AC 156, [1946] 2 All ER 471).

Comment

The first and second questions help to illustrate that the *ratio* is not set in stone but is subject to interpretation. The fact that textbooks give you the *ratio* of many cases only means that this is the conclusion the author reached after doing the same exercise. However, if lawyers have been doing this for centuries then it is not an impossible art to master. For instance, quite often (as in *Rylands* v *Fletcher* itself) a fairly clear idea of the *ratio* can be found in one sentence or paragraph. It is also part of a lawyer's skill to gather the *ratio* from reading the whole judgment (or judgments). This may test one's ability to deal with concepts and linguistics, but it is not an insurmountable task.

The third question illustrates the point that, even if the *ratio* is easy to spot, words do not always have a clear, single meaning. The word 'escape' was a major issue in the case of *Read* v *Lyons* noted in question (e).

One question we did not pose, which can only be dealt with by reading the case itself is: What earlier authorities were cited by the court? We noted in the introduction to this exercise that *Rylands* v *Fletcher* was criticised for 'inventing law'. Nevertheless, the judges still referred to a number of cases; cases which they said were analogous to this situation. Hence our previous comment that cases do not stand in splendid isolation.

The fourth and fifth questions lead us into a discussion on another vital aspect of reading a case—the question of what constitutes a *material fact*. This question exemplifies the idea that the *ratio* of a case strictly relates only to the actual facts of that case but is often expressed in wider terms. The fifth question asks you to decide whether changing a material fact (here, that *Read* was on the premises and not outside) might make such a difference that the original *ratio* should not be applied. But before analysing what is meant by the term *material fact* we will take the opportunity to note that not everything said by a judge when giving judgment can constitute a precedent. As Cross indicates (1991:39), the *ratio* can only relate to pronouncements of law, not the facts of the case; and then, only those pronouncements which he considers necessary for his decision are said to form part of the *ratio*.

Anything else said in the case that does not relate to the material facts is called *obiter dictum* (this means 'a thing said by the way'—the plural is *obiter dicta*). *Obiter dicta* statements are not binding on a later judge. MacCormick describes *obiter dicta* as 'statements of opinion upon the law and its values and principles in their bearing on the instant decision, statements which in some way go beyond the point or points necessary to be settled in deciding the case' (1987:156).

Obiter comments can arise in many ways—here are a few examples:

(a)   Where the judge makes a hypothetical pronouncement eg 'If the facts had been different (in some respect) then my decision would have been . . . '; or

(b)   The judge might say what he would have decided had he not been bound by *stare decisis;* or

(c)   The pronouncement by the judge might be entirely relevant to the material facts, but his judgment was in the minority. A minority judgment has its own *ratio*, but that cannot be the *ratio* of the case since that judge's view did not prevail.

(d)   The judge may make a number of general comments on the topic of law under discussion. In *Donoghue* v *Stevenson*, for instance, Lord Atkin made a number of observations about liability for negligent acts. One

observation was that one owed a duty of care not to injure one's 'neighbour'—
a person so closely affected by your acts that you must take reasonable
care not to injure them. This is an *obiter* statement because it is not directly
related to the facts; it proceeds far beyond that in its generality.

Most *obiter dicta* were never intended by the judge to be anything else.
However, as you will see (especially in Exercise 10) a later court may always
decide that what was said by a judge in the prior case was unnecessary
to the decision and therefore not part of the *ratio*. This 'reassessment' is
one of the devices used to overcome the binding element of precedent
discussed in Chapter Five.

A judge can decline to follow anything that is not the *ratio*. This is
why the classification is important. However, do not cast aside *obiter*
comments. For one thing, if the *ratio* of a case is an arguable point you
should not be too hasty in relegating a comment to the status of *obiter
dictum*; one man's *obiter* may be the next man's *ratio* to a case. For another,
obiter comments can turn out to be much more influential than the actual
ratio. Lord Atkins's 'neighbour principle' was not an irrelevancy; far from
it. Rather, it was used by later judges to form the basis upon which the
law of negligence was to develop. From a case about dead snails the
'neighbour principle' has been extended to consumer items, industrial
accidents, road accidents, misstatements, and many other areas.

Throughout the remainder of this chapter we concentrate on the two important
aspects of analysing *ratio decidendi:* 'how precedents develop' and the 'material
facts' of cases. These two topics are intertwined and, in our experience, it
would be ideal to consider them both simultaneously. Unfortunately, there
is no simple way of doing this. Therefore, by way of explanation and
introduction we will summarise the points to begin with:

(a)   In the section 'How Precedents Develop' we will seek to show that,
from the starting point of a single case, a line of cases can arise with similar
facts which can apply or modify the *ratio* found in the first case. This
exercise is something like analysing the history of computers. Forty years
ago it took a computer the size of a room a long time to produce fairly
simple results. Working from the same principles as that early computer
the next generation of computers were smaller and did the same job more
quickly. The use of silicon chips changed the size again and brought about
added refinements and advantages. The modern computer, with all the
advantages of networking or transputing, is the state of the art—but this
will change yet again, so that though the basic principles have probably
remained the same, the modern device is, in most respects, quite unlike
its ancestors. What we will stress is that it is the *reasoning* employed in
a case that is passed on for examination to the next generation, even though
the facts change with each case.

(b)   In the section 'Material Facts' we will attempt to explain which parts of the previous cases are considered vital to the decision. In other words, if the facts of each case are inevitably different to some degree, which facts do we consider material (vital) enough to say: 'That case was decided in a particular way and this case is sufficiently similar to it that it too should be decided in the same way'?

How Precedents Develop

Comparing the Reasoning in Cases

Once a case has been decided it falls to judges in later cases sitting in an inferior court to apply the case, or find reasons not to apply it. This much is demanded by the doctrine of *stare decisis*. Even if there is no binding element attached to the earlier decision, it will not simply be ignored (the persuasive nature of precedent should not be underestimated). The reality is that the later judge will (to a greater or lesser extent) formulate his own opinion as to the *ratio* of the earlier case. This may not be the same as the opinion held by the judge in that earlier case. There may be a difference of emphasis. It may be a wider *ratio* than the first judge intended; it may be narrower. It is rather like the writing and singing of a song: even when the same words are being sung the interpretation of different artists may be quite striking—consider the various versions of 'My Way' (eg that of Frank Sinatra and that of Sid Vicious).

A common mistake made by law students, however, is to ignore all this and, as we indicated above, to discover a similarity and take the analysis no further. A lawyer cannot rest like this. Various arguments might be presented regarding the similarities of cases, such as:

'This present case is on all fours with the previous case'; or
'The facts are dissimilar at first sight, but both cases illustrate the same principle'; or
'The present case is clearly distinguishable from the earlier case because one of the material facts of the earlier case is missing here'; or
'The present case is clearly distinguishable from the earlier case because there are additional material facts in this case which were not present in the earlier case'; or even
'When Lord Justice Bloggs formulated the principle in the earlier case he paid insufficient attention to fact (a) which he should have treated as material'.

There are therefore many ways in which one can try to use apparently dissimilar cases to argue your case; or argue that apparently similar cases are of little or no use at all. By way of illustration you will find below an example of how a case might develop. As we said, we shall return to the example of the road accident first used in Chapter Five. Remember, the facts were:

In *case (1)* a man driving a Ford Escort runs over an old lady who was lawfully using a zebra crossing. The man is found guilty of reckless driving. In *case (2)* a woman driving a BMW runs over an old man who was crossing the road.

We are not concerned with the real law relating to reckless driving. None of what follows is therefore a statement of real law. So let us say that the man (we shall call him Alfred) in *case (1)* was found guilty on the following facts:

(a)   *The old lady was lawfully and carefully crossing by a pedestrian crossing;*
(b)   *Alfred was speeding;*
(c)   *Alfred was not looking where he was going; and*
(d)   *The weather conditions were excellent.*

WE SHALL CALL THESE
THE MATERIAL FACTS OF
THE FIRST CASE.

CASE No 1
FACTS: (a), (b), (c), (d)
DECISION: ALFRED
GUILTY

We might say that the *ratio* of this case is: where a person is speeding in good weather conditions and not looking where they are going they will be guilty of reckless driving if they injure a pedestrian who is legitimately using a pedestrian crossing.

The fact that Alfred is male, that the victim is female, that the victim is old, or that the car was a Ford Escort, do not appear to have been relevant as *material facts.* But then, we cheated by telling you what facts we considered 'material' in the first place.

If we now apply the facts of *case (2)* to this decision: a woman driving a BMW runs over an old man who was crossing the road.

Fact (a) in *case (1)* appears not to be present, because the old man was not using a pedestrian crossing. For simplicity, we shall assume that *the woman was speeding, she was not looking where she was going either, and the weather conditions were still excellent.* Thus facts (b), (c), and (d) are the same. The absence of fact (a), however, may not paint the full picture. You might be asking, for instance, whether the old man was crossing over on a straight piece of road or, more dangerously, on a bend. We shall say that the new fact—(e)—is that the man was crossing over on a straight piece of road. The driver is called Brenda in this second case.

CASE 2:
FACTS: (b), (c), (d), (e)
DECISION: BRENDA IS
GUILTY
CASE (1) APPLIED

THIS TELLS US THAT IN CASE (2) THE COURT DID NOT CONSIDER THAT THE ABSENCE OF FACT (a), NOR THE PRESENCE OF FACT (e), MADE ANY DIFFERENCE TO THE APPLICATION OF CASE (1). CASE (1) APPLIED EVEN THOUGH THE OLD MAN WAS NOT ON A PEDESTRIAN CROSSING.

The *ratio* might be: where a person is speeding in good weather conditions and not looking where they are going they will be guilty of reckless driving if they injure a pedestrian who is carefully crossing a straight piece of road.

Our perception of the legal principles relating to reckless driving has been widened—ever so slightly; but still widened. Gone is any requirement for the presence of a Zebra crossing, but there still seems to be a requirement for a straight piece of road.

Now let us introduce a third case—*case (3)*. Here a woman, Carol, driving a Peugeot 205, runs over a student crossing the road.

The material facts are:

(a) *(see below)*
(b) *(see below)*
(c) *The woman was not looking where she was going.*
(d) *The weather conditions were excellent*
(e) *(see below)*
(f) *The student was crossing the road on a bend*

The student was crossing on a bend: thus *fact* (a) (using the pedestrian crossing) and *fact* (e) (crossing on a straight piece of road) do not apply. We shall say that Carol *was not speeding*. Thus *fact* (b) is missing.

Carol is found guilty.

THE DIFFERENCES BETWEEN CASE (*1*) AND THIS CASE SEEM TO BE THE QUESTION OF SPEEDING AND THE POSITION OF THE PEDESTRIAN ON THE ROAD. AS CAROL WAS GUILTY ANYWAY THIS CASE APPEARS TO TELL US THAT THE ABSENCE OF FACT (b)—*speeding*—WAS OF NO IMPORTANCE IN ASSESSING CAROL'S LIABILITY; NOR WAS THE ABSENCE OF FACT (a).

CASE 3:
FACTS: (c), (d), (f)
DECISION: CAROL GUILTY

APPLICATION OF CASE 1 MODIFIED

Further, you will recall that the absence of fact (a)—the use of the pedestrian crossing—was not significant in *case (2)* either; nor did the presence in *case (3)* of fact (f)—that the student was crossing on a bend—appear to be fundamental to the issue of liability. The position at which the pedestrian is crossing on the road appears to have become irrelevant, despite its presence in the original case. The judge in *case (1)* may have thought fact (a) important, but later judges have found that they can reach the same conclusion without it.

The *ratio* for *case (3)* might be: where a person is driving in good weather conditions and not looking where they are going they will be guilty of reckless driving if they injure a pedestrian who is crossing on the bend of a road.

It is tempting just to say 'crossing a road', but the next case might be about walking backwards across a road on a bend, on the brow of a hill where warning signs are posted. Sticking close to the facts is safer; though this also means that the ratio is of much more restricted use.

Compare the possible formulations of *ratio* in the three cases. Are the minor differences important?

CASE 1: where a person is *speeding* in good weather conditions and not looking where they are going they will be guilty of reckless driving if they injure a pedestrian who is *legitimately using a pedestrian crossing.*	*CASE 2:* where a person is *speeding* in good weather conditions and not looking where they are going they will be guilty of reckless driving if they injure a pedestrian who is *carefully crossing a straight piece of road.*	*CASE 3:* where a person is *driving* in good weather conditions and not looking where they are going they will be guilty of reckless driving if they injure a pedestrian who is *crossing on the bend of a road.*

This type of exercise is fine for examining decided cases—as you will do throughout your studies. But there is the practical 'prediction' aspect of law too. For instance, let us assume for a moment that you are a solicitor interviewing a client. The client tells you that he injured a young man in a car accident. The man was crossing the road, on a bend, in a wheelchair. Can you say that the cases we have discussed will apply? Is the introduction of a new fact—that he was in a wheelchair—sufficiently different from the precedents that they may have no application?

One thing you would certainly have to do is to read the cases. We have simplified things. There are no statements here from judges as to *why* they reached these decisions. It might even be that there is an *obiter* comment in one of the cases where a judge said that had the injured person been in a wheelchair or similar device the decision would have been different. This *obiter* comment is not binding but it might be highly persuasive to a later judge—the judge in your case.

Remember, though, that when the material facts are found to be sufficiently similar then the later court is bound to follow the decision of the earlier *superior* court (and possibly that of a court of equal status): it must apply the principle of law pronounced in the earlier case. The only other alternative is to **distinguish** the case. By this we mean that the lawyer or judge will seek to show a significant difference in the material facts or the reasoning employed in the two cases such that the court should not feel obliged to follow the earlier case. It is almost impossible to define coherently when courts will or will not feel inclined to distinguish a case. But do not be put off by the difficulty of predicting when a judge will distinguish cases. The ability to argue differences in cases, to argue why a case should or should not apply, lies at the heart of the Common Law. The fact that the judge finally disagrees with you may be annoying, but it's a fact of life. Sometimes your talents will be recognised even in the most hopeless of cases, as with Lord Donaldson's comment of David Pannick QC in *Attorney-General* v *Barker* [1990] 3 All ER 257 at 261e: 'My abiding impression of this case is that I have confirmed my admiration for counsel . . . as an advocate in his ability to dress up the wholly unarguable as if it had a scintilla of a basis of reason'.

Anyway you distinguish things every day. At its simplest level, you distinguish physical objects—a television from a video recorder for example. Their size, shape, and functions tell you that these objects are different. More inexplicably we all distinguish the faces of billions of people, despite the fact that they are built of the same, limited number of component parts. We would submit that, saying *exactly* why Deb and Jane are not the same person might, in the end, be more difficult than distinguishing between *case* (*1*) and *case* (*3*) in our examples above.

What the 'reckless driving' exercise tells us is that the analysis of the *ratio* of a *case* involves a high degree of interpretation—of applying the *principle* in one *case* to the different facts in another. The principles that emerge from a *case* can thus often only be seen in retrospect. Looking back at *case* (*1*), knowing that later cases have expanded upon such things as the position of the pedestrian on the road, we tend to generalise. Our account of the *ratio* of *case* (*1*) is much more general than it would have been immediately after *case* (*1*) was reported. When the decision in *case* (*1*) was given you could not say with any certainty that the presence of the pedestrian crossing or the fact the driver was speeding would be irrelevant to liability. It might be that now you feel you could extract a wide principle from the three cases, eg that a driver who does not look where he or she is going is guilty of reckless driving. Perhaps this is accurate—but would you have been confident in saying this when *case* (*1*) was the only decided case?

It is like watching a game of chess where you have not been told all the rules. You might see a knight move and conclude that chess pieces move in an 'L' shape. Only in subsequent observations do you find that this principle only applies to one piece; and you may not have deduced yet that the knight has the ability to jump over other pieces. The real attributes of the knight—the first case—are only seen as things develop and by comparison with other events. This comparison was once used by the late Richard Feynman to describe the discovery of scientific principles; it applies equally here. And, as with Feynman's analogy, there is always the possibility that just when you think you understand everything about chess (or science, or legal principles) something totally unexpected happens, such as 'castling'.

For instance, assume that a new major case has just been reported. At this stage you cannot say with certainty how it will be used in the future. How will later judges apply it to different facts? Is the *ratio* going to be restricted to the particular facts of the case, or used in many other similar (but possibly only remotely similar) cases? In other words, how will judges in later cases use the precedent?

If we might borrow and adapt an example of this form of reasoning from Dworkin (1987:chap 7) we can see that this twisting and turning of principles can apply outside the legal context too. Consider that Charles Dickens had never written *A Christmas Carol*. You have been commissioned to do so. In writing chapter one you have a completely free hand in deciding on the character of Scrooge and what will happen to him. Think of this as the first case in a line of precedents.

Now imagine that someone else is commissioned to write chapter two. They take your basic material, but place a different emphasis on it—maybe one you never intended. By the end of the novel (with even more authors having contributed) Scrooge, instead of being redeemed, is taught his lesson and still cast into hell. Your original idea has been changed out of all recognition, despite the fact that each chapter follows logically from the previous one.

Multiple and Inconclusive Rationes

It will not now come as a surprise that a case can be said to have different *rationes* in that there may be different interpretations as to what is the proposition of law for which the case stands as authority. Equally, you need to be aware that even 'crystal clear' judgments occasionally contain more than one *ratio;* and that in some cases no one can find the *ratio*.

On the first point we have in mind the position where a judge says: 'I find for X for the following reasons . . . I would also say that there is another (unconnected) reason for which I find for X'. Which is the *ratio?* This occurred in *Turner* v *London Transport Executive* [1977] ICR 952. The traditional answer is that both statements are *ratio*. Later judges do not, however, follow a consistent line when dealing with such cases; they 'relegate' one of the statements to mere *obiter dictum:* see Lord Denning's comments on *Turner* in *Western Excavating* v *Sharp* [1978] ICR 221, [1978] 1 All ER 713.

On the second point we have in mind a number of confusing cases which the lawyer usually relates as being 'an authority for any proposition of law for which you care to use it'. This will arise where the judges are agreed as to the decision (X won) but present their reasons in quite different formulations. *Bell* v *Lever Bros* [1932] AC 161 is one example which you will encounter in Contract Law. Another Contract case along the same lines is *Esso* v *Commissioners of Customs and Excise* [1976] 1 WLR 1, [1976] 1 All ER 117. The issue was quite simple. Esso had established a campaign whereby their garages were giving away free 'World Cup' coins (tokens bearing the faces of England's 1970 World Cup squad) with every four gallons of petrol. Customs and Excise claimed these coins were chargeable to purchase tax (the forerunner of VAT) because they were 'produced in quantity for general sale'. The customs officials placed a value on the coins and claimed £200,000.

The House of Lords held that Esso was not liable to purchase tax on the coins. But when one reads the judgments one finds that:

(a)   Two Law Lords held that there was no intent to create legal relations as regards the coins: they were gifts (see Viscount Dilhorne and Lord Russell).

(b)   Two Law Lords held that the advertisement on the garage forecourts was an offer which the customer accepted when he bought the petrol. However, the coins themselves were ancillary to the main contract and were only transferred when the motorist bought the petrol. Therefore the coins themselves were not produced for sale (Lord Simon and Lord Wilberforce).

(c)   Lord Fraser dissented, finding that there was intent to form a contract and the coins were part of that contract.

This summary ignores the many *obiter* statements which add greater confusion.

Exercise 10: Precedent and the congenital idiot

The following is an exercise on *ratio* and *stare decisis* based on the information above and that in Chapter Five. Its aim is to reiterate some of the points made and to show you a general plan in answering legal questions. It also gives us an opportunity to note that in legal education, if not in practice, you will be asked to write essays relating to quotations as well as analyse problem situations.

Lord Asquith once recounted a joke told to him regarding *ratio* and *obiter* that: 'The rule is quite simple, if you agree with the other bloke you say [the statement] is part of the *ratio*; if you don't you say it is *obiter dictum*, with the implication that he is a congenital idiot'.
Discuss.

Answer: This question asks you to analyse how a judge uses or avoids precedent: what do the terms *ratio decidendi* and *obiter dictum* mean; and is a judge really bound by the doctrine of *stare decisis?* Thus this is a specific question which demands a **specific** answer—not general comments. This style of question is one which is commonly found throughout all areas of law—a quotation questioning or denying the logic of a fundamental rule. For instance, the question might be: 'The formation of a contract is not based on assessing the parties' true intentions but on what the law defines as their intentions according to their conduct set against established case law. Discuss.' Or: 'When people talk of the United Kingdom losing its sovereignty on joining the EEC they fail to recognise that sovereignty is an economic fact, not a political aspiration. Discuss.' You are asked to perform four tasks:

(1) **IDENTIFY THE AREA CONCERNED.** In this case this hardly presents a problem because of the introductory words. But a quotation on theft, or misrepresentation in contract, may have hidden points.

(2) **LIMIT YOURSELF TO THE TOPIC IN QUESTION.** In the context of this chapter, this again is not difficult; but when such a question appears at the end of a course the task becomes more difficult. It is vital to see at what limited area the question is aimed. Not all the topics that fall within 'legal method' are relevant to the question posed here. Thus the poor student will tend to do one of two things:

(a) Launch into a lengthy discussion of various or all aspects of precedent. This is known as the 'shotgun' approach: something has to hit the target. With a question on provocation in Criminal Law, for instance, nearly every defence under the sun will emerge at some time.

(b) Spend too much time on introductory matters such as describing the court structure in detail. This would not be the crux of the question. This might be even more obvious when one glances down the examination paper to discover a question asking for just this type of information. With a question on Contract Law, for instance, there may be a page introduction setting out as many aspects of contract formation as possible when the question is only concerned with one aspect of offer and acceptance.

(3) **STRUCTURE THE ANSWER.** Do not leap into a discussion of the topic without planning the development of the essay. An examiner has difficulty following an answer that constantly repeats itself, re-states points or arguments for no apparent reason, or makes sense from sentence to sentence but not from paragraph to paragraph. A safe bet is to begin with some (we stress *some)* introductory words:

FOR EXAMPLE:
'The doctrine of precedent is central to the development of Common Law. The doctrine of *stare decisis* provides the mechanism for the operation of judicial precedent. *Stare decisis* demands that where a decision has been made on a particular point of law then later inferior courts (or courts of equal status in many cases) must not be merely persuaded by the earlier decision, but are bound to follow it. In its strictest form, therefore, this approach promotes certainty. However, the doctrine does not mean that all judges are simply machines; applying fixed rules already laid down. If that were so then the two sides would probably not be arguing the point. The difficulty is that the doctrine demands that *like cases should be decided in the same way.* This always leaves room for deciding when two cases are sufficiently similar that the doctrine of *stare decisis* should be applied: ie cases can very often be distinguished on their facts and the key point of *stare decisis* rests in the analysis of the *ratio* and *obiter dicta* of the earlier case. It is the principle in the earlier case that must be followed, not merely the decision.'

You might then go on to explain the difference between *ratio decidendi* and *obiter dicta*.

(4) **REFER TO THE QUESTION.** To obtain the best marks you should try to relate your comments to the quotation. At various points in your answer review the relevance of parts of your answer to the quotation. Here is an example:

> We have said that the doctrine of *stare decisis* provides certainty. Thus we can say that the 'law' on a topic can be discovered, and *stare decisis*, in particular, narrows down the enquiry. But such an approach assumes that the principle of a case (its authority) is not open to interpretation itself. If, however, **as the question implies or at least suggests**, the judge has at some early stage decided which way the case should go then his task is one of showing how the authorities that he wishes to follow are very similar to the case before him; and how the other 'apparently' similar cases are based on entirely different facts. But even if one does not take such a cynical line, it is also true to say that the *ratio* of any case is not fixed and immutable. Different judges perceive cases as authority for differently stated principles.

(5) **REFER TO SOME CASES TO ILLUSTRATE YOUR ARGUMENTS.** Here you could use cases which distinguished other cases on seemingly minor points, for instance—or cases where a judge felt compelled to follow earlier cases even when he believed them to be wrong. You could choose cases from areas you have studied eg Contract Law or Criminal Law. Legal method, remember, is about how law is analysed; it is not a separate subject in itself.

Cases are cited in a number of ways. We shall take this opportunity to look at these methods of citation. Here are five general examples of alternative methods. The case is on employment law and the legal definition of 'dismissal'. Do not worry about understanding the legal issues. The key point is that if an employee resigns he may still claim, in law, that he was dismissed. The aim of this provision is to prevent employers forcing an employee to resign without any remedy; it is referred to as 'constructive dismissal'.

(a) In *Western Excavating* v *Sharp* an employee was short of money following disciplinary action by his employer. He asked for an advance of his pay but, in keeping with company regulations, this was refused. He resigned in order to obtain his holiday pay; and because he felt his employer was acting unreasonably. The question before the court was: did a resignation because of 'unreasonable' conduct on the part of the employer fall within the legal definition of dismissal? The Court of Appeal held that a resignation could only constitute a dismissal where the employer had committed a serious breach of contract, not just because he may have been acting unreasonably. Hence there was no 'dismissal' here. **N.B. if you have** time to do this for each case you cite in an examination you can write more quickly than any student we know!

(b) The principle was established in *Western Excavating* v *Sharp* that an employee can resign but still claim he was dismissed if the employer has seriously breached the contract (**N.B. case names appear in italics in texts.** In essays it is always best to underline case names for clarity).

(c) The Court of Appeal in *Western Excavating* v *Sharp* stressed that the employer must be in serious breach of contract, not just acting unreasonably, before an employee can resign and still claim he was dismissed.

(d) A resignation cannot be classed as a dismissal unless the employer has seriously breached the contract: *Western Excavating* v *Sharp*.

(e) In the seventies there existed much judicial disagreement as to when a resignation might constitute a dismissal. One camp argued that if the employer acted unreasonably this would constitute a constructive dismissal. Others pressed the point that what was required was a serious breach of contract on the employer's part. The issue was apparently settled in *Western Excavating* v *Sharp* wherein the Court of Appeal pronounced in favour of the 'contract test'.

(6) **CONCLUDE.** The reality of the quotation is probably that some judges feel they must adhere to precedent at all cost because this promotes certainty; whilst others take a more creative standpoint. In the end it is probably true to say that judges do both things: they adhere to precedent and also use or adapt precedent to justify their decisions. The statement merely confirms that, despite our strict views of *stare decisis*, there exists the role of choice in our judicial process. Judges, after all, try to achieve 'fairness'.

The statement also recognises the interpretative element in describing the *ratio* of a case. The finer points of distinguishing cases, or showing how one case relates to others, can lead to a justifiable disagreement as to what is the *ratio* of a case.

Material Facts

The facts of a case are revealed in the documents, statements, affidavits, and evidence produced. All these are relevant to a case, but they are not all relevant to the *ratio* of the case. In our case of reckless driving, the legal reasoning is unlikely to hinge on whether the plaintiff was called Alfred, or what make of car he drove, or the colour of the car. Whether he was speeding is more **likely** to be material.

There is no set hierarchy of facts which will always be important or irrelevant. Change the issue before the court and different questions have to be posed. Alfred's name could be important where he is claiming that *he* is the 'Alfred' cited in a millionaire's will—so too his height, nickname and age. The colour of the car might be the whole issue at stake in a breach of contract action where Alfred has ordered a red car and is presented with a yellow car which he refuses to accept.

So one thing you need to be aware of is: what is the case about? What is the legal point at issue? Once you have established this, certain facts cannot be material. Secondly, be aware that facts can be viewed as 'narrow' or 'general'. This depends upon the level of **abstraction** with which one views the facts of a case; whether one takes only the literal facts as being relevant or one observes the facts as merely representing something wider. For instance, is a statement about the meaning of giving someone a red rose limited to red roses, indicative of all roses, all flowers, or representative of symbols of affection?

Consider the following columns based on the analysis by Stone (1959:597) of the case of *Donoghue v Stevenson*. We considered *Donoghue v Stevenson* in Exercise 8 in deciding why two cases should be decided the same way. To repeat the facts in brief: Mrs Donoghue and a friend went into a cafe in Paisley. The friend ordered ice-cream and ginger-beer for both of them. The shopkeeper poured out some of the ginger-beer over the ice-cream. Mrs Donoghue consumed some of the mixture. Her friend poured out the remainder of the ginger-beer for Mrs Donoghue and a decomposed snail fell out of the bottle. The bottle was of dark opaque glass so that the contents could not have been detected. Mrs Donoghue sued Stevenson (the manufacturer of the ginger-beer) for negligently causing her injury. She succeeded.

In the first column will appear a material fact that relates very closely to what happened. The next two columns go wider in their interpretation. Picture yourself as a judge and ask which level of generalisation you would adopt in a later case to see whether the decision in *Donoghue v Stevenson* should be applied. Our experience is that students are attracted to the 'widest interpretation of the facts' on points 1, 2 and 4; the 'wider facts' column tends to be preferred on points 3 and 5. You may feel different.

The point of this experiment is that the wider you set your *abstraction* of the facts the easier it is to apply one decision concerning a particular set of facts to another case concerning different facts.

NARROW FACTS	WIDER FACTS	WIDEST INTERPRETATION OF FACTS
1. The case is only about dead snails	1. The case is about the presence of any animal	1. The case is concerned with liability for any foreign body
2. The material point is that the liquid was ginger-beer	2. The material point is that the bottle was opaque—the liquid is irrelevant	2. The case is about articles in containers—not necessarily bottles
3. The defendant must be a manufacturer of ginger-beer	3. The defendant simply has to be a manufacturer	3. Anyone dealing with an item for consumption is potentially liable

| 4. It is material that the plaintiff was a Scottish widow | 4. It is material that the plaintiff was a woman | 4. Any person may claim |
| 5. A key point is that the snail was not visible. | 5. The snail was not discoverable without damaging the container. | 5. The defect must not be discoverable by anyone who could reasonably be expected to inspect the item. |

Assessing whether facts are 'material' or not can therefore be a difficult exercise. There is no set formula because it depends upon how narrowly or widely you view each fact. The case of *Donoghue* v *Stevenson* is about dead snails, ginger-beer and a Scottish widow, but if that was all it stood for as an authority we would wait centuries before those facts resurfaced in a new case. Meanwhile, the slightest difference in facts would mean that when your client asks you for advice and she is an English widow, the drink is Coca-Cola and a dead mouse has emerged you would be starting your argument afresh. Clearly you would abstract from *Donoghue* v *Stevenson* a slighter wider set of material facts.

In this light you might look again at *Grant* v *Australian Knitting Mills* in Exercise 8 and consider whether the court took a narrow or wide view of the material facts in *Donoghue*. You can follow this up by looking at a textbook on torts to discover what has happened to the principles enunciated in a simple 1932 case about dead snails.

One method we have tried in discovering material facts, which has proved successful with students is to analyse the importance of facts by removing them from the description of the case in hand and ask whether this would have made a difference to the decision. If the reasoning would have been altered and the decision would consequently have been different, it seems highly likely that something hinged on the now missing fact. Hence the removed fact would appear to be crucial to the formulation of the *ratio*.

Material Facts and the Question of 'What If?'

We can attempt to put this into practise with one of the most famous cases in law: *Carlill* v *Carbolic Smoke Ball Co.* [1893] 1 QB 256. The defendants placed an advertisement in various newspapers relating to their product, 'The Carbolic Smoke Ball'. The advertisement claimed that by using the smoke ball properly the purchaser could avoid influenza, colds, and a whole variety of other complaints ranging from neuralgia to whooping cough. The claim was made that many thousands of these smoke balls had been sold and in no ascertained case was influenza contracted by those using the smoke ball. It was stated that a £100 reward would be paid to anyone who used the smoke ball properly and who still contracted these illnesses. The advertisement went on to say that,' £1,000 is deposited with the Alliance Bank, Regent Street, showing our sincerity in the matter'. Mrs Carlill read the advertisement, bought one of the smoke balls, used it as directed, and caught influenza. She claimed the £100 'reward'.

The issue was whether the advertisement constituted an offer which could be accepted, or whether it was only an 'advertising puff'. If it was an offer, and had been validly accepted by Mrs Carlill correctly using the smoke ball, there was a contract and she was entitled to the £100. One of the main arguments propounded by the defendants was that the vagueness of the document showed that no contract was ever intended.

When her claim came before the Court of Appeal she won her case. The question for us to address, then, is what should be the *ratio* of the case? For a true appreciation of this, of course, one would have to read the judgments. If you do read the case, note how Lindley LJ and Bowen LJ stress quite different matters in their judgments. Here, however, we are concerned only with the idea of 'material facts'. So, in formulating a *ratio*, which facts would be material? Under the test proposed above we will eliminate or alter some of the facts. If this alters the reasoning and result of the case we can regard that affected fact as material.

If the advertisement had appeared in a shop window only, would that have made a difference to either the result or the *ratio*?
Unlikely. The case acknowledges that the offer was made to the 'world at large'. A smaller audience is hardly relevant. However, the use of a newspaper might carry with it more credibility than a shop window and so exhibit a greater degree of seriousness.

If Mrs Carlill had not used the smoke ball as directed, would that have made a difference?
This must be material because Mrs Carlill would otherwise not, in law, have accepted the terms of the offer. Hence, whatever the status of the advertisement, there could have been no contract.

If the sums of money had been £10 and £100, would that have made a difference?
The usual response to this is that the amount is generally immaterial. However, some would argue that the large amount (for 1893) indicated a serious intent on the part of the defendant and so is material. Recently, however, one of our students argued persuasively that the converse was true: that the sums of £100 and £1,000 set against the cost of the smoke ball (ten shillings) showed that the tenor of the company's claim was so extravagant that it was only on the outer limit of being taken seriously. A smaller 'reward' might indicate sincerity more easily.

If the defendants had not deposited the £1,000, would that have made a difference?
Our experience in conducting this exercise is that this question causes a split in the student vote. Many feel that it is this element which lent intention

to the defendants' claim. Others feel that the *promise* to deposit was the key point.

If the defendants had not promised that they had deposited a sum of money, would that have made a difference?
Most students draw the line here. The presence of the promise is seen as a vital factor in the case.

If Mrs Carlill had not known about the advertisement, but had bought the smoke ball anyway, would that have made a difference?
Here we enter the realms of the relevance of other case law. Other cases had tackled the problem as to whether one needs to know of an offer before performing an act in order to accept it legally. We put this question to reiterate that, though the analysis of material facts aids our understanding of the authority of a precedent, we must be aware that one case stands in relation to others eg here *Williams* v *Carwardine* (1833) 5 C & P 566.

One final question, to show that legal analysis need not be merely an abstract exercise but relates to the society in which it operates.

Influenza, at the turn of the century, was a more serious illness than it is now and large numbers of people died in the epidemics: so if the product claimed only to cure, say, bunions, do you think that that would have made a difference?
If you think there would have been a difference, is this because the question of seriousness and intent would have been affected; or might it be that the judicial attitude would have been different for reasons really unconnected with legal technicalities, ie the social setting? One of our part-time degree students, a medical practitioner, once added a gloss to this: the smoke ball claimed to *prevent* an illness, whereas the 'bunion product' would be claiming to *cure* an illness. Thus, although concerned with a less serious topic, the bunion cure was less speculative and, as a *cure,* might be taken more seriously.

We have been doing what many judges in later cases do when reviewing earlier authorities. Later judges must assess the extent to which the facts of the original case fit the case before them. In doing this they interpret the *ratio* of the earlier case by evaluating the importance of the facts: placing them in a narrow or wide setting. What we have not the space to do, however, is to consider whether the order in which one removes the facts might matter, or the effect of removing groupings of facts. You might wish to consider this with *Carlill.*

What Can Happen to a Case?

(a)   The case may be followed in its strictest form, or applied, in later cases. As we noted in Chapter Five, under the doctrine of *stare decisis* the earlier case may be followed even though the later judges disagree with it.

(b) Sometimes the later court may be superior in status to the earlier court. If it follows the reasoning of the inferior court it is said to have *approved* the earlier case. Obviously it might equally disapprove of or overrule the earlier case. Disapproval may diminish the status of the earlier case. In the case of overruling, the earlier case ceases to be an authority of any sort (unless an even more superior court reinstates it at a later date). Overruling is not that common, at least where the principle has been established for some time; but it does happen. In *R* v *R* [1991] 3 WLR 767, [1991] 4 All ER 481, for instance, we saw in Chapter Five that the House of Lords overruled a long line of case law on marital rape; in *Pepper (Inspector of Taxes)* v *Hart* [1992] 3 WLR 1032, [1993] 1 All ER 42 the House of Lords did the same in connection with the rules on statutory interpretation; in *Polkey* v *Dayton* [1987] AC 344, [1988] ICR 142 the House of Lords again overruled a decade's worth of Court of Appeal decisions on the question of determining fairness in an unfair dismissal.

(c) The term *overruling* tends to be applied when a court reviews previous precedents. However, if a court's decision is subject to an appeal the higher court obviously has to allow or dismiss the appeal. If the higher court reaches a different decision it is said to *overturn* or *reverse* the decision of the lower court. The higher court might not overturn the actual result of the lower court (ie, X still wins) but may reformulate the law or approve of only part of the decision in the lower court.

(d) When the facts are found to be dissimilar the later court is said to *distinguish* the earlier case. The art of distinguishing cases is a major weapon used by advocates; especially when confronted with problems of *stare decisis*. The attack is usually concentrated on showing a difference in the material facts of the two cases.

(e) The later case may decide that the decision in the earlier case was reached *per incuriam*.

(f) An Act of Parliament may change the law.

(g) The later case may state that the earlier case has no clear *ratio* and is therefore not binding. See on this, *Esso* v *Commissioners of Customs and Excise* detailed above.

Exercise 11: Tales from the grave

This exercise centres on the law of succession, in particular the requirement for a testator to sign a will in order for it to be valid. The purpose of the exercise is to examine the possible ways you might attack an earlier precedent to show why it should not be applied in your case. Although we have used a particular case this is by way of illustration only. The techniques and questions raised here can be used in any exercise on Criminal Law, Torts, Contract, etc. where you are comparing cases.

The earlier precedent: In *Wood* v *Smith* [1992] 3 All ER 556 the testator made a will two days before he died which started, 'My will by Percy Winterborne . . .'. He did not sign his name at the foot of the will and when the witnesses pointed this out to him he replied that he had signed it at the top (referring to the opening statement) and that it could be signed anywhere. The will was contested on the grounds that it was not validly executed. The Court of Appeal held that this was indeed a valid signature for the purposes of s. 9, Wills Act 1837 (as amended) so that the will was valid.

The relevant statute: Wills Act 1837, s. 9, states that no will shall be valid unless: '(a) it is in writing and signed by the testator . . . (b) it appears that the testator intended by his signature to give effect to the will; and (c) the signature is made or acknowledged by the testator in the presence of two or more witnesses present at the same time . . .'.

Your case: John Doe decided to make a will and purchased a 'will form' from a local shop. He started drafting it one day at work but was interrupted and did not complete the will until the following day. The first line of the will reads: 'John Doe—this is my last will and testament'. A witness pointed out to him that there was no signature on the will, but Doe said that this was all right since he had run out of space and provided wills were written on 'will forms' there was no need to sign them. The will was properly witnessed.

Question
What devices (eg, distinguishing the cases) could you use to argue that *Wood* v *Smith* does not apply to this case?

Answer

The best way to approach this exercise is to read *Wood* v *Smith* and all the cases it cites. You should concentrate on four things in particular:

(a)   Which court are you in? This matters in relation to questions of *stare decisis*. Assume in this exercise that you are in the Court of Appeal.
(b)   Exactly *why* did the Court of Appeal decide that the will was valid?
(c)   What precise words did Scott LJ use to explain the decision?
(d)   What differences in material facts can you find?

Whether or not you have had the opportunity to read the case, consider the following points in your argument:

Attack 1: Argue that the earlier case should not apply to the present one

(a) Is the case of *Doe* distinguishable on its facts from *Wood* v *Smith*?

(b) Is the case of *Doe* distinguishable as regards the issue of law raised in *Wood* v *Smith*?

Attack 2: If the case is not distinguishable, argue that *stare decisis* has no application

(c) Was there a clear *ratio* in *Wood* v *Smith*?

(d) Was the decision in *Wood* v *Smith* made *per incuriam*; or did it at least misinterpret the reasoning in earlier cases?

(e) When *Wood* v *Smith* had to decide matters that had not been raised in earlier cases, was the reasoning doubtful or unclear?

(f) Has *Wood* v *Smith* been doubted in other cases?

(g) Are there any decisions of the same level which conflict with *Wood* v *Smith*?

(h) Are there substantive conflicts in the reports of the case found in the *All England Law Reports* and the *Weekly Law Reports*?

(i) Were there any *obiter* statements which might help because they show that had the present facts arisen the court would have decided differently?

Attack 3: Argue that the case should be bypassed on more general grounds

(j) Has *Wood* v *Smith* been criticised by academic writers?

(k) Were the words used by Scott LJ clear as to why the will was valid; and were those words limited to the special circumstances of *Wood* v *Smith*?

(l) Have social conditions changed so radically that the earlier case should be doubted in a modern setting? (Not particularly useful in relation to *Wood* v *Smith* itself.)

One can see much of this at work in the cases flowing from *Donoghue* v *Stevenson*. However, by way of giving a different example we shall turn to the postal rules of acceptance in the Law of Contract to illustrate the development of a *ratio*.

Postal Rule Cases

In Chapter Five we took some of the 'postal acceptance' cases as examples of how judges use earlier authorities. We attempted to show that the doctrine of judicial precedent is not simply a mechanical process of matching similarities and differences; cases can appear to be similar at first glance, without necessarily proving to be so. As promised, we return to these cases to illustrate the development of a rule.

The format for this part of the chapter is to combine a description of the development of a simple rule with some exercise-type questions. You should be able to formulate opinions on the information provided; but, as always, you might devise better answers if you read the cases themselves.

As we explained in Chapter Five a contract is formed when there is an offer which is accepted, without the addition of new terms, by the other party. The general rule is that acceptance has to be communicated. If they communicate by post, when does the acceptance take place? When the letter of acceptance is posted, or only when it arrives with the offeror?

The first 'postal acceptance' case (some would argue, the first case on what we now term the rules of 'offer and acceptance') was *Adams* v *Lindsell* (1818) 1 B & A 681. Here an offer was made by post to sell some wool. The letter was sent on 2 September, reply to be by return of post. The letter was misaddressed and was not received until 5 September. It was accepted by post immediately. On 7 September the offeror had not received his reply by return of post and sold the wool elsewhere the day after. The letter of acceptance arrived on 9 September. Was there a contract established by these letters? If there was a contract then the seller was in breach because he had sold the wool to another person.

HELD: There was a contract at the moment the offeree posted the letter of acceptance.

Questions: *How would you present the ratio of this case?*
          Which facts should be seen as material; and how wide a description would you give to them?
          Should it be a material fact, for instance, that the offeror misaddressed the offer letter, but that the letter of acceptance did eventually arrive?

POSSIBLE NARROW *RATIO:* Where an offer to form a contract is sent by post but is late reaching its destination because the letter was misaddressed by the offeror, the acceptance will be valid from the moment of posting provided the offeree complies with the relevant conditions of the offer and the acceptance eventually arrives.

POSSIBLE WIDER *RATIO:* If the offeror chooses to use the post as a means of communicating an offer he must take the consequences. Thus, he will be bound by a postal acceptance from the moment the acceptance is posted.

Dunlop v *Higgins* (1848) 1 HLC 381; 9 ER 805 was the next case to deal with this problem, as we noted in Chapter Five. Dunlop wrote to Higgins offering to sell some iron; reply to be by return of post. The offer was accepted by Higgins in a letter but bad weather delayed the post. In the meantime there had been an increase in the price of iron. Dunlop maintained that because the reply had not been by return of post there was no contract— which would allow them to sell to other customers at the new price.

HELD: The House of Lords decided that a contract existed when the letter of acceptance was posted.

Questions: *How would you present the ratio of this case?*
Which facts should be seen as material?
Should it be a material fact that the parties were trading companies?
How does this decision alter the original principle established in Adams v Lindsell? Is the 'postal rule' now (in 1848) wider or narrower? For instance, does it now matter that, in Adams v Lindsell, the offeror misaddressed the offer letter?

POSSIBLE NARROW *RATIO:* Where an offer to form a contract is sent by post but the acceptance is late reaching its destination because of bad weather, the acceptance will be valid from the moment of posting provided there is a trade usage to use the post and the letter of acceptance is properly addressed.

POSSIBLE WIDER *RATIO:* The use of the post is an exception to the rule that communication of acceptance must be effective. If the offeror chooses to use the post as a means of communicating an offer he must take the consequences. Thus, he will be bound by a postal acceptance from the moment it is posted provided the letter eventually arrives.

EFFECT ON *ADAMS* v *LINDSELL:* The narrow *ratio* is formulated differently and one would now (in 1848) need to ask whether the offeror's error in *Adams* v *Lindsell* is crucial to the point. The possible formulation of the wider *ratio* has not changed substantially. However, you will remember that in Chapter Five we saw that the judges in *Household Fire* v *Grant* (below) disagreed about the real meaning of *Dunlop v Higgins*.

In *Household Fire Insurance Co.* v *Grant* (1879) 4 Ex D 216 Grant made an application in writing to the company for shares. A deposit was paid, the remainder to be paid within twelve months. The company allotted shares to Grant and posted the allotment to him. The letter never arrived. The company later went into liquidation and the liquidator sought the balance of Grant's application which was still outstanding. Grant maintained he had no contract with the company because his offer had not been accepted. No contract would mean no liability to pay. The company maintained that the offer had been accepted when their letter of acceptance had been posted even though it never arrived.

HELD: Grant was liable to pay the outstanding amount on the shares. The letter of acceptance was valid on posting even though it never arrived.

Questions: *How would you present the ratio of this case?*
Which facts should be seen as material?
Should it be a material fact that the letter of acceptance never arrived?
How does this decision alter the original principle established in Adams v Lindsell? Is the 'postal rule' now (in 1879) wider or narrower?

POSSIBLE NARROW *RATIO:* Where an offer to form a contract is sent by post the acceptance will be valid from the moment of posting even though it never arrives, provided the letter of acceptance is properly addressed and the parties expressly or impliedly agree to the use of the post as a means of communication.

POSSIBLE WIDER *RATIO:* If the offeror chooses to use the post as a means of communicating an offer he must take the consequences. The non-arrival of the letter of acceptance does not alter the general rule.

EFFECT ON *ADAMS* v *LINDSELL:* The narrow *ratio* is formulated differently and one would now (in 1879) need to ask whether the late arrival of the letter of acceptance in *Adams* v *Lindsell* was crucial to the point.

In *Henthorn* v *Fraser* [1892] 2 Ch 27 (CA) Henthorn visited Fraser's offices. Henthorn was given an option to purchase a house (ie an offer). Fraser withdrew the offer by letter, but not before Henthorn had accepted by post. So the letters crossed in the post. All letters arrived at their destinations on time.

HELD: The acceptance was valid when posted. The rule was not limited to trade usage but, in the words of Lord Herschell, extended to: 'Where the circumstances are such that it [the use of the post] must have been within the contemplation of the parties'.

Questions: *How would you present the ratio of this case?*
Which facts should be seen as material?
Should it be a material fact that Fraser was attempting to withdraw the offer by use of the post?
How does this decision alter the original principle established in Adams v Lindsell? Is the 'postal rule' now (in 1892) wider or narrower? For instance, has the fact that the offer was not made by post made a difference?

POSSIBLE NARROW *RATIO:* An acceptance which arrives at its destination will be valid from the moment of posting provided the letter of acceptance is properly addressed and the parties expressly or impliedly agree to the use of the post as a means of communication. This applies even where the offer was made in person and not by post.

POSSIBLE WIDER *RATIO:* Where the circumstances allow for the use of the post as a means of communicating an acceptance the offeror must take the consequences. Where the parties live in different cities, there may be an indication that using the post is acceptable.

EFFECT ON *ADAMS* v *LINDSELL:* The narrow *ratio* is again formulated differently and one would now (in 1892) need to ask whether much of what actually happened in *Adams* v *Lindsell* is now regarded as crucial to the point.

Finally, for our purposes, we have the case of *Holwell Securities* v *Hughes* [1974] 1 WLR 155, [1974] 1 All ER 161. Here an offer of an option to purchase property was sent by post. It stated: 'The option shall be exercisable by notice in writing to the vendor within six months'. Holwell accepted the offer, properly addressing the letter; but the letter never arrived.

HELD: There was no contract. The acceptance was not valid on posting. The specific wording of the offer letter showed that the acceptance was only valid when delivered to the offeror. The postal rules were held not to apply in all cases where there is postal acceptance: '[They] probably do not operate if their application would produce manifest inconvenience and absurdity'. *Adams* v *Lindsell* was distinguished.

Questions: *How would you present the ratio of this case?*
               Which facts should be seen as material?
               How does this decision alter the original principle established in Adams v Lindsell? Is the 'postal rule' now (in 1974) wider or narrower? For instance, can we now say that the postal rules can be excluded? If so, do we know which other forms of wording will be effective?

POSSIBLE NARROW *RATIO:* Where an option (offer) is granted in writing and specifies that the acceptance must be 'by notice in writing to the vendor' an acceptance which is never delivered will not be valid from the moment of posting.

POSSIBLE WIDER *RATIO:* The language used in the offer may be such that the express terms override the postal rules. The postal rules are rules of convenience only.

We can now pose four questions to conclude this discussion:

(a)   If you were writing a textbook on the Law of Contract how would you present a general principle which would summarise these cases and describe the 'postal rules of acceptance'?

(b)   If the cases had occurred in a different sequence, do you think the rule might have been differently formulated?

(c) Should these rules, by analogy, be applied to other forms of communication, eg telex, fax, or messenger rider?

(d) *Adams* v *Lindsell* was the seminal case from which all the other cases cited are directly descended. Do you think the judges in *Adams* v *Lindsell* could have forecast how their judgment would be applied in those later cases? After all, much of what seemed to matter in 1818 has probably disappeared. So is the position analogous to Dr Jacob Bronowski's comment on the 'Ascent of Man': that the ancestor of man two million years ago would not recognise us today as his own descendant?

The 'Uncertainty Principle' of Cases

Our final comment on the development of case law brings us to a theory in physics known as the 'Heisenberg Uncertainty Principle'. One of the themes we have tried to develop throughout this chapter is that later cases often change our perceptions of earlier cases. This often causes students problems, but, as we have said, discerning the *ratio* of a case is not like a hunt for buried treasure; it is one of interpretation and argument.

The problem is not unique to legal studies. The German physicist, Werner Heisenberg, argued in 1927 that as soon as you set about investigating an object you alter its state. If, for instance, you try to measure the temperature of a hot bath then the introduction of the thermometer alters the temperature—however slightly. The same is true with reading legal cases: the supposed *ratio* of an earlier case is open to reinterpretation by lawyers in later cases. Once the earlier case is looked at in the light of a new set of facts the perception of the case may be altered. Further, the way you phrase your question as to the meaning of the earlier case has an impact—which facts you concentrate on; which judicial phrase you subject to scrutiny.

In *Adams* v *Lindsell*, for instance, there is a marked difference in asking: (1) is the case authority for the rule that acceptance does not always have to be communicated?; and (2) is the case authority for the proposition that an offeror must always accept the risk for any mistakes he makes in *his* communication? The question posed as to the relevance of *Adams* v *Lindsell* will depend upon the facts of the case in front of you now and the issues thereby raised.

Exercise 12: Parking tickets and jiffy bags

1. PLEASE READ THE FACTS OF THE FIRST CASE—*Thornton* v *Shoe Lane Parking*—AND FORMULATE A RATIO DECIDENDI FOR THE CASE.

Question 2 follows the case description. It would be best if you could read the actual reports of the cases. Failing that, however, we provide a short summary of the issues raised.

THORNTON v SHOE LANE PARKING [1971] 2 QB 163, [1971] 1 All ER 686.

The plaintiff drove into the entrance to the defendant's automatic car park. A notice outside stated: 'All cars parked at owner's risk'. He took a ticket from the machine, the automatic barrier lifted, and he drove into the garage. He looked at the ticket to see the time printed on it. The plaintiff also noticed some printed words on the ticket which he did not read. When he went to collect the car an accident occurred in which he suffered personal injuries, partly through the negligence of the defendant garage.

The defendants admitted fault but relied on the ticket which contained the clause: '. . . *issued subject to the conditions of issue as displayed on the premises'*. These conditions were displayed inside the garage; they were lengthy, and excluded liability on the part of the garage for loss or damage to customers' property, or personal injury, howsoever caused. These, said the defendant, were contractual clauses which bound the plaintiff.

Mocatta J held the defendants liable. They appealed.

Lord Denning reviewed the relevant cases, some of which are noted here:

(1) *Parker v South Eastern Railway* (1877) 2 CPD 416. Here the plaintiff deposited a bag in a railway cloak-room. He was handed a ticket on which were the words 'see back'; on the back there were printed conditions excluding liability for loss or damage. The bag was lost. The Court of Appeal held that the key questions were:

(a) Did the plaintiff read the clause?

(b) Did the railway company do what was reasonably sufficient to give the plaintiff notice of the clause?

(2) *Olley v Marlborough Court Ltd* [1949] 1 KB 532, [1949] 1 All ER 127. Here it was held that a notice in a hotel bedroom which excluded liability for damage to guests' luggage was not valid as the contract had been made in the lobby of the hotel so that notice of the clause came too late.

Lord Denning dismissed the appeal. He indicated that the 'ticket cases' such as *Parker* were based on the theory that the customer, on being handed the ticket, could refuse it and decline to enter the contract on those terms. However real that theory was, it could not apply to a ticket which is issued by an automatic machine: 'The customer pays his money and gets his ticket. He cannot get his money back. He may protest to the machine, even swear at it; but it will remain unmoved.'

Olley v Marlborough Court applied. In *Thornton* the offer was contained in the notice at the entrance giving the charges for garaging and saying 'at owner's risk'. The acceptance took place when the customer put his money into the slot. The terms of the offer contained in the notice placed on or near the machine could only be binding if they were sufficiently brought to his notice before the contract was concluded. So, once the customer had accepted the offer, a contract was concluded on the terms known to exist which could not then be altered.

Parker v *South Eastern Railway* meant that, unless the customer knows that the ticket is issued subject to a clause to be found inside the garage, or the company did what was reasonably sufficient to give him notice of it, the company cannot avoid liability by relying on the later exclusion clause.

Counsel for the defendants admitted here that the defendants did not do what was reasonably sufficient to give the plaintiff notice of the exempting condition. Lord Denning held that the exclusion clause was:

> so wide and so destructive of rights that the court should not hold any man bound by it unless it is drawn to his attention in the most explicit way. . . In order to give sufficient notice, it would need to be printed in red ink with a red hand pointing to it, or something equally startling.

Lord Justice Megaw also dismissed the appeal. He declined to comment on what precise moment of time the contract was concluded. As regards the other points, His Lordship was in general agreement with Lord Denning MR. Under the three conditions noted in *Parker,* he concluded that the plaintiff in *Thornton* did not know of any printing on the ticket or, therefore, that these referred to contractual conditions. As well as this, however, His Lordship laid stress on the fact that the conditions in this contract contained the sorts of restrictions that were unusual. Thus:

> . . . at least where the particular condition relied on involves a sort of restriction that is not shown to be usual in that class of contract, a defendant must show that his intention to attach an unusual condition *of that particular nature* was fairly brought to the notice of the other party. (*emphasis added*)

Megaw LJ thus linked the type of clause in question (whether it was an unusual or usual clause in this type of contract) to the amount of effort needed on the defendant's part to bring the clause to the notice of the customer.

Sir Gordon Willmer agreed with Lord Denning and Megaw LJ: 'any attempt to introduce conditions after the irrevocable step has been taken of causing the machine to operate must be doomed to failure'.

2.   READ THIS SECOND CASE—*Interfoto Picture Library Ltd* v *Stiletto Visual Programmes Ltd* [1988] 1 All ER 348; [1988] 2 WLR 615—AND:

(a)   DECIDE WHETHER THE RATIO OF *THORNTON* APPLIES;
(b)   REACH A DECISION ON THE *INTERFOTO* CASE;
(c)   FORMULATE A RATIO FOR YOUR DECISION, EITHER APPLYING THE *THORNTON* RATIO (IN WHOLE OR PART) OR DISTINGUISHING *THORNTON* ON THE FACTS.

The defendant ordered certain photographic transparencies from the plaintiff. The photographs were consigned in a jiffy bag to the company messenger with the 'delivery note'. The defendant's manager ignored the note but, impressed by the contents of the bag, telephoned his acceptance.

There were a number of conditions contained in the delivery note. Condition 2 set the daily charge for retaining the transparencies beyond the stipulated date of return. These charges were exorbitant, representing a figure ten times higher than that charged by other comparable agencies.

The central issue was whether condition 2 was enforceable by the plaintiffs. Should it be enforceable?

We provide no answer for this exercise except to indicate one or two salient points. The first is that the *Interfoto* case is interesting because it posed the question whether the logic used for a number of years and in a number of cases regarding one type of clause—one which excluded liability—could be applied to a 'similar' type of clause: one which sought to impose onerous terms on the other party. The second is that if you read the case in full you will see that there were only two judges in the Court of Appeal. It is as well that they agreed with each other as to the outcome of the case.

The final point is that the judges did not fully agree with each other. The decision reached was the same: that condition 2 was not valid; but the reasoning employed by the judges differed greatly. Dillon LJ took a conventional line of arguing from precedents and drew a correlation between 'exclusion' clauses and 'onerous' clauses. Bingham LJ took a wider, more European, approach and looked to general notions of 'acting in good faith' to hold that the clause could not stand. This conceptual style of reasoning is very interesting; especially as there is no formula for defining 'good faith' in the English Law of Contract.

To see how academics reacted to this case we strongly recommend you to read the contrasting views seen in the following articles: Chandler and Holland, (1988) 104 LQR, 359; McLean, (1988) 47 CLJ, 172; MacDonald, (1988) LMCLQ, 294.

To see how the case has been employed in later cases, see *Circle Freight International Ltd* v *Medeast Gulf Exports Ltd* [1988] 2 Lloyd's Rep 427. This case involved two businesses which had frequently dealt with each other on standard terms. These terms, which included an exclusion clause, had never been read by the party who suffered loss. Were these terms effectively incorporated into the contract?

Conclusion

Discovering the *ratio* of a case and predicting how that *ratio* will be interpreted and applied in the future are some of the skills with which a lawyer must come to grips. There is no magic formula for acquiring these skills; they develop from practise. In turn, that practise must have some thought behind it. Reading a coaching text on your favourite sport will not, in itself, make you an Olympic athlete; and practising without analysing your play will only get you marginally further.

Perhaps the key point we wish to make with this chapter is that there is nothing resembling a template that can be placed over a decision to highlight and reveal the *ratio* of the case. Whether it is a student, a practitioner or a judge reading the case the exercise is still one of interpretation; and that form of exercise extends to persuasive precedents as well as binding ones.

REFERENCES

* Cross, R. (1991) *Precedent in English Law*, 4th Edition, Oxford: Clarendon Press.

Dworkin, R. (1987) *Law's Empire*, London: Fontana.

Goodhart, A. (1931) *Essays in Jurisprudence and the Common Law* Cambridge: Cambridge University Press.

— (1959) 'The *Ratio Decidendi* of a Case' *Modern Law Review*, vol. 22, p. 117.

Llewellyn, K. (1960) *The Bramble Bush*, Chicago: University of Chicago Press.

MacCormick, N. (1987) 'Why Cases have *Rationes* and what these are', in L. Goldstein (ed), *Precedent in Law*, Oxford: Clarendon Press.

Montrose, J. (1957) 'The *Ratio Decidendi* of a Case' *Modern Law Review,* vol. 20 p. 587.

Stone, J. (1959) 'Ratio of the *Ratio Decidendi*' *Modern Law Review*, vol. 22, p. 597.

Turow, S. (1988) *One L: what they really teach you at Harvard Law School*, London: Sceptre.

Twining, W. & Miers, D. (1991) *How to Do Things With Rules*, 3rd Edition, London: Weidenfeld and Nicolson.

Chapter Seven

The Drafting of Statutes

The aim of this chapter is to introduce you to the techniques and problems of drafting statutes. We do not intend here to turn you all into potential statutory draftsmen. Rather, by looking at the problems underlying the drafting process, we can shed some light on the process of interpretation, and the relationship between styles of drafting and techniques of interpretation.

In so doing we have divided this chapter into three parts. The first concentrates upon drafting in the Common Law world; the second will contrast this with European (Civil Law) approaches to drafting legislation, which will lead us specifically into a consideration of drafting in the context of EC law.

The Problems of Drafting in English Law

Although for constitutional purposes primary legislation is created by Parliament, the drafting of Statutes is the province of civil servants. Most of the work is done by the various Government departments together with Parliamentary draftsmen in the Office of Parliamentary Counsel. There are only about 30 of these specialist draftsmen. Their job is to translate the political objectives behind a proposed Bill into the appropriate legal form, to assess its impact upon the existing law, and to make sure that changes to the existing law are effected properly. This is a demanding task.

So, how do the draftsmen approach that task? In a major article published some years ago Francis Bennion (1978), a Parliamentary Counsel, identified nine targets of the draftsman's work; these he describes as:

(a) legal effectiveness;
(b) procedural legitimacy;
(c) timeliness;

(d) certainty;
(e) comprehensibility;
(f) acceptability;
(g) brevity;
(h) debatability;
(i) legal compatibility.

Although we can describe them as targets they are not all mutually compatible; as a result, drafting tends to be rather like negotiating a path through a maze of both political and technical legal constraints, as we shall now see.

Legal Effectiveness

Legislation starts off as a sometimes very generalised political policy which, to take effect, requires Parliament to introduce a new law, or to change the existing law in some way. The job of civil servants in the relevant Department, and ultimately of the Parliamentary Counsel is to convert that political will into a legal form without losing sight of its intended aims. As Sir Noel Hutton (1979) expressed it, the draftsman must:

(1) Master the subject matter; (2) ascertain in detail what primary and secondary effects the client wishes to secure or avoid; and (3) express the result in plain and unambiguous language.

This is not always straightforward, particularly as one Bill may reflect a range of intentions, not all of which may be equally practicable, and all of which may (or may not) be significantly amended as the Bill passes through Parliament.

Procedural Legitimacy

The Bill must comply with the formal procedures for legislation laid down by both Houses of Parliament. These procedures govern not only the process whereby legislation is debated and amended, but also the matters of form which we considered in Chapter Three. The final shape of any legislation is thus prescribed in part by influences beyond the direct control of the individual draftsman.

Timeliness

The draftsmen are constrained by the fact that they must work within the time constraints created by the Parliamentary timetable. A Government wishing to push through large quantities of reforming legislation will inevitably impose considerable pressure on the draftsmen thereby.

The difficulty is compounded by the fact that most people, including the draftsmen, are inclined to underestimate the amount of time it takes to draft an Act. The late Professor Driedger (1976:xix) cited one such incident in Canada where a government department requested a Bill within three weeks; gave public assurances that it would be ready on time, and then had to wait the 18 months it took an experienced draftsman (working full-time) to prepare the Bill!

The lack of time may mean that there is not only an increased risk of making errors under pressure, but also more generally a lack of opportunity finally to review draft legislation with a view to tidying up its structure, or simplifying its language, with the result that Bills entering Parliament may be, as one Member of Parliament has put it, 'ill-formed, ugly or premature progeny'—Rhys Williams (1987:138)

Certainty

This is probably one of the most debatable points about English drafting. It is accepted that it is desirable that a provision should normally only have one clear meaning, and that is the established target of English drafting. However, it is an ideal that is often difficult to achieve, for a number of reasons.

(a)   As we sought to show in Chapter Four the English language itself is not always a very precise tool. This problem has to be confronted by the draftsman, who is required to make his meaning as clear and certain as possible. In achieving certainty the draftsman has to bear in mind the ordinary, or if necessary, technical meaning of the term he wishes to use. He must also be aware of the approach that the courts are likely to take when approaching questions of interpretation. Let us illustrate each of these points.

For instance, using a Thesaurus, look up any word, eg *invention*. The range of synonyms is: contraption, design, device, discovery, gadget, fabrication, fantasy, fiction, illusion, creativity, ingenuity, innovation, inventiveness, originality.

But if you perform the same exercise with one of the words in the above list, *eg fabrication* then you get a further list: falsehood, fib, lie, prevarication, story, construction, manufacture, production.

A sentence in a statute that therefore reads:

*An employee must surrender to his employer any **invention** made in the course of his employment*

is unlikely to mean

*An employee must surrender to his employer any **fantasy** made in the course of his employment*

but it could mean

An employee must surrender to his employer any *fabrication* made in the course of his employment

or

An employee must surrender to his employer any *design* made in the course of his employment

A design and a fabrication are not, however, the same thing, even accepting that 'fabrication' does not mean 'lie' or 'fib' in this context. 'Design' and 'fabrication' for instance, would have a different meaning in the fashion industry from that in the computer industry when applied to any definition of 'invention'. Clearly, the context of the word in the statute and the problem before the court must affect the meaning and accuracy of the application of the word.

Anticipating the reaction of the courts is not always easy. The word, or wording, does not even have to be complicated to cause problems. The statute can be about a very simple topic, and yet lead to many odd cases. Consider, as an example, the Wills Act 1837, s. 9. This section originally stated that the signature to a will must appear at *'the foot or end'* of the will. But did this mean the physical positioning at the end of a document, or that the signature was the last thing written on the will, ie that the signature could appear anywhere as long as, in terms of time, it came at the end of making the will? Signatures appeared everywhere on wills because people always manage to do strange things. Some judges were lenient as to the physical positioning of the signatures; others were not. In 1852 the Act had to be amended to read that the signature should come:

At or after, or following, or under, or beside, or opposite to the end of the will, that it shall be apparent on the face of the will that the Testator intended to give effect to the will.

The wording to this section was changed again in 1982, by the Administration of Justice Act of that year. It became:

No will shall be valid unless:
. . . it appears that the testator intended by his signature to give effect to the will . . .

This removed any reference to the position of the signature, so that should have resolved all the earlier problems. Nevertheless, the case of *Wood* v *Smith* shows that, even with the amended wording, the judges can still manage to disagree about the effect of the section. In this case the deceased had signed his will at the top, then written out the various bequests, and finally had it signed by his witnesses. At first instance, the High Court held that it was not a valid will (see *The Times*, 10 July 1990). It was the natural construction of the words of the Act that the maker should sign the will after making the various dispositions, not before. There has to be something in the nature of a disposition before a will exists and can be signed. The Court of Appeal took a rather different view of the issue—see [1992] 3 All ER 556. It decided that a signature did *not* have to be appended after the dispositive provisions of the will had been written, provided that the writing of the will and its signing by the testator constituted 'one operation' (a concept which is barely defined by the courts). So, on this point the High Court was overruled, since there was no doubt on the facts that the testator had completed his will as a single operation. In its final version *Wood* v *Smith* thus appears to have done what the legislation intended, and, for the majority of cases, the decision shifts the court's focus away from the position of the signature, and on to the issue of testamentary intent. Ironically, however, it is certain that the Court of Appeal, by introducing the extraordinarily vague 'one operation' criterion, has relocated rather than resolved some of the basic problems of determining that a will is validly signed. The case thus provides a good example of how case law actually creates litigation about statutory criteria through attempts to clarify or define the ambit of the legislation.

(b)   The desire for certainty frequently leads to undue verbosity, precisely because the drafter is seeking to delineate meaning to such a high degree. That is why we find examples of such extremely dense prose as:

If a person is more than 5 years below pensionable age on the qualifying date in any period of interruption of employment then, subject to the following provisions of this section, in respect of every day of that period in respect of which he is entitled to an invalidity pension, he shall also be entitled to an invalidity allowance at the appropriate weekly rate specified in relation thereto in Schedule 4, Part I, paragraph 3; and 'the qualifying date' means the first day in that period (whether before the coming into force of this section or later) which is a day of incapacity for work or such earlier day as may be prescribed. (Social Security Act 1975, s. 16(1).)

Not exactly light reading is it? If we look at what makes it so difficult, we can see a number of factors. One is the cross-referencing to other technical issues, both implicit in the use of terms such as 'pensionable age' or 'relevant amount', which are defined elsewhere in the Act, and explicitly in the reference to Schedule 4. A second is the actual length of the sentence, and the number of dependent clauses it contains. By the time we reach the end there is a real risk that we will have forgotten what the subsection first set out to do (ie, define entitlement to invalidity allowance). The third factor is the use of terms which would be redundant in ordinary usage, but are used to emphasise the interrelationship between different parts of an Act. Here there are two such examples in the phrases 'subject to the following provisions of this section' (could we not work that out by reading it?) and 'specified in relation thereto' (if it was not so specified, why mention it in the first place?)

The poor quality drafting of s. 16 has been acknowledged, and when

that provision was consolidated into the Social Security Contributions and
Benefits Act 1992, it was amended. Section 34 of the 1992 Act duly reads:

> *(1) If a person is more than 5 years below pensionable age on the qualifying
> date in any period of interruption of employment then, subject to the
> following provisions of this section, in respect of every day of that period
> in respect of which he is entitled to an invalidity pension, he shall also
> be entitled to an invalidity allowance at the appropriate weekly rate specified
> in Schedule 4, Part I, paragraph 3.*
>
> *(2) In this section 'the qualifying date' means the first day in the period
> of interruption of employment (whether that day falls before the coming
> into force of this section or later) which is a day of incapacity for work
> or such earlier day as may be prescribed.*

See if you can identify the main changes that have been made. Do they
significantly increase the intelligibility of the section? Are there any other
textual changes you would want to make?

(c)   Sometimes it may happen that a provision is left deliberately vague.
As Bennion points out this may well happen where the framers of the
Act are themselves uncertain of how to handle it.

Comprehensibility

Despite what we have just said, draftsmen do aim for legislation that is
understandable. However, in so doing they tend to have a specialist audience
in mind, in that legislation is designed to be read first and foremost by
lawyers. Ideally it should also be comprehensible to Members of Parliament,
who may not share the same degree of expertise as a legal audience. How
effectively it reaches the latter audience is certainly debatable (eg, Rhys
Williams, 1987:140). What is beyond doubt is that legislation is not drafted
for lay people to read and understand with ease.

Comprehension also implies some degree of clarity and logical structure.
We have already illustrated how linguistic problems affect clarity. However
clarity can also be influenced by the overall structure of an Act, particularly
in the way it is broken down into composite parts and sections. It is
considered good practice that draftsmen should start with matters of general
principle, before getting buried in consequential detail. Yet this principle
seems to be frequently overlooked. Sir William Dale, one of the sterner
critics of English drafting, has cited a number of examples of poor
arrangement in an article published some 12 years ago. One of those Acts,
the Unfair Contract Terms Act 1977 (UCTA), was briefly introduced in
Chapter Three. According to Dale (1981:148–9) UCTA is drafted quite
illogically. Section 1 of the Act is purely a definition section, which makes
no sense at all until we have read the rest of the Act. The key provisions,
regarding exclusion and exemption of liability, are relegated to ss. 2 and
3 (though even then s. 2 commences with excluding liability in negligence,
rather than contract). This is particularly curious given that the Act was

based upon a draft Bill proposed by the Law Commission, which *began*, more logically, with exemption clauses in contract.

Even where definitions do not dominate the substantive provisions, they can still make legislation more difficult to follow by what Dale (1977:331) calls 'centrifugence', which involves 'a flight from the centre [the section under consideration] to definition and interpretation clauses' often located in very different parts of the Act. As he concludes: 'an English statute often cannot be read—it must be perambulated.' (1981:149).

Acceptability

The language of legislation has to be 'acceptable'. By this Bennion means that it must obey the rules traditionally prescribed. These were essentially laid down in the latter half of the last century, at the time the Office of Parliamentary Counsel was created, which means that the language used is traditional (if not archaic) with a very flat prose style. Continued reliance on such language cannot be blamed solely on the Counsel themselves, but also upon those they serve. Bennion describes the difficulty faced by a draftsman who seeks to break the mould. He once drew considerable criticism from within the House of Commons for using the phrase 'tried his best' rather than the more conventional 'used his best endeavours'.

Brevity

Draftsmen are also encouraged to be as brief as possible. Brevity, however, is a relative term, and the desire for brevity can conflict both with the demand for an acceptable style, and the aim of certainty. As we shall argue below, in terms of brevity, there is little comparison between most English and continental drafting. The latter seems frequently to achieve similar ends with notably less verbiage. One cannot but feel that in the competition between brevity and tradition, it is brevity which is inevitably the loser.

Debatability

Legislation should ideally be framed in such a way that the general principles are debatable in Parliament. This requires Counsel to consider carefully both the complexity and even the order of clauses. However, as Bennion again points out, the draftsman may be subject to political pressures in this respect. If the government wishes to limit debate and make amendment difficult, it can do so by seeking to impose a more complex structure on the Bill. (This is, of course, in addition to its procedural power to restrict the time for debate once a Bill enters Parliament—which is a more significant, though less subtle, mechanism for limiting effective opposition to legislation than drafting devices.)

Legal Compatibility

The draftsman must finally work out how the proposals fit in with the existing law. This apparently simple statement disguises a number of difficulties.

First, the draftsman needs to know what the existing law actually says. In that respect, the briefings from the instructing department are often an essential starting point, but any draftsman would then engage in research to determine not just what the law says but *how* it says it. As a general principle, a draftsman ought to attempt to use the same form of wording as appears in other legislation covering the same subject matter. With old or already complex legislation, this principle may act as a further constraint on the draftsman, as he may be obliged to import the same archaic terminology, or complex concepts into the amending Act

Note also that Parliamentary Counsel do not generally have extensive precedents to guide them, so how far Counsel can and will spend time searching out a model from earlier legislation may well depend upon the time or other pressures upon them.

Secondly, the draftsman should also indicate the manner and extent to which existing legislation is amended by the proposed Bill. This not only requires further, sometimes difficult, research, but also some important questions of drafting style.

Amendments may be either **textual** or **non-textual**. The difference between them is quite significant. A textual amendment is one which amends legislation by making precise changes to the wording of the earlier text by a process of substitution. A non-textual amendment does not replace one set of words with another, or just add a new phrase to the end of a section. Instead, it will normally introduce a new concept or point of interpretation to the existing text, so that both have to be read together.

The Renton Committee (1975) gave examples of both types drawn from the Town and Country Planning Act 1968. This made two amendments to s. 149 of the Town and Country Planning Act 1962. The first of these, by s. 37(3), is non-textual. It reads:

> *For a person to be treated under section 149(1) or (3) of the principle Act (definitions for purposes of blight notice provisions) as owner-occupier or resident owner-occupier of a hereditament, his occupation thereof at a relevant time or during a relevant period, if not occupation of the whole of the hereditament, must be, or as the case may be, have been occupation of a substantial part of it.*

The second, effected by s. 38 and sch. 4 of the 1968 Act, is textual. It states:

> *Section 149*
> *In subsection (1)(a), (1)(b), (3)(a) and (3)(b), for the words 'the whole or part' (wherever occurring) there shall be substituted the words 'the whole or a substantial part'.*

Of course, neither form of amendment makes a great deal of sense when read in isolation, both need to be read in the context of the Act they amend. A non-textual amendment is probably less incomprehensible, because it is at least drafted in a narrative style, and usually offers a little explanation of how it affects the principal statute (a 'hereditament', by the way, is another term for land or a house).

Textual amendments are usually wholly meaningless out of context, but they do have the virtue of simplicity. It is immediately clear on comparing the principal and amending Acts what effect the one has upon the other. This may not be the case with non-textual amendments, whose effects may be far more debatable. It is thus argued that generally textual amendment is to be preferred, though not all amendments are equally susceptible to the textual form. Even where textual amendments are used, the result can be extremely difficult to decipher where the provisions of the principal Act have received multiple amendments. This is particularly so as amended Acts are not re-issued (with the exception of *Statutes in Force)* to take amendments into account. As a result, a lot of a lawyer's time can be taken up working out precisely what an amended Act says.

Thirdly, an increasing problem is one of ensuring compatability with EC law. The drafting complexities created by Community membership are twofold. First there is a general obligation on member states to avoid legislating in contravention of Community law. This adds a substantial body of rules to the existing law, which should be considered when domestic legislation is being proposed. Second, there is the further problem of implementing Community directives. Implementation involves expressly translating a piece of community legislation into the form of domestic law. Ideally, it should be achieved without misinterpreting the substance of the original legislative Act. The difference in styles between Community and UK or Irish legislation may make this problem more acute in Britain and the Republic of Ireland than elsewhere in the EC. The difference in style is a point to which we shall return in more detail later in this chapter.

European Legislative Drafting

The Drafting Process

The English style of drafting is not universal. It can be directly contrasted with the somewhat different techniques adopted in the Civilian systems of continental Europe, which have also come to dominate the form of European Community law.

You will recall that in Chapter One we made the point that the great majority of Civilian systems are built upon principles of codified law. That emphasis on codification has, of course, had an impact on the whole legal process, not just on the drafting of legislation. For that reason, before we focus on the specifics of drafting technique, it is worth thinking about the general characteristics of codified as opposed to uncodified law. We shall focus on five key features.

Coherence: one of the problems with the Common Law, it is said, is that it lacks coherence. It is fragmentary and dispersed through a variety of sources, with negative consequences for both the clarity and certainty of the law. Restatement in a codified form potentially overcomes this problem, by bringing the law together within a single document or coherent set of documents.

Comprehensiveness: to a greater or lesser extent, codes claim to be complete restatements of the area of law to which they apply. This is not always easy to achieve, and may require a degree of complexity that is ultimately undesirable—an extreme example of such was the *Allgemeines Landrecht* promulgated in Prussia in 1794 which ran to an unmanageable 17,000 articles. The extent to which codes are complete statements depends on a variety of factors; most notably the extent to which the code has been updated by subsequent codified and uncodified legislation. Codes are difficult to replace in their entirety (for one thing it is an extremely lengthy legislative process), and attempts to dismantle an established Code may be politically sensitive. For example, the revolutionary roots of the French Civil Code give it a 'sanctity' which would make its repeal an extremely emotive issue. Such problems encourage a policy of tinkering, by amending the 'outdated' parts by new legislation. Such amendments may take their place either as a textual amendment to the Code itself, or as a separate legislative act, or in the introduction of whole new codes to deal with issues beyond the original schema. Inevitably this results in a reduction of the supposed simplicity and comprehensiveness that the original codification process sought to achieve, though supporters suggest that the overall effect can still be more coherent than an uncodified approach.

Knowledgeability: in theory, codification has been seen as a means of democratising law by extending knowledge of the law to the ordinary citizen and curbing the power of the judiciary—the original French Civil Code, the *Code Napoleon*, is one example of codifying law passed with this aim in view. The extent to which the Common Law lacks knowledgeability is a long-standing criticism. Jeremy Bentham (1748–1832), one of the most influential English members of the codification movement, pointed to this in his famous statement that the Common Law was 'dog law': the pragmatic, case by case development of the Common Law meant that people were punished for their actions *ex post facto*, as you would beat a dog only after it had misbehaved. (For further discussion of Bentham and the movement for codification in nineteenth-century England, see Lobban, 1991.) However, a lack of knowledgeability is not a characteristic unique to the Common Law. As the range of human activities demanding regulation has expanded, knowledgeability has been the chief victim, and is one attribute that is not widely found in modern codified systems, other than as an idealised notion of how the law ought to be.

Clarity: knowledgeability and clarity are obviously related concepts, since clarity of language and exposition can greatly influence the knowledgeability of the law. But clarity is also a relative concept; some codes may seek to achieve a very high degree of brevity and simplicity in their formulation, while others may settle for a more technical level of clarity. However, one aim of codification has always been the clarification of law by the removal of what Vanderlinden (1967) calls (to paraphrase) obscurity, doubt, and ambiguity in the formulation of legal rules. Most Common Law draftsmen would share those aims. They are not easily achieved, and demand a high-quality drafting process. It is possible to argue that, in many instances, both Common and Civil Law systems have been tried and found wanting so far as clarity is concerned—see the discussion later in this chapter.

The absence of contradiction: The process of *redaction,* of converting uncodified law to a codified form, gives the lawmaker an opportunity to resolve contradictions which may be present in uncodified law—eg, in conflicting customary or case law. On the positive side, it is thereby possible to create greater certainty, but it may involve the lawmaker in a more or less subjective choice of one formulation of a rule over another. This part of the codifying process will often prove controversial. Problems of this sort have arisen in the recent attempts to produce a Draft Criminal Code for England (see de Búrca & Gardner, 1990).

As the preceding discussion suggests, the benefits of codification are somewhat debatable. Before you make up your own mind, let us consider how these general principles (and problems) come to be reflected in the technicalities of continental drafting.

Once again, generalisation is a little difficult. Most European states have laws that are not fully codified; in Spain, for example, the Civil Code *(Código Civil)* is often of only subsidiary force in some of the regions where the *Fueros,* or local law can still hold greater sway. Similarly, some states have a federal system, or other form of subsidiary legislature capable of legislating in its own right—for example, the codification of the *fueros* by some Spanish regional governments; or the legislative activities of the German *Länder.* The following comments are only really exemplary of the more 'conventional' systems of codified national laws.

The drafting process in many European countries is, in some senses, a less specialised activity than in England. The initial drafting is usually completed solely by lawyers within the relevant ministries, or else by external commissions set up both to review a problematic issue and propose a draft law upon it. The latter, of course, has its analogy with the English use of Royal Commissions or bodies like the Criminal Law Revision Committee, though in the European context the draft proposal seems less likely to be significantly tampered with than is the case in England.

After the initial drafting, the proposal will be revised. In France, this is the function of the *Conseil d'État,*—a consultative as well as judicial body—which is empowered to propose detailed changes to the legislation, and though the government is not obliged to follow that advice, it generally does so (see Ducamin, 1981). A similar system exists in Italy and in the Netherlands, while in Germany that function is performed by the Ministry of Justice. In all these countries it is only after this first revision by legal experts that further revision before Parliament takes place—a significant variation on the British pattern of legislating.

In the EC itself, there is again no equivalent of the Parliamentary Counsel, with the actual drafting normally being undertaken by staff within the European Commission—one of the key law-making institutions of the Community. This is normally followed by a detailed consultation period involving committees of experts appointed from within the member states, and the Legal Service of the Commission, which must ultimately approve the draft before it goes before the Commission itself. Once approved, the proposal is set before the Council of Ministers (the other body with direct law-making power); it may sometimes be placed simultaneously before the European Parliament. From there, the process becomes extremely complex, with procedures depending upon the nature of the legislation and the criteria laid down for its revision and implementation. In most cases, consultation with Parliament is required before the Council can adopt the proposal, though this is not always necessary; in other cases, under the Single European Act, the Parliament has been given greater power to propose amendments to legislation, though the Council retains the last word. Only when legislation has finally been adopted by the Council is it signed by the President and thus capable of having the force of law. The roles of these institutions in the legal process will be discussed further in Chapter Ten.

The Style of Drafting

In most codified systems much of the basic legal structure is now firmly established, and drafting styles broadly reflect the forms adopted by the eighteenth or nineteenth century authors of their codes. To a lawyer trained in any other tradition, English legislation comes as something of a shock; as a Bulgarian commentator has suggested:

> It is a challenging and arduous task to find one's way through the intricacies of English law when, as a translator, or professionally as a continental lawyer, one has to acquire a working knowledge of this uncommon law.' (Dodova, 1989:69)

In this section we shall therefore try to identify the key distinguishing features of Civilian forms of drafting, then look at some of the specific drafting issues surrounding EC law.

Structure: We have already said that one of the arguable failings of English drafting is its poor arrangement—for example, the lack of rational distinction between points of principal and of detail, or its tendency towards centrifugence. By comparison, Civilian law often shows a far greater concern to establish a rational overall structure. One of the clearest examples of this is the German Civil Code—*Bürgerliches Gesetzbuch* (BGB).

The BGB consists of five books and approaching 2,500 paragraphs. The five books reflect the main conceptual divisions of the German Civil Law, which tend to follow the classical 'institutional' divisions of the French Civil Code. Thus, Book One is the General Part; Book Two covers the Law of Obligations; Book Three, Property; Book Four is on Family Law and Book Five contains the Law of Succession. The provision of a General Part carries an explicit message about the purpose of those provisions. It denotes a high degree of conceptual abstraction, whereby the rules of Book One are of widespread application and are not tied to a specific institution.

This movement *from the general to the particular* is a common feature of codified laws and greatly aids interpretation by allowing us to establish general rules clearly before we look for exceptions. Thus, the General Part of the BGB contains the rules governing the legal personality of individuals and corporations; and more specific principles governing, eg, avoidance powers in cases where legal intent is lacking; or provisions concerning the capacity of parties to act (ie, by reason of age, mental capacity, etc.). Such a structure can also help us in interpreting the legislative purpose behind particular rules, and also sometimes ease the process of actually *finding* specific principles (though some commentators would argue that some divisions within the BGB are so abstract that it is not as easy to use as many later codes). The structure of the BGB can be contrasted with English law, where often general rules either do not exist, or lack a unified legislative source, or appear illogically ordered within the Act (eg UCTA as above).

Let us take the capacity of minors as an example. In German law the basic principle is expressed by para. 1 of the BGB, which states '[t]he legal capacity of a human being begins at the time of his birth.' This is of course somewhat qualified by other provisions, which will appear in the relevant Book, so, for example, para. 1893 enables a child in the womb to acquire certain inheritance rights and para. 104 qualifies the contractual capacity to act of children under eighteen. So, even in such a codified system, provisions on capacity may be somewhat scattered. By comparison, in English Law, the age of full legal capacity is defined as 18 by the Family Law Reform Act 1969; though there are many situations where a young person has some capacity well below that age. For example, the contractual capacity of children is then separately governed by the Minors' Contracts Act 1987, while the various inheritance rights of a minor are governed chiefly by provisions in the Law of Property Act 1925, the Administration of Estates Act 1925 and the Inheritance (Provision for Family and Dependents) Act 1975. This seems an even more disparate manner of dealing with essentially the same problems.

Linguistic simplicity: Here, there is perhaps much greater practical variation in style with continental systems. The Swiss Civil Code of 1907 and the original Napoleonic Code of France are frequently cited as good examples of legislative simplicity, whereby principles are expressed in clear, naturalistic language. This ideal is not always sought, let alone achieved, even within a codified system. The BGB, for example, is noted for its technical language, though it still maintains a high degree of clarity for all that, and some of the later French Codes are similarly of greater complexity than the *Code Napoleon*—perhaps not least because they are dealing with modern legal phenomena such as social security rights, which are not as amenable as some areas of law to (relatively) simple exposition.

Brevity: Connected with our second point, we can often see in Civilian legislation an attempt to keep legal statements brief and to the point. English proponents of the 'European approach' to drafting often cite this as a key difference between English and continental styles (eg, Dale, 1981).

Both these differences can be seen more clearly by comparing the following extracts from the Sale of Goods Act 1979 and the French Civil Code (taken from Smith, 1980).

Sale of Goods Act	French Civil Code
41 (1) Subject to the provisions of this Act the unpaid seller of goods who is in possession of them is entitled to retain possession of them until payment or tender of the price in the following cases, namely:	1612. The seller is not bound to deliver the property if the buyer does not pay the price for it, unless the seller has granted him time for payment.
(a) where the goods have been sold without any stipulation as to credit;	1613. He shall also have no duty of delivery, even if he shall have granted time for payment, if after the sale the buyer has become bankrupt or insolvent so that the seller is in imminent danger of losing the price, unless the buyer gives him security for payment on the due date.
(b) where the goods have been sold on credit, but the term of credit has expired;	
(c) where the buyer becomes insolvent.	
(2) The seller may exercise his right of lien notwithstanding that he is in possession of the goods as agent or bailee.	

A fairly quick scan of the wording tells us that each of these provisions is doing essentially the same thing: defining the rights of an unpaid seller in respect of both cash and credit sales. There are comparatively few differences in terms of content, the main exception being that the Code contains no equivalent to subsection (2) of the Act.

The French text is obviously simpler, even though Article 1613 is rather verbose by the standards of the Civil Code. So, what is it about the Code which makes it seem so much more approachable than the Act?

First, it is a question of the language used—technical terms like 'lien' and 'bailee' are notable for their absence in the French text. Also, European drafting techniques place less emphasis on explicit definition. This reflects a general determination to use ordinary words in an ordinary way wherever possible. An absence of lengthy definitions can substantially simplify and shorten legislation. It is hardly surprising, therefore, that one common difference that has been much commented upon is the relative length of English and continental legislation. Dale provides a graphic example by a comparison of various national copyright laws. He concludes:

All these copyright laws give effect to common international obligations, and . . . are much the same in substance. The United Kingdom Act is twice as long as the German, more than three times as long as the French, and five times as long as the Swedish. (1981:145)

(Note also that this article helpfully lays out a number of provisions from each system, and thus provides a more extensive example of drafting styles than we have room for here.)

English lawyers argue that a lack of definition actually creates uncertainty. As we have seen, certainty has always been the great virtue claimed by the English for their legislation. But if it is so certain, why do our courts spend so many hours arguing over questions of construction? In part, the answer to that has been given in Chapter Four—it is a question of shades of meaning and, to that extent, exactly the same problems arise in Europe (see also Chapter Eight). However, one can argue that the English make a further rod for their own backs by attempting to produce lengthy and 'exhaustive' definitions, both of specific words and of situations in which the Act is to apply. As Sir William Dale has long argued, however, definition does not make for certainty; his own position (which we support) is to agree with the Italian jurist Calamandrei that 'The statutes cannot foresee all the cases that reality, much richer than the most fervid imagination, brings before the judge' (1981:159). In other words definition can often cause, as much as alleviate, uncertainty by creating doubt as to whether certain fact-situations are covered.

Secondly, approachability is also a matter of the form into which those words are put. The two Articles cited represent a more 'normal' narrative form than the sections of the 1979 Act. English legislation does not reflect the way people talk or think. We do not normally have to break concepts down into highly structured, itemised, lists. Why do we do it for legislation? The answer seems to lie in the density of the language used. The verbosity of English statutes is a throwback to the style of drafting which existed prior to the 1860s. Then sections were very densely written, with minimal punctuation (resulting in sentences that could run to many lines), and virtually no attempt to separate criteria within sections. Compared with this the highly technical structure of modern English statutes provides far more clarity, but the form of language is not wholly dissimilar.

The problems of drafting become more apparent when you try to draft a document yourself.

Exercise 13: The minimum speed limit

In this exercise you are a Parliamentary draftsman appointed to deal with the problems of slow-moving traffic. Assume that you have been instructed to draft legislation which will introduce a 'minimum speed limit' in country areas and on motorways. The purpose of this exercise is:

(a)   to explore the style of wording you use—how many clauses; how concise the wording;

(b)   to see how difficult it is to anticipate all the possible situations that may occur.

Answer: There is of course no single right answer to this problem. Instead here are a few situations which we think your legislation should allow for. Glancing through them you may feel your drafting covers them, more or less. Our experience is that it is a sobering (or exasperating) exercise to get a friend to compare the situations with your piece of draftsmanship. The chances are that at one stage (at least) you will find yourself saying: 'Yes, but I meant it to cover that . . .' or 'Of course it covers that'. But does it?

Consider whether your legislation covers:

Stopping at junctions or traffic lights; stopping at hazards such as temporary roadworks; breakdowns; having to slow down because of moving hazards such as tractors; separate criteria for tractors and other agricultural vehicles—if so, how do you define an agricultural vehicle; for that matter, how did you define 'vehicle'; did you have the same speed limits for different roads eg the B3212, the A4018 and the M5; did weather conditions come into the definition, such as fog or bad visibility?

(c)   Now, without necessarily re-drafting your version, think how your answer might differ if you were drafting this in a European style.

Would you want the same degree of definition, eg, of concepts such as 'vehicle'? How easy is it to find a dividing line between principle and detail—

what could you safely leave to the court? Is your answer 'Of course it
covers that' now more valid?

Before we jump to the conclusion that Civilian drafting styles are *always*
superior, we should remember that Civilian lawyers today are facing many
of the same legislative problems as their English counterparts. As Jean-
Eric Schoettl, a member of the French *Conseil d'État* explains:

> In France the situation is far from being satisfactory . . . the main reasons
> for this are well known. The first is the rapidity with which changes
> take place under the pressure of events, or under the imperious pressure
> of political will. We can be very hasty in the way we prepare provisions.
> They are superimposed one on another without clearly fitting with
> previous law. The chief draftsman at the Ministry of the Interior, M.
> Latournerie, calls this 'panic' legislation.
>
> The second reason is the fact that legal language is no longer reserved
> for a small circle of people brought up in the same nursery. All branches
> of human activity are involved. Technical government departments,
> independent administrative authorities, local authorities, trade unions,
> employers—all these people take a part in drafting, and they have not
> necessarily had the same intellectual preparations. They come to law
> in different ways, and they have very different concerns. The result of
> this is what M. Latournerie calls 'legal babel'—the law is expressed in
> a multitude of dialects. (Dale, 1986:36)

Plus ça change, plus c'est la même chose?

The Style of Community Legislation

Not surprisingly, the structure of EC legislation more closely reflects Civil
as opposed to Common Law style. For example the important equal pay
Directive 75/117 states in Article 1:

> *The principle of equal pay for men and women outlined in Article 119
> of the Treaty, hereinafter called 'principle of equal pay', means, for the
> same work or for work to which equal value is attributed, the elimination
> of all discrimination on grounds of sex with regard to all aspects and
> conditions of remuneration.*
>
> *In particular, where a job classification system is used for determining
> pay, it must be based on the same criteria for men and women and so
> drawn up as to exclude any discrimination on grounds of sex.*

Again, it is apparent that the Article concentrates heavily upon general
principle. The Directive as a whole is also silent on technical detail, such
as the matter of proof which creates some of the greatest difficulties in
this area (particularly the question as to *how* we evaluate 'work of equal

value'). This is the kind of detail that is left to the courts to fill in—see on this point case 61/81 *European Commission* v *United Kingdom* [1982] ECR 2601 and case 237/85 *Rummler* v *Dato-Druck GmbH* [1987] 3 CMLR 127.

This lack of technical detail is not a consistent feature of all EC legislation; some Directives and Regulations can be highly detailed and technical *where the subject matter so requires*—for example, Directive 82/501 on health and safety at work, which lays down a fairly complex notification scheme for certain hazardous industries. But even there the layout and language of the provisions is less dense than much English legislation.

There are two further, special, dimensions to EC law which make questions of drafting/interpretation rather interesting.

First, there is a problem of language. In respect of the Treaties, 'authentic' (ie. fully official) versions do not exist in all Community languages. The European Coal and Steel Community Treaty has only the original French version as authentic; the Treaty of Rome is authentic in German, French, Italian and Dutch, though the Treaty of Accession does, of course, have an authentic English version. Other EC legislation has to be translated from the language in which it was originally drafted (which may be any of the Community languages, depending upon the preference of the team engaged in drafting) into all Community languages. In both cases, this can create an element of doubt. Can we be sure that translation effectively carries the legislative intent of an act across the linguistic divide?

This is not solely a problem within the EC, but afflicts any state where legislation is enacted in more than one language. Canada provides a good comparative example, where, since 1982, all legislation has been enacted in both English and French. McEvoy (1986) illustrates the problem by reference to s. 8 of the Canadian Charter of Rights and Freedoms, which reads:

Everyone has the right to be secure against unreasonable search or seizure.

Chacun a droit à la protection contre les fouilles, les perquisitions ou les saises abusives.

One assumes that the legislature intended these to be equivalent provisions. Certainly, both cover seizures (*'les saises'* in French) and searches, though the French is actually more precise than the English as *'les fouilles'* and *'les perquisitions'* clearly cover both searches of persons and property. The difficulty arises in the apparent equation of 'unreasonable' and *'abusive'*. *Abusive* in French denotes something which is excessive or unauthorised. As McEvoy argues, therefore, 'it is not a true cognate' (1986:158) of the English 'unreasonable'; though there is clearly an area in which the terms overlap (something which is excessive is surely unreasonable), the fit is not exact: is something unreasonable necessarily unauthorised? This may seem to be a (semantic) storm in a teacup, and may be a lesser problem in countries where the lawyers are less inclined towards literalism than the Common Law orientated Canadians. Even so, as McEvoy shows, there is a case for saying that courts dealing with bilingual enactments should not just *assume* linguistic equivalence.

In the EC, this seems to have been acknowledged. There are many cases where the Court's attention has been drawn to linguistic differences as part of the interpretative process; see, eg, case C–372/88 *Milk Marketing Board* v *Cricket St Thomas Estate* [1990] 2 CMLR 800 (a comparison of French and German versions of the Treaty with the English version). Sometimes the nuances may be so fine as to make no practical difference in the context; though occasionally the Court of Justice has found conflicting versions, and been forced to adopt a version which either seems to accord with the majority of the texts, or with the presumed legislative intent. For example, in case 13/61 *de Geus* v *Bosch* [1962] ECR 45, the Court was faced with a provision in the Treaty of Rome where all four authentic texts conveyed a different meaning. Advocate General Lagrange submitted that the Court was free to decide the issue according to the spirit of the text. Certainly no single language is treated as having primacy in interpretation.

Secondly, a further problem in EC law arises out of the use of Directives. We mentioned in Chapter One that a Directive only becomes fully effective in a member state once implemented by domestic law. In the United Kingdom alone, implementation requires a major transition of style. There is as yet little evidence that the Westminster draftsmen are adopting different stylistic techniques in respect of EC-based as opposed to 'home-grown' legislation. So, how effectively can a broadly drafted Directive be converted into the form and language of a British Act or Statutory Instrument?

An interesting example of the problem arises with the Consumer Protection Act 1987. This was passed in line with the United Kingdom's obligations under the Product Liability Directive 85/373.

Section 4(1)(e) of the Act contains what is called the 'development risks defence'. This enables manufacturers of products to escape liability if they can prove that the defect in their product was not discoverable, considering the state of scientific or technical knowledge at the time. Let us now use this to create another Exercise:

Exercise 14: The Consumer Protection Act—a defective product?

The wording used by the Act states:

> *In any civil proceedings by virtue of this part against any person in respect of a defect in a product it shall be a defence for him to show that the state of scientific and technical knowledge at the relevant time was not such that a producer of products of the same description as the product in question might be expected to have discovered the defect if it had existed in his products, while they were under his control.*

The Directive, on which this was based, stated at Article 7(e):

> ... *the producer shall not be liable* ... *if he proves that the state of scientific and technical knowledge at the time when he put his product into circulation was not such as to enable the existence of the defect to be discovered.*

Consider:

(a)   Do the Act and the Directive have the same effect?

Answer: Ignoring the excess baggage in s. 4(1)(e), the Act certainly provides a development risks defence, however, the last three lines are not simply ineffective verbiage. They bring in a second element to the defence that does not appear in the Directive, so that, under UK law, the producer of a defective product can rely not only upon evidence which shows that the development risk was not discoverable, but that it was, objectively speaking, of a sort which a manufacturer would not have *expected to have discovered.* Now consider

(b)   Which of the Act or Directive better protects consumers?

Answer: On a strict interpretation, the answer has to be the Directive. It is surely easier for the manufacturer to prove that no equivalent producer could have discovered the defect, than to prove that *no one* could have discovered it.

In this instance, it is debatable as to how far the difference between the Directive and the Act is reflective simply of drafting styles, or of an underlying political argument as well. The European Commission has argued that the Act does not meet the requirements of the Directive in this respect. The UK Government seems adamant that it does. As a result there is much potential uncertainty about the scope of the UK development risks defence. That uncertainty is complicated by the fact that s. 1(1) of the 1987 Act requires *(inter alia)* s. 4 to be construed so as to comply with the Product Liability Directive. Whether the UK courts will be willing to use s. 1(1) to override what appears to be the inconsistent provision of s. 4(1)(e) remains to be seen.

Conclusion

Perfecting any legislation is a very difficult task. The balancing of clarity, generality, conciseness, precision, and the avoidance of excess verbiage to achieve a satisfactory statute requires a great deal of skill. Further, certain words are, as we saw in Chapter Four, probably beyond universally applicable definition—words such as 'reasonable' or 'practicable'.

Which of the English and European styles is ultimately the more effective? In some cases that is possibly debatable, but it would be a hardened Anglophile who would support the case of English drafting without hesitation.

In terms of structure, the way in which an English Act is put together can, at best, aid interpretation by clarifying the relative degree of dependency that sections, sub-sections and paragraphs have on each other. Sometimes, however, the structure imposed by the English draftsman can seemingly obscure that very same relationship. Much depends upon the quality of the drafting, which as we have seen may be affected by a number of variables.

In terms of the detailed language used, there seems to be much in English legislation that is redundant, or redolent of a formalised language that is largely unrecognisable to the majority of the community. The greater emphasis on detail and definition in English legislation certainly does not make legislation any more litigation-proof. One suspects that what it does do is to shift the level of judicial debate from a consideration of the purpose and effect of legislation, to a dispute over semantic detail. The reasons for this can be briefly explained.

Once a question of interpretation arises, European judges are normally given substantial discretionary powers. For example, Article 1 of the Swiss Civil Code entitles the judge, in the absence of clear statutory authority, to decide an issue 'in accordance with the rule he would establish as legislator'. In this sense, Civilian systems imply a partnership between Parliament and court, whereby the latter is there (to paraphrase Lord Denning) 'to fill the gaps and iron out the creases' left by the former. It is often expressed as a power to interpret legislation according to its objectives, or the intention of its authors. This power may be explicit in the legislation itself, or in the jurisprudence of the court—see eg, para. 133 of the BGB; also the decision of the Court of Justice of the European Community in case 22/70 *European Commission* v *Council* of the *European Community* [1971] ECR 263.

In England judges also seek to implement the will of Parliament. But unlike the codified approach seen on the Continent, English judges have not (at least until recently) shown much inclination to claim extensive powers to look at the general purpose of the Act. For the most part they will therefore adhere to the plain meaning of the words, so far as that proves possible. The way in which they go about these tasks forms the subject of the next chapter.

REFERENCES

* Bennion, F. (1978) 'Statute Law Obscurity and the Drafting Parameters' *British Journal of Law and Society*, vol. 5, p. 235.

Dale, W. (1977) *Legislative Drafting—A New Approach*, London: Butterworths.

* Dale, W. (1981) 'Statutory Reform: The Draftsman and The Judge' *International and Comparative Law Quarterly*, vol. 30, p. 141.

Dale, W. (ed.) (1986) *British and French Statutory Drafting*, London: Institute of Advanced Legal Studies.

de Búrca, G. & Gardner, S. (1990) 'The Codification of the Criminal Law' *Oxford Journal of Legal Studies*, vol. 10, p. 559.

* Dodova, L. (1989) 'A Translator Looks at English Law' *Statute Law Review*, p. 69.

Driedger, E. (1976) *The Composition of Legislation*, 2nd Edition, Ottawa: Department of Justice.

Ducamin, B. (1981) 'The Role of the *Conseil d'Etat* in Drafting Legislation' *International and Comparative Law Quarterly*, vol. 30, p. 882.

Hutton, N. (1979) 'Legislative Drafting in the United Kingdom' *The Parliamentarian*, no. 253, p. 100.

Lobban, M. (1991) *The Common Law and English Jurisprudence 1760–1850*, Oxford: Clarendon Press.

McEvoy, J, (1986) 'The Charter as a Bilingual Instrument' *Canadian Bar Review*, vol. 64, p. 155.

* Renton Committee (1975) *The Preparation of Legislation*, Cmnd. 6053, London: HMSO.

Rhys Williams, B. (1987) 'Legislation and Parliament' *Statute Law Review*, p. 138.

Smith, J (1980) 'Legislative Drafting: English and Continental' *Statute Law Review*, p. 14.

Vanderlinden, J. (1967) *Le Concept de Code en Europe Occidentale de XIIIe au XIXe Siècle*, Brussels: Editions de l'Institut de Sociologie, Université Libre de Brusselles.

Chapter Eight

Interpreting Statutes—The Rules

Most people are willing to believe that case law can present problems because facts are never precisely repeated; at the same time most people also believe that statutes are precise and accurate—that anyone can 'look up' the law in a statute. For the most part the implementation of statutory provisions will indeed be a routine matter. But you will have seen from your experience in trying to draft a statute that this is not universally true. Once words appear in a statute they are open to all manner of argument and interpretation. Those arguments may be about the meaning of the language used in the statute (a sort of translation exercise), or about the application of the language to the facts (application exercise), or about both.

By a 'translation' exercise we mean the court having to deal with phrases such as: '. . . equipment includes any plant and machinery, vehicle, aircraft, and clothing'. The first question to ask here is whether the word 'includes' means that the subsequent items fall within the definition of 'equipment' and everything else is excluded; or whether 'includes' means that the list is not closed, ie, that vehicles etc are included, but other things might also be included. This problem arose in *Coltman* v *Bibby Tankers Ltd* [1988] AC 276, [1987] 3 All ER 1068. We will return to this case later. The 'translation' was that the list was not closed. The House of Lords then had to consider whether the phrase, as translated, applied to ships: the application exercise.

The same problems arise, of course, in ordinary life with insurance policies, contracts, and even the rules of games. Take a look, for instance, at the rules of 'Monopoly'. Under the heading *Landing on 'Chance' or 'Community Chest'* the rules state: 'A player takes the top card from the pack indicated and after following the instructions thereon, returns the card face down to the bottom of the pack'. Let's say you land on 'Chance'. You know (because you have been concentrating) that the only card still to come is a property repairs card; a fact which will cause you severe problems.

Do you have to take the card? What arguments could you use not to? Do you have to show the card to anyone? Would the type of argument be the same as when you argued (but presumably lost) that you did not have to take the card at all?

When you look at any document the meaning attached to words is often influenced both by the fact that you wish your interpretation to be accepted and also by your general approach to life. What we mean by this last point is that some people are by nature apt to take words at their literal meaning—'it says X so it should mean X' (or, the Monopoly rules say 'take the card' so you must take the card)—whilst others naturally find themselves looking for the purpose behind the words—'what are these words trying to do?' (or, what is the point in having cards marked 'Chance' if they leave you no choice whether to take them or not; surely there is a difference between 'Chance' and 'Community Chest'?).

The same is true of judges. Thus we find two main approaches to interpreting the words of a statute: *The Literal Rule* and *The Golden (or Purposive) Rule;* some texts also refer to a third approach—*The Mischief Rule.* Before looking at these 'rules of interpretation' there are two general warnings to bear in mind:

(1)   Many general textbooks present the rules as though they were fixed and adhered to logically. The reality is much less certain. Particular judges tend to favour one or other rule. Most commonly judges have leant toward a literal approach, but this is not necessarily true today.

(2)   These 'rules' are not really rules at all; they are different approaches which a lawyer will try to persuade a court to use, or which a judge will use to justify his decision. Very often, one lawyer will therefore try to argue a literal interpretation ('the words say this and nothing more') whilst the other seeks a more purposive approach ('the words may say this but they cannot mean that when you look at the purpose behind the Act'). Interpretation is an art, not a science.

So do not get too worried about these rules for now. You must know what they are seeking to do, but only as a tool for the way you argue your case; and so that you can make some guess at how the judge might decide the issue. Instead of thinking about statutory interpretation as just another legal topic—like homicide, theft or offer and acceptance—you should think about the ideas outlined below and try to make use of them, either in academic discussion or in practice, across the whole range of legal subjects.

But we must emphasise that these are not fixed rules of law; for the most part they are examples of the use of language generally. Cross, for instance, refers to cases which decided such awe-inspiring questions as 'Is a bicycle a "carriage"? Is a goldfish an "article"?' and concludes:

Conundrums of this sort are part of the daily bread of judges and practitioners. In solving them the courts usually pay due regard to the context, but, in many instances, the answer must . . . be treated as a matter of common sense. (1987:76)

Understanding the 'rules' of statutory interpretation is important, therefore, because:

(a)   Judges are not robots; their personality affects the way they will approach a problem of interpretation. Judges do not follow a 'critical path' analysis, progressing from one rule to another in a logical fashion. You need to be aware, therefore, what range of analytical options are open to a judge.

(b)   When arguing your case, or analysing the advantages and disadvantages of pursuing that case, you need to know the framework in which you are operating. It is often said that a bad workman always blames his tools; a workman who does not even know which tools exist deserves all he gets.

(c)   It helps if you can combine (a) and (b), but that means you need to know how the judge is likely to react to the approach you have chosen. An argument based on the grand purpose of a statute delivered to a judge who believes firmly in a literal interpretation of words will fall on stony ground. You will discover from reading cases which senior judges favour which approach. This may not help on your first appearance in court before an unknown junior judge—which is why point (b) is important.

These traditional 'rules' may be explained as follows.

The Literal Rule

The 'literal rule' is founded on the assumption that the words chosen by Parliament in the Act clearly show their intentions in passing that Act. The rule demands that one looks at what was said, not at what it *might* mean; that one is concerned with linguistics rather than considerations of the purpose of the Act or the wider context in which the statute was enacted. To do otherwise, as was said in *Duport Steel v Sirs* [1980] 1 WLR 142, [1980] 1 All ER 529, 541, might mean that the court is not interpreting the Act but really making law. There, Lord Diplock said:

Where the meaning of the statutory words is plain and unambiguous it is not for the judges to invent fancied ambiguities as an excuse for failing to give effect to its plain meaning because they consider the consequences of doing so would be inexpedient, or even unjust or immoral.

Presented in this way the rule is seen as a safe bet—judges simply apply what is there. Safe bet or not, it is not a true reflection of reality. If the words were that clear nobody would have brought the case in the first place. The literalist is prepared for this challenge. What the literalist would be looking for is the *primary* or most *obvious* meaning of the word, not any *general* or *secondary* meaning. And he will usually do this by looking at the way the word or sentence fits into the rest of the section or even the Act as a whole (see Summers & Marshall, 1992:213). The literal rule at its most extreme echoes the approach of a fundamentalist: consideration of the word or phrase as written is sacrosanct. The rule does not demand that the word be viewed in isolation from the rest of the sentence or section; but demands steadfastly that the investigation as to meaning does not stray beyond this point.

Thus the literal rule does not call upon a judge to consider the consequences of the interpretation. Sometimes this can still lead to what appear to be pretty odd results. The literal rule does not always generate a feeling that justice has been done even though it may be linguistically precise. Nor does it bear mathematical precision. As Willis stated:

> it is quite possible for all the members of the court to agree that the meaning of a section is so plain that it cannot be controlled by the context and yet to disagree as to what the plain meaning is. (1938:2)

Many examples can be given of judges relying upon the literal rule. But if we listed one hundred cases all we would see is a hundred different examples of the rule being used. The examples would not necessarily tell us how to interpret the next case. However, here are two examples that might help to give a flavour of literal interpretation in action.

In *R v Harris* (1836) 7 C & P 446 a statute made it an offence to 'stab, cut or wound' another person. Harris bit off her friend's nose in a fight— and then the policeman's finger. Was she guilty under the statute? The answer was no. The words in the statute pointed towards the use of a *weapon*. Teeth (even false?) are not a weapon. This conclusion was given further force by the fact that elsewhere in the section were references to the use of weapons, such as the word 'shooting'. You may think she should be guilty of something, but she was not guilty as charged. See also *R v Munks* [1964] 1 QB 304, [1963] 3 All ER 757 in a similar vein on the meaning of the word 'engine'.

In *Fisher v Bell* [1961] 1 QB 394, [1960] 3 All ER 731, an Act of 1959 made it an offence to 'sell or hire or offer for sale or hire . . .' certain offensive weapons such as flick-knives. Bell placed a flick-knife in his Bristol shop window with a price-tag on it. Was he guilty of the offence? Again the answer was no. As you will see in the Law of Contract, placing an item on display is not the same thing as 'offering it for sale'. If the statute had used the phrase 'expose for sale' the answer would, on this analysis, have been different.

Exercise 15: Are we still on strike?

Take a look at the following case summary. We pose a few questions at the end of the account.

Stock v *Frank Jones (Tipton) Ltd* [1978] 1 WLR 231, [1978] 1 All ER 948 concerned the dismissal of employees who were on strike. Under the Trade Union and Labour Relations Act 1974 (TULRA) an employee who was dismissed for striking could not claim unfair dismissal unless 'one or more of the employees, who also took part in that [strike], were not dismissed for taking part'. So all employees taking part in the strike had to be treated the same way. If one employee, eg, the shop steward, was victimised by being the only person dismissed, he could claim that the dismissal was unfair (which would be decided on the facts). In this case the employees were on strike and, following fairly normal industrial relations tactics, the employer threatened them with dismissal if they did not return to work. Some did return. The employer dismissed those who did not return and they claimed unfair dismissal.

(a) Using the literal rule, what do you think the words 'employees who took part in that [strike]' mean? Do they mean:
(i) all the employees who originally took part in the [strike]? or
(ii) those employees who were still taking part in the [strike] when some of the others had returned to work following the threat?
(b) What are the consequences of choosing each option?

Answer: The House of Lords decided that 'employees who took part in the [strike]' could only refer to those employees who were participating in the strike **when the strike began**. Thus, when some employees returned and were not dismissed they still counted in the number of those who 'took part in the [strike]'. The employees who had been dismissed had therefore been 'victimised' and could claim unfair dismissal.

If the House of Lords had taken the second and less literal option then, provided all those who stayed out on strike had been dismissed (which had happened) the employer would have been protected against any claim for unfair dismissal. After this case employers argued that this made nonsense of industrial relations. Under this case, if the employer threatened to dismiss anyone not returning to work and one person out of a thousand did return the employer would either have to dismiss no one or dismiss everyone, including the one who returned!

The law on this topic has taken several twists and turns via a number of statutes since *Stock* v *Frank Jones* (in 1978, 1980, 1990 and 1992). In essence, the law now is that the employer is protected provided all those participating in the industrial action at the time of dismissals are treated in the same way and there is no victimisation present in re-employing selected individuals within three months from that date. You might wish to think how you would redraft the statute to achieve this result—the real wording can be found in Trade Union and Labour Relations (Consolidation) Act 1992, ss. 237, 238 and 239.

It is often said that the literal rule will not be used when it would lead to inconsistency or absurdity. This must not be taken too widely. Many people would disagree with the above cases; this is not the same thing as saying that relying on a literal approach produced an absurd result. So, when will judges deem the literal rule inappropriate?

The Golden Rule

The golden rule can be best described as an *adaptation* of the literal rule. We use this form of interpretation every day when reading signs such as 'Stop Children'; hardly an instruction to act like Herod! The context aids the interpretation. The classic exposition of the rule is to be found in *River Wear Commissioners* v *Adamson* (1876–77) 2 App Cas 743 at 764–5, per Lord Blackburn:

> . . . I believe that it is not disputed that what Lord Wensleydale used to call the golden rule is right, viz, that we are to take the whole statute together and construe it all together, giving the words their ordinary signification unless when so applied they produce an inconsistency, or an absurdity or inconvenience so great as to convince the court that the intention could not have been to use them in their ordinary signification and to justify the court in putting on them some other signification which, though less proper, is one which the court thinks the words will bear.

Sadly, his Lordship did not offer us much assistance as to **how** the interpretation is to proceed once we have discovered the absurdity. We can overcome this by arguing that the only logical way to deal with an absurd interpretation is to correct it by assessing what Parliament was trying to do. We can do this by looking at the *purpose* of the Act. For that reason it is sometimes called a 'purposive approach'—though some care is required when employing that term because the judiciary have been highly inconsistent in their use of it, as we shall see below.

In *Stock* v *Frank Jones (Tipton) Ltd* [1978] ICR 347, [1978] 1 All ER 948 Lord Simon advocated departure from the literal rule only when:

    (a)   there is a clear and gross anomaly;

    (b)   Parliament could not have envisaged the anomaly and would not have accepted its presence;

    (c)   the anomaly can be obviated without detriment to the legislative intent; and

    (d)   the language of the statute allows for such modification.

This is in keeping with the tenor of statements made by judges in the nineteenth century, particularly Lord Wensleydale in *Grey* v *Pearson* (1857) 6 HL Cas 61, which linked the idea of absurdity with the situation where a literal meaning would prove repugnant or inconsistent with the rest of the section or Act (the *internal* context). The emphasis is laid on establishing that the literal meaning would be a nonsense when the rest of the statute is considered; it clearly does not mean that an absurdity can be said to arise merely because a literal meaning might offend one's sense of justice.

Viewed this way the golden rule can be seen as an accessory to, or shadow of, the literal rule. It does not exist independently of the literal rule but only comes into play as a backup when the literal rule has failed; usually focusing on the range of secondary meanings of the word or phrase in question. The literal rule will be departed from mainly where there is confusion *within* the Act—that a clear interpretation is not possible because of surrounding words and sections. It is interesting to note, however, that many of the cases which developed the golden rule were in fact cases on the interpretation of another type of document: testators' wills. And even a cursory study of the interpretation of wills in the law of succession reveals that there has always been a major conflict of judicial attitude here: do you follow only what the testator wrote, or do you look for other evidence of his intentions? The law of succession has had the same problems as seen in statutory interpretation. It has not produced a satisfactory answer. Even Lord Wensleydale, the sometime father of the golden rule, was known to adopt a strong literal approach when interpreting wills (see, for instance *Abbott* v *Middleton* (1858) 7 HLC 68).

It is respectfully submitted that Lord Simon's guidelines are useful, although they still leave us with the one major problem with the golden rule: how do we know when something is an anomaly, an ambiguity, or absurd? This is a question most frequently avoided by commentators. Cross, however, does make a number of helpful points on this problem (1987:84–96).

First, the primary meaning cannot be abandoned, 'simply because it produces a result which [the judge] believes is contrary to the purpose of the Act. No judge can decline to apply a statutory provision because it seems to him to lead to absurd results'. Equally, however, judicial treatment of the topic does not lend itself to simply saying judges are only concerned with the *internal* context of the words. Cross is forced to conclude that judicial applications of the rule tend to show that 'absurdity' 'does mean something wider than repugnance or inconsistency with the rest of the document' (1987:92). In other words, some judges at least will go beyond merely examining the words of the section etc and probe into the purpose of the Act. Discovering whether something is absurd when matched against the purpose of the Act may involve examining the wider legal, and even social, setting of the Act. That is to say, judges, to a greater or lesser extent, will look to the *external context* of the statute.

Again there are many cases which illustrate the rule, but that is all they do—*illustrate*. As a lawyer you are concerned with using the rule to argue—it is of little value citing a case which simply proves that the courts do occasionally use the rule if the case cited has nothing to do with your argument.

Here, however, are two famous examples of the golden rule in operation:

R v *Allen* (1872) LR 1 CCR 367: Allen, who was already married, married a woman called Harriet Crouch. The statute in question said: 'whosoever being married shall marry any other person during the lifetime of his spouse' shall commit bigamy.

Now, Harriet was in fact closely related to Allen so this apparently bigamous marriage was actually void. Thus Allen argued that he had not married Harriet (because at law this was impossible) and so had not committed bigamy. He argued that the second marriage had to be a legal marriage before bigamy could be committed.

But this would of course produce an absurdity because logically no bigamous marriage is lawful by its own definition; so, if Allen's argument was accepted, the judges would have had to pretend that the section was meaningless. Therefore they took a more purposive approach and read the words in the section 'shall marry' as meaning 'going through the ceremony'.

Re Sigsworth [1935] Ch 89, [1934] All ER Rep 113: Mrs Sigsworth was found dead. An inquest found that she had been murdered by her son, who was also found dead. Mrs Sigsworth's will left everything to her son. However, old rules of public policy dictated that the son (and therefore his estate) could not inherit in these circumstances. Therefore Mrs Sigsworth died intestate. But, under the Administration of Estates Act 1925, s. 46, the person entitled on intestacy was her son, and through him, his estate. The money had gone round in a circle; and the statute dealing with intestacy said nothing about murderers being barred from inheriting.

The court held that the statute could not have been intended to allow murderers to inherit, despite being silent on the point. The old rule which applied to inheriting under a will was applied to intestacy on the grounds that cases such as *Sigsworth* would be 'obnoxious' to that old principle and must be read as being subject to it.

Exercise 16: Not all there; or, present and correct?

Please read the following case summary. We pose only one question at the end of the account.

Under the Statute of Frauds 1677 it was a requirement that a will had to be signed by the testator 'in the presence' of witnesses.

In *Casson* v *Dade* (1781) 28 ER 1010 Miss Honora Jenkins went to her attorney's office to execute her will. She signed the will but then felt faint and was taken outside to sit in her carriage with her maid. The witnesses to the will remained in the office and gave their signatures to the will. The maid gave evidence that at the moment the witnesses were signing the carriage horses reared up, causing the carriage to move into a line of sight with the office window. The maid stated that, had Miss Jenkins looked through the window she would have seen the witnesses sign.

Was the will validly witnessed?

Answer: The court held that the will had been properly witnessed. Miss Jenkins was 'in the presence' of the witnesses even though she was not physically present in the same room. The fact that she was in the line of sight of the witnesses and could have seen them sign had she looked was enough. For, as had been said in *Shires* v *Glascock* (1687) 21 ER 1134, to demand otherwise would mean that 'if a man should but turn his back, or look off, it would vitiate the will'. In modern parlance, it would be absurd to hold otherwise!

The Mischief Rule

Akin to the golden rule is a much older aid to interpretation called the mischief rule, or the rule in *Heydon's Case* (1584) 3 Co Rep 7a, 7b.

Like the golden rule, the mischief rule stresses the need to interpret an enactment in such a way as to give effect to its objectives. However, the mischief rule is, formally, of narrower application, in that the approach is located purely in the context of an identifiable common law status quo which existed prior to the Act. Thus the courts are required to consider four things:

1. What was the common law before the Act?
2. What was the 'defect or mischief' for which the common law did not provide?
3. What remedy did Parliament intend to provide?
4. What was the true reason for that remedy?

Great care must be taken when relying upon this rule in argument:

First, when *Heydon's Case* was determined the mischief could in fact be discovered within the Act itself because the reason for the Act's existence was always stated in the **preamble**. Thus a judge did not have to go beyond the bounds of the Act to discover the mischief it sought to remedy. The *internal* context was sufficient. A classic example of the use of preambles comes in the **Charitable Uses Act 1601** which states:

WHEREAS Lands, Tenements, Rents, Annuities . . . have been heretofore given, limited, appointed and assigned, as well by the Queen's most excellent Majesty, and her most noble Progenitors, as by sundry other well disposed Persons; some for Relief of aged, impotent and poor People, some for Maintenance of sick and maimed Soldiers . . . which Lands, Tenements, Rents, Annuities . . . nevertheless have not been employed according to the charitable Intent of the givers and Founders thereof, by reasons of Frauds, Breaches of Trust, and Negligence in those that should pay, deliver and employ the same: For Redress and Remedy whereof, Be it enacted . . .

Lord Diplock recognised this in *Black-Clawson International Ltd* v *Papierwerke Waldhof-Aschaffenburg Aktiengesellschaft* [1975] AC 591, [1975] 1 All ER 810 when he said:

> So, when it was laid down, the 'mischief rule' did not require the court to travel beyond the actual words of the statute itself to identify the 'mischief and defect for which the Common Law did not provide' . . . the mischief rule must be used with caution to justify any reference to extraneous documents for this purpose.

The point concerning 'extraneous documents' is significant. As we will see below, judges have not, traditionally, been allowed to look at any and every source in order to discover the mischief. Recently this approach has altered.

Secondly, 'mischief' itself can be difficult to define. All Acts came about for **some** reason, be it social, economic, political, or because of some technical legal defect. This latter reason is a reasonably safe basis upon which to attach the tag 'mischief'. One can easily find out what the law was before the Act came into effect; and thereby see the apparent changes the Act sought to make in the law. The other means of identifying the mischief are fraught with danger because they clearly involve making value judgments.

Two good examples of the mischief rule in operation are the cases of *Gorris* v *Scott* (1874) LR 9 Ex 125, and *Smith* v *Hughes* [1960] 1 WLR 830, [1960] 2 All ER 859.

In *Gorris* v *Scott*, Scott contracted to transport some sheep by sea. The sheep were swept overboard because they had not been fenced in. Orders in Council made under the Contagious Diseases (Animals) Act 1869 required that the sheep should have been put in pens. Gorris thus claimed that Scott was in breach of the Act.

The Court of Exchequer held that the purpose of the Act (which was clear from the preamble) was to prevent the spread of diseases amongst sheep or cattle en route to Britain; not to give a right to claimants like Gorris.

In *Smith* v *Hughes*, s. 1 of the Street Offences Act 1959 stated: 'It shall be an offence for a common prostitute to loiter or solicit in a street or public place for the purposes of prostitution'. Prostitutes began trying to attract customers by signalling to the men from balconies or from windows. The report notes that the prostitutes would indicate the price by raising three fingers—and that on one occasion they received a counter-offer of two raised fingers! The Divisional Court of the Queen's Bench Division (on an appeal by way of case stated) decided that the mischief of the Act was to 'clean up the streets'. The words of section 1 did not indicate **who** had to be in the street; and so an offence had been committed under the section.

It is probably fair to say that, today, the distinction between the mischief and golden rules is, in the minds of some judges, so fine as to be virtually non-existent. It could even be argued that both rules have become subsumed within a general purposive approach. An example of such thinking can be seen in Lord Diplock's approach to the Abortion Act 1967 in *Royal College of Nursing* v *DHSS* [1981] AC 800, [1981] 1 All ER 545. His lordship began by defining his method for discovering the purpose of the Act:

> . . . one starts by considering what was the state of the law relating to abortion before the passing of the Act, what was the mischief that required amendment, and in what respect was the existing law unclear.

He continued his analysis by looking at the whole context of the abortion problem—its social and economic aspects, as well as its legal history. He then concluded that:

> . . . the wording and structure of the section are far from elegant, but the policy of the Act, it seems to me, is clear. There are two aspects to it: the first is to broaden the grounds upon which abortions may be lawfully obtained; the second is to ensure that the abortion is carried out with all proper skill and in hygienic conditions.

Be careful, however, not to assume that, in discovering the 'purpose' of an Act the judges are dealing with some sort of absolute, clearly definable, objective. Discovering the purpose of a rule is often an act of creative interpretation by the judge. Purposes and reasons for legislating are at least as indeterminate as the rules themselves.

Secondary Aids to Construction

The three 'Canons of Construction' so far considered are sometimes called **primary** aids to interpretation. It is now necessary to consider a set of secondary rules that can be employed within the framework of the primary aids to facilitate interpretation. These relate either to the use that can be made of parts of the statute itself, or to external (*extrinsic*) materials. Many of the rules noted below are simply rules of grammar which are not unique to legal terminology. For instance, to borrow part of the exercise we set at the end of this chapter, consider the following list: *cats, dogs, horses, cattle, sheep, pigs, and snakes or insects common to the British Isles.* Is it only snakes and insects that have to be common to the British Isles?

The title of the Act: It is very tempting to point to the long or short title in order to show the purpose of the Act. It should be stressed that the long title is rarely used for this purpose and the short title is practically irrelevant. A classic example of this is the case of *R* v *Galvin* [1987] QB 862, [1987] 2 All ER 851. Galvin acquired 'restricted' Ministry of Defence documents. When Galvin was charged under the Official Secrets Act 1911 he argued that the documents had ceased to be secret and had never actually been 'official'—which, he said, is what the title of the Act demanded. Nevertheless he was found guilty because the section only referred to 'documents' and the title, being merely a label, had to give way to the words actually used in the section. The conviction, however, was quashed on other grounds.

On the use of the long title, see *Vacher v London Society of Compositors* [1913] AC 107. Note also that special rules will apply to the use of the Schedules that often appear at the end of an Act: see *Buchanan & Co. Ltd v Babco Forwarding & Shipping Ltd* [1978] AC 141, [1977] 3 All ER 1048.

Inclusory words and lists: A word which often arises in a statute is 'include': thus you find a section which might read:

> *For the purposes of this Act references to sending include delivering, causing to be sent or delivered, transferring and posting.*

The question would then be whether the word 'include' meant all the subsequent terms were included **and everything else was excluded** or that the subsequent terms were examples only so that other terms might also be included. For instance, should 'distributing' or 'handing out' be included?

As we noted above, this problem was considered in *Coltman v Bibby Tankers* [1988] AC 276, [1987] 3 All ER 1068. The House of Lords solved the problem by looking at other sections in the Act which listed things. These other lists were very specific when not introduced by the word 'include'. This tended to indicate that when the word 'include' did occur it was merely stating examples, so that items not stated in the list might still fall within the definition of 'equipment' in the Act. Thus a ship was 'included' in the definition of equipment when that definition read: '. . . equipment includes any plant and machinery, vehicle, aircraft, and clothing'. However, Lord Oliver also noted that this list actually read: 'equipment includes any plant and machinery . . .'. He stated at page 1073a:

> The key word in the definition is the word 'any' and it underlines, in my judgment, what I would in any event have supposed to be the case, having regard to the purpose of the Act, that is to say that it [the subsection] should be widely construed so as to embrace every article of whatever kind furnished by the employer for the purposes of his business.

Thus the mere fact that a list is introduced by the word 'includes' does not automatically mean that the list is open-ended. Much more needs to be considered. Indeed, we would strongly recommend you to read this case as it encompasses many of the techniques of statutory interpretation discussed in this chapter—including a reference to the long title of the Act which is introduced without excuse or explanation.

Closely connected to this problem is the position where a simple list of words appears. Can other words be added to the list? As always there is a latin maxim to cover this: *expressio unius est exclusio alterius* (the expression of one thing is the exclusion of others). Using this maxim one can argue that if the legislature produces a list of items then it is logical that all other items were specifically excluded. Thus one might use this rule to decide whether a faith healer fell within 'clairvoyant, fortuneteller or diviner'. This maxim might have applied in *Coltman* had it not been for the presence of the word 'include'.

A rather different problem arises where an Act employs a generic but non-exhaustive list—for example an Act may state that it is to apply to 'dogs, cats, budgerigars and **other animals'**. Would you consider that a cow could be included on that basis? Obviously it is difficult to say without more information about the context in which those words appear. We can, however, identify a specific legal method of dealing with such a problem by saying that: where general words follow a list of specific words then the general words must be read according to the *genus* (ie, type or group) of the preceding specific words. [It is the legal equivalent of explaining what one means by 'etcetera'.] Thus, we must discover the *genus* which our named categories have in common and then interpret the general words ('other animals') so that they do not conflict with the specific words ('dogs' etc.). This is called the *eiusdem generis rule.*

In the example given we could therefore argue, depending upon context, that 'other animals' could refer to **any** commonly domesticated animal, or to any commonly domesticated animal normally **kept as a pet**. Either interpretation might be feasible, which is why it is important to remember that such rules are secondary aids—and therefore used only within the context of our understanding of the provision as a whole. See, for examples of this rule in operation: *Powell* v *Kempton Park Racecourse* [1899] AC 143 on whether Tattersall's Ring fell within 'other place' in the phrase 'house, office, room or other place'—it did not; *R* v *Staniforth, R* v *Jordan* [1976] 3 WLR 887, [1976] 3 All ER 775 on whether pornographic material could fall outside the definition of obscene material under the Obscene Publications Act 1959 as being 'in the interests of science, literature, art or learning, or of other objects of general concern'. The argument was that the obscene material had psychotherapeutic value, so falling within the definition. The argument failed in the House of Lords.

Linked with this is the maxim *noscitur a sociis*—a word is known by its associates. The meaning of a word is affected by the surrounding words and should be interpreted accordingly. This rule is similar to the *eiusdem generis* rule and students often confuse the two. The *eiusdem generis* rule only comes into effect when dealing with general words at the end of a list. Thus if we take Wills Act 1837, s. 20 as an example, one of the ways of revoking a will is by 'burning, tearing, or otherwise destroying'. The *eiusdem generis* rule tells us that 'or otherwise destroying' is to be read in the light of burning and tearing; the cases showing us that this requires an act of physical violence rather than, say, amending the text. The *noscitur a sociis* rule cannot be used here. It could only apply if the section read: 'burning, tearing, mutilating, or defacing'. Then one would ask: what if the will had been partially destroyed by fire? How should you read the word 'burning'? Does the burning have to be complete before the will is revoked, or is partial burning enough? From the surrounding words, especially 'mutilating' and 'defacing', it seems that this act does not have to be complete—that burning could be read as including partial burning.

To take one final example of the *noscitur a sociis* rule: the rule would be useful in ascertaining what *type* of fortuneteller would be covered in the list: 'clairvoyant, fortuneteller or diviner'. Would a palmist be covered?

The Interpretation Act 1978: You should be aware of the existence of this Act, but it is not as helpful as it first sounds. The Act simply states that certain words will have a standard meaning unless specifically changed.

Thus 'month' means a calendar month and not 30 days; 'he' is read as including 'she'; singular words include the plural, and so on.

Punctuation: The modern view is that punctuation can be used as an aid to interpretation. Traditionally, however, this is not true of headings and marginal notes in a statute, though occasional references can be found to headings in particular if they help to resolve an ambiguity: see *Dixon v British Broadcasting Corporation* [1979] ICR 281, [1979] 2 All ER 112.

Dictionaries: Dictionaries can be used by judges where a word has no specific legal meaning. One must be careful here, however, as words can change meaning by dint of time, usage and context.

One example of a court using dictionaries to interpret sections arose in *Flack* v *Baldry* [1988] 1 WLR 393, [1988] 1 All ER 412. The case concerned the legality of possessing a 'stun gun' which could administer an electric shock of 46,000 volts. Did this offend against the Firearms Act 1968 as a 'weapon designed for the **discharge** of any noxious liquid, gas or other thing'? The court found that 'discharge' had a dictionary meaning of 'emit' rather than 'physical ejection', so that the stun gun was caught by the Act.

One has to tread carefully here, though. Different dictionaries often give different slants to the meaning of words. For instance, in one exercise we give to our students a key question arises whether a person has committed an act of 'violence' when they have been found guilty of causing criminal damage to a snack bar. Depending upon which dictionary is used you tend to get definitions which will either stress that 'violence' relates only to causing injury to people, or that it includes damage to property as well as injury to people.

Travaux préparatoires: This translates literally as 'preparatory works'. In the English context it refers to the consideration of public materials by the courts in order to discern the purpose of the legislation. A common example would be the reports or working papers (though not the recommendations) of law reform bodies such as the Law Commission or Criminal Law Revision Committee. The question as to whether White Papers may be referred to in aid of interpretation has been inconclusively mooted by the Court of Appeal in *Thomas* v *Chief Adjudication Officer and Secretary of State for Social Security* [1990] IRLR 436, [1990] 3 CMLR 611 (see Webb, 1992:395 for comment). In the European context, the willingness to consider *travaux préparatoires* has traditionally been greater. EC case law, for instance, thus includes references to the use of legislative proposals as published in the *Official Journal;* parliamentary debates in Member states, though never to the deliberations of the Council or Commission.

In contrast, the English courts have until recently taken a restrictive view as to the range of documents which may be so used. For instance, all Parliamentary debates in the House of Commons and House of Lords are recorded in *Hansard.* Traditionally, *Hansard* could not be referred to explicitly by a court in order to gauge Parliament's intention (although some judges have admitted over the years to looking at the debates anyway). In the international context, such as dealing with the interpretation of international treaties, the English courts have taken a more relaxed attitude: see *Fothergill* v *Monarch Airlines* [1981] AC 251, [1980] 2 All ER 696. And, in the European context, as more and more legislation has owed its origins to the European Community the House of Lords has referred to *Hansard* on several occasions and moved more towards harmonisation with European methods of interpretation in the use of *travaux préparatoires*: see *Pickstone* v *Freemans* [1988] 3 WLR 265, [1988] 2 All ER 803; *Litster* v *Forth Dry Dock* [1990] AC 546, [1989] 1 All ER 1134 and *R* v *Secretary of State for Transport, ex parte Factortame Ltd* [1990] 2 AC 85, [1989] 2 All ER 692.

In 1992, however, the House of Lords delivered a blockbuster in the case of *Pepper (Inspector of Taxes)* v *Hart* [1992] 3 WLR 1032, [1993] 1 All ER 42. By a six to one majority (Lord Mackay LC dissenting) the House of Lords decided to allow reference to be made to *Hansard* in limited circumstances. Reference to Parliamentary materials will therefore be allowed where:

(a) legislation is ambiguous or obscure, or leads to an absurdity;

(b) the material relied upon consists of one or more statements by a minister or other promotor of the Bill together if necessary with such other Parliamentary material as is necessary to understand such statements and their effect;

(c) the statements relied upon are clear.

In this case, the effect of permitting reference to *Hansard* was that the literal meaning of the statute in question was not followed.

Some comments by their Lordships are worth noting here. Lord Bridge stated (at 1039H, WLR) that:

It should, in my opinion, only be in rare cases where the very issue of interpretation which the courts are called on to resolve has been addressed in Parliamentary debate and where the promoter of the legislation has made a clear statement directed to that very issue, that reference to Hansard should be permitted.

Lord Oliver commented (1042H, WLR):

> It can apply only where the expression of the legislative intention is genuinely ambiguous or obscure or where a literal or prima facie construction leads to a manifest absurdity . . .

Lord Mackay (dissenting) observed:

> I believe that practically every question of *statutory* construction that comes before the courts will involve an argument . . . [on (a) to confirm the meaning of a provision as conveyed by the text, its object and purpose; (b) to determine a meaning where the provision is ambiguous or obscure; or (c) to determine the meaning where the ordinary meaning is manifestly absurd or unreasonable] . . . It follows that the parties' legal advisors will require to study Hansard in practically every such case to see whether or not there is any help to be gained from it. I believe this is an objection of real substance. It is a practical objection not one of principle . . . (1037G, WLR)

> Such an approach appears to me to involve the possibility at least of an immense increase in the cost of litigation in which statutory construction is involved. (1038B, WLR)

Lord Bridge further commented on the issue of additional costs (1039H, WLR):

> Provided the relaxation of the previous exclusionary rule is so limited, I find it difficult to suppose that the additional cost of litigation or any other ground of objection can justify the court continuing to wear blinkers which, in such a case as this, conceal the vital clue to the intended meaning of an enactment . . . (W)here Hansard does provide the answer, it should be so clear to both parties that they will avoid the cost of litigation.

Between November 1992 and March 1993 the House of Lords has made express use of *Hansard* in three important cases: *Chief Adjudication Officer* v *Foster* [1992] 2 WLR 292, [1993] 1 All ER 705; *Stubbings* v *Webb* [1993] 2 WLR 120, [1993] 1 All ER 322; *R* v *Warwickshire County Council, ex parte Johnson* [1993] 2 WLR 1, [1993] 1 All ER 1022. In the last case, for instance, a question arose on the interpretation of Consumer Protection Act 1987, ss. 20, 39 and 40. A shop had displayed a misleading 'price promise'. The probem was: could an employee who refused to honour the advertised price be guilty under the Act or was this limited to the employer/owner? The case hinged on the meaning of the rather curious and ambiguous phrase that liability rested on such notices appearing in 'any business of his'. Reference to *Hansard* showed that it had been clearly intended that only the employer should be liable.

In contrast to this, however, one can also find reservations or scepticism concerning this new-found research source. Thus in *Sheppard* v *Commissioners of Inland Revenue*, 23 February 1993 (LEXIS transcript) Aldous J expressed concern regarding the problem of determining what is an ambiguity for the purposes of reference to *Hansard* and on the level of clarity required in a Minister's statement specifically on the issue in question.

There is some division in the legal world as to the efficacy of *Pepper* v *Hart*. Indeed, there is some division between the authors of this book. There are undoubted advantages in making use of all relevant materials to interpret a statute: the cases to date have allowed perceived justice to win over technicalities. The rule was being eroded anyway, in practice if not in law. Equally, Lord Mackay's words as to the extra level of research and costs involved in litigation should not be disposed of lightly. And on the evidence of the past few months, perhaps the cases are not as rare as Lord Bridge thought. Possibly more pertinent to this book is the fact that practitioners, academics and law students will now have to come to terms with a new source of material in their research. Given the appalling indexing for *Hansard* this should prove interesting.

It is also somewhat ironic that although English courts are embracing a brave new world of *travaux préparatoires*, the Court of Justice of the European Communities has at times shown a more cautious attitude: see Case 136/79 *National Panasonic UK* v *EC Commission* [1980] ECR 2033. It is also worth noting the recent article by Summers and Marshall (1992:213) advocating the interpretation of statutes based on using the 'ordinary' meaning of words as opposed to wide purposive or teleological methods— an article published just before *Pepper* v *Hart* appeared.

Two final comments: first, given this seachange in interpretation techniques, we cannot state categorically that the 'rules' noted above concerning matters such as the bars on reference to the long and short titles to statutes are still sacrosanct. Secondly, once again we are instructed to refer to material extraneous to the statute only when the words are 'ambiguous' or 'obscure'. Do you feel you have heard these terms before? These are classic terms for preferring a purposive to a literal approach. But, as we commented earlier, there is a problem in defining these terms in the first place. We await further developments on all these points.

Other statutes: Provided statutes are in *pari materia* a word in an Act can be given the same meaning it had in an earlier Act. *In pari materia* means concerning the same matter. Thus the way the word 'horse' was interpreted in an Act concerning breeding rights, could not be used readily to interpret the same word in an Act pertaining to the definition of a dangerous animal.

See, for instance, *R* v *Wheatley* [1979] 1 WLR 144, [1979] 1 All ER 954 on whether 'explosive substance' in Explosive Substances Act 1883, s. 4, included a pyrotechnic device. The 1883 Act gave no definition, but the Explosives Act 1875 dealt with the same subject matter and encompassed pyrotechnic devices in the term 'explosive'. Note also *British Amusement*

Catering Trades Association v *Westminster City Council* [1988] 2 WLR 485,
[1988] 1 All ER 740, in which, in order to decide whether video games
in an amusement arcade fell within the meaning of 'exhibition of moving
pictures' in the Cinematograph Act 1982, the court considered every
occurrence of this phrase within the long line of Cinematograph Acts dating
from 1909 and the Cinemas Act 1985.

From Rules to Reality

The question posed by all students at some stage is: in what order will
the rules be applied? The analysis of statutory interpretation found in many
textbooks begs the same question. Most of them fail to answer it. The
reality is that not only is there no answer; it is the wrong question to
ask.

The right question is: how do judges choose to explain the construction
they have placed on the statute? Posed this way the question recognises,
as Willis put it, that there is not 'one great sun of a *principle,* "the plain
meaning rule"', around which revolves in planetary order a series of minor
rules of construction . . . Any one of these approaches may be selected
by your court.' (1938:1) There is no rule that says a judge must look at
the literal meaning of words first. The fact that many judges do this is
simply the recognition that most English judges do not want to be seen
to be *creating* law, and a logical starting point in reading any document
is to see what has actually been written! By examining the literal meaning
of the words judges appear to take a logical and safe line. However, if
they wish then to rely on a more purposive argument they will do so by
finding absurdity or inconsistency; they have at least guarded against some
criticism.

We would suggest that interpretation is a question of *style,* not rules.
By emphasising the *style* of judging we would draw a parallel with Llewellyn's
analysis of how judges use case law. In 1960 Llewellyn drew attention to
two different approaches used by judges; he termed these 'grand' and
'formal'. The 'grand' style reflects a judicial willingness to base a decision
on public policy and to take a creative or flexible approach to precedent.
Conversely, the 'formal' style demands rigid adherence to traditional
doctrine and the denial of a creative judicial function.

So too, we submit, is this the case with statutory interpretation. Judges
who employ the 'grand' style place substantial emphasis on the external
context of the statute. They place less weight on the dictionary meaning
of words, preferring to seek out the sense of the provision in question.
One who adopts the 'formal' style, however, is more concerned with the
form the statute takes, the internal context, and the perceived hierarchy
of the rules.

The formalist will, therefore, frequently seek to find a safe embarkation
point in a literal approach. This does not prevent the formalist then making
use of the golden and mischief rules; but this method of 'follow the pathways'
analysis provides appropriate justification for departing from a strictly literal

interpretation. Such 'formalism' can be seen extensively in the House of Lords' decision in *Duport Steel* v *Sirs* (cited above).

On the other hand, the 'grand' style will encompass those judges who will tend to move much more easily to reliance on the external context for interpretation. Such can be seen in *Royal College of Nursing* v *DHSS*; but equally its ranks will also be filled by judges prepared to go beyond this point to using a 'teleological' approach. A teleological approach is a rather grandiose name for an interpretation which is based on the purpose or object of the text confronting the judge. It goes beyond the inquiry as to the external context of the Act; examining instead the broader social, economic, perhaps political reasons behind the Act. It thereby attempts to give the fullest effect to the grand design of the law. It is, in the end, not really different from a purposive approach; it is more an extreme method of discovering that purpose and surfaces more in the analytical styles of European judges than in English Law.

The hallmark of the 'grand' style is often that the approach is extremely credible from a common sense viewpoint: the authority for such (often) sweeping statements is less clear.

In support of this analysis any examples are inevitably somewhat selective. However, we suggest that a good illustration of these styles in action is a case we first mentioned in Chapter Five concerning *stare decisis: Davis* v *Johnson* [1979] AC 264, [1978] 1 All ER 841 (CA) and 1132 (HL).

Jennifer Davis and Nehemiah Johnson were joint tenants of a council flat. Davis was subjected to extreme violence by Johnson and eventually fled the flat with her infant child. She applied to the county court, under the Domestic Violence and Matrimonial Proceedings Act 1976 (DVA), s. 1, for an injunction restraining Johnson from assaulting or molesting her or the child and ordering him to vacate the flat and not return. At first the injunction was granted and then withdrawn. We are concerned with the case in the Court of Appeal and the House of Lords. The case illustrates the points we have been making because, even when the various judges were agreed as to the outcome, their approaches to the question of interpretation differed extensively.

The case is dealt with in texts mainly as regards the issue of *stare decisis* raised by the Court of Appeal's judgment. We will not dwell on that aspect of the case in this analysis. However, the case is a fine example of the areas of judicial precedent and statutory interpretation overlapping; and this is an aspect of statutory interpretation that is worth noting. As with judicial precedent, cases concerning statutory interpretation do not exist in isolation. When a court is considering the meaning of a statute it will frequently have to interpret it in the light of previously decided cases.

Returning to *Davis* v *Johnson:* in the Court of Appeal Lord Denning MR, Sir George Baker P, and Shaw LJ found in favour of Ms Davis and the injunction was granted. Goff and Cumming-Bruce LJJ dissented. The House of Lords unanimously dismissed Johnson's further appeal.

What Was the Question of Interpretation?

Section 1 of the DVA stated:

> *(1) Without prejudice to the jurisdiction of the High Court, on an application by a party to a marriage a county court shall have jurisdiction to grant an injunction containing . . . [(a) and (b) are irrelevant here] . . . (c) a provision excluding the other party from the matrimonial home. . .*
> *(2) Subsection (1) above shall apply to a man and a woman who are living with each other in the same household as husband and wife as it applies to the parties to a marriage and any reference to the matrimonial home shall be construed accordingly.*

So, did this section apply to the case in hand? It was argued that s. 1 was procedural in its effect; it had not changed the existing law on property rights and could not have been meant to do away with these rights. In other words, if the man had property rights in the home (eg as a joint tenant, as was the case here) he could not be excluded from the property.

The *stare decisis* point (see Chapter Five) was that there were two binding Court of Appeal decisions where similar applicants to Davis had failed: *B v B* [1978] Fam 26, [1978] 1 All ER 821, and *Cantliff* v *Jenkins* [1978] 2 WLR 177n, [1978] 1 All ER 836.

How Did the Judges in the Court of Appeal Set About the Question of Interpreting the Statute?

Lord Denning began by recounting the history of the Act—an Act designed to protect 'battered wives'. He then commented that 'No one, I would have thought, could possibly dispute that those plain words (section 1 above) by themselves cover this very case.' One sees here a reliance on the literal reading of the section (though without full explanation) and hence the 'formal' style in operation.

In reviewing the two earlier Court of Appeal decisions, Lord Denning set about proving they had inadequately interpreted the section. If *B v B* was right, he argued, the only woman who could obtain an injunction would be one who owned the property solely. Thus, he said, 'In order to give s. 1 any effect at all, the court must be allowed to override the property rights of the man' (849b). Even when faced with House of Lords' authority which appeared to give preference to the protection of property rights, Lord Denning reacted: 'Social justice requires that personal rights should, in a proper case, be given priority over rights of property . . . I prefer to go by the principles underlying the legislative enactments rather than the out-dated notions of the past' (849 e–f). This is a purposive approach in the 'grand' style. The term 'social justice' looks like a logical and analytical argument, but in fact it has appeared from nowhere. Try to look up 'social justice' as a legal term of art: you will have difficulty.

Lord Denning then returned to the history of the Act and investigated

Reports of Select Committees and statements made in Parliament. This was more than simple reliance on the 'mischief rule' and again demonstrates a 'grand' style purposive approach.

Sir George Baker P began by discerning the 'mischief' on which the DVA centred by reference to legal history and the long title of the Act. There is nothing apparently unconventional in this. On the whole this is still a 'formal' approach; though it moves away from the strict canons of interpretation by its premature use of the long title. That mischief was the protection of family partners (married or unmarried) from violence. His analysis continued on a 'formal' basis: he rejected the idea that only a woman who was a sole owner could bring such an action. This interpretation he justified on the grounds that any other interpretation would deprive the Act of any practical meaning or purpose. Although Sir George Baker talks of 'purpose' the style of the judgment is still 'formal'. He had to make the point as to 'purpose' in order to overcome the decision of *B* v *B*. What he is actually saying is that:

(a)   a literal reading of section 1 produces this solution; it gives the woman a right to have the violent male excluded; it does not even mention a limit to be placed on this; and

(b)   it was the earlier cases which had gone beyond this literal reading by importing into the wording the sanctity of property rights and, in doing so, had not implemented the purpose of the Act. He is therefore arguing that it is the use of a 'formal' style which produces the real purpose and not the 'grand' style.

Shaw LJ first considered that the meaning of the section was plain: nothing in the wording took account of the 'other party's' property rights so it could not have intended this to be relevant. He reviewed the arguments to the contrary, and, though attracted by them, concluded that the 'section would be utterly stultified' if nobody but a sole owner could gain the injunction. The general theme of the section was to subordinate property rights to the need to protect the victim of violence. Shaw LJ's decision thus has a strong 'formalist' feel about it, though there are odd hints of a wider approach such as: 'The construction of a statute dealing with a morbid aspect of society must, it seems to me, be pursued in the practical context of the evil sought to be remedied rather than with analytical detachment' (876a).

Goff LJ (dissenting) dwelt on the *stare decisis* aspect and felt bound by the earlier decisions although he expressly did not agree with them. However, he made some comment on the interpretation of the section. He reiterated the point that a woman should not have to be sole owner of the home in order to make the application, for this would deprive the section of all effect. Goff LJ continued in a classic 'formalist' vein by analysing the relationship of section 1 to other parts of the Act. He concluded that, if he were free of binding precedent, he would adopt a 'liberal approach' and grant the injunction because:

... the strict construction ... virtually strikes the power of eviction in s 1(1)(c) ... since where the (woman) is sole owner of the property she does not need it ... yet where she is not sole owner and so the Act is needed to protect her from just the same evil, it is held inapplicable. (874:d)

His Lordship was prepared to make reference to the mischief of the Act, but only by discovering that mischief on the accepted (limited) grounds. The meaning of Parliament, he said, must still be found in the words used in the Act.

Cumming-Bruce LJ (also dissenting) agreed with the decision in *B* v *B* and, for the most part, with Goff LJ; but concentrated his reasoning on points of precedent. The tenor of his judgment is in the 'formal' style. This is particularly noticeable in his references to the mischief rule and his consequent disapproval of using debates in Parliament to assess the purpose behind the Act on which he says (at 885):

The task of this court is to decide what the words of the Act mean. The subject should be able, as in the past, to read the words of an Act and decide its meaning without hunting through Hansard to see whether the Act has a different meaning from that which is to be collected by application of the subtle principles of construction that this court has worked out over the last three centuries.

How Did the House of Lords Interpret the Statute?

The House of Lords unanimously dismissed Johnson's appeal but the Law Lords were not of one mind in their reasoning.

Lord Diplock stated a preference for a narrow 'formal' approach to the interpretation of section 1; to which he added adverse comment on the practice of looking at reports on Parliamentary debate to discern the meaning of a statute. This latter point was treated in the same way by the other Law Lords.

Viscount Dilhorne stated (at 1145) that the 'language is clear and unambiguous and Parliament's intention apparent'. To differentiate between married and non-married women would 'frustrate the intention of Parliament'. At first sight this appears to be a 'formal' style; but it is difficult to see from where Viscount Dilhorne derives his conclusions apart from the line (at 1145): 'Subsection (1) is not concerned with property rights'.

Lord Kilbrandon took a literal approach to the section; expressly agreeing with Lord Salmon and Lord Scarman.

Lord Salmon adopted a 'formal' style, moving from a literal reading ('It has been said that its (section 1) meaning is as plain as a pikestaff. I agree') to a more purposive stance based on an examination of the legal history of the Act and the mischief it sought to remedy.

Finally, Lord Scarman also looked to the mischief the Act was designed to remedy. Out of this Lord Scarman identified the purpose of the Act and had no difficulty extending this purpose to allow an unmarried woman with no property rights to be, nevertheless, granted the injunction. His Lordship's speech lies between the 'formal' and 'grand' styles. Lord Scarman concentrates on the mischief. There are wide statements of purpose (at 1156): 'I would expect Parliament, when dealing with the mischief of domestic violence, to legislate in such a way that property rights would not be allowed to undermine or diminish the protection being afforded'. But, having said that, the tenor of the speech is that of a formalist. He refuses, for instance, to look at *Hansard* to determine either mischief or purpose; and the other pillar to his decision is effectively that Parliament has stated a right clearly so if it affects property rights by a side wind, so be it.

Thus when one just adds up the decisions of all the judges (merely who won and who lost) in this case as well as *B* v *B* and *Cantliff* v *Jenkins* one finds seven Lords Justices on one side and the Master of the Rolls, the President of the Family Division and two Lords Justices, together with five Law Lords on the other. And, as we have shown, this simple arithmetic does not reveal the diversity of approach.

As to the styles adopted: we have made some comment as to 'formal' or 'grand', but it must be admitted that we were occasionally in some healthy disagreement as to which side of the line the judge's approach fell: and this is the very point we wish to emphasise. There are gradations even within these approaches; there can be no fixed formula. To the extent, for instance, that nearly every judge examined the mischief of the Act one could classify these remarks as being in the 'grand' style. But this does not always follow. Their approach may have been a standard example of turning to the literal meaning first, and only then falling back on the mischief. One needs (in good literalist fashion?) to read what they actually said. With this in mind we have been conservative in classifying every purposive approach as 'grand style'. In the end we would prefer you to make up your own mind and then ask: is the classification absolutely vital? And to this we would reply 'No', because our classification has only been designed to underscore our wider point that it is *styles* of interpretation that matter, not the rules.

Even where the judges are in agreement as to the outcome, the route they followed in getting there is not always shared by others. And one judge does not always maintain a consistent style. You may recall that Lord Denning, in *Davis* v *Johnson,* relies on a literal reading of the section at one stage, only to turn to the purpose of the Act later. He was not alone. There was, for instance, another problem with section 1: subsection (2) speaks of the woman having the right to claim the injunction if the parties are a man and a woman 'who *are living* with each other in the same household'. A literalist view would be that once she left she was no longer 'living' with the other party. Thus she could not bring her application.

Some judges who commented on this eg, Sir George Baker and Cumming-Bruce LJ stated that this could not mean that once the woman left (once 'the door shuts behind her') she lost her right to apply. Since most women, faced with violence, would have fled the home, such a literal interpretation would be a nonsense. Thus whilst one major point in the case is, on the whole, decided by using the 'formal' style, this second point could be said to have been decided: (a) in the 'formal' style (effectively the absurdity triggering the golden rule); or (b) in the 'grand' style—never mind the words, look at the purpose of the Act.

Two final points need to be made here. First, it is very tempting to criticise those who adopt the 'grand' style as inventing reasons to fit decisions they have already reached. But on closer examination, when a judge adopts a more 'formal' style it is still often difficult to understand exactly where *the purpose* to which he refers came from, as we can see with the treatment of the phrase 'living with each other' above. The 'formal' style, ranging from literalism through to a more purposive approach, is not automatically entitled to be termed logical.

Secondly, if you approach the problems of interpretation by only asking 'which rule will be used?', you will miss the point. To adapt the chess analogy we used in Chapter Six: knowing that your opponent can 'castle' does not tell you that he will 'castle'. There is no set moment when your opponent will 'castle'—if at all. And if you are playing chess and do not know what 'castling' is, and when it may be used, you are at a serious disadvantage. Thus the rules describe the limits of what *may* happen; and they tell you what will *not* happen. Your opponent cannot move his pawn as if it were a knight, for instance. Equally there are limitations placed, by convention and common sense, on even the most purposive of judges. The rules may tell you *what* will happen in terms of basic structure; they cannot tell you *how* the game will progress. Each player has his own style.

We would agree, therefore, with Twining and Miers that, 'We do not believe that there is one right answer in hard cases or that problems of interpretation can be solved primarily by rules' (1991:376) and with Zander that, 'The rules and principles of interpretation therefore do little or nothing to solve problems. They simply justify solutions usually reached on other grounds' (1989:148). It is not unfair for a student new to legal studies to ask which rule will be used; it is unfair, however, for us to pretend there is a 'right' answer.

However, most of your academic life will be spent presenting an argument for one side (the same will be true if you go on to practise law). Your problem does not therefore lie in which approach you should use to *determine* a case: that will not be your function. Instead, your problem lies in determining which approach to adopt so that your argument is at its most convincing. Consequently, if you can master the types of reasoning available to you described above and learn to judge when one style is more applicable than another then you will have done all you can in presenting your argument professionally. The fact then that there is no single correct way to read a statute becomes a less daunting prospect.

Interpretation and the European Community

The influence of the European Community and the Civil Law's more 'purposive' approach to interpretation may also begin to produce changes in judicial technique, even as regards legislation unconnected with the Community.

We have seen throughout this book that the Civil Law tradition is different from ours as regards case law. Here we must recognise that European legislation is structured in a manner that is also very different from English Acts of Parliament. The former follows the *Civilian* tradition in emphasising simplicity of drafting and a high degree of abstraction which is quite different from the exhaustive approach adopted by English draftsmen. This means that a wide-ranging purposive approach (a teleological approach) is even more central to the interpretative process in the context of European Community legislation. Here, questions of broad economic or social aims are regularly considered by the courts, in a way that could be attacked in the English courts as a 'naked usurpation of the legislative function'.

This difference in approach has increasingly been recognised by the English judges when considering Community legislation, or even when considering English legislation that has been passed to fulfil an obligation under European Community law. Indeed recently the House of Lords completely (and openly) ditched the literal approach in *Litster* v *Forth Dry Dock* [1990] AC 546, [1989] 1 All ER 1134, where the statute in question was derived from a Directive of the European Community. Instead of the literal approach the Lords adopted a very wide purposive approach in line with European judges.

This does mean, perhaps rather unsatisfactorily, that the judges are seeming to apply two different standards of interpretation; depending upon whether the legislation is purely domestic, or founded in Community law. It is difficult to generalise, as the judges have yet to develop a consistent approach to European Community influences—for example, the decision in *Litster* can be compared with that of a differently constituted House of Lords in *Duke* v *GEC Reliance (formerly Reliance Systems)* [1988] AC 618, [1988] 1 All ER 626, which took a far more traditional (ie, narrow) approach to a related problem of interpretation. Few English judges have followed the line taken by Lord Denning in *Bulmer* v *Bollinger* [1974] Ch 401, [1974] 2 All ER 1226, to argue that the English courts should generally adopt a broad purposive approach, akin to the European style, in all cases. However, one can detect an increasing tendency towards this approach: see *R* v *Registrar-General ex parte Smith* [1991] 2 QB 393, [1991] 2 All ER 88.

We have left describing the methods utilised by European judges and lawyers to interpret legislation until Chapter Ten.

Interpreting Secondary Legislation

When looking at the rules of statutory interpretation, it is easy to forget that much legislation is not created by statute but by statutory instrument or byelaw. You will recall that we considered the growth, and importance, of this whole area of 'secondary legislation' in Chapter One. We now need to consider the principles of interpretation that apply to secondary, or delegated, legislation.

As a starting point, we can say that generally the same rules do apply; which is a relief. The courts will look at the words used in a regulation, and interpret them according to their immediate linguistic context, only straying beyond this point in cases where the judge finds some absurdity or ambiguity demanding a more purposive approach. However, within this framework there are a number of substantive differences which reflect the fact that delegated legislation is, ultimately, a different creature from primary legislation.

This is because delegated legislation does not stand alone, in the way that an Act of Parliament does; it forms part of a legislative 'package' which includes the parent Act, and possibly other sets of regulations, which may affect our assessment of meaning. It is also because the courts are less constrained by problems of sovereignty when dealing with secondary as opposed to primary legislation.

These various differences can be explored in relation to two issues: the way in which we define the context of secondary legislation; and the way in which the courts handle questions of validity.

Defining the Context

As we have said, delegated legislation is to be read within a potentially wider context than statute law. The meaning of a particular provision is to be ascertained from the whole body of regulations of which it forms part, the parent Act and the Common Law. Exceptionally, the environment within which the regulations operate may also be considered as part of the context. The part played by each of these will be considered.

The regulations: The principle here is the same as that applied to statute. Just as you would not take one section of an Act out of context, so you should not consider a regulation outside of its instrument. This may be particularly important if a reading of the parent Act offers alternative interpretations.

The parent Act: This is of central importance in defining meaning. This is emphasised by the fact that s. 11 of the Interpretation Act 1978 requires words used in secondary legislation to be read as having the same meaning as in the parent Act, unless a contrary intention appears. This is fine, of course, so long as the meaning in the empowering legislation is clear! If it is not the court has to work it out for itself, from possibly a variety of competing explanations. Where there are doubts about the meaning of a word used within the parent Act, then it seems permissible for the court to look at both the parent Act and the regulations in assessing meaning: see *Nurse* v *Morganite Crucible Ltd* [1989] AC 692, [1989] 1 All ER 113.

The Common Law: This can also be of significance. The courts will be reluctant to interpret any delegated legislation in such a way that it conflicts with an established and fundamental principle of Common Law. For example, in *R* v *Secretary of State for the Home Department ex parte Anderson* [1984] QB 778; [1984] 1 All ER 920, the court had to assess the validity of order 5A (34) made by the Secretary of State under powers contained within the Prison Rules 1964, which were themselves made under the authority of s. 47(1) of the Prison Act 1952. The order sought to prevent prisoners from obtaining visits from their legal advisers regarding complaints about their treatment in prison. Section 47(1) was silent in respect of such rights of access, so the court resorted to the Common Law. As a result it held that the fundamental right of access to the courts was wide enough to include a prisoner's right of access to legal advice. Parliament could not be deemed to have legislated against that right purely by implication, so order 5A (34) was held invalid. The courts' powers to declare secondary legislation invalid is a point to which we shall return.

The Principle of Validity

We noted in Chapter One that the courts have the power to declare secondary legislation invalid where it involves an exercise of power exceeding that granted by Parliament. The decision to invalidate is thus dependent upon a question of interpreting, first, the scope of the powers contained within the delegated legislation, and secondly, the scope of the grant within the parent Act. In dealing with these situations, the courts have developed a number of principles.

First, in some specific instances, they have ruled that delegated legislation may only do certain things if there is express authorisation within the parent statute. There are two particularly significant situations where this applies:

(a) the courts apply a presumption against retrospectivity to prevent instruments having an effect on events which precede their introduction. The presumption may be used to require not only that the possibility of retrospective effect is specifically alluded to within the instrument, but that it was also within the ambit of the original grant of power by Parliament— see, eg, *Marshall's Township Syndicate Ltd* v *Johannesburg Consolidated Investment Co. Ltd* [1920] AC 420; *Webb* v *Ipswich Borough Council* (1989) 21 HLR 325.

(b) Parliament will not be presumed to have authorised the amendment of primary by secondary legislation without clear authority within the parent Act. Thus, in the case of *McKiernan* v *Secretary of State, The Guardian,* 28 October, 1989, the Court of Appeal refused to imply that social security regulations modified an otherwise mandatory condition laid down under the parent Act in the absence of express authority. Even where such powers have been granted, the courts have tended to construe them narrowly. However, in *R* v *Secretary of State for Social Security ex parte Britnell* [1991] 1 WLR 198, [1991] 1 All ER 726, the House of Lords appeared significantly to depart from such a restrictive interpretation. In this case, their Lordships determined that a transitional provision in social security regulations could properly modify the parent Act so as to allow the Department of Social Security to recover an overpayment of supplementary benefit made some 15 years earlier. This was despite the fact that such a conclusion required the court to find that what was, in reality, a radical policy innovation towards overpayments constituted no more than a 'modification' of the parent Act. The *Britnell* decision is, it is submitted, a worrying development, for as Professor David Feldman (1992:212 at 217) has argued:

[i]f the courts are prepared to adjust principles of interpretation in order to legitimate a questionable exercise of delegated legislative power, this creates a threat to the principle of legality and, by implication, to the legislative supremacy of Parliament.

Secondly, the courts have, as we suggested at the beginning of this section, shown a marked reluctance to allow secondary legislation to be invalidated purely because of problems of ambiguity. The courts have used the maxim *ut res magis valeat quam pereat* ('it is better for a thing to have effect than to be void') to justify whichever of competing interpretations would be a valid exercise of power. This principle has become widely used in Common Law jurisdictions to avoid treating delegated legislation as *ultra vires*. Strictly speaking, it should not be adopted in cases where the meaning of the regulation is clear from the face of the document, or where its application would require a virtual re-writing of the legislation. In that respect it is no more than a manifestation of the rules against ambiguity.

Thirdly, in cases where delegated legislation is only partially invalid, the courts recognise that they have a power of 'severance'. Severance is a process whereby invalid portions of a document may be separated from those which are valid, leaving those valid parts still standing: see *DPP* v *Hutchinson, DPP* v *Smith* [1990] 2 AC 783, [1990] 3 WLR 196. As such, it can be seen as a derivative of the principle of validity. The concept of 'severance' is extremely complex and we do not recommend that you consider it in any greater detail.

Exercise 17: Perilous poodles and rabid fish

This exercise explores the basic methods of interpreting statutes.

In Exercise 19 (Chapter 10) and in the Appendix to the book we have set out two more extensive exercises, based on examination papers we have set our students in the past. The problems set there combine both case-law and statute and therefore more accurately reflects the skills you need to master.

We recommend that you do not attempt those problems until you are quite happy with the techniques involved in this more simple exercise.

Problem: It is to be assumed that, as a result of a recent outbreak of rabies (and following a consequent Law Commission recommendation) the **Rabies and Dangerous Animals Act 1993** has been passed. It states:

Section 1:	It is an offence to leave animals unattended in any hotel, public house, restaurant or other public place.
Section 2:	The keeping of any animal, other than a domesticated one, without an appropriate licence, is an offence. The form and cost of such a licence will be determined by orders issued from time to time by the Minister. A domesticated animal is one so defined by Schedule 9 of this Act.
Section 3:	Private dwelling houses are exempted from the provisions of this Act.
Schedule 9:	For the purposes of this Act a 'domesticated animal' includes cats, dogs, horses, cattle, sheep, pigs, and snakes or insects common to the British Isles.

Using the rules of statutory interpretation that have been developed, present arguments **AS IF YOU WERE COUNSEL FOR THE DEFENCE** in the following cases.

(1)	*R v Alfred*	Alfred left his poodle in the changing rooms at his local tennis club while he played tennis. He is charged with contravening section 1 of the Act.
(2)	*R v Bert*	Bert keeps piranha fish in a pond in his front garden. The garden is unfenced. He is charged with not having the appropriate licence under section 2.

Points to note in this exercise:

1. **Alfred.** The defence may rest on three grounds.

(a)   The Act refers to 'hotel, public house, restaurant or other public place'. Does a tennis club, therefore, come within that last, general, category? The phrase 'or other public place' could be read *eiusdem generis* to restrict the general words to the genus of the preceding specific words. What is the genus of the preceding words? The prosecution will argue that these words show that the tenor of the section is to prevent animals being left in a place to which the public have general access. The defence could argue that the words indicate a place restricted to food and drink establishments.

Further, if the tennis club is private (or has a limited membership) there might be a defence here. The express exclusion of private dwellings under s. 3 could also be cited in support of this interpretation (since we are entitled to look at the effect of the **whole** Act). This is a weak point but could be used by ignoring the problematic word 'dwelling' and concentrating on the privacy element.

(b)   In the alternative, the defence could argue that the above phrase is not sufficiently specific to create a genus, and that therefore, since a literal interpretation of such general words is virtually meaningless, the court should enquire into the purpose of the Act. A formal style of discovering 'purpose' would be to analyse the Act mainly by referring to the internal context. The short title of the Act is the Rabies and Dangerous Animals Act. This cannot itself be used, unlike the long title, as an aid to construction: *R* v *Galvin*. However, it does suggest that the Act is particularly concerned with the threat of dangerous animals (note the exclusion of domesticated animals by s. 2 and sch. 9). This argument could be used to deny the application of the section to pet dogs, and the long title of the Act (if it has one) could be cited in support (if it offers that support—the question is silent on this). See *R* v *Galvin*, where it was stressed that the long title could be used as a minor aid to construction, provided it did not contradict the express language of the Act.

Seeking the purpose in the 'grand' style one can move away from the Act itself to matters such as social conditions. Similarly, the Law Commission's report could also be used in support, if that was the case (*Black-Clawson*), and even *Hansard* might prove useful on this point.

(c)   Finally, one could argue that 'unattended' does not mean the animal always has to be in the owner's presence (or that 'presence' simply means 'in the line of sight' as in *Casson* v *Dade*).

2.   Bert.   Note: Section 2 covers animals. Fish are animals and so require a licence unless Schedule 9 exempts them. The defence is threefold:

(a)   The most obvious line of attack is the purposive argument that, although fish may be animals, they are incapable (to the best of the authors' knowledge) of carrying rabies. The prosecution may well point out that the Act is concerned with both rabid *and* dangerous animals; a dangerous fish falls within the provisions of the Act. However, the purpose of the Act, as exemplified in the title and gained through an examination of the social setting for the Act, would probably demonstrate that the two ideas were connected.

(b)   The offence created by s. 2 is absolute, save for the exclusion of domesticated animals in sch. 9. Though a literal approach apparently catches Bert he might be able to utilise s. 3. One must argue an extended meaning to 'private dwelling houses'. Land is usually included in such terms. Bert could try to argue that as the fish are kept in his garden they should be excluded under s. 3. This could be argued on the basis that the purpose of the Act is only to protect the public in places to which they normally have resort. As such, there is an argument that an individual's garden is as much his private property as his house, and that any wider meaning could create absurd results. One might try to find other statutes which have defined the term in an acceptable way for the defence. Finding one *in pari materia* might be more difficult. One such possible example might be the Dangerous Dogs Act 1991. And, indeed, the very question of whether a garden path constituted a 'public place' under s. 10 of the Act arose recently in *Fellowes* v *DPP*, *The Times*, 1 February 1993. The Queen's Bench Divisional Court held that it was not a public place because of the purpose of the Act and that people only entered the private premises as visitors, not as general members of the public. You would have to be sure that the statutes were *in pari materia*, however. You would also have to be aware that, regarding the same section of the same Act the QBD Divisional Court has also recently decided that a dangerous dog in a private car had to be muzzled because the car was on a public highway and this constituted a public place for the purposes of the Act (*Bates* v *DPP*, *The Times*, 8 March 1993). Further, if the mischief in our fictitious Act is perceived as relating to 'danger', the unfenced pond is still a problem in our argument.

(c) The categories of animals referred to in sch. 9 are wide; wider, perhaps, than a literal reading of the word 'domesticated' would lead us to expect; although it is presented as an inclusive definition. The case of *Coltman* v *Bibby Tankers* [1988] AC 276 considered the dual meaning that can be given to 'inclusive' definitions. The list might be either exemplary or exhaustive. It is notable that fish are excluded, and so if the definition is exhaustive, the prosecution might seek to argue the principle *expressio unius est exclusio alterius*. This would be difficult to counter, and the defence's only response, it is submitted, might be to argue that the definition is exemplary; that 'domesticated' here is sufficiently wide to include all animals that are in fact kept as 'pets'. Whether piranhas are on that basis common to the British Isles might nonetheless be a difficult point to argue!

Conclusion

By way of conclusion we would like to suggest a rough guide on how you might approach the problem of interpreting a statute.

1. *Read the section(s) carefully.* This may include referring to:

(a) related sections in the Act;
(b) schedules;
(c) interpretation sections;
(d) related statutes.

2. *Understand the mischief*

(a) refer to annotations of the Act;
(b) Law Commission Reports;

(c) the social, economic or political background;
(d) *Hansard*;
(e) the long title of the Act.

3. *Check for any European derivation.*

4. *Research academic texts*

(a) textbooks;
(b) monographs;
(c) articles and case notes;
(d) practitioners' texts.

5. *Research existing or related case law.*

6. *Be aware of any technical meanings of the words in question.* For example: 'property'; 'possession'; 'dismissal'; 'recklessness'. In particular, check whether the word is covered by the Interpretation Act 1978.

7. *Be aware of any technical rules of grammar.* For example, the *eiusdem generis* rule.

8. *Be aware of judicial trends in methods of interpretation.* Are judges now more purposive in their approach?

9. *Be aware from which perspective you are viewing the problem.* Are you acting as an advocate? Are you arguing the general possibilities?

10. *Adopt the appropriate style of argument.* You must decide how to pitch your case in terms of a formal or grand style.

11. *Decide how to marshal your authorities to substantiate your approach.* For example, what degree of emphasis will you put on each case? How will you present the *ratio* of the case? How will you deal with *obiter dicta*?

12. *Decide how you are going to distinguish unhelpful authority.*

REFERENCES

* Cross, R. (1987) *Cross: Statutory Interpretation,* 2nd Edition (by Bell, J. & Engle, G.), London: Butterworths.
Feldman, D. (1992) 'Commencement, Transition and Retrospective Legislation' *Law Quarterly Review*, vol. 108, p. 212.
Llewellyn, K. (1960) *The Common Law Tradition*, Boston: Little Brown.
* Summers, R. & Marshall, G. (1992) 'The Argument from Ordinary

Meaning in Statutory Interpretation' *Northern Ireland Legal Quarterly*, vol. 43, p. 213.

* Twining, W. & Miers, D. (1991) *How To Do Things with Rules,* 3rd Edition, London: Weidenfeld & Nicolson.

Webb, J. (1992) 'Limiting Reliance on Discriminatory Pensionable Ages: The Possible Consequences for Other Benefits' *Modern Law Review*, vol. 55, p. 393.

* Willis, J. (1938) 'Statute Interpretation in a Nutshell' *Canadian Bar Review*, vol XVI, p.1.

* Zander, M. (1989) *The Law-Making Process,* 3rd Edition, London: Weidenfeld & Nicolson.

Chapter Nine

Exploiting Legal Reasoning

In this chapter, we will consider explicitly the theories underpinning legal reasoning, and the way reasoning techniques are employed in legal contexts. In so doing we will examine, first, the logical foundations of legal reasoning, and then explore the extent to which legal reasoning requires us to consider criteria beyond those imposed by the strict necessity of logic (eg, social values).

Law is often described as a system of 'practical reasoning'. We can see what this means when we think about what 'doing law' involves. Thus, a judge has to give judgment, lawyers have to advise their clients, legislators have to predict the impact of their laws. The key link between all these activities is that they are built upon some kind of reasoning process. The answers found by judges, lawyers and legislators are not simply based upon some pre-existing knowledge of the law. Although the ability to find and use the various kinds of legal material is important it is not enough, because your sources may not actually provide you with an answer. To be sure, there are some legal questions which can be resolved simply by looking the answer up in a book. If you wish to know what is the maximum compensation payable for, say, an unfair dismissal, you can find the answer in statute and statutory instrument, or in a textbook. But determining whether Jane Smith is likely to win her case, and what level of compensation she is likely to obtain cannot simply be looked up in a book. There is an important element of creativity, of working out an answer according to a whole range of supposedly rational criteria. In this and the following section, we are concerned with how lawyers must go beyond the legal texts, to *construct* their own answers to discrete legal problems. It is this process that constitutes what we shall call the process of **legal argumentation**.

Let's start by thinking about thinking itself. This is perhaps not something we are too used to doing, even in an educational setting. Obviously 'learning' is about acquiring new information—but don't forget that we have to be able to *use* that knowledge. Studying maths provides a good example. Mathematical skills reflect an ability to apply the appropriate formulae (knowledge) to a particular problem, eg, calculating the sine of angle x in a triangle where the length of the sides are known. You might well know that the formula for that calculation is represented as:

$$sine\ x = \frac{opposite}{hypotenuse}$$

but that is not the end — you need to use that knowledge to produce a *specific* answer. That answer will of course vary according to the data you use. Similarly when structuring legal arguments we are working from a source of knowledge about law, and using that to construct an answer to a specific legal problem. It is the process of getting from knowledge to answer that involves our skills of practical reasoning. In setting up this legal process we shall consider three elements under the following heading.

Logic and Legal Reasoning

Legal argument is first based upon fundamental reasoning skills that are common to most disciplines. By 'reasoning', we mean, in essence, the process of deciding on a given course of action. It is important to distinguish 'reasoning' from the colloquial idea of 'having a reason'. Because we are rather careless in our use of language, it is easy, but wrong, to think of reasoning as simply a matter of cause and effect. It is not; reasoning reflects the ability to arrive at a rational, calculated decision.

Let us try to illustrate what we mean. If A hits B because B called him names, he has a reason. A is angry with B and has decided to hit him. Of course, since this is an emotional response, one could say it lacks rationality; in fact it is unlikely to be 'reasoned' at all in the true sense, since A's anger has probably prevented him from thinking through his actions. Would A have been so quick to hit B had he thought about it and realised that later B would come looking for him, with his brother, the champion boxer, seeking revenge? This emphasis upon rationality means that we are essentially grounding legal decisions in the mental process we call *logic*. This point is hardly new. Philip Leith (1991), for example, traces the contact between law and logic back through history to the Ancient Greeks, though, as his work shows, interest in the relationship has been given a modern boost by attempts to create computer models of legal decision-making. The link between law and logic has been frequently acknowledged by the judiciary, and notably by Lord Devlin in *Hedley Byrne* v *Heller & Partners* [1964] AC 465 at 516, where he said:

The common law is tolerant of much illogicality, especially on the surface; but no system of law can be workable if it has not got logic at the root of it.

This is not to suggest that law is unusual; in much day to day life we are using basic logic without really knowing it. If I go out in the morning with only enough money for my bus fare back home, I have a simple choice: either I spend that money while out and walk home, or save it for the return bus ride. I know that I cannot do both. The conclusion that I have to choose is founded on a commonsense form of logic. Logic thus provides a commonplace basis for decision-making, by helping us plan our actions in a way that 'makes sense'. At this level, it is hardly surprising that logic is equally significant in helping us to make sense of legal argumentation; however, it is only fair to point out that the image of logic represented in this chapter is an extremely simplified one. Logic is a complex subject of academic concern in its own right, and, as Leith points out, the view that most individuals have of logic as clear and precise is erroneous; logicians are as prone to arguing about the merits of different theories and systems of logic as academics of other disciplines!

The Nature of Reasoning

Let us begin by formalising our notion of reasoning a little more clearly. We know that it reflects a particular kind of decision making process, which, so far, we have described simply as 'rational'. By this, we mean that it is a structured form of discourse which involves passing from one proposition already known or assumed to be true, to another distinct from the first, but following from it. The classic example of the logical reasoning process is the Aristotelian 'syllogism', a verbal structure which draws a true conclusion from a major and minor premise, each of which is verifiable in its own right, thus:

All men are mortal
Socrates is a man
Therefore Socrates is mortal

In this case the logic is impeccable. We know as a matter of fact that men are mortal, we also know that Socrates' is a man. The conclusion of Socrates' mortality is therefore inescapable.

Logicians tell us that the reasoning process employs two particular modes of thinking, called **inductive** and **deductive** logic. Robert M. Pirsig uses the example of locating a fault in a motor cycle to illustrate these logical modes in the process of scientific method. If the analogy seems rather out of place, persevere, because it is as applicable to lawyers as it is to scientists:

Two kinds of logic are used, inductive and deductive. Inductive inferences start with observations of the machine and arrive at general conclusions.

For example, if the cycle goes over a bump and the engine misfires, and then goes over another bump and the engine misfires . . ., and then goes over a long smooth stretch of road and there is no misfiring, and then goes over a fourth bump and the engine misfires again, one can logically conclude that the misfiring is caused by the bumps. That is induction: reasoning from particular experiences to general truths.

Deductive inferences do the reverse. They start with general knowledge and predict a specific observation. For example, if from reading the hierarchy of facts about the machine, the mechanic knows the horn of the cycle is powered exclusively by electricity from the battery, then he can logically infer that if the battery is dead the horn will not work. That is deduction. (1974:107)

There is an important distinction between these modes of reasoning. The form of deductive reasoning is such that, so long as the major and minor premises are correctly constructed, the conclusion has to be true. Thus the syllogism we have just considered is a representation of the form of deductive reasoning. Inductive reasoning does not provide us with the same degree of certainty. We can reach an answer inductively on the basis of an assumption that our particular experience is of general application. In some cases, such as Pirsig's for example, our assumption is likely to be pretty accurate, and obviously the more information we have supporting our hypothesis, the more likely it is to stand up in the future. But, in terms of formal logic, we cannot say that our conclusion is conclusive. There is always the possibility that some other conclusion exists.

For example, Patrick Shaw (1981) tells of an experiment conducted in Birmingham some years ago. Drivers in the city were urged to use only dipped headlights at night. During the experiment, it was shown that the number of road accidents had fallen sharply. The local papers immediately declared the experiment to have been a major success. However, it was subsequently found that there had been fewer vehicles on the road than usual during the experiment, so the press had not really got it right. There may have been some correlation between the dipped headlights and the reduction in accidents, but the connection was not as great as had been assumed. The relative inconclusiveness of inductive reasoning is a point to which we shall return shortly.

Lawyers use both inductive and deductive reasoning, and legal decision making will often be a reflection of *both* those modes, used in conjunction with each other to produce a reasoned conclusion. In the legal context, it is, however, also helpful to distinguish between two separate processes: reasoning about legal rules, and reasoning about facts (what we shall call, following Alexy (1989), **empirical reasoning**).

Reasoning and Legal Rules

The first issue is to consider the ways in which such legal reasoning employs inductive and deductive modes. Using Pirsig's analogy, look at the following and give your own reasoned conclusion.

Exercise 18: Zen and the art of legal reasoning?

Statement	*Event*	*Conclusion*
(i) Statute requires that whosoever takes property belonging to another, with the intention of permanently depriving the other of it, shall be guilty of an offence.	X deliberately takes Y's bicycle and sells it to Z.	

This is, of course, a simple example—but in reaching the logical conclusion that X is guilty, were you using inductive or deductive reasoning?

The process you used is in fact deductive. Our starting point is a general rule, laid down in a statute, which we are then applying to a specific instance. We could convert this into a syllogism, thus:

An individual who takes another's property
with the intention permanently to deprive that
other of it, shall be guilty of an offence.

The accused X has committed the prohibited act

Therefore X is guilty of the offence

Another, perhaps simpler, way of looking at deductive reasoning is to talk of it as involving an 'IF-THEN' clause. We could thus describe the above process as requiring that the following proposition be satisfied:

IF the accused has taken another's property with the necessary intent, THEN he is guilty of the offence.

It is easy to fall into the trap of equating deduction with the whole process of logical reasoning, and to treat any other form of argument as illogical. Fans of the *Sherlock Holmes* stories have already come across that fallacy; many of Holmes's supposed 'deductions' are in fact examples of inductive reasoning! This is of particular importance here because deduction by itself is not practically of much assistance to the lawyer. That may seem rather surprising, since, at first sight, legal reasoning seems to depend heavily on deduction. But that conclusion is not tenable if one analyses legal reasoning more thoroughly. Let us explain this by reference to the processes of both statutory interpretation and precedent.

In the legal context, as we have seen, we conventionally distinguish between two distinct reasoning contexts: the interpreting of statutes and the use of precedent through case law. In terms of logic, however, they are not so different. On the face of it, statutory interpretation seems to be chiefly a deductive process, hence the above example. However this is itself an oversimplification. Statutory interpretation will often involve inductive reasoning, where, for example, as Twining and Miers (1991:262) suggest, there are doubts about the scope of a statutory rule, and there may be an argument from competing analogies. In this respect it is a mistake wholly to separate case law and statute in your mind. It is not unusual for cases which turn on a question of statutory interpretation to require the court to look at competing arguments as to statutory meaning which have existing authority derived from case law. For example, in _R_ v _Shivpuri_ (1986), a case we have already considered, the essential problem was one of interpreting the scope of s. 1 of the Criminal Attempts Act 1981. However, the House of Lords could not treat that simply as a question of interpreting the Act; they were required, by the rules of precedent, to consider the meaning given to the Act by an earlier House of Lords decision in the case of _Anderton_ v _Ryan_ (1985) and had to justify their decision accordingly. Whether this same emphasis on induction holds for Civilian (codified) systems is more debatable, as we shall argue below; though given that even codified legal systems often have vestiges of precedent which may help determine interpretation, these too are probably best seen as involving a hybrid reasoning process.

Using precedent also, in theory, involves both deductive and inductive reasoning. In applying a rule of law in a particular case, a judge is thinking deductively. One of the clearest judicial statements to this effect comes from Lord Hailsham in _DPP_ v _Morgan_ [1976] AC 464 at 516. The case concerned the question of whether an honest but unreasonable belief that the victim consented to sexual intercourse could negative the necessary intent on a charge of rape. His lordship identified the following legal propositions as being correct: 'If. . . the prohibited act in rape is non-consensual sexual intercourse **and** the guilty state of mind is an intention to commit' the prohibited act, **then**, he argued, an honest but mistaken belief as to consent must result in an acquittal. In effect, all he is saying is that the accused lacked the necessary intent, but the strength of the argument lies, in his lordship's view, in the fact that to convict would result in a logical impossibility.

Conversely, deciding what rules should be applied is an inductive process, whereby the court must frequently choose between competing rules, or competing interpretations of the same rule. The operation of the doctrine of precedent is particularly important in shaping the reasoning process in case law. Precedent involves the hardening of what are (in inductive terms) examples from earlier cases into rules of law in their own right. These rules may then be applied deductively to future cases. Edward Levi (1949:2) developed this idea into what he called a 'three step process'. Step one is where a judge sees a relevant factual similarity between an earlier case, or cases, and the present one. In step two, the judge identifies the rule of law on which the previous case(s) rested. Finally (step three) he or she applies that rule to the present case. It is this final stage which, in effect, requires the judge to decide IF-THEN. That means that, of these steps, one and two can be seen as inductive and only step three as deductive. This means that, logically, once a judge has decided upon the rule of law, he or she should apply it: that rule is conclusive.

Equally, it follows that the earlier stages inevitably involve a degree of discretion. Levi's first step gives the judge freedom of action in deciding what similarities—and differences as well—are relevant. In step two, the judge again has some freedom in deciding what rules of law are discoverable from the earlier cases. A judge is only obliged to follow a precedent once satisfied that *the precedent fits*. By this we mean that the judge must have first accepted that the facts are, in material respects, sufficiently similar, and that the legal principle established in the earlier case should apply. A similar degree of freedom will exist where the decision turns on a question of statutory interpretation. In either situation, the judge will be engaged in a comparison of the example created by precedent or statute and the circumstances of the present case. This tells us that a judge is using a particular kind of inductive process, commonly called **reasoning by analogy**. In the following sections we shall consider the role of reasoning by analogy, first in the Common and then in the Civil Law context.

Common Law: Reasoning by analogy refers to a very common process whereby we can come to a conclusion in a new situation by drawing comparisons with known examples. It is a technique that we have all used. A child may well reason that it is safe to climb a tree in a friend's garden, because that friend has just done so without falling. That child has reasoned from the analogy, or example, of his or her friend. The basic premise underlying reasoning by analogy in law is simple. It can be summarised as follows:

In case x, factors A, B and C existed. Judgment was given for the plaintiff.
In case y, factors A, B and C existed. Judgment was given for the plaintiff.
In case z, factors A, B and C exist. Judgment should, therefore, be given for the plaintiff.

In practice, the process of reasoning by analogy is not quite as straightforward as the example given. More often, it involves weighing up and balancing a whole variety of differences and similarities. It will be unusual for the analogy to be so clear, and what is more likely is that only a few of the common factors (for example, **A** and **B**, but not **C**) will be present in the later case, so the judge must weigh up the relative importance of **C** in deciding whether to apply the analogy. We have already given you an example of that kind of technique in Chapter Six. **This means that reasoning by analogy cannot be conclusive.** To use our earlier example, the child will not know conclusively that the climb will be safe. His or her friend may be lighter, stronger or taller, all of which might make a difference to the outcome of the climb. It will be up to the child to weigh up the risks and decide if the example is good enough to follow.

The inconclusive nature of analogy goes quite some way to explaining why the inductive stages of legal reasoning create so much potential ambiguity and discretion in legal method, and thence why even a fairly basic logic can have only a restricted role in legal decision-making. However, it is not the whole story, as we consider under the heading of 'The Limits of Logic'. In the interim, we change our focus to the other side of the English Channel.

Civil Law: In this section we shall consider, briefly, whether the Civilian tradition reflects a significantly different approach to legal reasoning.

Michel Villey makes the point that

> Even today English law is the closest to the casuistic art of the classical Roman jurists. The law for the [English student] . . . , is above all a matter of science; or rather of case law; because the law is to be induced from nature, and by the study of each case. (1975:700)

So do we assume from this that the role of induction, and hence of analogy, is of far less significance in continental European legal systems? Unfortunately it is not that simple. Legal theorists recognise that, in Civilian systems too, legal reasoning takes on a hybrid form which is neither wholly deductive nor inductive. There are, however, two distinctive features of Civilian systems which suggest substantive differences from the Common Law lawyer's logic. First, the codes are often said to provide an **axiomatic** basis for legal rules. By this we mean that they constitute often complete, self-contained principles of law. Secondly, as we have seen, precedent plays a lesser role in Civil Law systems, because of the interpretative traditions connected with codified law. Taken together these might indicate that deduction plays a larger role in Civil Law systems. However, the axiomatic basis of many of the codes only *reduces* (but does not obliterate) the need for the judges to reason from analogy in the manner suggested by Twining and Miers (above). The relative lack of binding precedent might similarly reduce the inductive significance of case law. But, as we have said before, there is a danger that by overstating the doctrinal differences between the systems, we could equally overstate the differences in the reasoning techniques used.

Ultimately, we would suggest that much of the supposed divergence between Civil and Common Law techniques probably involves drawing a distinction without a measurable difference. Bergel makes it clear that Civilian legal method is irreducible to a deductive base, because:

> The law is full of departures from logical solutions deduced from an axiom. These exceptions result from other preoccupations, other principles and other axioms of which the sheer number, the complexity and the differing intensity make an expression of positive law in mathematical terms impossible. (1985:290)

Empirical Reasoning

Solving legal problems, we know, is not simply a question of reading the law. Legal arguments are not constructed in a vacuum, but arise out of real, human, situations. Legal rules are expressed only in very general terms. The application of a rule to a particular case is dependent ultimately on the court or tribunal deciding that the facts of that case fit the rule. This conceals what are in reality, as Ivainer (1988) notes, two distinct processes: the proving of alleged facts (see Chapter Four); and the subsequent interpretation of those same facts. The latter involves a reasoning process. It is up to the lawyers to construct a legal argument to the effect that the facts are *x, y & z*, and that on those facts the rules should be applied in such-and-such a way. It is this aspect of the law-fact relationship that we shall concentrate upon for the remainder of this section, as the actual implications of finding that *x* is fact rather than law is best left to courses on the law of evidence, or on the particular area of substantive law concerned.

At the heart of empirical reasoning is what Ivainer (1988:22) defines as *'une démarche hermeneutique'* ie, a *hermeneutic,* or interpretative, process which seeks to draw a conclusion from the known facts in each case. This emphasis on interpretation is valuable in that it highlights again the extent to which the use of facts in the legal system involves a creative process, which we shall now examine.

From the perspective of the trial lawyer, as opposed to the judge, there are two discrete reasoning techniques that are central to the process of fact analysis. At the early stages of a case, the body of evidence relating to the case is likely to be incomplete; the first task of the lawyer is thus to establish what is sometimes called 'a theory of the case' (see Inns of Court School of Law, 1992) — ie, a plausible explanation as to what may have happened and its legal consequences, which can then be used to assist further information-gathering. Developing a theory of the case itself involves two elements: the creation of both legal and factual theories. By *legal theory* we mean simply the creation of arguments for one or more potential causes of action, ie, a claim for breach of contract, negligence, etc. Although a legal theory is triggered by the factual information you have available, it also underpins the process of fact analysis. A lawyer's legal theory is critical in determining how he or she organises and explains the facts of the case. As Paul Wangerin explains:

Surprisingly, few lawyers and students seem to realize that creating a statement of facts must follow, rather than precede, creating the legal arguments. This chronology must be observed because the statement of facts plays two crucial roles for the advocate. The second role necessitates this order of preparation . . . [T]he statement of facts' first role is to generate psychological sympathy for the represented client. This role has nothing to do with the merits of any legal position . . . The statement of facts' second role is to prepare the reader for the legal arguments to follow. This is its key role, which explains why the legal theory must always be planned first. (1986:435–6)

Creating a *factual theory* involves what is termed abductive reasoning. Anderson and Twining define this as 'a creative process of using known data to generate hypotheses to be tested by further investigation' (1991:443). It is thus a style of reasoning that is essentially based on *inference* — on using your existing knowledge to infer potential facts and explanations. For example, assume that Amanda approaches you for advice. She tells you that her husband, Bart, was recently killed when his car ploughed through a motorway barrier and overturned. The road was quite wet when the accident happened, but no other car was involved in the accident. She cannot tell you whether there are any witness statements relating to the accident. She is convinced that there must be some explanation, other than Bart's own negligence. The accident occurred soon after he left home; he was not overtired, and he was an experienced and careful driver.

You know that, if you are to help your client, you need to establish that someone (other than Bart) was negligent, or the vehicle was defective. So you would start by thinking about a legal theory of the case based either on negligence or, possibly, product liability. What factual theories might you develop? If no other car was involved, you might infer that you should rule out the negligence of another driver. So, alternatively, there is the possibility of a mechanical defect. You could hypothesise along the following lines — was the steering faulty; did a tyre burst, and if so, was the burst due to a manufacturing defect, or some other cause? And so on. Equally, you would have to consider the possibility of driver error: despite his wife's protestations, could Bart have fallen asleep at the wheel, for instance? To get an idea of abductive reasoning in action, see if you can construct a theory suggesting that there was negligence by another driver. (We pause here while you write.)

There are a number of possibilities. Perhaps a vehicle pulled into the lane too close to the front of Bart's car, causing him to break hard and lose control on the wet road. Perhaps a vehicle in front temporarily lost control, because the driver fell asleep, or lost concentration, causing Bart to take avoiding action from which he was unable to recover, given the conditions. In both situations it is quite conceivable that the car causing the accident was not then caught up in it.

The key point to remember is that these are no more than hypotheses based on limited information. This means that, though akin to the inductive form of reasoning, the results of abductive reasoning are far more tentative, and would not be sufficient to persuade a court in your favour. To take the example above, it is pretty obvious that you would not get very far alleging that the accident was due to a burst tyre without evidence from a police accident report that a tyre had indeed burst, and expert evidence supporting your theory that the burst was due to defective manufacture. However, you must recognise that abductive reasoning techniques are necessary to establish the possibility that such an argument exists, before you can think about obtaining the evidence to change the possibility into a specific, supportable, theory at a later stage in the pre-trial process.

Once you have the evidence to establish a supportable theory, the reasoning process moves on to a second stage. Now your empirical reasoning falls firmly within the inductive sphere. Shakespeare, as usual, offers a suitably gory illustration (from *Henry VI*):

Who finds the heifer dead and bleeding fresh,
And sees fast bye a butcher with an axe;
But will suspect twas he that made the slaughter.

Inductively, the conclusion that it was the butcher who did it is acceptable. It is not of course, in formal logic, the only possible answer, but it is *probable*. In any given case of induction the probability will vary by degrees from the slight to the overwhelming—as we have seen already, the law sets its own standards of probability in fact-finding. Deductive reasoning, because it requires that the formal conclusion is absolute, not merely probable, plays little part in empirical reasoning, because the facts are seldom conclusive. The process, therefore, is essentially one of mustering the information that you have, and using it to draw logical inferences regarding the guilt/innocence/liability of a particular person.

In seeking to resolve factual problems there are a number of useful techniques, though in the end much of this boils down to careful application of common sense.

First, think dialectically: essentially all this means is that you need to think through alternative explanations. Do not be afraid to challenge your own assumptions. It is not advisable to develop your own theory of why or how something happened, and ignore other possibilities. This applies as much to the student answering a problem question (where there will often be gaps in the facts waiting for you to construct alternative solutions) as it does to the practitioner preparing a case.

Secondly, be systematic. It is usually important to have an accurate picture of the nature and course of events in order to create a structure within which you can develop your argument.

Thirdly, and following from the above, proceed step by step in presenting the facts of a case. Proof is best built up in small stages. Making major quantum leaps from fact to conclusion may help in developing an initial strategy, but it is unlikely to build a convincing case. This too doubles as sound advice in dealing with problem questions as a student.

Lastly, remember that, in the courtroom, mastery of fact and law may not be enough. A common piece of advice given to young advocates is to 'go for the jugular'. This is what Twining and Miers call 'the principle of concentration of fire' (1991:274–5). It suggests that the best tactic is to concentrate on the weakest points in your opponent's argument, and reminds us of the traditional image of the adversarial process as a battle between opposing sides. Such techniques are a matter of persuasion rather than logic, but then, as we have seen, the ability to persuade can be as important as the logic of a lawyer's arguments. Whether techniques of persuasion should play such an important part in the legal process is a far weightier question, which we leave for you to consider.

The Limits of Logic

In looking at the limits of logic, we shall again divide the issues into their two constituent areas of legal rules and facts.

Reasoning About Legal Rules

Under this heading there are two points to make. Firstly, it follows from what we have already said that the form of logic in legal reasoning is qualitatively different in legal as opposed to scientific method. Secondly, the courts are willing to impose practical or policy-based limits on the extent to which they will apply logic. Let us consider each point in turn.

Earlier we suggested that reasoning is about discovering the truth. In law, we are not concerned with truth (or facts, if you prefer) in a scientific, ie, verifiable, sense. The statement 'water is wet' is verifiable—no one would question the truth of that. Also in scientific method, logic enables prediction, so that it is possible to say that if conditions A and B are satisfied then C will follow as a matter of necessity. In law, we are dealing with rules which are—to use the technical jargon—**normative statements**. This means that they are based essentially upon a value judgment made by Parliament or a judge that a particular consequence *should or ought to* follow certain behaviour. The normative nature of law does not mean that we are stepping outside the realm of induction, but it does introduce the qualitative difference between legal and scientific method that was intimated. This was explained by the American jurist Karl Llewellyn (1960):

> . . . in law your logical system refuses to remain on the level of description, of arranging existing observation. Backed by the fact and doctrine of precedent, your logical system shifts *its content* to the level of Ought (this does not affect the logic). Its remarks change in tone and substance. Now they run: '*If I am a correct description of the accepted doctrine, the future cases a* and *b are to* have the outcome *x*—they *should* have that outcome, and if the judge is on the job he will see to it that they do.' . . . No longer are these initial data statements *merely* of how courts have held on given facts. They have—thanks to the addition of

precedent—become each one a statement simultaneously of how a court *has* held, and in addition how future courts *ought* to hold.

Let's look more closely at this statement in respect of two issues: first, the problem of defining accepted doctrine, and secondly, the question of the relationship between prediction and what we shall call 'public policy'.

Defining legal doctrine: Llewellyn's 'if' in the above extract is crucial. As we have already seen from Levi's three step process, the existence of competing analogies means that the arguments in law are not necessarily just about the logical deductions in step three, but about the premises upon which deduction is to be based. The difficult questions for law tend to be located at the point of defining 'accepted doctrine', and it is there that pure logic is often of little help. We can illustrate this by looking at two contrasting decisions of the Employment Appeal Tribunal (EAT) in the cases of *Kidd v DRG (UK) Ltd* [1985] ICR 405 and *Clarke v Eley (IMI) Kynoch Ltd* [1983] ICR 165. Both cases arose on very similar facts whereby the applicants had alleged that redundancy schemes operated by their respective employers were contrary to the Sex Discrimination Act 1975 in that, by selecting part-time workers for redundancy first, they indirectly discriminated against women, and married women in particular, who were disproportionately dependent upon part-time employment. The legal basis of the women's claim, and the defence raised by the employers in each case were also closely comparable. In *Clarke,* the EAT had found in favour of the women applicants, but in *Kidd* a differently constituted tribunal came to the opposite decision. How could this be? Had a strict analogy been applied, then *Kidd* should have followed *Clarke.* In departing from the latter, Waite J, giving the decision of the EAT in *Kidd,* recognised that their decision left the concept of indirect discrimination 'exposed to criticism by the orderly minded as lacking form or precision' (p. 417). Clearly this did not unduly worry the tribunal; in fact, just the reverse, since they justified the refusal to apply *Clarke* on the ground that they wished to preserve flexibility in this area of law by avoiding drawing general principles from specific cases. In other words, the tribunal was really *rejecting* the need to define a precise legal doctrine in the first place!

Prediction and public policy: Llewellyn's reference to outcomes means that we are preserving the element of prediction based upon logical deduction, but the legal context changes the nature of that prediction from one of fact to one of value, or, if you prefer, from 'is' to 'ought'. This change is vital. We can see that there is a major qualitative difference between 'is' and 'ought' statements. A parent's comment that a naughty child *is* going to be smacked obviously has a very different meaning from an onlooker's observation that the child *ought* to be smacked.

Precedents in law are very much the second kind of statement. They show that there may be an answer which logic predicts should apply, but what if that runs contrary to the system of values held by the judge deciding a case which is analogous to the precedent? Is he bound to follow it? The answer is plainly no. The judicial ability to distinguish what are perceived to be 'awkward' precedents can often provide a judge who is sufficiently determined not to apply precedent strictly with the means of so doing. Similarly, in statutory interpretation, the element of choice between literal and purposive approaches also reduces predictability. In short, differences within accepted legal methods can justify different results.

The role of theoretical logic is thus limited by the fact that it may only take the judge as far as identifying a number of rational options. From there, the values that the legal system is seen to serve will play a significant part. This is often explicitly recognised in the legal process by reference to such terms as 'public policy' or 'public interest' (for a similar exposition in a Civil Law context, see Ghestin & Goubeaux, 1983:46–7). The idea of public policy has always played some part in the legal process. Many of the more recent innovative developments in the law have come about precisely because the judges have stopped to ask 'what is the best policy for the law to adopt'? Examples of this kind of reasoning have influenced developments in both the Common Law, and in the application of statute law. Thus, Lord Atkin's 'neighbour principle', developed in *Donoghue* v *Stevenson* [1932] AC 562 was clearly actuated by his lordship's belief that a generally applicable test for negligence was desirable. The case could have been resolved without the 'neighbour principle', as established criteria already existed which could have included the issue of manufacturer's liability raised by the facts of that case. Similarly, questions of value cannot be excluded from the process of statutory interpretation. We cannot just sit down and logically analyse an Act of Parliament without taking any account of a whole variety of variables; including not least judicial attitudes to that legislation. In particular, any judicial claim to be adopting a broadly purposive approach to statutory interpretation is likely to disclose some element of policy analysis—as in the abortion law case of *Royal College of Nursing* v *DHSS* [1981] AC 800, [1981] 1 All ER 545.

Sometimes, the extent to which judges depend upon policy arguments is not openly acknowledged, for fear that the judges would be seen as adopting a 'political' law-making role as opposed to a 'legal' interpretative role (see Frank, 1947), though this narrow view of judicial intervention has been largely rejected by academics and even by some members of the judiciary in recent years. As a result, we can even begin to recognise some fairly formalised kinds of policy argument which are frequently applied by courts. These range from the pragmatic, such as the so-called 'floodgates principle' which may be used by the courts to reject a claim, on the basis that to allow it would open the floodgates to so many additional claims that the courts might be overwhelmed thereby (see, eg, the minority decision of Lord Wilberforce in *McLoughlin* v *O'Brian* [1983] AC 410, [1982] 2 All ER 298), to the political (eg, the tendency of the courts to regard the needs of national security as an issue for the Government, and therefore non-justiciable: *Council of Civil Service Unions* v *Minister for the Civil Service* [1984] 3 All ER 935).

Equally the judge may not be endorsing a specific public policy argument, but arguing from a more generalised sense of what is right. This is sometimes signalled in the courts by reference to concepts such as 'justice' or 'equity'. The meaning of such terms is, of course, virtually impossible to pin down with any degree of certainty—and indeed they have been the subject of debate among legal theorists for centuries! Nevertheless they provide a useful, but unpredictable, mechanism for a lawyer to favour one (more or less) rational answer over another. This can be illustrated by the case of *DPP v Majewski* [1977] AC 443. Like *Morgan,* this was a case dealing with the problem of mens rea in rape. However, here, the court refused to be swayed by the logical argument that if a person is incapable through drink of forming the requisite intent to commit the crime, he cannot be guilty of it. In finding that an intoxicated accused lacking intent could still be guilty of rape, certain members of the House of Lords recognised that they were departing from logic, but in the words of Lord Salmon, to do so in this case accorded with 'justice, ethics and commonsense' (p. 484).

The point is that pure logic does not necessarily give the desired answer, and may be, therefore, of limited value in predicting future decisions. To return to our original simile, the observer's prediction that the child ought to be smacked will be a pretty poor predictor if the parent is actually opposed to corporal punishment. Legal arguments and decisions are inevitably influenced by the values of the actors within the legal process, and there is thus no guarantee that what is formally logical will necessarily be 'right'.

In recognising this gap between logic and 'good law' (whatever that may be), we must recognise that the limiting of logic carries with it a definite cost. That is, that the introduction of policy or of notions of 'justice' creates greater uncertainty in legal reasoning. We might argue that it is worth the cost, because it enables the judges, and hence the law, to be responsive to changes in (say) social or economic conditions, or to cases which are taken to be exceptional. In responding to such changes, the judges are inevitably acting subjectively, and, in a sense partially. This is not to imply political bias, but given the homogeneity of the English judiciary, there is some recognition that the judiciary tend to speak with the voice of the 'Establishment'. As a senior judge admitted some years ago:

> Impartiality is rather difficult to obtain in any system. I am not speaking of conscious impartiality, but the habits you are trained in, the people with whom you mix, lead to your having a certain class of ideas of such a nature that, when you have to deal with other ideas, you do not give as sound and accurate judgments as you would wish.
>
> (Scrutton LJ 1923:8)

Whether, therefore, the judiciary are well-placed to evaluate the demands of public interest or policy is a debatable question, though one that goes beyond the scope of this book. It is, however, worth noting that a number of academic critiques (notably Griffith, 1991) have suggested that they frequently fail in that evaluation. Ultimately, the significance of such value-based reasoning might also lead us to question whether there is, in reality, any truly deductive basis within legal reasoning as practised; though this too would seem to remain an issue over which legal theorists are themselves divided.

The growing recognition amongst philosophers that formal logic perhaps does not play a major part in legal reasoning has, in recent years, re-opened interest in a sister-discipline called **Rhetoric** (see Goodrich, 1986:168–208). Put simply, rhetoric is the art of constructing an argument. Like logic, it recognises that a persuasive argument must be built upon certain rules. The father of what is now called the 'New Rhetoric', Professor Chaim Perelman, argued that:

> the domain of argumentation is that of the likely, the plausible, the probable, to the extent that the latter escapes mathematical certitude (1963:134).

In this way rhetoric has always recognised that truth is contingent, and the establishment of any version of 'the truth' is dependent upon argument. Historically this meant the religious, political and legal emphasis on oral argument central to Ancient Greek and also Roman society; hence the colloquial understanding of rhetoric as oratory or 'speechifying'. Current legal interest in rhetoric has understandably centred upon this emphasis on argumentation, and its opposition to formal reasoning processes. As an alternative view on the construction of legal arguments it has been significant in the development of elements of European Critical Legal Theory (Goodrich, 1986; cf. Alexy, 1989).

Empirical Reasoning

In empirical reasoning, the quality of our decisions on the facts of a case will be dependent upon the quality of the fact finding process, and it is this relationship which probably constitutes the greatest limit on the role of logic in empirical reasoning. We have already considered, in Chapter Four, some of the problems of fact finding. Here, we intend to develop some of those issues in a more abstract and theoretical fashion.

Most cases that come before a court concern a dispute over the facts. *R* v *Wallace*, discussed in Chapter Four, is a prime example. The difficulties referred to by the Court of Criminal Appeal in that case did not concern tricky questions of law, but arose in trying to sort out what actually happened.

The first limitation we explore concerns the way in which lawyers perceive facts. In the classic type of problems set by law teachers, that issue normally does not arise. You will be given a set of 'facts' and asked to advise on the law. Though such exercises have practical value in developing problem solving skills, they inevitably by-pass this rather fundamental issue.

Formal definitions of 'fact' in the abstract are, as we have shown, thin on the ground; though there are plenty of cases where the judges have to decide whether a particular issue is one of fact or law. This reflects the commonsense approach to facts, which says (to put it a little crudely): 'we all know what a fact is, don't we? Facts are things we know to be true. They just exist. So what's the problem?' We would argue that this level of certainty itself is a problem. Our sense of what is fact is largely based upon observation (what we perceive with one of our five senses) or else some more abstract form of knowledge (generally 'received wisdom', or, eg, in a more specialised sense, a forensic scientist's, or other specialist's, expertise). The danger is of treating instances of 'observation' or 'knowledge' as absolute truths. When we talk of 'facts' it is very easy to get caught up in a pseudo-scientific mode of thinking, in which facts appear to have the force of objectivity—a fallacy we first discussed in the context of Chapter Four. In law, fact-finding is not that simple. We know that one and one make two, but in the courts facts have to be established from a very unscientific source—us! Kohler's famous drawing of the goblet/faces is an example of the kind of difficulty we must deal with.

If I tried to describe this I might simply say that I saw the profiled faces of two people, staring at each other from close to. That might be an accurate, and therefore 'true', description, because it might be all that I saw. If another person described accurately a drawing of a goblet they had been shown, would you necessarily realise that each of us was describing the same thing? Two individual perceptions of the same fact may thus

be very different, because there may well be equally valid alternative forms of explanation.

This example does not take into account another variable, which is the quality of the observation. Considerable psychological research into skills of observation has emphasised human fallibility (Lloyd-Bostock, 1988:3–23). To put it bluntly; we are not particularly good at remembering what we have seen or heard or done. To make matters worse, the more time that passes between the event and the point of recall and the more stress we were under at the time the event happened, the less accurate our recollections are likely to be.

Stress or external factors may not be the only cause of unreliability. The internalised values of a particular witness may, consciously or unconsciously influence testimony; personal expectations or prejudices may well play an important part. For example, Mr Brown lives in a wealthy suburb of town which has suffered a recent spate of burglaries. One day he sees two cars drive slowly down his road. The first is driven by Mrs Smith, the second by Mr Jones. He informs the police about Mr Jones, but does not mention Mrs Smith because he does not think it relevant. Why? Because Mr Brown may be influenced by his own value judgments of what is suspicious behaviour. He may assume that a woman is less likely to be engaged in criminal activity than a man; if Mrs Smith is well-dressed, and in a smart car, while Mr Jones is badly dressed and in a battered old car, he may be more likely to consider Mr Jones's behaviour deviant, and so on. In recent decades, some scientists and social scientists have come together to argue that we too easily disregard the extent to which what we call 'knowledge' is not wholly objective, but socially constructed. This is what Hanson means by his observation: 'seeing is a theory-laden undertaking' (1958:19). This applies not just to lay witnesses, but also to expert evidence.

Expert evidence is quite commonly used in court to establish technical evidence outside the competence of lawyers and ordinary witnesses—the cause of an accident, the handwriting on a letter, the ballistics of a particular gun are all likely subjects of expert testimony. Given the adversarial nature of proceedings, each side may have its own experts, whose opinions may well be diametrically opposed. This is because expert testimony, which may reflect on not only what has happened, but also a version of how or why, will depend heavily upon the individual's perspective on his or her subject. Courtrooms can often become a point at which different 'world views' meet head-on.

This is a tendency which is exacerbated by the manner in which such evidence is used in the trial process. To explain this, let us consider an example from a real, American, case which is of some notoriety.

On 30 March 1981, John Hinckley attempted to assassinate the US President, Ronald Reagan. The assassination attempt failed, though four people, including the President, received bullet wounds from Hinckley's gun. Hinckley was arrested on the spot and subsequently put on trial for attempted murder (see Low et al., 1986). His (successful) defence was one of insanity, and it was the facts that would be used to establish that defence which, even more than the celebrity of his intended victim, caught the public attention. It soon emerged that Hinckley was obsessed with the actress Jodie Foster, then a student at Yale University. He had written to her, phoned her, and followed her repeatedly, and, a fact that was to take on major significance in the trial, watched her in the film *Taxi Driver* over 15 times.

Taxi Driver became a key piece of evidence in establishing Hinckley's insanity. It was alleged that Hinckley had been particularly influenced by a leading character in the film, the lonely and mentally unstable taxi driver Trevis Bickle, who was befriended by the young prostitute portrayed by Jodie Foster. Of critical importance was the fact that, in the film, Bickle was stalking and preparing to assassinate a politician who employed a woman with whom Bickle had unsuccessfully tried to form a relationship. Using *Taxi Driver* as evidence, the defence sought to show that Hinckley's behaviour was consistent with schizophrenia. It was argued that there were clear links between the actions of Bickle and the formulation of Hinckley's bizarre plan to assassinate Reagan and thereby 'rescue' Foster. In essence, it was argued that Hinckley had adopted the persona of Bickle, and turned the fantasy into his own 'reality'. Conversely, the prosecution sought to show that although he may have held certain false beliefs or delusions, this proved only that Hinckley was a 'dreamer' — an essentially ordinary man — and not that he was mentally ill. In an intriguing re-evaluation of the case, Rosanne Kennedy (1992) has focused on the ways in which expert explanations of Hinckley's behaviour and beliefs were polarised by the advocates into sets of binary images: rational/irrational; real/imaginary; mad/bad. As she concludes:

> Over and over, the trial lawyers force essentially indeterminate medical testimony into categories of truth or falsity, thereby masking the undecidability on which the insanity defence is based. (1992:21)

The role of the advocate in creating an image of the 'facts' of a case, therefore, should not be overlooked. It is worth thinking back to the quote from Paul Wangerin, cited earlier in this chapter. What Wangerin is stressing is not just an analytical technique, but a *rhetorical* device. It is a creative use of fact whereby the statement of facts is constructed so as to support the legal argument and persuade an adjudicator of its correctness. Do not forget that this is not only a technique used by advocates. Judges will also use the statement of facts as a rhetorical device, as we have seen from Lord Denning's judgment in *Miller* v *Jackson*, in Chapter Four.

This lack of real objectivity in fact-finding has important implications in the legal context. It means that there is often something to be said both supporting or denying the existence of a supposed fact, to the extent that it may be difficult to establish that one party's assertion constitutes fact at all. It is hardly surprising that many cases revolve around disputed testimony from witnesses about their observations. The uncertainties of fact-finding in law led some legal theorists to become what have been described as 'fact-sceptics'—theorists who have used the uncertainty of the fact-finding process to challenge the rationality of legal decision making— the most famous of these was the American Jerome Frank, who once, succinctly if provocatively, argued that 'facts are guesses' (1949). Although such fact-scepticism may seem negative, it provides an important insight into the legal process. It emphasises that the trial is not a place for establishing 'truth' in an *objective* sense of that term. By recognising that 'truth' in the courtroom is established by the court arriving at an agreed view of events, rather than by discovering objective reality, we are recognising both the extent to which facts have to be created in court, and the extent to which that means that inferences drawn upon legally established facts may be based upon uncertain foundations. This much has been admitted extra-judicially by the Australian judge, Fox J when he said:

> When it is said that the rules of evidence tend to the ascertainment of truth, the most that can be meant is that by their application a particular piece of evidence may be more reliable, or may be the more correctly assessed by the tribunal. This may or may not be the effect in relation to a particular piece of evidence, but one cannot by any process of aggregation of those pieces have any assurance that what is seen as the resultant situation (the ultimate proposition, or finding on the issue) accords with the truth. (1982:152)

The extent to which facts are established according to rules of evidence and procedure may itself set a further limit on the value of logic to empirical reasoning. The point is that the application of such rules may not accord with strict logic, but with other values endorsed by the legal system. As Fox J points out, these rules frequently depend upon the demands of expediency, such as expense or delay to proceedings, or upon substantive claims of public policy (for example the assumption, only recently challenged, that the evidence of young children is inherently unreliable, and therefore insufficient by itself to ground a criminal conviction), rather than any devotion to the ascertainment of truth.

We would thus support Professor Julius Stone in his description of the limits of logic:

> . . . the outcomes of 'pure' logical procedures do not correspond to what necessarily is (or will become) law of any actual community. They may be invaluable for criticising existing legal propositions by reference to a hypothetical model of internal logical consistency or . . . to test the extent to which a legal system can be conceived as a logically consistent set of legal propositions . . . These are all legitimate outcomes of logical analysis; but they must always be carefully distinguished from erroneous uses of these outcomes. (1985:45–6)

The various forms of uncertainty we have discussed suggest that the best that *we* can try to achieve is to ensure that our arguments or decisions are essentially rational in the way they are structured, and that they take into account the considerations of legal principle and/or public policy that seem to apply. In this final section which follows, we suggest a practical technique for structuring legal decisions that you will be able to use.

The Decision Analysis Method

The technique we are about to describe is derived from techniques of decision analysis in business decision-making. The idea of decision analysis is a useful one. Keeney and Raiffa summarise its aims succinctly:

> The major role of formal analysis is 'to promote good decision-making' . . . As a process, it is intended to force hard thinking about the problem area: generation of alternatives, anticipation of future contingencies, examination of . . . effects, and so forth. (in Moore & Thomas, 1988:245)

Do not be put-off by this; the model we have adopted is a much simplified version of the original, which has been adapted to fit the legal context more closely. It also builds on the basic techniques of problem solving that we have already discussed. The stages to using this method are displayed in the following figure.

STAGE 1	STAGE 2	STAGE 3
Structure the problem.	Assess known consequences of alternatives.	Integrate information to evaluate alternatives.
Identify alternatives.	Identify (and quantify) uncertainty.	
Determine your objectives.		

These steps can be taken as a number of relatively discrete stages.

Structure the problem: make sure you know who you are and for whom you are acting; in practice, begin to establish the parameters of your theory of the case (in a 'law school' problem, simply identify your relevant facts).

Identify alternative courses of action: eg, do the facts disclose an action in contract and/or tort (eg, the possibility of an action on the basis of both negligent misrepresentation and negligent misstatement); civil and/ or criminal proceedings; multiple or alternative grounds for proceeding (eg, theft and handling of stolen goods; innocent or negligent misrepresentation); a court action or some alternative form of resolution (eg, a common law action for wrongful dismissal and an unfair dismissal claim before an industrial tribunal)?

Determine your objectives: what does the 'client' want—compensation; some other remedy (eg, injunction, specific performance) or just advice as to his or her liability?

Assess the consequences: will each of your alternative courses of action achieve the objectives you have identified? For example, it may be little consolation advising X that he might be able to sue Y for trespass (by Y stealing fruit from his orchard), if X is concerned at his own liability to Y for the injuries that Y suffered being chased off the land by X's Doberman dog! Discard any alternatives that are clearly incompatible with your objectives. By this stage you should have a clearer idea of the facts that will be material to your case.

Identify uncertainty: what are the main uncertainties you face—are there gaps in the facts, or alternative arguments that may be constructed from the same facts; contradictory precedents; ambiguous wording in the Act creating liability, etc (in which case, can you create rational arguments supporting your case)? Are there strong policy arguments which might sway a court one way or another?

Evaluate your remaining alternatives: taking into account any different levels of uncertainty, decide which alternative(s) come(s) closest to achieving your objective(s).

This technique is not foolproof—none is! Ultimately it can only be as good as your initial preparation. Do bear in mind that a decision-making technique such as this is dependent upon your doing sufficient thorough research into the issues first—it cannot make a poorly prepared argument look good!

REFERENCES

Alexy, R. (1989) *A Theory of Legal Argumentation* (trans. R. Adler & N. MacCormick), Oxford: Clarendon Press.

Anderson, T. & Twining, W. (1991) *Analysis of Evidence*, London: Weidenfeld & Nicolson.

Bergel, J-L. (1985) *Théorie générale du droit,* Paris: Dalloz.

Fox, Mr Justice R. (1982) 'Expediency and Truth-Finding in the Modern Law of Evidence' in Campbell & Waller (eds) *Well and Truly Tried,* Sydney: Law Book Co.

*Frank, J. (1947) 'Words and Music: Some Remarks on Statutory Interpretation' *Columbia Law Review*, vol. 47, p. 1267.

—— (1949) *Courts on Trial,* cited by W. Twining. 'Some Scepticism about Some Scepticisms' in *Rethinking Evidence: Exploratory Essays*, Oxford: Basil Blackwell, 1990.

Ghestin, J. & Goubeaux, G. (1983) *Traité de droit civil: introduction générale*, 2nd Edition, Paris: Librairie générale de droit et de jurisprudence.

*Goodrich, P. (1986) *Reading the Law*, Oxford: Basil Blackwell.

Griffith, J. (1991) *The Politics of the Judiciary*, 4th Edition, London: Fontana Press.

*Hanson, N. (1958) *Patterns of Discovery: an inquiry into the conceptual foundations of science*, Cambridge: Cambridge University Press.

Inns of Court School of Law (1992) *Evidence and Casework Skills*, 4th Edition, London: Blackstone Press.

Ivainer, T. (1988) *L'interprétation des faits en droit*, Paris: Librairie générale de droit et de jurisprudence.

Kennedy, R. (1992) 'Spectacular Evidence: Discourses of Subjectivity in the Trial of John Hinckley' *Law and Critique*, vol. III(1), p. 3.

Leith, P. (1991) *The Computerised Lawyer*, London: Springer-Verlag.

Levi, E. (1949) *An Introduction to Legal Reasoning*, Chicago: University of Chicago Press.

*Llewellyn, K. (1960) *The Bramble Bush*, New York: Oceana Pub.

*Lloyd-Bostock, S. (1988) *Law in Practice*, London: British Psychological Society/Routledge.

Low, P. et al. (1986) *The Trial of John W. Hinckley, Jr.: A Case Study in the Insanity Defence*, New York: The Foundation Press.

Moore, P. & Thomas, H. (1988) *The Anatomy of Decisions*, 2nd Edition, London: Penguin Books.

Perelman, Ch. (1963) *The Idea of Justice and the Problem of Argument* (trans. J. Petrie), London: Routledge & Kegan Paul.

*Pirsig, R. (1974) *Zen and the Art of Motor Cycle Maintenance*, London: The Bodley Head.

Scrutton, Lord Justice (1923) 'The Work of the Commercial Courts' *Cambridge Law Journal*, vol. 1, p. 6.

Shaw, P. (1981) *Logic and Its Limits*, London: Penguin.

Stone, J. (1985) *Precedent and Law: Dynamics of Common Law Growth*, Sydney: Butterworths.

*Twining, W. & Miers, D. (1991) *How to do Things with Rules*, 3rd Edition, London: Weidenfeld & Nicolson.

Villey, M. (1975) *La formation de la pensée juridique moderne*, 4th Edition, Paris: Les Éditions Montchretien.

Wangerin, P. (1986) 'Skills Training in Legal Analysis: A Systematic Approach', *University of Miami Law Review*, vol. 40, p. 409.

Chapter Ten

European Legal Method

Britain's membership of the European Community has meant that the English Legal System is increasingly having to take account of the European dimension. As we have noted before, and shall explore in this chapter, Community law takes precedence over national law and can even take precedence over legislation. Not only does this mean that some of the law affecting us is created by institutions of the European Community rather than by our national Parliament and courts, it also involves us in a different way of thinking. We have touched upon these matters throughout the book but, as the role of the Community tends to run parallel with English law rather than fit clearly into the hierarchy, we felt that too much detail on Community law in the earlier chapters might lead to confusion. This chapter therefore explores the topics of Community institutions and legal method in greater depth:

(a)   with a brief description of the sources of Community law;
(b)   by noting the institutions which will have an increasingly important role in our law-making;
(c)   by exploring the effect of the analytical techniques employed by European lawyers; and
(d)   by examining the legal method employed in the Court of Justice.

The Sources of Community Law

In the simplest of outlines, Community law is made up from the originating and amending Treaties of the Community (what might be seen as the Community's constitution), the 'acts' of the various Community institutions (sometimes referred to as secondary sources), and the judgments of the Court of Justice. The four major institutions—the Council, the Commission, the Parliament, and the Court of Justice—all play a part in law-making within the Community. Two other institutions, the Economic and Social Committee and the Court of Auditors, will not be dealt with here.

The Treaties

The European Community began life in 1957 under the Treaty of Rome, signed by France, Germany, Italy, Belgium, Luxembourg and the Netherlands. The same six states had already created the European Coal and Steel Community in 1951; and added the European Atomic Energy Community to the list on the same day as the EEC itself was formed. The aims of the signatories were not limited to economics—a fact becoming more evident today. The Court of Justice of the European Communities and the Parliament (originally called the Assembly) were the only institutions that these Communities shared until 1965; at which date the institutions with overlapping functions in the different Communities effectively merged.

The United Kingdom joined the Communities in 1973. As Treaties are not part of our law, the United Kingdom Parliament passed the European Communities Act in 1972 to incorporate the Treaty provisions. In 1986 the member States signed the Single European Act with its aim of removing trade barriers by 1992 and providing a framework for political unity. This European provision was incorporated into UK law by the European Communities (Amendment) Act 1986.

At the time of writing Parliament is locked in what seems an interminable debate on the Treaty of European Union 1992 (TEU 1992)—the *Maastricht Treaty*. As this chapter is concerned with legal method rather than the substantive law of the European Community we will not make extensive reference to *Maastricht* except where necessary; especially as we do not yet know what will be the final form adopted by Parliament (if any).

The Aims set out in the original Treaty and its modifying Treaties are, with some exceptions, expressed in general terms and broad principles. Each 'section' of the Treaties is referred to as an *Article*. Thus Article 3 of the Treaty of Rome lists the activities of the Community such as finance, trade, social welfare, and politics. When we refer to an Article it will relate to the 1957 EEC Treaty unless otherwise stated.

To these general aims in the Treaty are added various powers by which the European Community can give detail and definition to the general requirements. Under Article 189 the institutions of the Community, therefore, have powers to create law under the Treaties; officially styled 'acts' of the institutions.

Acts of the Institutions

Clearly someone has to have the power to make law within the Community on a year-by-year basis. That power falls to two bodies, termed *The Council of Ministers* and *The Commission*. We will deal with these two institutions below.

As we first mentioned in Chapter One these laws are termed:

(a)   *Regulations;*
(b)   *Directives;* and
(c)   *Decisions.*

Regulations and Directives are sometimes referred to as secondary sources of legislation. However, we prefer to adopt the view taken by L. Neville Brown (1989:5) that the acts of the institutions are too fundamental and broad to be relegated to a 'secondary' tag; they are, along with the Treaties, 'Community legislation'.

A *Regulation* has a general application. Like the Treaty itself, the Regulation applies to all member States and individuals, and is binding without further action on the part of the member States. Regulations have to be published in the *Official Journal* of the Community.

A *Directive* also has general application in that it is binding on member States as to the **result** to be achieved, but leaves open to each state the **form and method** of implementation. This enables the Community to establish the legal principle whilst allowing member States to incorporate that principle, within their own national legislation, in the way they see fit. As we will see below this idea can lead to problems when the wording of the Directive and the national legislation do not correspond. Member States are invariably given a time period for implementation. A Directive has no effect in law until it is implemented by the state (unless the time period has passed), and the method of implementation will vary from state to state according to their own special conditions. The general aim must, however, be satisfied.

A *Decision* is not something of judicial origin, though it sounds as if it should be. Instead it is a binding 'order' issued by an institution of the Community and addressed to an individual or state. These frequently arise in competition cases with the Commission determining the legality of agreements.

To these three binding legal provisions we can also add *Recommendations* and *Opinions* which will be of persuasive authority.

The Court of Justice of the European Communities

We shall deal with the Court of Justice below. Suffice it to say for the moment that the Court of Justice is modelled on European systems, and most of its procedure and legal method bears little relationship to the Common Law world.

Direct and Indirect Effect of Community Legislation

The national courts of member States of the EC are under a duty to interpret and apply Community law to any relevant matters arising in domestic courts. They are also bound to interpret domestic legislation to maintain consistency with Community law. The nature and extent of the courts' duty is fundamentally bound up with two concepts: direct applicability and direct/ indirect effect.

Direct Applicability

Direct applicability denotes the situation where a rule of Community law *automatically* becomes part of the law of a domestic legal system without the need for formal enactment by the legislature of the member State. We noted this above, regarding provisions of the EEC Treaty and Regulations of the Commission or Council.

The other major source of EC legislation, Directives, do not have direct applicability as such. However, Directives are still significant in two ways:

(a) They are binding on Governments, which have an obligation to implement a Directive, normally within a specified time period. If a Government fails to implement the Directive within that period, then the Directive will acquire direct applicability (see Case 262/88 *Barber* v *Guardian Royal Exchange* [1991] 1 QB 344, [1990] 2 All ER 660) becoming an operative part of Community law and therefore taking precedence over any contrary provisions of national law.

(b) Directives continue to provide an interpretative source in relation to domestic law. Thus, English courts are required to construe any domestic legislation passed after related Community Acts in a manner that is consistent with that EC legislation.

Direct Effect

The basic idea underlying direct effect is straightforward. *Direct effect* means that someone may cite a Directive as law without having to cite any domestic legislation which was meant to implement that Directive. It may seem strange that this is not done all the time. But remember that a Directive is designed to be implemented by the member States rather than stand as national law in its own right. So what we are dealing with here is the situation (an increasingly common one) where a Directive is exceptionally used as the governing source of law, thus by-passing the national legislation. In a famous judgment (Case 26/62 *NV Algemene Transport—en Expeditie Onderneming Van Gend en Loos* v *Nederlandse Administratie der Belastingen* [1963] ECR 1, [1963] CMLR 224) the CJEC said that where EC legislation creates 'clear and unconditional' obligations on member States, these were capable of creating individual rights enforceable in domestic courts. All forms of EC legislation are *capable* of having direct effect, provided the acts meet certain conditions. There are normally three overlapping conditions for direct effect:

(a) *The provision of EC law must be clear and unambiguous.* The approach of the CJEC to this issue is highly flexible; eg, in the joined cases of *Francovich and Bonifaci* v *Italy* (C-6/90, C-9/90) [1992] IRLR 84 the Court recognised that the provisions of Directive 80/987/EEC, guaranteeing compensation to individuals for loss of employment through insolvency of the employer, gave member States a wide element of discretion (and so were not unambiguous). Nevertheless, the CJEC felt that it could discern a sufficient 'minimum guarantee' to make the provison precise enough to be capable of direct effect.

(b) *It must be unconditional.* For example, it must not be subject to conditions requiring implementation by member States, or giving member States substantive discretion in respect of the period for implementation.

(c) *It must be capable of taking effect without further action by the EC or a member State.* For example, the EC legislation should not be dependent upon further clarifying regulations being passed in each member State. Again, this test is of crucial significance in respect of both Treaty obligations and Directives which are initially expressed to be conditional *but become unconditional with the passing of time* and thereby become directly effective.

The operation of the principle of direct effect has spawned an extensive body of case law, both before the CJEC and domestic courts. This has added greatly to the complexity of the principle. Much of the difficulty centres upon a further distinction that is made between *vertical* and *horizontal direct effect.*

Vertical direct effect Vertical direct effect is the ability of an individual to use an obligation under the Treaty (etc.) against an organ of the state (see *Van Gend en Loos*) or some other body having special powers to provide public services under the control of the state—this would include, for example, a privatised industry under a statutory duty to provide a public utility—see Case C–188/89 *Foster v British Gas* [1991] 1 QB 405, [1990] 3 All ER 897 (CJEC); [1991] 2 AC 306, [1991] 2 All ER 705 (HL).

Horizontal direct effect A horizontal direct effect is one that is capable of enforcement against another person or non-state organisation—ie, it is horizontal because you are suing someone of equivalent legal standing to yourself—unlike the state which exists in a superior (therefore vertical) relationship with the individual. In Case 43/75 *Defrenne v Sabena (No. 2)* [1976] ECR 455, for example, an employee successfully sued her airline employer (Sabena) for breach of Article 119, EEC which ensures equal pay for men and women doing equal work.

It is accepted by the CJEC that Directives may have a vertical direct effect, for to deny a vertical direct effect (ie, an individual against an organ of the state) would thus enable a member State to rely upon its own non-implementation of Community law. Whether Directives can have a horizontal effect has been hotly debated for many years and we will return to this in discussing the legal method employed in the CJEC.

Indirect Effect

The case of *Von Colson v Land Nordrhein-Westfalen* (14/83) [1984] ECR 1891 is credited with creating a further principle, termed indirect effect. Indirect effect sidesteps some of the problems created by the vertical/ horizontal direct effect distinction. If a Directive does not have horizontal direct effect it may be effective *indirectly* by means of domestic courts adopting an appropriately purposive form of interpretation for related national legislation. In other words, courts can read into the wording of the national legislation the *purpose* declared in the Directive. A court may thus give the citizen a right under domestic law where there would otherwise be none because the EC Directive lacks direct effect. The relationship between direct and indirect effect is a problematic feature of the European jurisprudence, and one to which we shall return later in this chapter.

The Institutions

There are four major institutions considered here. All institutions are equal, at least on a formal basis.

The Council of Ministers

Article 145 of the Treaty states that the Council will ensure that the objectives set out in the Treaty are attained.

The Council is based in Brussels and is a political body which has the final say on nearly all legislative matters. The Parliaments of the member States do not create Community legislation; nor is Community legislation subject to the approval of the national Parliaments. The responsibility of the national Parliaments is merely to implement the Regulations, Directives and Decisions of the Community.

However, power is not given up so easily. The Council is effectively the sovereign body of the Community and is made up from one ministerial representative appointed by each member state. The representative sent by each state varies according to the issue at hand; economic matters will draw the Chancellors, other matters will require the appropriate minister. At the highest level the Heads of State will meet—indeed they are required to meet twice a year. When this occurs the Council is referred to as the European Council, or more informally as a 'summit'.

The Council does not itself generate legislation. That function, as we shall see, rests with the Commission. The importance of the Council, however, is that it decides whether proposals from the Commission shall take effect. The Council is not a fixed body, it is not in permanent session, and the ministerial representatives change frequently in 're-shuffles'. In order to work effectively, therefore, there exists the full-time Committee of Permanent Representatives (COREPER), as well as a system of Management Committees. COREPER comprises state representatives of ambassadorial rank, and their function is to examine the Commission's proposals and sift through them to decide on the level of controversy they might generate when they come before the Council. Those issues which receive unanimous approval from COREPER are put on one list for the Council to 'rubber stamp'. The Council can then dwell on discussing, or disagreeing, on the more contentious issues.

Voting on issues is a complicated business in the Community. Some matters require an unanimous vote in the Council (eg, fiscal measures); and in some cases of vital national interest one state may insist on an unanimous vote even though the Treaty does not demand this, ie, the state may exercise a veto. Other issues can be carried by a simple majority or by a qualified majority. The phrase 'qualified majority' relates to the fact that voting takes place on a weighting system so that the larger states (eg, UK and France) have more votes than the smaller ones such as Luxembourg. The Single European Act allowed more issues to be decided by qualified majority than was the case before.

Further changes to the majority voting rules have been initiated under the *Maastricht Treaty*. For instance, the Community Charter of Fundamental Social Rights (the 'Social Charter') was blocked by the United Kingdom. In an attempt to sidestep the UK's objections the *Maastricht Treaty* contained a specific Protocol (effectively an appendix) on social policy. This allowed the other 11 Member states to introduce the Social Charter in those states as Community law. It also allowed for areas of social policy to be passed (*among the eleven*) by a 'qualified majority' rather than requiring unanimous voting—which had been the case before. This raises an interesting point of legal principle. It means that, if the Treaty is implemented in this form by the United Kingdom, the UK will not be directly bound by any measure introduced using the new post-Maastricht procedures, rather than the old system of unanimous voting. We therefore face the possibility that there will be a 'two-track' Europe with regard to the applicability of future EC social laws.

At the time of final editing, the situation is even more confused than when we wrote the paragraph above. During the passage of the Bill implementing the *Maastricht Treaty* the government was forced to accept an amendment which may have provided the means of re-introducing the Social Charter into English law. Whether this is the effect of the amendment is hotly debated and turns on some complex questions of international law which are likely to be the subject of litigation. This is a matter on which the authors do not feel competent to comment any further! What we can say is that if the Social Charter becomes part of English law the 'qualified majority' principle described above would govern the United Kingdom as well.

The Commission

The Commission is based in Brussels. It consists of nationals drawn from each member State (with weighting for the larger states) and at present comprises 17 members. They are not representatives, and are supposed to act independently of their national governments. Each Commissioner is allocated a special task. The Commission plays a vital role in the legislative process of the Community. It has three responsibilities:

(a) To act as an initiator of legislation;
(b) To safeguard the objectives of the Treaty; and
(c) To act as the Community's executive.

Initiator: The Council may have the final say on nearly all matters of legislation, but it is the Commission which formulates and proposes that legislation. Thus, instead of legislation being simply a list of state interests, the Commission is designed to act with the separate and distinct interest of the Community in mind. The Council of course then applies the nationalistic political factor. Under the original Treaty the Commission's proposals only took effect if the Council agreed to them unanimously. Under the Single European Act this is no longer necessary on all issues, a point which effectively increases the powers of the Commission.

The Commission prepares its proposals after consultation, to varying degrees, with national governments and experts. Political and economic reality plays a part, however, in that the Commission knows that ultimately the proposal has to prove agreeable to the Council members.

Watchdog: The Commission, under Article 169 of the Treaty, has the power to investigate and take proceedings in the Court of Justice against member States infringing Community law. The term 'state' here includes the legislature, the executive and the judiciary. The Commission will first issue an opinion on the failure by the state. Only if the state does not comply with the opinion will action be taken. However, even if the action proves successful no punitive measures will be levied by the Court of Justice, though it is rare for a state not to comply at this stage.

One such action occurred in one of the *Factortame* cases. The issues underlying the *Factortame* cases are complex (for fuller details of the background, see Gravells (1989:569–73)). At the centre of a lot of legal activity was a challenge to the legality of s. 14, Merchant Shipping Act 1988 by a number of Spanish nationals affected by the changes. It was alleged that s.14 effectively prevented other EC nationals from registering fishing boats as British vessels (and hence entitled to greater fishing rights in British territorial waters) unless those vessels were at least 75 per cent British owned, and British managed. This, the Spanish fishermen argued, constituted unlawful discrimination against other EC nationals under Article 7 of the EEC Treaty.

The challenge to the Act was mounted first in the English courts, where the case went as far as the House of Lords, which then made a reference to the CJEC under Article 177 (see *R v Secretary of State for Transport ex parte Factortame* [1989] 2 WLR 997). In the meantime, the European Commission itself began proceedings against the UK under Article 169.

In May 1989, the Commission issued an opinion, to the effect that the Act was inconsistent with Community law. The British government disagreed, so, in October 1989, the CJEC, using its power to grant interim relief, ordered the British government to suspend the operation of s. 14; see Case 246/89R *European Commission* v *United Kingdom* [1989] ECR 3125. Despite backbench mutterings about 'British sovereignty', the government rapidly complied, by means of the Merchant Shipping Act 1988 (Amendment) Order 1989. For the sake of completeness, and to try and dispel some of the confusion caused by the volume of litigation in the case, it is worth mentioning briefly the history of *Factortame* after 1989. If nothing else, it provides a good example of just how complex EC litigation can become.

Since the ruling in October 1989, the case has been flying back and forth between Strasbourg and London like the proverbial shuttlecock. In June 1990, the CJEC gave its preliminary ruling under Article 177 in Case C–213/89 *R* v *Secretary of State for Transport ex parte Factortame* [1990] 3 CMLR 807, [1990] 2 Lloyd's Rep 351, in response to the question on powers to grant interim relief posed by the House of Lords in 1989 (see Chapter One). The House of Lords then gave its decision on this issue in October 1990 (see *Factortame (No. 2)* [1991] 1 AC 603, [1991] 1 All ER 70). Following that, the High Court's original request for a preliminary ruling on the legality of the relevant provisions of the Merchant Shipping Act (see Gravells, 1989) finally reached the CJEC in January 1991. Unsurprisingly, in a judgment which mirrored the reasoning in *European Commission* v *United Kingdom*, the CJEC held that the Act was contrary to the principles of free establishment and non-discrimination contained in Article 52 of the EEC Treaty (see Case C–221/89 *Factortame (No. 3)* [1991] 3 CMLR 589, [1991] 3 All ER 769. And that, thankfully, is where the reported litigation stops.

The Commission can also take action against individuals in relation to breaches of Community competition law.

Executive: The Commission is largely subject to the political control of the Council. However, the detail of legislation is the work of the Commission, and certain matters such as competition law and the rules on agriculture are decided on by the Commission.

The Parliament

This body sits in Strasbourg, though many of its activities are carried out in Luxembourg (its administration) and Brussels (its committees). It was originally called the Assembly and its members were drawn from national Parliaments. It was not a directly-elected democratic body until 1979. Consequently it never was a legislative body in the way we would understand the term 'Parliament'. Rather it had the function of supervising and advising. This is still largely true today, despite the introduction of direct elections.

Except in the case of the budget it is a body exerting influence rather than power.

Despite being restricted to a debating forum, the Council must consult (though not negotiate with) the Parliament on important issues. Failure by the Council to do so can render legislation ineffective; and there are other procedural brakes that Parliament can put on the actions of the Council or Commission. Further, the Commission must report to the Parliament, and this includes answering questions. Ultimately, Parliament may dismiss the Commission collectively or force individual members of the Commission to resign. This has never happened. The Council likewise reports to Parliament on a formal basis, though Parliament exercises no control over the Council. Finally, the Parliament can bring an action in the Court of Justice against the Council or Commission for failure to act under Article 175.

Under the TEU 1992, however, it is proposed that Parliament's powers of veto will be extended in certain areas, eg health and consumer protection, under a new procedure of taking decisions in conjunction with the Council.

The Court of Justice of the European Communities

The Court of Justice sits in Luxembourg and pre-dates the Economic Community. It was created when the European Coal and Steel Community was founded under the Treaty of Paris 1951. The Court is often referred to as the European Court of Justice or (as in the European Communities Act 1972) the European Court. We have used the more accurate title to emphasise that the court deals only with Community law; it is not some supreme European Court of Appeal. 'Communities' is used in the plural because as well as the Economic Community there are Communities of Atomic Energy (Euratom) and Steel and Coal over which the court has jurisdiction.

We consider three points below:

(a)   *What is the jurisdiction of the CJEC ?*
(b)   *What is the composition of the Court?*
(c)   *How does a case come before the CJEC?*

What is the jurisdiction of the CJEC?   Article 164 states: 'The Court of Justice shall ensure that in the interpretation and application of (the Treaties) the law is observed'. The Court is therefore the supreme authority on the law relating to the European Community. It deals only with the interpretation and validity of Community-generated law. Further, it is the national courts and tribunals which apply the interpretations handed down by the Court of Justice. On most issues, therefore, the Court of Justice is a court of reference; it is not a court of appeal.

The court has a wide jurisdiction given to it under the Treaties. Here are a few examples:

(a)   it exercises judicial control over the institutions of the Community such as the Commission;

(b)   it exercises powers of judicial review on the validity of Community legislation such as Regulations and Directives—in other words it can annul Community legislation;

(c)   it hears cases brought by member States or Community institutions against other member States regarding violations of the Treaties;

(d)   it decides whether international agreements entered into by the Community are compatible with the provisions of the Treaties; and

(e)   it gives *preliminary rulings* under Article 177 when asked to do so by a court of a member State concerning the interpretation of Community legislation.

Since 1989 it has also acted as an appeal court to a new court, the *Court of First Instance,* which deals with, amongst other things, cases relating to the staff of the Community.

As this is just one chapter of a book concerned with legal method, and we cannot hope to do more than to show the impact and influence of Community law on our system, we will concentrate most of our attention on *preliminary rulings* (see below).

What is the composition of the court?   There are 13 judges at the moment (1993): one for each member State plus an additional judge drawn from the larger states (France, Germany, Italy and the United Kingdom) in rotation, in order to ensure an odd number. Appointment is for six years, though re-appointment is possible. The judges also elect one of their number to be President of the court for a term of three years. The quorum for the full court (referred to as sitting in *plenary session)* is seven (and must always be an uneven number because the President has no casting vote).

The court is sub-divided into six 'Chambers'. The term 'Chambers' bears no relation to the grouping of advocates we see with the English bar. The term simply means that smaller groups than the whole court can hear cases of lesser importance; perhaps with some degree of specialisation in each Chamber. The presidency of each chamber changes annually.

A Registrar deals with the procedure and administration of the court. His role is perceived as something more important than the title would imply under our system—he even sits with the judges in court, but takes no part in the decision. Each judge, rather like the American system, then has a team of legal experts and secretarial back-up to help him.

As one would expect, the official languages of the member States are the official languages of the court (10 at present, including Irish which has not yet been used). To cope with this there is of course an extensive interpretation organisation. The language preferred by the court is French.

None of this is surprising. The real difference between our system and that of the Community lies with the use of a person called an 'Advocate General'. The idea of an Advocate General is a familiar one in continental legal systems. The Advocate General is an 'adviser' to the court; performing a task which might be likened to 'sifting' through the law on behalf of the court in each case. Article 166 describes his function thus:

> It shall be the duty of the Advocate General, acting with complete impartiality and independence, to make, in open court, reasoned submissions on cases brought before the Court of Justice, in order to assist the court in the performance of the task assigned to it in Article 164.

In practice this means that the Advocate General receives all the details of the case from the parties, investigates the law relating to the issues raised, and delivers his opinion on the case to the court as to what decision they should reach. He sits with the judges on the Bench (opposite the Registrar) but plays no part in their deliberations. He delivers his opinion after the case has been heard by the court, and often at a later hearing. The court is not bound to agree with the Advocate General.

The Advocate General is thus a member of the court, subject to many of the same conditions of appointment as a judge; but one who has no say in the actual decision. As you will see below, whereas the court delivers a very limited and concise judgment, the Advocate General has a wider brief and may often comment on many aspects raised in the case. The Advocate-General's opinion appears with the judgment in any case report and is a persuasive authority in later cases.

Note that since 1982 there is no hyphen in the spelling of Advocate General, except when referring to the possessive case, thus: *The Advocate General said* . . . but *The Advocate-General's opinion was* . . . The plural of an Advocate General is Advocates General. So much for formality.

How does a Case come before the CJEC?

(a)   The style of proceedings. The most common way that a case will come before the Court of Justice is where a reference is made to the court *by a national court* for a *preliminary ruling* under Article 177 of the Treaty of Rome. It is possible for actions to be taken against member States (eg, by the Commission) and for action to be taken against Community institutions. We shall concentrate on Article 177 because it is this procedure that is generally most pertinent to the practising English law lawyer or student. Through the use of Article 177 we get a chance to see how our courts regard the Community and its institutions. To a great extent one can leave specialist Community law to the European Law expert; but the impact of Community law is wider than the individual pieces of legislation.

It is the duty of each court in member States to apply Community law; and remember that Community law takes precedence over national law. The interpretation of Community law may be a straightforward matter, but where authoritative interpretation is needed then that can only be supplied by the Court of Justice. Under Article 177 any country's domestic courts or tribunals can ask the Court of Justice for a ruling on Community law; but it is that domestic court or tribunal which implements the decision.

Thus, once a national court or tribunal is faced with a problem involving the application of Community law it may ask the Court of Justice for an authoritative interpretation of the Treaty Article or, for instance, a Community Directive. It does this by posing questions in the abstract; it does not ask for the solution to the particular case. The case is now lodged with the Court of Justice—and joins the backlog! A reference to the Court of Justice is, in this procedure, a step in the action before the national court; it is not an appeal because the case in the national court has simply been adjourned pending the opinion of the Court of Justice. Thus, although we call it a 'preliminary ruling' this is a little misleading: the reference to the Court of Justice is made **during** the case in front of the national court, not before the case has started. The closest thing to this in our system is probably the appeal by way of case stated.

Once the case comes before the Court we see a difference in approach from the Common Law system. As we argued in Chapter Four, English law still bears some relation to its roots in 'trial by battle'. The champion is now replaced by the solicitor or barrister, the swords replaced by words; but the basic plot is the same. Our system concentrates on the adversarial approach and depends greatly on oral argument. The continental approach depends far more on an inquisitorial procedure and written argument (though note that our Court of Appeal is increasingly demanding written submissions in advance of oral argument). Indeed, if the case is concerned with a *preliminary ruling* there are, strictly speaking, no parties involved— the national court has sought an opinion, not a fight. Significantly, notes issued by the Court of Justice ask counsel, if making any oral statement, not to exceed 30 minutes. In a court of English law it sometimes seems it takes this long for counsel to say good morning.

All documents are sent by the Court of Justice's Registry to the parties in the national court, member States, the Commission and (possibly) the Council. All these parties have a right to make submissions on the case. For instance, in a case concerning part-time workers in Germany (case 171/88 *Rinner-Kühn* v *FWW Spezial Gebäudereiningung GmbH and Co. KG* [1989] IRLR 493) a number of member States (recognising that the case was of great importance) made submissions to the Court even though they were not directly involved. The next major difference lies in the presence of the Advocate General, as mentioned above.

Remember, the Court of Justice is concerned only with ruling on the abstract question of law, not on deciding the case. There is thus no appeal from a judgment of the Court of Justice (though there are various mechanisms where the Court can review its own decision). Further, as we shall note again in relation to legal method below, there is only one judgment given by the Court; no dissenting voices are heard. And that judgment is short and usually without detailed reasons. One can find the presentation of reasoning which resembles that of the English judge in the opinion delivered by (accepted or not by the Court) the Advocate General.

(b)   When will a case go to the Court of Justice? We said above that it is for the national court to decide whether it wishes to refer a matter to the Court of Justice. Article 177 states that where a question of interpretation of the Treaties:

> . . . is raised before any court or tribunal of the member State, that court or tribunal may, if it considers that a decision on the question is necessary to enable it to give judgment, request the Court of Justice to give a ruling thereon.
> Where any such question is raised in a case pending before a court or tribunal of a member State, against whose decisions there is no judicial remedy under national law, that court or tribunal shall bring the matter before the Court of Justice.

So, any court has a discretionary power to refer a case to the Court of Justice; and if a court is the final appeal court it *must* refer the matter. National rules of precedent have no effect on a court's power to refer a matter to the CJEC. Thus the House of Lords should be bound to refer all cases to the Court of Justice which involve a problem of Community law. Further, there are instances where a case reaches a point where there is no further appeal and that court is not the House of Lords. If this is so then that final court of appeal, for that case, must refer the matter to the Court of Justice.

The House of Lords and other final appeal courts do not, however, refer all relevant cases to the Court of Justice. The key word in Article 177, applied to both the discretionary reference and the mandatory reference, is 'necessary'.

(c)   What does 'necessary' mean? Article 177 states that the national court need only make a reference where it considers that such a reference is necessary to enable it to give judgment. If the same question was decided upon by the Court of Justice last week, for instance, then making a reference would seem pointless.

A major point to establish, then, is that the decision to refer lies with the national court alone. This was decided early in the Court's life in *Costa v ENEL* [1964] ECR 585. It cannot be restricted by any national system of precedent, nor does it matter whether the parties request such a reference to be made.

In *CILFIT Srl v Ministro della Sanita* [1982] ECR 3415 the Court of Justice ruled that a reference is not 'necessary' if:

(a)   *the question of Community law is irrelevant; or*
(b)   *the provision has already been interpreted by the Court of Justice;*
or
(c)   *the correct application is obvious.*

Steiner (1992:295) draws the parallel with this formulation and the French

Administrative Law doctrine of *acte clair*, in which there can be no question of needing to interpret a provision if the meaning is clear. As Steiner points out, this is a deceptively simple idea: because what is clear to one person is not necessarily clear to another, as we saw in the chapters on statutory interpretation. Indeed this was illustrated in *R* v *Henn* [1978] 1 WLR 1031, [1978] 3 All ER 1190, where the Court of Appeal did not ask for a preliminary ruling on the grounds of *acte clair;* the House of Lords did not find the matter so obvious and pursued a reference (*DPP* v *Henn and Darby* [1980] 2 CMLR 229). Equally, as we noted before, the Court of Justice is not bound by *stare decisis* and so is free to change its mind on a matter.

Taken to an extreme the notion of *acte clair* could spell disaster for the Court of Justice because there is no mechanism to force a national court to make a reference. But with one or two exceptional bursts of chauvinism from national courts the spirit of co-operation and collaboration has prevailed.

A reference is made in the form of a question. The Court of Justice is keen to convert any question which seeks an answer as to how to *apply* the law into a more abstract question as to what the Treaty or other provision *means* or whether the provision is valid.

European Legal Method

In the text above we have attempted to give a very brief description of the workings of the EC institutions. We will return to this topic later when we examine the specific legal method employed by the CJEC. To better understand the CJEC's techniques of legal analysis, however, we must first explain how it is that European lawyers approach legal problems in a quite different way from Common Law lawyers.

Traditionally the English lawyer has a distrust of theory and principle and places his faith in pragmatism. The development of the Common Law has been the work of practitioners, not philosophers. The Civil Law tradition, on the other hand, is different; here case law is an application of deduction from established and more abstract principles. An attempt is made to rationalise and arrange fundamental principles by way of legislation; known as a Code. From these principles contained in the Codes the whole law can, it is hoped, be deduced. French judges, for instances, are expressly forbidden to create general and regulatory principles; they must decide the case before them only and their decisions relate to the text of the Code. It is the Code, therefore, that is ultimately authoritative, not the case law; though this does not mean at all that case decisions are irrelevant to the Civil lawyer.

A Comparison of Concepts

It is interesting, for instance, to compare the different treatment rendered to one concept—that of 'good faith'—in English, French and German law. We will confine our very brief remarks to the law of contract. The aim is to sketch the different approaches, not to analyse contract law. Most people instinctively know what 'acting in good/bad faith' is. It should be said, however, that no legal system has ever constructed a succinct legal definition of the term. This is why we chose it!

The notion of 'good faith' centres on principles of fair dealing. Traditionally, in English law, the search for a theory of 'good faith' offers little reward. It is, however, possible to unearth the odd clue and the occasional judicial or statutory reference to the requirement to act in 'good faith'. This is especially true of those cases or statutes owing their origin to Mercantile law; but then the development of Mercantile law owes a heavy debt to Continental influences. Allusions to elements of 'good faith' such as 'honesty', 'fair dealing' and 'reasonableness' can therefore emerge through the cases; but there is no overriding principle to be applied.

Consequently, the term sometimes emerges as an endorsement of other ideas, but it rarely stands on its own as justifying a decision. If a judge wishes to rely on such an indefinable notion as 'good faith' he will wrap it up, disguise it, with references to more orthodox, technical, conventional terminology such as terms being *implied* into a contract. Bowen LJ utilised the concept this way on a number of occasions in the late nineteenth century. One of the authors once described this process as 'judges trying to pummel equitable notions such as good faith into a contractual setting like a Victorian belle being prised into her whale-bone corset'.

Sometimes however judges can surprise us. Such was the case with Bingham LJ's judgment in *Interfoto Picture Library Ltd* v *Stiletto Visual Programmes Ltd* [1988] 1 All ER 348, [1988] 2 WLR 615 to which we referred in Chapter Six. There, Bingham LJ recognised that English law has often supported the principles of good faith by the device of *ad hoc* solutions (though it has not lent support to the concept itself) when he said (at [1988] 1 All ER 352, 353):

> In many civil law systems, and perhaps in most legal systems outside the common law world, the law of obligations recognises and enforces an overriding principle that in making and carrying out contracts parties should act in good faith. . . English law has, characteristically, committed itself to no such overriding principle but has developed piecemeal solutions in response to demonstrated problems of unfairness . . . Thus equity has intervened to strike down unconscionable bargains.

There is no theory of 'good faith' evident here, nor the acknowledgment of any overriding principle; but there is a more outright recognition of an underlying theme in the law of contract. This is an exception. On the whole we are still governed by the idea of contract as an economic exchange; by the notion of *caveat emptor* (let the buyer beware) and the limitation of being bound primarily by express terms regarding performance of the contract.

The French regard their contract law as part of a theory of obligations. This last word demonstrates quite a difference of approach. Accordingly, in France we find express reference to the concept of 'good faith' in the *Code civil*. Contracts must be performed in good faith: *Code civil* (1804) article 1134(3). Thus, as regards **pre-contractual dealings** (such as negotiations), Nicholas states that, 'the wider context is more favourable in French law to the importation of ideas of good faith or fair dealing (*loyauté*)' and 'there is a greater disposition to seeing silence (as to a fact which determined the other party's consent) as reprehensible' (1982:98). However, Nicholas also notes that when it comes to analysing whether the **performance** of the contract has been fair, 'The French courts have made very little express use of Article 1134 . . . It may be that, like the English courts, they are reluctant to set loose such a wide-ranging principle'. (1982:148)

Harris and Tallon, however, paint a slightly different picture. Whereas French law insists on exact performance of contractual obligations, the Anglo-American attitude presents a choice between performance and paying damages. 'It follows that French law resorts to issues of morality, such as fraud, serious fault, or good faith, more readily than does English law' they conclude. (1989:386). Indeed, under Article 2268, *Code civil*, good faith is presumed and it is for the party who alleges bad faith to prove it.

A description of the German approach proves interesting here. Sections 138, 157, 242 of the *Bürgerliches Gesetzbuch* (BGB, which is the German Civil Code relating to private law) all contain references to the principle of good faith. Section 138 creates obligations of a general nature, rendering a legal transaction void if it conflicts with good morals. Section 157 deals with the construction of contracts and relates that contracts are to be construed as good faith requires. Most important of all, perhaps, is the apparently innocuous s. 242 which states: 'The debtor is obliged to effect performance in such a manner as good faith requires, regard being paid to general practice'. This section regulates the manner in which contracts are performed. Horn, Kötz and Leser (1982:135) describe this so:

> Unimpressive though it looks, s. 242 BGB is one of the most astonishing phenomena in the Code . . . a statutory enactment of a general requirement of good faith, a 'principle of legal ethics', which dominates the entire legal system.

The discussion which follows this quotation is well worth reading. However, Cohn's comments are also noteworthy: 'Section 242 has . . . considerably increased the freedom of the courts in interpreting contracts. No similar liberty is enjoyed by English courts.' (1968:154) The strength of s. 242 can be seen in the case law. Horn *et al.* comment: 'The numerous [contractual] duties that have been created . . . include duties of care, duties to supervise the manner and form of the principal performance, duties to assure performance, duties of co-operation, and duties of information and explanation.' (1982:139) Good faith has even been used (in 1923) to revalue debts during times of hyperinflation. Debts incurred before inflation set in could be paid off easily once the effects of that inflation had made the currency practically worthless. The German courts revalued these debts by expressing them in the equivalent new currency to match the original sum. This was done even where the debt had already been paid off.

Finally, to complete this brief comparative survey, it is worth noting the approach adopted in the United States. Here we see the Common Law system in action. Yet we also find that the vague concept of 'good faith' is embraced in the case law through reference to the Uniform Commercial Code (UCC). Now this is not a *code* in the pure Civil Law sense. It is more like the original English Sale of Goods Act 1893, whereby the case law has been pulled together into a more systematic general restatement. The UCC is law in most jurisdictions in the US by virtue of local (rather than federal) enactment.

In the UCC we find Articles 1-201, 1-203 and 2-103, along with many others, give a general definition of good faith. Article 1-201 states that good faith means honesty in fact in the conduct or transaction concerned. Article 1-203 imposes a general obligation of good faith performance and enforcement; and Article 2-103 says that, in the case of a merchant, it means honesty in fact and the observance of reasonable commercial standards of fair dealing in the trade. These provisions have given rise to varied judicial and academic debate; not least as to whether there is a requirement for objective good faith to be found ('reasonableness', 'fair dealing') or only a subjective test—what has been referred to as the 'pure heart and empty head test'. Here we see that the Common Law still cannot rid itself of its fixation with the need to define terms through the cases. It is unable to cope easily with pure conceptual thinking.

It may be, therefore, that the conventional contrast between the two traditions—experience and pragmatism on the one hand, concept and doctrine on the other—is not always as clear cut as it seems. The German system *should* be systematic as per the usual perception of a Civil Code system; but it is not. Case law *should not* play a creative role of law-making; but it does. The French system *should* allow for greater use of the concept of 'good faith' than the English system; but this is not guaranteed. The American system *should* pay as little heed to such an indefinable concept as we do; but it does so through a 'code'. And it is quite possible for all these systems, through different explanations, to arrive at the same conclusion eg, on the construction of the contract. This demonstrates the difficulty in finding even a common starting point for lawyers in the two systems. Szladits and Germain (1985:ix) describe the problems thus:

Because of a different training, of a different 'legal method', there is an unavoidable inclination on the part of the Anglo-American lawyer to evaluate the importance of code provisions, of decisions of a higher court or of writings and comments in the light of his own background knowledge. He may attach undue importance to some decisions 'as precedents', and underrate the value of treatises or commentaries . . .

He may also underrate the importance of cases and attach too exclusive force to code provisions

The continental lawyer in contrast, will usually find himself at a loss among the innumerable precedents which are binding, but yet can be distinguished out of existence. . . and will vainly look for precise concepts among the legal synonyms, loosely phrased decisions and unsystematic textbooks . . .

In the first edition of this book we chose the idea of 'good faith' for comparison of approaches because it was an interesting topic and one with which all jurisdictions have experienced difficulty. Since that time, further developments have occurred so that we are now faced with a draft EC Directive on Unfair Contract Terms which will rely heavily on the concept of good faith. Thus English law may yet have to tackle the meaning of 'good faith'. There is, however, opposition to the proposed Directive and it is not likely to take effect, if at all, before 1995.

The Use of Precedent in European Legal Method

We have already seen in Chapter Five that a major distinction between how Civil lawyers (and courts) reason and the reasoning of Common Law lawyers is the use of *stare decisis*. As the quote from Szladits and Germain indicates, however, it is wrong to say that case law is unimportant to the Civil Law lawyer. Reference to case law and a loose idea of precedent clearly exists in the Civil Law tradition. David and Brierley (1985:133) point out that statements which flatly exclude cases as a source of law in the Civil system,

> are somewhat ridiculous when used in countries such as France or Germany, where cases have been of primary importance in the evolution of some branches of law.

Cases are a source of law in that a line of cases demonstrates a consistent pattern of thought. But whereas the Common Law judge draws openly on case law for his analysis, the Civil Law lawyer often hides behind the veil of 'interpretation' of legislation. The cases provide guidance on legal rules; but the rules do not carry with them any sense of obligation. Judges are not compelled to analyse earlier cases or justify departure from them. Indeed, in France, judges may not simply cite earlier authorities to support their decisions. This does not mean that the judges are unaware of the case law; though the structure of French judicial decisions is generally terse and fairly uninformative as to reasoning (to the English lawyer's eye). Equally, decisions of the French Supreme courts are likely to be followed in practice, as are those of the *Cour de cassation,* which deals with judicial matters such as contract law, and those of the *Conseil d'État* which deals with administrative matters. In fact, 'There can be little doubt that the (case law) of the *Conseil d'État* is a true source of law, since most of the *general* principles and rules of administrative law have been created by its decisions' (David & Brierley, 1985:30).

Furthermore, as David and Brierley (1985:144–5) also note, though a general principle of Civil Law may be that case law is descriptive rather than prescriptive, there are instances where the notion of *binding* precedent is not alien to Civil Law jurisdictions either. Thus,

> it may on occasion happen that a judge must observe a judicial precedent or a line of previously decided cases. The authority of binding precedent is attributed in Federal Germany to the decisions of the federal Constitutional Court . . . The creative role of decided cases is officially recognised in Spanish law by the concept of *doctrina legal* (a judicial practice based on several decisions of the Supreme Court).

Legal Method in the Court of Justice

The Court of Justice of the European Communities was created by Civil Law lawyers. It therefore bears the hallmarks of the points noted above.

These hallmarks are important in a number of ways:

(a)   first, as to whether the Court of Justice really regards every question as being open to re-examination;

(b)   secondly, in investigating how our national courts should approach the status of preliminary rulings;

(c)   thirdly, as to the future role of precedent in our courts;

(d)   fourthly, as to the possible effect on the drafting and interpretation of legislation as noted in Chapters Seven and Eight; and

(e)   finally, in examining the other sources of law used by Civil lawyers to analyse legal problems.

We shall deal with these issues in turn.

Does the Court of Justice really regard every question as being open to re-examination?   As we noted in Chapters Five and Six, the absence of any *ratio decidendi* in the decision rather destroys the essence of precedent as we know it. The judgments are short, even terse, and bear little relationship to those of our courts; not least because they are given as a collegiate decision. By this we mean that, whether the court was unanimous or there was only a bare majority, only one decision is delivered. There is no record of dissent; no variant judgments dispensed.

The Court of Justice does, however, allude to earlier judgments and prefers to follow those decisions. But the court is quite free to change its mind, develop principles and create conflicting precedents as between Chambers. Part of this may be due to the fact that the court sees its role as 'filling the gaps' in Community legislation. It is therefore openly creative and plays an active part in the law-making of the Community.

The Advocate General in a case will more frequently cite earlier cases;

and the Advocate-General's opinion will be of persuasive authority in later cases, even where the court did not follow it.

The answer, therefore, to the question posed is that every question is open to re-examination; nothing precludes a national court, for instance, from seeking a further ruling on exactly the same point discussed in an earlier case (see *Da Costa en Schaake* [1963] ECR 31 and *NV Algemene Transport—Van Gend en Loos* [1963] ECR 1). The notion of *acte clair* is not *stare decisis* in another form.

In practice, of course, there is a strong tendency to try to establish and maintain a coherent, or settled, jurisprudence, which does require some reference to precedent. Indeed there seems to be some evidence to suggest that direct reference to case law is a growing judicial practice—for example, in Case C–229/89 *European Commission* v *Belgium* [1991] IRLR 393, the Court went to some lengths to justify its decision by reference to the earlier cases of *Teuling* (30/85) [1987] ECR 2497, which had decided a closely analogous point of law, and *Rinner-Kühn* v *FWW Spezial Gebäudereiningung GmbH and Co. KG* [1989] IRLR 493. However, this still does not mean that the Court regards itself as strictly bound by its own earlier decisions.

How should our courts approach the status of preliminary rulings? Two points arise here: first, if the Court of Justice is simply interpreting Community law, is any decision retroactive? That is to say, is the interpretation to be applied from the date of judgment onwards (as with our system) or does it also have effect from the date the provision originally came into force? Secondly, how binding is a decision of the Court of Justice?

On the first point: in general, the ruling will take effect from the date the legislation was brought into force—a retroactive approach. The Court is declaring what already existed. The Court may however choose not to do this (only the Court can decide this) on grounds of, say, the need for legal certainty. It did this in relation to equal pay rulings in *Defrenne* v *SABENA* [1976] ECR 455 and recently regarding equal pay and pension rights in *Barber* v *Guardian Royal Exchange Assurance Group* Case C–262/88 [1991] 1 QB 344, [1990] 2 All ER 660. This idea of retroactive decisions has always been a controversial matter. So much so that, because of the ruling in *Barber* v *Guardian Royal Exchange* a Protocol to the *Maastricht Treaty* creates a broad principle of non-retroactivity in relation to pension rights.

On the second point, given that a national court can always ask the Court of Justice for a ruling (even on matters previously decided) the Court of Justice's decisions are not binding as such. They are binding, however, in as much as the national court must either apply them or seek a new ruling; it cannot simply ignore the Court of Justice. This point is reinforced by European Communities Act 1972, s. 3(1).

There is no hierarchical system as between the various courts in member States. What is decided in the national courts of Germany or France has no direct effect (it may have a persuasive one) on our courts. As the Court of Justice is the only authority which can interpret provisions anyway, this should cause no problems.

What will this mean for the future role of precedent in our courts? First, much of our law still has no relationship with Community law. To this end the line of precedents on what constitutes an 'offer' or an 'invitation to treat' will continue to carry the same significance as 20 or more years ago. Where Community law is concerned it is clear that the higher courts in our system can no longer bind the lower courts; only the Court of Justice can make authoritative rulings. The Court of Appeal, for instance, is not bound by a decision of the House of Lords on the *interpretation* of Community law. It may, however, be bound by a decision on the *application* of Community law to particular facts.

All this is unlikely to bring about the abandonment of *stare decisis* and all its intricacies. Thus we now have two systems of precedent. In practice the presence of Community cases can lead to some doubt as regards advising clients. We are not yet adept at treating wide statements of principle as having just as much effect as 70 pages of judgment by the House of Lords. For instance, in Employment law we were faced with the decision of the Court of Justice in *Rinner-Kühn v FWW Spezial Gebäudereiningung GmbH and Co. KG* [1989] IRLR 493. The case concerned Article 119 of the EEC Treaty and Equal Pay Directive 75/117 and arose from a preliminary ruling given to a German Labour court in relation to the right of part-time workers to receive sick pay.

The specific details on employment rights are different across member States, but as with the UK a worker usually has to work for a minimum number of hours a week in order to qualify for certain rights. In the UK, for instance, that minimum number of hours is usually 16 per week. As a considerably smaller number of women than men can comply with such time qualifications, this form of limitation, Frau Rinner-Kühn argued, was discriminatory. The Court of Justice held that Article 119 is to be interpreted as precluding legislation which had such an effect.

For the practitioner, let alone the academic, this now presents a problem as to application. The English lawyer instinctively asks: should one apply this to other 'time qualification' rights such as unfair dismissal and redundancy? The English lawyer immediately seeks to compare or distinguish, to see what the ramifications of the decision will be. Further, whatever the legal analysis, it takes a brave advocate to cite such rulings in the middle of an industrial tribunal case when they clearly drive a coach and horses through some of the provisions of the UK statute (the Employment Protection (Consolidation) Act 1978). Integration into Community law is sometimes easier in books than in English courts and tribunals!

We wrote the above account of *Rinner-Kühn* in the first edition. Since that time there have been developments in this area, though the general problems recounted remain valid for other cases of European origin. In 1992 the Equal Opportunities Commission (EOC) brought an application in the English courts for judicial review against the Secretary of State for Employment, requesting an alteration in our law to comply with the *Rinner-Kühn* decision: *R v Secretary of State for Employment ex parte Equal Opportunities Commission* [1993] 1 All ER 1022. The EOC failed, partly because it was decided that the EOC had no standing to bring the particular case. The Court of Appeal, however, was divided as to whether the UK could have established a justifiable case for the differences in rights for full-time and part-time workers.

What might be the effect on the drafting and interpretation of UK legislation? There are three problem areas here:

(a)   The style of statutory interpretation;
(b)   The direct effect of Community legislation;
(c)   The indirect effect of Community legislation.

(a)   The style of statutory interpretation.   As we noted in Chapter Eight, the Civil Law approach to rules of statutory interpretation is far more 'purposive' than ours; an approach that could be attacked in the English courts as a 'naked usurpation of the legislative function'. But, as noted in Chapter Seven, European legislation is structured in a manner that is very different from English Acts of Parliament. The *Civilian* tradition emphasises simplicity of drafting and a high degree of abstraction. The question then is, should our national courts adopt this more purposive style of interpretation—the 'grand' style, as we termed it?

We noted in Chapter Eight that this difference in approach has increasingly been recognised by English judges when considering Community legislation, or even when considering English legislation that has been passed to fulfil an obligation under European Community law. In *Bulmer* v *Bollinger* [1974] Ch 401, [1974] 2 All ER 1226 Lord Denning MR proposed the view that, when considering Community legislation, the national court should adopt the Civil method of interpretation. Again, in *Macarthys* v *Smith* [1979] 1 WLR 1189, [1979] 3 All ER 325, and *Buchanan and Co. Ltd* v *Babco Forwarding and Shipping (UK) Ltd* [1977] 2 WLR 107, [1977] 1 All ER 518 the Court of Appeal, and particularly Lord Denning, stressed the use of the Civil method on the more general level.

The House of Lords has proved inconsistent in tackling this problem. Thus we find Lord Diplock advocating that *all* legislation passed since the UK's membership of the Community should be interpreted in the light of Community laws: see *Garland* v *British Rail* [1983] 2 AC 751, [1982] 2 All ER 402. Movement towards a more purposive approach (here, the use of *Hansard*) was seen in *Pickstone* v *Freemans* [1988] ICR 697, [1988] 2 All ER 803 and has been seen again in *Pepper* v *Hart*. But this more relaxed view is not reflected in the traditional approach evident in *Duke* v *GEC Reliance* [1988] AC 618, [1988] 1 All ER 626.

Again, the House of Lords completely (and openly) abandoned the literal approach in *Litster* v *Forth Dry Dock* [1990] AC 546, [1989] 1 All ER

1134 where the legislation in question (the Transfer of Undertakings (Protection of Employment) Regulations 1981) was derived from a directive of the European Community. Instead of relying on a literal approach the Lords, particularly Lord Oliver, adopted a very wide purposive approach in line with European judges. However in *Finnegan* v *Clowney Youth Training Programme Ltd* [1990] 2 All ER 546, we have seen the House of Lords take an attitude which had all the hallmarks of 'We will fight them on the beaches . . .' written all over it. This was yet another addition to the long line of discrimination cases fought out between British and EC law. As a Northern Irish case, however, it added a further twist to the story. Whereas the Sex Discrimination Act 1975 had pre-dated the Equal Treatment Directive (76/207) so that it could be argued that the Act was not made in compliance with the Directive; the Northern Irish equivalent, the Sex Discrimination (Northern Ireland) Order 1976, was enacted some four months after the Directive. The relevant section was, however, worded in identical terms to its equivalent provision in the 1975 Act.

This was presented by counsel for the employee as a crucial difference, so that following the approach of the CJEC in case 14/83 *Von Colson* v *Land Nordrhein-Westfalen* [1984] ECR 1891, as applied in *Pickstone* and *Litster,* it was argued that the court must interpret the domestic legislation so as to give effect to the Directive. The House of Lords accepted this view of the law, but rejected its application here, and with it counsel's invitation to use the 1966 Practice Statement to depart from *Duke* v *GEC Reliance.* Lord Bridge, with whom the rest of their Lordships concurred, followed Lord Templeman's line in *Duke.* He thus argued (at p. 551) that the legislative history of the 1975 Act suggests that the British government saw no inconsistency between the Act and the Directive, and that the 1976 Order, being in identical terms, should be deemed to have the same effect. This ignores, as does *Duke* itself, the *purpose* of the Directive, and the broad principles of construction adopted by the CJEC in the *von Colson* case, which Lord Templeman in *Duke* saw, in a most un-European manner, as limited to its own facts.

This highlights one of the main (self-imposed?) difficulties faced by the English courts: that is, their seeming unwillingness to comprehend the *jurisprudence* of the CJEC. This problem also arose in the *Factortame* case. The House of Lords deflected the arguments on interim protection by arguing (per Lord Bridge at [1990] 2 AC 85, 151) that the principles cited by the applicants were drawn, in effect, from *obiter* statements of the CJEC. Yet, as Gravells notes, 'the distinction between *ratio decidendi* and *obiter dicta* has no place in the jurisprudence of the European Court' (1989:586). This view has been confirmed by the CJEC's reliance on the broad principles enunciated in those very cases when giving judgment both in the Art 177 proceedings in case C–213/89 *R* v *Secretary of State for Transport ex parte Factortame (No. 2)* [1991] 1 AC 603 and in the reference from the Divisional Court in the same matter—reported as Case C–221/89 *R* v *Secretary of State for Transport, ex parte Factortame (No. 3)* [1991] 3 CMLR 589, [1991] 3 All ER 769.

All this means, perhaps rather unsatisfactorily, that the judges are seeming to apply two different standards of interpretation, depending upon whether the legislation is purely domestic, or founded in Community law. And as yet the pro-European lobby has only been seen at work on secondary legislation; the full-blown Civil Law approach has not surfaced in relation to a statute.

(b)   The direct effect of Community legislation.   We noted above, the rather confusing idea that some aspects of Community legislation are *directly applicable* in the UK (Regulations for instance) which means that no UK legislation needs to be passed to give effect to them; but that Directives are not directly applicable because Directives have to be implemented *via* UK legislation. If they are not implemented or they are not implemented properly there is the question as to whether a UK citizen can nevertheless enforce the rights given under the Directive. We saw above that if the Directive has vertical effect then the answer is generally 'yes'; but if an individual wishes to sue another individual he/she must argue that the Directive has horizontal effect. This is more problematic. To give Directives horizontal direct effect, it is argued, equates them with Regulations—so what would be the distinction?

In one of the leading equal treatment cases, Case 152/84 *Marshall v Southampton and South West Hampshire AHA* [1986] 1 CMLR 688, [1986] 2 All ER 584 the CJEC denied the possibility of giving horizontal effect to Directives on the basis of the wording in Article 119 EEC. Both the CJEC and the Advocate General agreed that the Directive could only be relied upon in actions against the state. On the facts, Ms Marshall succeeded in her claim as it was conceded that her employer (the health authority) was an emanation of the state (see, by way of contrast, the House of Lords' cases of *Duke* and *Finnegan* above).

So the effect on drafting and interpretation here is that a failure to implement a Directive or to implement it properly (though what this means is obviously debatable in itself) will mean: (i) in the case of Directives of vertical effect the government will run the risk of enforcement proceedings being commenced by the Commission under Article 169 of the EEC Treaty; (ii) Directives continue to provide an interpretative source in relation to domestic law. The European Communities Act 1972, s. 2(4) expressly requires British courts to construe domestic legislation so as to give effect to Community obligations under s. 2(1) of that Act. Courts will thus interpret legislation passed after related Community Acts in a manner consistent with that EC legislation; (iii) it is vital to establish whether the legislation has direct effect or whether the only legislation one can refer to is the wording contained in the enacting UK statute.

(c)   The indirect effect of Community legislation.   To this we must add a third category. *Marshall* has not resolved the problem of direct effect once and for all in European law. As we have seen, the earlier case of *Von Colson v Land Nordrhein-Westfalen* is credited with creating a further principle of 'indirect effect'. *Indirect effect* enables a court to 'read in' to the statute the wording and even the aims of the original Directive. It is called indirect effect for this reason, since it gives an individual a right of action through national law, but based *indirectly* on the Directive. This takes us full circle because we are now back in the field of *how* the courts interpret statutes as seen in (a) above.

We have to say that the position is becoming more and more convoluted. The guidelines issued by the Court of Justice in *Von Colson* were less than clear. Courts in some Member states have taken the view that the rules of construction laid down in that case could not apply to national legislation enacted before the Directive. Thus, the United Kingdom and, to a lesser extent, France, have argued that *Von Colson* creates no more than a rule against ambiguity for use in situations where the meaning of the domestic implementing legislation is unclear (see the discussion above on *Duke* and *Finnegan*; for the situation in France, see Galmot & Bonichot (1988)). In Case C-106/89 *Marleasing SA* v *La Commercial Internacional de Alimentación SA* [1992] 1 CMLR 305 the CJEC reaffirmed the views expressed in *Marshall* but introduced a further complication by adding that in cases where there is direct effect, national law (not just legislation) must comply with Community legislation whether the Directive has been implemented, implemented improperly, or not implemented at all. In coming to this conclusion, the CJEC has greatly extended the importance of indirect effect. Docksey and Fitzpatrick (1991:113) go so far as to suggest that indirect effect is now set to become the normal mechanism whereby individuals may enforce rights contained in Directives, though this view is not universally supported—see Snyder (1993:43). However, it is still open to debate whether, if domestic legislation is deemed clear and unambiguous, *Marleasing* should be taken to authorise domestic courts to go directly against national law.

English courts had to grasp this particular nettle in the recent case of *Webb* v *EMO Air Cargo (UK) Ltd* [1990] ICR 442 (EAT), [1992] ICR 445, [1992] 2 All ER 43 (CA), [1993] 1 CMLR 259 (HL) which posed the question whether the dismissal of an employee on grounds of pregnancy constituted sex discrimination when the dismissed employee had been engaged specifically to cover for another employee's absence. The Employment Appeal Tribunal and the Court of Appeal thought not (see Harrison, 1992). They said that a claim only lies under the Sex Discrimination Act 1975 where a pregnant woman is treated less favourably by her employer than a hypothetical man would be in 'comparable' circumstances; for example, where he is suffering from an illness of similar severity and duration. Ms Webb had argued that the dismissal was discriminatory, based on the fact that a man can never be in the same position as a pregnant woman.

However, there is contrary authority derived from the Equal Treatment Directive EC/76/207, as applied in Case 177/88 *Dekker* v *Stichting Vormingscentrum voor Jong Volwassen Plus* [1991] IRLR 27. Ms Webb's counsel argued that the Directive as interpreted in *Dekker* (although not having direct horizontal effect) should be applied according to *Marleasing* principles. In the latest development of the *Webb* case, the House of Lords ([1993] 1 CMLR 259, [1992] 4 All ER 929) has indicated that, in its view, there is no discrimination here on a 'proper construction' of the 1975 Act. But their Lordships also stated that (*per* Lord Keith [1993] 1 CMLR 259 at 270):

[I]t is for a United Kingdom court to construe domestic legislation so as to accord with the interpretation of the directive as laid down by the European Court, if that can be done without distorting the meaning of the domestic legislation . . . This is so whether the domestic legislation came after or, as in this case, preceded the directive: *Marleasing* . . .

Their Lordships found that the *Dekker* case was not direct authority on the facts in *Webb* (and so implicitly not 'binding' upon them), but have sought a preliminary ruling from the CJEC on the meaning of the Directive.

Finally in this saga we should note joined cases C–6/90 and C–9/90 *Francovich and Bonifaci* v *Italy* [1992] IRLR 84, where the CJEC held that, under certain conditions, a member state is liable to make good damage to individuals if loss is suffered because the state failed to implement a Community Directive. This form of reasoning may yet have set up another means whereby an individual might be able to rely on EC legislation directly (see Steiner, 1993). Once again, we await further developments.

What are the other sources used by Civil lawyers to analyse legal problems? Common to both traditions are sources such as legislation, case law and custom. As we noted in Chapter Eight, preparatory materials leading to legislation *(travaux préparatoires)* are given greater importance in statutory interpretation by the Civil system. Again in Chapter Eight we noted the different approaches used by Civil Law lawyers and the Court of Justice, in contrast to Common Law lawyers in interpreting legislation. We shall now explore these in greater detail under three headings.

(a) Principles of interpretation. In considering questions of interpretation Brown details the options available to the court. These he describes as the literal, historical, contextual, comparative, and teleological methods. We shall briefly consider each of these in turn, but you are advised to refer to the fuller account in Brown (1989:271). It should be stressed that the CJEC is not bound to use only one approach; any one case may legitimately reflect a whole variety of judicial styles.

Like the English lawyer, the Civilian lawyers, too, recognise and make use of different styles of interpretation. First, there is the **literal** approach: it should come as no surprise that every court, not just English courts, turns first to the words of the text. But this is not the English law 'Literal Rule' in disguise. It is simply a common sense embarkation point which does not require the declaration of 'ambiguity' before it can be discarded. For a major difference between Common and Civil Law judges lies in the degree of willingness and freedom to move beyond the ordinary meaning of the words used.

In the Court of Justice, adherence to a literalist approach becomes even more difficult because, as we have already noted, texts have to be translated from one language to another: see, for instance Case C–372/88 *Milk Marketing Board* v *Cricket St Thomas Estate* [1990] 2 CMLR 800 on the meaning of 'pasteurised milk'. As Miers and Page note, however, there may also be a positive side to these linguistic differences: it may also be that 'the scope for doubt as to the meaning in one language may often be closed down by the language of the others' (1990:184).

Having at least noted the wording of the text, European judges have four methods at their disposal. The **historical** approach is described by David and Brierley as one, 'clarifying present texts in the light of previous circumstances and taking into account the legislator's intention' (1985:125). Traditionally, European judges have been prepared to unearth the purpose behind legislation by examining what was actually intended by the legislature (ie, by asking what was their 'subjective' intent). This has been achieved by turning to all manner of source documentation in the form of *travaux préparatoires*. Brown argues that the English mischief rule bears resemblance to this approach, though concentrating on a more limited and 'objective' assessment of legislative intent, as we saw in Chapter Eight. There is an irony here. Whilst English lawyers are moving (slowly) towards admitting more in the way of *travaux préparatoires,* European lawyers have placed less reliance on such material.

The **contextual** approach, like the literal approach, concentrates upon the meaning of the words, except that it does not confine itself to investigating only the wording of *that* Act, but rather considers the whole legislative context. By this we mean that the court must consider the 'framework of Community law'—the interrelationship of all aspects of Community law: see Cases 90–91/63 *European Commission* v *Luxembourg and Belgium* [1964] ECR 625; Case 6/64 *Costa* v *ENEL* [1964] ECR 585. Brown regards this as one of the most important techniques used by the CJEC.

By **comparative** we mean that the judges of the CJEC are, by their very background, bound to draw upon their own experience as lawyers within the Member states. This means that inevitably the Court will seek to evaluate and maybe utilise solutions provided by the legal systems from which the judges are drawn, eg, the adoption of the French Administrative law doctrine of *Acte Clair* to define when an Article 177 reference is 'necessary': see Cases 28–30/62 *Da Costa en Schaake NV* [1963] ECR 31; *French Republic* v *Deroche, Cornet et Soc Promatex-France* [1967] CMLR 351. The term 'comparative' should not be taken as a euphemism for 'compromise'. The aim is to extract the appropriate principle, not to create some sort of mishmash.

Looking at the style of judicial pronouncements rather than any substantive law, it is also interesting that in recent years the influence of British judges has surfaced in CJEC decisions. Taking the case report as a whole, one can detect a greater tendency to explain decisions, analyse the points raised, and even consider previous cases in depth: a style of presentation more in keeping with Common Law than Civil Law: see, for instance, Case C-262/88 *Barber* v *Guardian Royal Exchange Assurance Group*.

The last, but probably the most important, approach we need to consider is the **teleological** method (also known as the *schematic* approach). As we noted in Chapter Eight, this may be defined as a broad 'purposive' approach which requires courts to place the legislation within the entire setting and spirit of Community law: see Case 106/77 *Amministrazione delle Finanze dello Stato* v *Simmenthal Spa* [1978] ECR 629. It is widely used by the CJEC, and increasingly employed by national courts in interpreting Community law. Thus, in *Murphy* v *An Bord Telecom Eirann* [1988] 2 CMLR 753, the Irish High Court held that where there was a right to 'equal pay for equal work' in accordance with Article 119 EEC, this must automatically include a right to equal pay for work of *greater* value. The Irish legislation stated only that equal pay was to be given for work 'equal in value'; and this had to be interpreted in keeping with the spirit of Article 119. As Keane J said: 'the literal construction . . . must give way in the present case to the teleological construction.'

(b)   Doctrine. Legal writings (referred to as *Doctrine)* hold a different place in the Civil system from that of the Common Law tradition. The status and influence of such writings is greater on the Continent than here. As we have seen, if one is seeking influence and authority as a writer on English law the general advice is to be ancient and dead. The continental academic lawyer is not required to make the same sacrifice. So, *Doctrinal* writings hold a much more important place in the Civil system, though they are still not a formal source of law. The same is true of the American legal system, demonstrating that the relegation of legal writing is not a Common Law tradition, but an English law approach. Why this difference should exist is a question of history, prejudices, and attitude. The difference may be in the process of being eroded so that more heed will be paid to legal writers in English law.

(c)   General principles. Finally, when all else fails—whether it is the analysis of a Code or the application of precedent—there is the ultimate fallback of 'general principles'. Some countries draw upon these unwritten rules because their Code allows them to do so, eg, Spain and Italy. Others, such as France, discover them in the spirit and tradition of the law; often more assumed than debated. As Szladits and Germain point out (1985:44), it is in the systematising of these general principles that the role of *Doctrine* can have its greatest effect. The Common Law too knows of 'general principles', though for the most part authority is still sought. Ultimately the Common Law lawyer will fall back on the notion that there exists an amorphous mass of laws termed 'The Common Law' from which the rules can be derived, or will refer to 'Equitable principles'.

The Court of Justice has developed its own sense of 'general principles' in the protection of fundamental human rights such as those found in the European Convention of Human Rights and Fundamental Freedoms. Thus we can discover principles of proportionality, equality, certainty, natural justice and due process in the rulings of the Court of Justice (for a full discussion see Steiner (1992:chapter 4)).

Exercise 19: Product liability—woodworm, oysters and pesticide

The following exercise, which builds on Exercise 14 (on Chapter 7, above), is based on one we have used with our students. It is an exercise which places a premium on legal research skills, but one that also asks you to bring together your knowledge of English and European legal method. We do not provide a full answer to the problem, but offer some advice on techniques and issues you might explore. The exercise centres on problems of interpretation created by sections 2 and 4 of the Consumer Protection Act 1987. To get you started, we have reproduced the relevant parts of those sections below. However, do bear in mind that those may not be the only provisions that are useful to you. You are also advised to consider the relevant wording of the EC Product Liability Directive, which the 1987 Act was intended to implement.

CONSUMER PROTECTION ACT 1987

2.—(1) Subject to the following provisions of this Part, where any damage is caused wholly or partly by a defect in a product, every person to whom subsection (2) below applies shall be liable for the damage.

(2) This subsection applies to—
   (a) the producer of the product;
   (b) any person who, by putting his name on the product or using a trade mark or other distinguishing mark in relation to the product, has held himself out to be the producer of the product;
   (c) any person who has imported the product into a member State from a place outside the member States in order, in the course of any business of his, to supply it to another.

4.—(1) In any civil proceedings by virtue of this Part against any person ('the person proceeded against') in respect of a defect in a product it shall be a defence for him to show—
   . . .
   (e) that the state of scientific or technical knowledge at the relevant time was not such that a producer of products of the same description as the product in question might be expected to have discovered the defect it it had existed in his products while they were under his control;
   . . .

YOU ARE TO ASSUME THAT THE FOLLOWING CASE IS LISTED TO BE HEARD BY THE COURT OF APPEAL

PRESTWICK v *ROSEBERRY'S SUPERMARKETS* [1993]

The plaintiff, Pamela Prestwick, has brought an action against the defendants, Roseberry's Supermarkets alleging breaches of the Consumer Protection Act 1987 (CPA).

The case arose out of events following the birth of Pamela's daughter, Sarah, in October 1990. Sarah was born with a congenital heart defect which has required major surgery and has left Sarah dependent on drugs to counteract a residual weakness in the heart which would otherwise cause irregular heartbeat and palpitations.

About a year ago, Pamela read an article in *The Inquirer* newspaper which stated that research published in America in 1988 had shown that a particular pesticide used on vegetable crops, called DZT, could cause defects to the internal organs of unborn children. This had led the American Food and Drugs Adminstration to ban the use of DZT early in 1989. The article further stated that no steps had been taken by the Ministry of Agriculture to ban its use in Britain, and that various British supermarkets were known to use suppliers who have sprayed crops with DZT, including Roseberry's Supermarkets. In June 1992, the Minstry of Agriculture removed DZT from the list of pesticides safe for use on foods intended for human consumption.

Pamela and her husband have always done their weekly shopping at Roseberry's and were therefore concerned that Sarah's disability might have been caused by DZT. They have since obtained expert medical opinion indicating that Sarah's disability is consistent with the known effects of DZT. This is not disputed by the supermarket.

Pamela commenced proceedings, on Sarah's behalf, against Roseberry's alleging that they had produced and supplied a defective product causing Sarah injury contrary to the 1987 Act.

Roseberry's admitted that their main supplier of vegetables, Archer's Farms Ltd was, at the relevant time, a user of DZT, but deny liability. Archer's Farms went into liquidation in May 1992.

In the High Court, Purchase J held:

(1)   Roseberry's Supermarkets could constitute a producer of agricultural products under CPA s. 2(2)(b); Roseberry's were responsible for the final packaging of the goods displayed in their shops, and by marking all such goods with their own trade mark, had held themselves out as producers of those products.

(2)   However, following *The Mighty Mussel Co. Ltd* v *Seldon* [1992] the packaging of the goods undertaken by Roseberry's did not constitute an 'industrial process' within the meaning of the Act. Accordingly, Roseberry's

were suppliers of unprocessed agricultural products and could not be liable for defects within those goods—CPA, s. 2(4) applied.

(3) In the alternative, even if the defendants' liability under s. 2 could be established, the defendants were entitled to rely on the development risks defence contained in s. 4(1)(e). At the time the plaintiff suffered damage, the American evidence was little known in Britain. It was certainly not knowledge within the public domain, and the Ministry of Agriculture had not issued any warnings against the use of DZT. It was not, therefore, a defect which, given the circumstances, the defendants might have been expected to discover. There was no basis in English law for allowing the wider defence of the Product Liability Directive 85/374/EEC, Article 7(e), to displace the clear meaning of s. 4(1)(e). The view of Bramley LJ in the *Seldon* case was to be preferred to that of Cox J in *Halsbury v Coke's Wood Products Ltd* [1991].

The plaintiff's claim was therefore dismissed.

YOU ARE REQUIRED TO PRESENT THE CASE FOR PAMELA PRESTWICK IN HER APPEAL TO THE COURT OF APPEAL AGAINST PURCHASE J'S DECISION.

The following are the fictitious cases cited in the judgment (NB: they are extracts from the judgment only):

Halsbury v Coke's Wood Products Ltd [1991]
(High Court, QBD)

Cox J: This claim is brought by Mrs Halsbury as an action for damages in respect of the death of her husband, which she alleges was caused by the defective product produced by the defendant company.

The facts in this tragic case are essentially simple. In July 1990 the plaintiff and her husband purchased an old cottage on the edge of Dartmoor which they intended to renovate for use as a holiday home. Mr Halsbury was a keen 'do-it-yourself' enthusiast and undertook much of the renovation work himself. One of the tasks undertaken by Mr Halsbury was the spraying of the roof timbers with woodworm treatment. To complete this task, he purchased a quantity of 'Zap-o-Worm' fluid, manufactured by the defendants. However, whilst appying the fluid to the timbers, Mr Halsbury suffered severe breathing difficulties and collapsed before he could get out of the loft. By the time Mrs Halsbury had been able to summon help to bring her husband down, he had asphyxiated and died.

Mr Halsbury was asthmatic. His asthma was not chronic, but serious enough to require regular medication. It is accepted by all concerned that the cans of fluid used by Mr Halsbury carried explicit instructions warning against the risk of inhaling high concentrations of vapour from the fluid. It is not contested by the defendants that Mr Halsbury had taken such precautions as would generally be sufficient to protect a normal person from any serious risk to health. Evidence brought by the defence has also persuaded me that, in most environments, an asthmatic, other than a chronic asthmatic, would not be at any mortal risk from using the fluid. However, in this case, the environment in which the fluid was used appears to have been exceptional . . . The results of tests carried out on behalf of the plaintiff show that, in these circumstances, concentrations of vapour at a level dangerous to someone of Mr Halsbury's sensitivity could have built-up in the upper reaches of the roof void, that is, at the level of the deceased's head. The defendants have not contested these findings.

Let us now turn to the law as laid down in the Consumer Protection Act 1987. For liability to rest with the defendants it must be established that they constitute the producers of a consumer product which was defective within the meaning of s. 3 of the Act and which caused injury or loss under s. 2(1). That the defendants constitute producers of the product is not at issue; nor is it contested that the fluid caused Mr Halsbury's death, even though it may have done so in an unforeseeable way. The outcome of this case thus turns ultimately on two questions of law: was this product defective, and was this a defect which the producer should have guarded against . . .

Finally, we come to the second question of law. The defendants in this case have sought to rely upon the development risk defence provided by s. 4(1)(e) of the 1987 Act. This makes it a defence to show that the defect was not one that the producer should have discovered at the stage of manufacture. The defendants brought considerable evidence to show that, while the risk to chronic asthmatics, or to others with serious breathing problems, was widely recognised in the industry (and product warnings issued accordingly), the combination of personal sensitivity and environmental conditions in this case had not been foreseen by the industry as a whole, and could not have been easily recreated in laboratory conditions.

The ambit and effect of s. 4(1)(e) is a matter for doubt, not least because this appears to be the first opportunity that a superior court has had of ruling upon its operation.

Section 4(1)(e) states that it shall be a defence to show:

that the state of scientific or technical knowledge at the relevant time was not such that a producer of products of the same description as the product in question might be expected to have discovered the defect if it had existed in his products while they were under his control;

In the instant case, the section as drafted would appear to be wide enough to provide the defendants with a defence. This was not a defect which a producer of such products would have expected to discover—we have ample evidence that the British industry was unaware of the risks. However, expert evidence brought by the plaintiff has also shown that research in Germany, which was published in the German scientific press at the time this product was under manufacture (though not published in England until considerably later), had established that tests existed to show that the risk of serious breathing difficulties being caused by woodworm treatments had been seriously underestimated. Counsel for the plaintiff has used this information to argue, following the Product Liability Directive 85/374/EEC, that there is no defence. The Directive states in Article 7(e):

> . . . *the producer shall not be liable . . . if he proves that the state of scientific or technical knowledge at the time when he put his product into circulation was not such as to enable the existence of the defect to be discovered.*

It is said, therefore, that, strictly and objectively, the state of scientific knowledge at the time was such that the defect was discoverable. Counsel for the plaintiff has presented the Court with two options. Either we can apply s. 1 of the 1987 Act and interpret s. 4(1)(e) purposively to reach the conclusion that the defect was discoverable, or we can avoid doing damage to the language of the Act by relying on the Directive itself. If either of these arguments find favour, the Court is obliged to rule against the defendants.

So, counsel in this case thus present us with a clear anomaly. On the one hand we are apparently obliged by the literal meaning of s. 4(1)(e) to find for the defendants, while on the other, we are obliged to adapt or avoid the language of the Act to give effect to what might be called the 'Euro-meaning' of the development risk defence.

In resolving the issue, we cannot disregard the purposes for which this Act was passed. We must recognise that the Act is concerned, as the preamble to Directive 85/374/EEC makes clear, to create a principle of strict liability for defective products, as the only means of fairly apportioning risk. To put it succinctly, the purpose of the Act is to protect the consumer. It was also created to meet our obligations as members of the European Community, following the passing of that Directive. The defective drafting of s. 4(1)(e) means that we risk failure on both counts. To correct that defect, I can see no difficulty in relying upon the Directive itself as a source of action. As the European Court of Justice made clear in *R* v *Secretary of State for Transport ex parte Factortame* (C-213/89) [1990] 3 CMLR 807, it is for national courts to ensure the full effect of the rules of Community law, a principle which must apply equally to all forms of Community legislation.

This leads me, finally, to consideration of Article 7(e). On the wording of the Article, the defence places the onus upon the defendants to show that no one could possibly have discovered the defect at that time. This is a strict construction, but it is one which is consistent with the primary purpose of the Directive. On the facts before us, however, the safety of products of this type plainly had been put into question, albeit outside the British timber treatment industry. The existence of this knowledge made the defect discoverable, and it is no defence in those circumstances for the defendants to say that they were unaware of the defect. Accordingly, I find that the development risk defence is not available to the defendants, and the plaintiff therefore succeeds in her action.

The Mighty Mussel Co. Ltd v Seldon [1992]
(Court of Appeal)

Lord Sturmer MR: The respondent in this case brought an action against the appellant company under the Consumer Protection Act 1987, alleging injuries caused by severe gastroenteritis after eating contaminated oysters supplied to a restaurant by the defendant company. The company has sought to defeat Mr Seldon's claim on two grounds. First, it argues that the harvesting and supply of oysters did not constitute an industrial process within the meaning of the Act. Second, it argues that, if the oysters were capable of being a defective product, the company was protected by the development risks defence in s. 4(1)(e) of the Consumer Protection Act.

Have the oysters undergone an industrial process?
The term industrial process is used to determine the limits of product liability for agricultural produce under Part I of the 1987 Act. Under ss. 2(4) and 1(2) liability does not extend to agricultural products (which are defined so as to include the products of the seas) unless they have undergone an 'industrial process'. The 1985 Product Liability Directive similarly uses the phrase 'processing of an industrial nature' in the preamble. These phrases are nowhere defined in the legislation. It behoves the court to apply the ordinary meaning of such terms. The term 'process' requires no definition; 'industrial' simply implies a system of manufacturing, that is, a conversion of the product from its natural state into something else. This conclusion, I would suggest, is supported by the language of s. 1(2)(c) which emphasises the need for an industrial process to have imparted some essential characteristic to the product.

On the facts of this case, the oysters have merely been harvested, sorted and distributed to various culinary destinations. Sorting and distribution clearly lack the necessary 'processing' characteristics of manufacture, and so cannot be an industrial process. In my view, harvesting also is not an industrial process. An industrial process under the legislation can only be undertaken in respect of produce. Logically, the oysters can only be produce once they have been harvested. It follows that the oysters have not been subjected to an industrial process, and are not within the scope of the Act.

Can the appellants rely on the development risks defence?
One of the more curious facets of this case is the cause of contamination. The Court below was presented with clear evidence that contamination in this case was caused by a novel cocktail of chemicals which polluted the company's oyster beds following illegal inshore dumping of industrial waste by persons unknown. Although the defendants routinely test samples of their shellfish for common forms of contamination, they had not tested for the contamination which actually took place. The Court was also presented with evidence that tests existed which could have identified the chemicals involved, but that their occurrence in shellfish in any injurious

concentrations had not been encountered before, with the result that the tests had not been adapted for use by companies such as the defendants. The appellants accordingly sought to rely on s. 4(1)(e) of the 1987 Act, or, in the alternative, on the possibly wider defence of Article 7(e) of the 1985 Directive, both of which provide a defence to producers where the state of scientific knowledge at the time of manufacture was not such as to enable them to discover the existence of the defect.

My lords, it seems that this is a clear instance of a situation to which s. 4(1)(e) must apply; to find otherwise would be absurd, and the judge at first instance erred in not applying the defence. The fact that discovery of contamination was a technical possibility, although, practically, so improbable as to be discounted, should not be used as a reason for denying a defence to the producers.

Since this issue can be resolved on the terms of the 1987 Act, I see no need to consider the question whether Article 7(e) of the Directive could be used to displace the clear language of s. 4(1)(e).

Accordingly I would allow this appeal on both grounds.

Bramley LJ: I have had the advantage of reading the judgment of Lord Sturmer MR, and would allow this appeal for the reasons he has given. I would only add that, in my view, some comments on the perceived conflict between the development risks defence as laid down by the Consumer Protection Act 1987 and by the Product Liability Directive of 1985 may be of assistance for the future development of this area of law.

The differences in wording between s. 4(1)(e) of the Act and Article 7(e) of the Directive have been alluded to by a number of commentators. Opinions are divided. There are those who perceive the differences to be of no practical effect, and others who suggest that the drafting of the defence in the 1987 Act is more generous to producers of products. Whichever is true (and for the reasons given by Lord Sturmer MR, this Court does not consider it necessary to rule on that point), the underlying question must be whether the English courts are entitled to override the provision of an Act of Parliament by reference to the Directive it is intended to implement. In the present context, this is a question of some difficulty.

It is well established within the jurisprudence of the European Court of Justice that obligations contained in a Directive are enforceable against the state, if the state has failed to take the necessary steps to implement that legislative act. This principle was recently emphasised in the case of *Francovich* v *Italian Republic*, reported in *The Times*, 21 November 1991. But that is not the situation in the instant case. The Consumer Protection Act is the implementing legislation, so is it still possible to rely on the Directive in actions before the domestic courts? In my view there are two distinct possibilities.

First, it is possible to argue that the Directive may be directly effective against individuals, regardless of the implementing legislation. This view was adopted in the English High Court by Cox J in the case of *Halsbury* v *Coke's Wood Products Ltd* [1991]. I have to say that I am unconvinced by the learned judge's reasoning in that case. It has been well established since the case of *Van Duyn* v *Home Office (No. 2)* [1974] ECR 1337, [1975] 3 All ER 190 that Directives lack the necessary horizontal direct effect to ground an action between private individuals. I am not persuaded that the European jurisprudence has significantly changed since that case was decided.

Second, an alternative view would be to argue (as did counsel for the defendant in this case) that the domestic Act must be interpreted so as to give effect to the meaning of the Directive—see *Von Colson* v *Land Nordrhein-Westfalen* [1984] ECR 1891. Section 1 of the Consumer Protection Act puts this obligation into statutory form. It requires us to construe provisions in the Act in a manner that is consistent with the Product Liability Directive. It follows that such a duty requires English courts to adopt a purposive approach to the implementing legislation. But does this mean that the courts must always adopt a purposive approach to this legislation? I think not. I cannot accept that Parliament intended by this wording to empower the courts to disregard the clear meaning of the enactment. Rather, it is my view that s. 1 merely expresses the established rule against ambiguity which is derived from the *Von Colson* case. As Lord Templeman explained in the case of *Duke* v *GEC Reliance* [1988] AC 618, [1988] 1 All ER 626 at 637, an English court is not obliged to distort the clear meaning of an enactment to achieve consistency with a Directive which does not have direct effect—a view which has since been followed by this Court in *Marshall* v *Southampton and South West Hampshire Area Health Authority (No. 2)* [1991] ICR 136, [1990] 3 CMLR 425. If the approach I have outlined is correct, it is only if the language of s. 4(1)(e) is ambiguous that a court must turn to the wording of the Directive. Although I see no necessity to rule on this point in the instant case, I must express some doubt that any such ambiguity can be found.

Russet LJ: I concur with the views of my learned brethren Lord Sturmer MR and Bramley LJ. For the reasons they have given, I too would allow this appeal.

Comments: This is a difficult and demanding exercise which requires you to use three specific skills (i) to do library-based research; (ii) to construct an argument from conflicting precedents, and (iii) to apply principles of statutory interpretation.

One mistake that some of our students make with these exercises is to rely too heavily on the materials given, and little else. This does not help you to develop a critical perspective on the cases, and makes it all the more likely that you will miss erroneous reasoning or incorrect statements of principle that appear.

As a preliminary, there are a number of basic and obvious research strategies you should follow to develop an understanding of the area. Obviously you should look at the text of the Act—ideally an annotated version, which will give you some commentary. Do not focus just on the sections at issue, but look at definition sections and any related provisions that might help assess the purpose of the Act. Similarly, look at the Directive, particularly the relevant articles and preamble.

Are there any cases on the Act or Directive which would be of assistance? Do not assume that because none is cited in the materials, they do not exist. Authority on the effect of s. 1, and on the scope of ss. 2 and 4 of the Act would be particularly useful. Sources like *Current Law*, *European Current Law*, LEXIS and JUSTIS-CELEX could be used in addition to a search for relevant textbooks or articles.

Once you get into the problem itself, it is important that you concentrate on the grounds of appeal. These are as identified by Purchase J, and provide a basic structure for your answer.

(a)   *Is Roseberry's a producer of agricultural products?*
The High Court found in your favour here—but that is little help given that Purchase J's judgment is the subject of the appeal. Is it sufficient to reiterate the judge's finding to support your argument, or should you do something more? If so, what?

The distinction between this and the second point of appeal looks highly artificial—do you need to clarify the relationship between s. 2(2) and (4)?

(b)   *Have the goods undergone an industrial process?*
You have authority for this term in the *Seldon* case. It is a Court of Appeal decision, and therefore the *ratio* is binding on later Courts of Appeal. You should consider:

(i)   Whether all the judges in *Seldon* agree on their interpretation? If so this is the *ratio* of the case, if not, your Court is not bound.

(ii)   Could the Court of Appeal have erred in law? Is there an established legal meaning for 'industrial process' or is the ordinary meaning approach correct—use dictionaries, *Words and Phrases Legally Defined*, etc. to confirm. If there is an alternative interpretation is *your* Court of Appeal free to adopt it?

(iii)   Is there any basis for *distinguishing* the present case? Is packaging a significantly different process from 'harvesting, sorting and distributing'?

(c)   *Can the defendants rely on the development risks defence?*
This part of the problem creates the greatest difficulties. The courts in the fictitious cases have got into a mess here, and you have to try and sort it out.

Unless you think you can get round most of these difficulties by distinguishing, the ultimate question you need to determine is as follows. The Directive has supposedly been implemented by the 1987 Act. Is there an argument that it has been improperly implemented in respect of the defence? If so, what should the Court do about it? Apply the Act regardless? Give the Directive horizontal direct effect as per *Halsbury* (this is persuasive authority only; but also cf. the Court of Appeal's comments in *Seldon* on that approach)? Give the Directive indirect effect by means of a purposive interpretation of the Act? This question thus contains a whole range of issues you might consider:

(i) Is there a clear meaning to s. 4(1)(e) or is the provision ambiguous? You cannot argue it is ambiguous because it conflicts with the Directive— we are looking for an internal ambiguity.

(ii) If there is a clear meaning to s. 4(1)(e), what is it? If there is an ambiguity, what is it? What is the meaning of Article 7(e) of the Directive? Is there any appreciable difference between the meanings? Look at *Halsbury* and *Seldon* on these points, but do not disregard the possibility of further research for binding or persuasive authorities.

(iii) If there is a clear meaning, must the Court apply it, even if it is contrary to the wording of the Directive? You will need to consider the various conflicts of authority here, notably between the cases cited— *Duke, Marshall* on the one hand and the CJEC decision in *Von Colson* on the other. What about *Marleasing* and *Webb* v *EMO*? Does *Marleasing* empower the Court of Appeal to overlook *stare decisis*? Could you argue that the case here is distinguishable from the situation in *Duke et al.* anyway?

(iv) If there is an ambiguity within the Act, should your Court adopt a purposive approach to avoid it? Given that the Act is expressly to be interpreted in the light of the Directive (CPA, s. 1) this could be a fairly good line to follow. You could use *dicta* from cases such as *Bulmer* v *Bollinger* or *Buchanan* v *Babco* in support. However, you still have to try and reconcile this approach with the views expressed in *Seldon*.

(v) Alternatively, can you rely on the Directive directly? Cox J says you can, but cf. Bramley LJ in *Seldon*—is this *ratio* or *obiter*? What *are* the principles governing the direct effect of Directives in situations where implementing legislation exists? How do these principles apply to the Product Liability Directive?

Conclusion

There is a perceived difference between how the English lawyer and the continental lawyer approach their tasks. Much of the difference may, in the final analysis, be more to do with form than fundamentals. However, the difference is perceptible, and the reality is that it is the English lawyer who will have to change, more than his continental counterpart. Our system of precedent has been described as a system whereby 'we never clean our slates', or, more candidly, as an 'ungodly jumble'. It depends upon an immense network of narrow rules. It avoids working from general principles. It is only now, reluctantly, beginning to embrace a purposiveness in interpretation. It rests on the sanctity of case law.

The contrast with Civil Law is obvious; perhaps the battle-lines are drawn. We may have to reassess the (perhaps apocryphal) headline in *The Times* early this century: 'Fog in the Channel—Europe isolated'.

REFERENCES

* Brown, L. (1989) *The Court of Justice of the European Communities*, London: Sweet and Maxwell.
Cohn, E. (1968) *Manual of German Law*, (2 vols) London: British Institute of Comparative Law.
* David, R. & Brierley, J. (1985) *Major Legal Systems in the World Today*, 3rd Edition, London: Stevens.
* de Búrca, G. (1992) 'Giving Effect to European Community Directives' *Modern Law Review*, vol. 55, p. 215.
Docksey, C. & Fitzpatrick, B. (1991) 'The Duty of National Courts to Interpret Provisions of National Law in Accordance with Community Law' *Industrial Law Journal*, vol. 20, p. 113.
Galmot & Bonichot, (1988) 'La Cour de Justice des Communautés Européenes et la transposition des directives en droit national' *Revue français de Droit administratif*, vol. 4, p. 1.
Gravells, N. (1989) 'Disapplying an Act of Parliament Pending a Preliminary Ruling: Constitutional Enormity or Community Law Right?' *Public Law*, p. 568.
Harris, D. & Tallon, D. (1989) *Contract Law Today: Anglo-French Comparisons*, Oxford: Clarendon Press.
Harrison, K. (1992) 'Pregnancy in the Court of Appeal' *New Law Journal*, vol. 142, p. 462.
* Horn, N., Kötz, H. & Leser, H. (1982) *German Private and Commercial Law: An Introduction*, Oxford: Clarendon Press.
Lasok, D. & Bridge, J.W. (1991) *Law and Institutions of the European Communities*, 5th Edition, London: Butterworths.
* Miers, D. & Page, A. (1990) *Legislation*, 2nd Edition, London: Sweet and Maxwell.
Nicholas, B. (1982) *French Law of Contract*, London: Butterworths.
* Snyder, F. (1993) 'The Effectiveness of European Community Law: Institutions, Processes, Tools and Techniques' *Modern Law Review*, vol. 56, p. 19.
* Steiner, J. (1992) *Textbook on EEC Law*, 3rd Edition, London: Blackstone Press.
* Steiner, J. (1993) 'From Direct Effect to *Francovich:* Shifting means of enforcement of Community Law' *European Law Review*, vol. 18, p. 3.
Szladits, C. & Germain, C. (1985) *Guide to Foreign Legal Materials: French*, 2nd Edition, New York: Oceana Pub.

Appendix

The following exercise was set as an examination for our students in 1991. The students were given a fictitious Act (here the *Access to Health Records and Medical Reports Act 1989*) which was based on two real Acts but changed so as to allow us to explore specific issues in the study of Legal Method. The students were given the fictitious Act together with the fictitious precedents and allowed approximately three months to submit their answer. This is the usual form for our Legal Method examination. By the time the students take the exercise they will not only have completed the Legal Method course but they will also have completed the major part of the substantive law subjects such as Contract or Criminal Law.

The aim of this exercise was to create a more realistic setting for the examination of Legal Method skills, by bringing together the areas of statutory interpretation and precedent as well as research and presentation skills. The statute is deliberately drafted so as to present problems. The judgments are helpful on some points and puzzling on others. Many of the phrases in the statute and in the judgments are taken from real Acts and cases. We have tried to incorporate as many aspects of Legal Method techniques covered in this book as we could manage. You should be able to work through the problem with some confidence.

We have decided in this edition to reprint two LLB I student answers to this exercise (with their kind permission and that of the University Academic Registrar). You will see from the answers that they are quite different in approach, showing that there is never one set method of answering a legal problem. They are good answers. They are well-structured and the arguments (whether we agree with them or not) are well-researched and presented. Equally, they are not perfect.

We would recommend that you attempt the exercise yourself first before looking at the students' submissions. Note also that the law is always changing so that the law regarding such matters as reference being made to *Hansard* has altered since the papers were written in 1991.

Legal Method Assessment Material: Instructions

The following material provides the basis for the Legal Method assessment (*1991*).

Word limit: the word limit (*to be adhered to strictly*) is 2,000 words.

It is to be assumed that the following fictitious Act (the Access to Health Records and Medical Records Act 1989) is law. This fictitious Act is based on two real Acts: the Access to Medical Reports Act 1988 and the Access to Health Records Act 1990.

There are a number of differences in wording between the fictitious Act and the real Acts. Thus it should be stressed that for the purposes of this assessment the version below is to be taken as the Act in force and the real Acts deemed never to have been passed.

Any annotations to the real Acts may be useful. In particular, the history of the real Acts and any mischief they sought to remedy may be helpful to you in determining the purpose of the fictitious Act in this assessment.

Any regulations created by way of Statutory Instruments under the real Acts are deemed, for the purposes of this assessment, not to exist.

Marks will be awarded for:

1. Evidence of research skills
2. Analysis and application
3. Awareness of rules of precedent
4. Application of statutory interpretation techniques
5. Quality of presentation of argument.

No particular weighting will be given to any of these factors.

ACCESS TO HEALTH RECORDS AND
MEDICAL REPORTS ACT 1989

An Act to establish a right of access to health records by the individuals to whom they relate and other persons; to provide for the correction of inaccurate health records; and for connected purposes. [3rd October 1989]

Right of access to health records

1. (1) An application for access to a health record, or to any part of a health record, may be made to the health professional who is the holder of the record (hereinafter, the 'holder') by any of the following, namely—

   (a) the patient;

   (b) a person authorised in writing to make the application on the patient's behalf;

   (c) where the person is a child, a person having parental responsibility for the patient;

(d) where the patient is incapable of managing his own affairs, any person appointed by the court to manage those affairs;

(e) where the patient has died, the patient's personal representative and any person who may have a claim arising out of the patient's death.

(2) Where an application is made under subsection (1) above the holder shall give access to the record, or the part of the record, to which the application applies within a reasonable time.

Exemptions

2. Access shall not be given under section 1 above to any part of a health record—

(1) which would be likely to disclose—

(a) information likely to cause serious harm to the physical or mental health of the patient or of any other individual; or

(b) information relating to or provided by an individual, other than the patient, who could be identified from that information; or

(2) which was made before the commencement of this Act, except in so far as this excluded information is necessary, in the opinion of the holder, to make intelligible any part of the record to which access is required to be given under section 1.

Rights of access to medical reports

3. It shall be the right of an individual to have access, in accordance with the subsections below, to any medical report relating to the individual which is to be, or has been, supplied by a health professional for employment purposes or insurance purposes.

(1) A health professional shall not be obliged to give an individual access to information or to any part of a medical report where disclosure would be likely to cause serious harm to the physical or mental health of the individual or others or would indicate the intentions of the practitioner in respect of the individual.

(2) A health professional shall not be obliged to give an individual access to information or to any part of a medical report where disclosure would be likely to reveal information about another person, or to reveal the identity of another person who has supplied information to the practitioner about the individual, unless that person has consented.

Correction of inaccurate records or reports

4. (1) Where a person considers that any information contained in a health record or medical report, or any part of a health record or medical report, to which he has been given access under section 1 or section 3 is inaccurate, he may apply to the holder of the record for the necessary correction to be made.

(2) On such an application the holder of the record shall—

(a) if he is satisfied that the information is inaccurate, make the necessary correction;

(b) if he is not satisfied, note this point on the record; and

(c) in either case, supply the applicant with a copy of the correction or note.

(3) In this section 'inaccurate' means incorrect, misleading or incomplete.

Applications to the court

5. Application may be made to the High Court or a county court in order to effect the requirements laid down in this Act.

Interpretation
6. For the purposes of this Act—
'health record' means any record made by a health professional relating to the physical or mental health of a patient.
'health professional' shall include medical practitioners, pharmaceutical chemists, registered nurses, occupational therapists and psychologists.
'access' means viewing, reading, examining, inspecting or other such actions.
'make', in relation to a record, includes compile.

CASES ARISING UNDER THE ACCESS TO HEALTH RECORDS AND MEDICAL REPORTS ACT 1989

[*NB: These cases are fictitious*]

BLACKSTONE v COKE [1990]
COURT OF APPEAL

STORY LJ:
The facts of this case are straightforward. Earlier this year Mr Blackstone applied for a job with Widgets International Ltd. As is their usual policy, the company offered the job to Mr Blackstone subject to a satisfactory medical examination. Mr Blackstone underwent such an examination by a Dr Coke and two weeks later was told by the personnel officer at the company that we would not be employed at Widgets International owing to the nature of the medical report submitted by Dr Coke. The company refused to explain their reasons or show Mr Blackstone the report. Mr Blackstone then approached Dr Coke and sought access to the report under s. 3, Access to Health Records and Medical Reports Act 1989. Dr Coke refused Mr Blackstone access to the report on the grounds that the identity of another person who supplied the information to the practitioner about the individual would be revealed by allowing access to the report contrary to s. 3(2) of the Act.
Mr Blackstone now demands that Dr Coke's decision regarding access should be reviewed by this court and that Mr Blackstone should be able to exercise the rights stated in s. 4. In the court below Scalpel J held that s. 3(2) allowed the health professional absolute discretion to withhold such information. Mr Blackstone's argument has been that: (i) s. 3(2) is subject to objective assessment; and (ii) he should, in the course of litigation, be allowed to see the report in order to challenge its accuracy.
Under this Act an individual's right of access is not absolute. There are a number of limitations. Thus, on Mr Blackstone's first point I agree with Scalpel J's analysis: it is for the medical practitioner to decide whether the information should be revealed or not. Dr Coke is convinced of the authenticity of the information; the information arising from his treatment of another patient. That is enough for this Act: the test in s. 3(2) is subjective. On the second point, if Mr Blackstone is allowed to see the report in order to challenge its accuracy, he will have achieved his wider purpose because he will have gained access to the report. On the other hand, if he does not see the report he is somewhat at a loss. The information, for all we know, could have been supplied in error or maliciously. Sections 33 and 34 of the Supreme Court Act 1981 permits a paitent to gain access to his medical records if he contemplates litigation, but this can only apply (as far as I can see) where the patient is suing the practitioner in respect of personal injuries and so needs the records to prove his case. That does not apply here.

Equally, s. 4 of the present Act allows a person to challenge the accuracy of a report but only one 'to which he has been given access under section 1 or section 3'. There is no easy answer to this rather circuitous point. Given my finding on the first point I can see no alternative but to hold that Mr Blackstone cannot be allowed to see the report. I therefore dismiss the appeal.

TALE LJ and FABLE LJ agreed without expressing opinions.

HALSBURY v MANSFIELD [1990]
COURT OF APPEAL

LEGEND LJ:

This case is only the second to come before this Court under the Access to Health Records and Medical Reports Act 1989. It is a case of some difficulty, and, indeed, has raised some novel issues in respect of which we have found the decision of our learned brethren in *Blackstone* v *Coke* [1990] to be of little or no assistance.

The facts of the case are easily stated. Mr Halsbury applied to the High Court under s. 5 of the Act seeking a declaration that the defendant Ms Mansfield, a registered ophthalmic optician, should disclose her records concerning the appellant's consultations with her in the period since the Act came into force. The defendant refused to disclose these records on two grounds. First, that she is not a 'health professional' within the scope of this Act, and, secondly, even if caught by the terms of the Act, it was her opinion that disclosure would not be in Mr Halsbury's interest at this time, since it was information likely to cause serious harm to his mental health, and therefore exempted under s. 2(1)(a).

The appellant had, at the time, no inkling of any problem, and hence no reason for seeking disclosure, other than a general desire to discover what information was held on him by various health practitioners. This is, in fact, only the first of a number of different claims to access being made by Mr Halsbury, and while such behaviour may, at first sight, suggest some vexatiousness about his litigation, let us say that the Act (perhaps a little surprisingly) requires the applicant to make no justification for claiming access. It is his statutory right, and should not be interfered with without good reason. In this case, the High Court found that there was, indeed, good reason. While it held that Ms Mansfield's records were subject to the Act, it accepted, following *Blackstone* v *Coke*, that the words 'would be likely to' as used in ss. 2 and 3 connote a subjective test. Accordingly, the Court felt unable to interfere with Ms Mansfield's professional judgment, and refused disclosure. Mr Halsbury now appeals against that decision to this Court.

The first question we must consider is whether the records of an ophthalmic optician are within the scope of this Act. This issue is to be decided according to provisions contained in ss. 1 and 6 of the Act. Section 1 provides a right of access to 'health records' held by a 'health professional'. Each of these rather inelegant terms is then defined by s. 6. The concept of health record seems of limited assistance in the present context, being heavily dependent upon the definition of a health professional. If we consider Ms Manfield to be a health professional, it would surely be ludicrous to consider her patients' records to be anything other than 'health records' for the purposes of the Act.

So, turning to that issue, it is notable that the Act does not offer an exhaustive definition of the term 'health professional'. That being the case, it seems obvious to me, as it was to the learned judge in the court below, that an ophthalmic optician is capable of inclusion within the broad class of person implied by the list contained in s. 6, and should, logically, be included.

Having found that Ms Mansfield's records are governed by the access right, it is necessary to decide whether her claim to exemption under s. 2 is valid. While I am loathe to suggest that a court is a competent body to challenge the professional opinion of specialist practitioners within their own field, I find the breadth of s. 2 somewhat disturbing. If, as our learned brethren in *Blackstone* v *Coke* decided, the standard applied in assessing what is likely to cause harm is purely subjective, then the views of the professional involved will be virtually conclusive, however insubstantial they might be. Surely it cannot have been the intention of the legislature to enable those health professionals (few though they may be) who would seek to hide their mistakes and infelicities behind a cloak of feigned paternalism to succeed in this deception? Accordingly, I would find that the test in s. 2 is objective, not subjective.

In so doing, I am conscious that precedent obliges me to follow the decision in *Blackstone* v *Coke*, unless there appears to be some valid basis for distinguishing that case. Given that the point of interpretation in that case arose in respect of s. 3, I have no difficulty in so doing.

There is another problem: should the court have the right to examine the records? How is a court to assess (either on a subjective or objective test) the decision of the health professional if the court never sees the records? What surprises me is that this point was not raised in *Blackstone* v *Coke*. Even on a subjective test, the court must be able to say, in those cases where there is clear evidence of bad faith or of the most outrageous irrationality, to the professional: 'you could not, even on a subjective test, believe that such a disclosure would cause physical or mental harm'. But if it never sees the records, how will it know whether bad faith exists? With the objective test we have adopted, the court's right to examine the documents is self-evident. We have therefore examined the documents in the absence of the parties; and have formulated our views accordingly. We would have adopted the same procedure under a subjective test.

Thus, turning to the facts of the case, we must consider whether, objectively, this was information likely to cause mental harm to the appellant. Ms Mansfield is not a specialist in matters of mental health, but neither, one assumes, is any other ordinary ophthalmic optician. It is a decision we must assess according to the standards of her profession. We have no evidence before us that such non-disclosure would be viewed as professional misconduct by the defendant. Indeed, she has done no more than many doctors who will be selective in what they disclose to their patients. Having examined the records I can find no basis, even objectively, for denying Ms Mansfield the exemption provided by s. 2(1)(a). Accordingly, I would dismiss the appeal.

TALE LJ:

I have had the advantage of reading the judgment of my learned friend Legend LJ and would join him in dismissing this appeal. However, in so doing, I would take issue with his reasoning, persuasive though his arguments may be.

It is an established principle that an Act must be read in its entirety, not simple section by section. Does this therefore mean that, where the same phrase is used in different sections it should automatically have the same meaning? Having examined the authorities I find they are divided on this point. On the language of this Act I would favour the reasoning set out in the Court of Appeal's decision in *Dixon* v *BBC* [1979] 2 All ER 112 to that of *Bracey* v *Read* [1962] 3 All ER 472. Thus, the words common to s. 2 and 3 must be read the same. Accordingly, in keeping with *Young* v *BAC* [1944] KB 718, I feel bound by the precedent established in *Blackstone* v *Coke*.

I would therefore say that s. 2 encompasses a subjective test. Nevertheless, applying that test I can find no basis for interfering with the decision of the court below.

YARN LJ:

I have had the advantage of reading the judgments of my learned brethren, Legend and Tale LJJ, and find myself in full agreement with the views expressed by Legend LJ. Accordingly, I too would dismiss the appeal.

You are to assume that the following case is listed to be heard by the Court of Appeal.

GLANVIL v BRACTON [1991]

In January 1990 a Mrs Fitzherbert died. For the last five years she had been a national figure and leading campaigner for the introduction of greater penalties for drink-drive offences. Fitzherbert died without making a will and the first person entitled to take out letters of administration (and thereby become Fitzherbert's personal representative) was her estranged brother, Mr Bracton.

As Fitzherbert and Bracton had not talked to each other for 20 years, Bracton was at first reluctant to become her personal representative. However, a leading national newspaper contacted Bracton offering him a large amount of money if he could obtain proof that Fitzherbert had been a secret alcoholic. Bracton therefore took out letters of administration and set about obtaining Fitzherbert's health records. He found that Fitzherbert had not made use of general practitioners but instead had always referred to a homeopath, one Mr Glanvil who possessed no traditional medical qualifications.

Glanvil refused to give Bracton access to the records because: (i) he claimed that the records would identify other people under s. 2(1)(b) of the 1989 Act; and (ii) he had ben informed of Bracton's true motive and objected strongly to such conduct.

Bracton later became convinced, but could not prove, that Glanvil was not telling the truth about the fact that the records would reveal the identity of another person. He applied to a county court to gain access to the records under s. 1(1)(e) and s. 5 of the 1989 Act.

Bracton's application was granted by Forceps J on the grounds:

(i) *Halsbury* v *Mansfield* should be preferred to *Blackstone* v *Coke*. This decision was more apposite to the case in hand as it concerned s. 2 and so was binding in this case. The court had therefore examined the relevant documents (without revealing them to the plaintiff). Mr Bracton's assertion that Mr Glanvil was telling lies could not be substantiated, but there was an area of doubt. In the court's view, on an objective test, the conditions set out in s. 2(1)(b) were not met.

(ii) It was distasteful to allow the 1989 Act to be used in the manner proposed by Bracton, but the court was bound to follow the strict wording of the Act.

(iii) Although a homeopath who is not otherwise medically qualified does not *prima facie* fall within the definition of 'health professional' as set out in s. 6, the case of *Coltman* v *Bibby Tankers* shows that when the word 'includes' introduces a list of words then that list is not exhaustive. A homeopath could fall within the definition.

(iv) In the definition of 'access' contained in s. 6 the phrase 'or other such actions' must be read *eiusdem generis* with the preceding words. The genus is that only actions which do not tamper with or alter the state of the documents is permitted. Duplication and reproduction of the documents are therefore 'other such actions' for the purposes of the Act.

DIRECTIONS:

YOU ARE REQUIRED TO PRESENT THE CASE FOR GLANVIL ON HIS APPEAL TO THE COURT OF APPEAL AGAINST FORCEPS J'S DECISION.

STUDENT PAPER NUMBER ONE

My Lords, Mr Glanvil's case that Mr Bracton should not be given access to these records, rests upon three submissions. Firstly, that under the terms of the Act, Glanvil is not a 'health professional'. My second submission is that even if your Lordships find Bracton has a right of access under

s. 1, access should not be given because the provisions of s. 2(1)(b) and s. 2(2) apply. I finally submit that even if your Lordships find the s. 2 exemptions do not apply and consequently Bracton should be given access, that right of access does not include the right to duplicate and reproduce any of the information contained in the documents.

My first submission is that Glanvil is not a 'health professional' under this Act. Section 6 of the Act states: 'health professional', shall include medical practitioners, pharmaceutical chemists, registered nurses, occupational therapists and psychologists'.

However, are homeopaths also to be defined as health professionals? That depends upon whether this interpretation clause creates an exemplary of exhaustive definition. A similar clause was considered by the House of Lords in *Coltman v Bibby Tankers Ltd* [1988] AC 276. In the leading judgment, Lord Oliver of Aylmerton states that when considering a list which 'includes' certain items, to ascertain whether that list is exemplary or exhaustive, one should look at the matter in the context of other interpretative lists. He contrasts three lists which are prefixed by 'includes', with two lists prefixed by 'means'. He concludes that the draftsman of the statute must have intended these lists to have different purposes, for the 'meaning lists' are to be exhaustive while the inclusory lists give examples. Applying this reasoning to the interpretive lists in this Act it can be seen that, 'inaccurate', 'health record', and 'access', are said to 'mean', something, while, 'health professional', and, 'make', include certain items. Consequently, the 'health professional' list should be interpreted as giving examples only.

However, such a decision does not mean that a homeopath should automatically be considered to be another example of a health professional. As the list is exemplary it should be treated in a similar manner to other non-exhaustive lists; the *eiusdem generis* rule should be applied. For homeopaths to be health professionals they must conform to the genus of the items listed. Admittedly, the *eiusdem generis* rule has traditionally been applied to lists including a number of specific terms followed by a general term, but the use of the rule here places limits upon an otherwise limitless (and merely exemplary) definition. I submit that the genus here is that all the health professionals are registered and qualified under legislative provisions, either by Act of Parliament or in the case of psychologists under a scheme established by the Privy Council. All these registration schemes prescribe qualifications of training conditions.

There are two broad categories of homeopaths. Firstly, medical doctors who have studied for an received a postgraduate Diploma of Homeopathy from the Faculty of Homeopathy. These doctors are thereby both homeopaths and health professionals. As the appellant has no traditional medical qualifications he cannot be included in such a category. The appellant falls into a second category, what you may call, 'lay homeopaths'. He may be knowledgeable in his subject, yet he is not qualified and registered in a manner recognised under legislative rules. Therefore Glanvil cannot be included under the same genus proposed, and is consequently not a health professional.

A further point substantiates that Glanvil is not a health professional. This Act was intended to bring the law on manually-held health records into line with the law on computer-held health records as prescribed by the Data Protection Act 1984 and modified by the Data Protection (Subject Access Modification) (Health) Order 1987 (SI 1987 No. 1903). The aforementioned Order includes a schedule which gives an exhaustive definition of health professionals, and does not included any reference to homeopaths. Therefore, for there to be consistency between the two Acts, a homeopath cannot be a health professional.

Proceeding to my second submission: that access should not be given because of the provisions in s. 2 of the Act. Considering s. 2(1)(b) first, this states that access should be denied in circumstances:

(1)   which could be likely to disclose—
    (b)   information relating to or provided by an individual, other than the patient, who could be identified from that information;

Glanvil claims his records contain such information. Bacton disputes this. Two issues arose when Glanvil's claim was tested by the county court. First, should the test which assesses Glanvil's claim be from a subjective or an objective perspective? Secondly, in order for access to be denied what degree of likelihood must there be that the releasing of the document would reveal someone's identity? These can be called the 'perspective', and the 'probability' questions. It appears that the perspective question has received greater consideration than the probability question in the case law, nevertheless both questions are crucial to this appeal.

Considering the perspective question first, the court has to decide whether the professional assesses whether someone's identity would be revealed (a subjective test), or whether the court makes the assessment (an objective test)? *Blackstone* v *Coke* states any claim to exemption must be assessed by a subjective test. *Halsbury* v *Mansfield* states, 'the test in s. 2 is objective, not subjective'.

Since *Halsbury* v *Mansfield* is the subsequent decision, with reference to s. 2, it should usually be followed. However, I submit this is one of those rare occasions where the Court of Appeal can depart from its previous decisions. Lord Greene MR listed those occasions in *Young* v *BAC* [1944] KB 718 at 729:

(1)   The court is entitled and bound to decide which of two conflicting decisions of its own it may follow.
(2)   The court is bound to refuse to follow a decision of its own which, though not expressly overruled, cannot, in its opinion, stand with a decision of the House of Lords.
(3)   The court is not bound to follow a decision of its own if it is satisfied that the decision is made *per incuriam*.

Occasion two does not occur because no House of Lords decisions are involved. Furthermore, *Halsbury* v *Mansfield* cannot be said to be *per incuriam* for failing to take into consideration the authority of *Dixon* v *BBC* [1979] 2 All ER 112. A case is not *per incuriam* simply because; 'the authority in question does not mention some relevant rule' (per Lord Simon of Glaisdale in *Miliangos* v *George Frank (Textiles) Ltd* [1976] AC 443 at 477 F-G). Even though Legend and Yarn LJJ failed to cite *Dixon* v *BBC*, it was clear from Tale LJ's speech that the court was aware of the case. Furthermore, *Duke* v *Reliance Systems Ltd* [1987] 2 WLR 1225 states that a case can only be found *per incuriam* if the omission of an authority *must* result in a contrary decision. If the overlooked authority only *might* have changed the decision, then the case is not *per incuriam*. With the conflict of *Dixon* v *BBC* and *Bracey* v *Read* [1962] 3 All ER 472, these authorities only *might* have changed the decision.

So the only way in which a decision cannot be followed is if the court finds there are conflicting decisions. But how extensive is this doctrine? Holland and Webb, in *Learning Legal Rules*, take a restrictive view of this exception; such conflict arises because the Court of Appeal does not hear one case at a time; different Lord Justices may be sitting hearing different cases at more or less the same time. It is also possible that some earlier cases might not have been reported.

According to this view, there would be no conflict in this case. However, Cross (in *Precedent in English Law*) cites a conflict between *Morrison* v *Sheffield Corporation* [1917] KB 866 and *Woodhouse* v *Levy* [1940] 2 KB 561. These two cases were both reported and were decided 23 years apart. In *Fisher* v *Ruislip-Northwood UDC* [1945] KB 584, the Court of Appeal held a conflict existed and chose the earlier case in preference to the latter. Therefore, I submit it is possible for the conflicting decisions exception to have a wide application. I suggest the ratio of *Halsbury* v *Mansfield*, which provides separate tests for ss. 2 and 3, conflicts with *Dixon* v *BBC*, which states that a statute should be read as a whole. Therefore your Lordships are able to choose which authority to follow. I submit for reasons of consistent interpretation *Dixon* v *BBC* should be followed, and as this court is still bound by *Blackstone* v *Coke*, a subjective test should be adopted.

A further reason why a subjective test should be followed is that under the Data Protection (Subject Access Modification) (Health) Order 1987 a subjective test is specified. Again for reasons of consistency, the provisions in this Act should follow the Data Protection provisions.

However, if the court still opts for an objective test I submit that Glanvil should still be given exemption from releasing the records. The basis for making this submission is the 'probability', question. This Act states exemption will be granted in a situation, 'which would be likely', to reveal someone's identity. Therefore, for exemption to be granted it must be more likely than not someone's identity will be revealed. Forceps J found that: 'Mr Bracton's assertion that Mr Glanvil was telling lies could not be substantiated, but there was an area of doubt'.

If this assertion could not be substantiated, it is likely the record would reveal someone's identity. Therefore applying the strict wording of the Act, Glanvil should be granted exemption.

Additionally, under s. 2(2), access should not be given to any part of a health record, 'made before the commencement of this Act'. The only exception to this is if, 'in the opinion of the holder', previous information would be required to make the record intelligible. The appellant does not hold such an opinion, therefore Bracton can only have access to records compiled between 3 October 1989 (the date the Act came into force) and Mrs Fitzherbert's death in January 1990.

My third submission: is that the right of access does not include the right to duplicate and reproduce any of the information. Section 6 of the Act states: 'access means viewing, reading, examining, inspecting or other such actions'.

As Forceps J rightly says, 'other such action' should be read *eiusdem generis* with the preceding words. Therefore, one has to identify the genus of those words. Forceps J suggests the genus is actions which do not tamper with or alter the state of the document, hence including duplication and two reasons. Firstly, the purpose of this Act is to give people a right of access to their health records. But surely it does not permit representatives to make a profit at the expense of a deceased person's reputation? If such a genus is adopted, a legal absurdity will result. Consequently, this court is able to use the Golden (or Purposive) Rule, as expounded by Lord Blackburn in *River Wear Commissioners* v *Adamson* (1876–77) 2 App Cas 743 and to give the word, 'access', a restrictive definition which does not include duplication or reproduction. Such a decision would give Bracton access, but prevent him from making a profit.

Secondly, if duplication and reproduction are included in the terms of the access, this Act will be in conflict with the Copyright, Designs and Patents Act 1988 (CDPA). Under the terms of CDPA, Glanvil's records are a 'literary work'—CDPA, s. 1(1)(a)—and hence the copying of the work and issuing copies to the public are prohibited: CDPA, s. 16(1). Therefore, this definition of access would be too wide since these would breach the provisions of CDPA. A possible genus which would not conflict is actions which involve merely looking at the records. Such a decision gives access but would prevent Bracton from executing his 'distasteful' plans, as Forceps J rightly described them.

Bibliography

Introduction to Legal Method—Farrar & Dugdale
Learning Legal Rules—Holland & Webb
Medical Law—Kennedy & Grubb
Precedent in English Law—Cross
Precedent and Law—Stone
Homeopathy—Scott & McCourt
Homeopathy—Ruthven Mitchell

Length: 1982 words

STUDENT PAPER NUMBER TWO

In order to succeed in an appeal to the Court of Appeal against Forceps J's decision it is necessary to counter the reasons for his decision and it is intended to do so following the order in which his reasons are given.

(i)   There would appear to be several arguable points against Forceps J's reasoning on this point, as follows:

(a)   Although the Court of Appeal in *Halsbury* v *Mansfield* distinguished the case of *Blackstone* v *Coke* by the fact that it was concerned with a different section of the Access to Health Records and Medical Reports Act 1989, Forceps J was incorrect in finding *Halsbury* more apposite. Whilst the instant appeal is concerned with the same section, s. 2, as in *Halsbury*, the relevant subsection in *Halsbury*, s. 2(1)(a), seeks to afford protection to the physical or mental health of the patient or another. Section 2(1)(b), on the other hand, under which Glanvil seeks to shelter, deals with protection against breach of confidentiality which may affect a third party. This is also the objective of s. 3(2) upon which, in *Blackstone* v *Coke*, it was decided that the test for whether or not access should be given is a subjective one. Therefore, due to the similarity in purpose of ss. 2(1)(b) and 3(2) *Halsbury* should be distinguished and *Blackstone* applied; a subjective test should be applied thereby disallowing access to the records by Bracton.

(b)   If my reasoning in (i)(a) is not seen to be sufficient to enable the Court to distinguish *Halsbury* then, as expounded by Tale LJ in the *Halsbury* case, *Dixon* v *BBC* [1979] 2 All ER 112 should be applied in this appeal. Following *Young* v *BAC* [1944] KB 718 the instant court is entitled either to choose between previous contradictory decisions of the Court of Appeal or, alternatively, to find the decision in *Halsbury* to be *per incuriam* due to that court's oversight of the judgment in *Dixon* v *BBC*, ie, that the Act should be read as a whole, and that a different test (objective) should not have been applied in *Halsbury* simply because the point in question came under another section of the Act.

(c)   As Forceps LJ has already seen fit to apply the objective test applied in *Halsbury* by the court's examination of the relevant documents, one must look to the words 'which would be likely to disclose' in s. 2(1) to ascertain where the burden of proof lies. These words imply that, where there is a possibility of the consequences as foreseen by ss. 2(1)(a) and 2(1)(b) occurring, it is for the party seeking disclosure to show positively that this is not the case. As stated by Legend LJ in the case of *Halsbury* v *Mansfield*, this is extremely difficult to do without perusal of the document itself, and therefore the court in *Halsbury* did indeed examine the documents. However, Legend LJ then went on to say that ' . . . even on a subjective test . . . where there is clear evidence . . .'. In the instant case there is no 'clear evidence' and therefore it is Bracton who has not met the conditions necessary to satisfy the implications of s. 2(1)(b).

(ii) It is unfortunate that Forceps J felt unable to look beyond the strict wording of the Act but it is preferable to deal with this point at a later stage.

(iii) Forceps J's application of *Coltman* v *Bibby Tankers* (1988) is questionable in seeking to ascertain the parameters of the word 'include' under s. 6 of this Act, in listing persons under the heading of 'health professional'. In *Coltman* the House of Lords reached its decision that a list is not exhaustive where introduced by 'includes' by looking to other lists within the Act pertinent to that case, as well as considering the mischief that Act sought to remedy. In that case, because lists which were not introduced by 'includes' were very specific, where 'includes' was used in introducing lists they concluded that the latter were merely stating examples. This is not the case in this instance. For example, under s. 6 'access' means . . . or other such actions' is clearly not exhaustive nor strictly specific but the word 'includes' is not used. Therefore it seems unlikely that *Coltman* should be applied in this case and consequently two approaches may be taken to show that a homeopath (Glanvil) does not fall within this category. Firstly, that, if the list is not exhaustive, a homeopath does not fall within the same genus as the other examples and, secondly, that the list is indeed exhaustive. On the first point, in order to pinpoint the genus implied by the list, it may be necessary to look beyond this Act to the history behind it.

The introduction of the Data Protection Act 1984 created an anomaly in the law that access could be gained to records by patients whose doctors stored that information on computer whilst access was denied to patients whose doctors kept manual records. Prior to the introduction of the Access to Health Records and Medical Reports Act 1989 this anomaly was rectified by the introduction of a statutory instrument in the form of The Data Protection (Subject Access and Modification) (Health) Order 1987 which exempted 'health professionals' from the provisions of the Data Protection Act. Within that statutory instrument 'health professionals' are clearly identified in the Schedule to it. The Act in question in this case is a clear attempt by Parliament to make provisions for those persons wishing access to records held by 'health professionals' and, given its legislative history, it would seem entirely acceptable to look to the Schedule of SI 1987 No. 1903 for a definitive definition where there is any doubt about the wording of the instant Act. Homeopaths are not included within that Schedule and, given the breadth of its ambit, which includes all those professionals stated in the relevant list in this Act amongst others, it is surely not merely an oversight in draftsmanship. Therefore, Glanvil cannot be considered a 'health professional' in which case an action brought under this Act cannot effect disclosure of his records.

Alternatively, turning to my second point, that the list under s. 6 is exhaustive, it is necessary to examine the construction of the other lists under that section. The first of those lists used the word 'any' whilst the list relating to 'access' includes the phrase 'or other such actions'. Had Parliament intended the list of 'health professionals' to be non-exhaustive it seems likely that they might have made use of either or both of these means to do so. They did not, which would imply their intention to create an exhaustive list and list, again, Glanvil would not fall within the scope of this Act.

(iv)   Forceps J is correct that 'or other such actions' must be read *eiusdem generis* with the preceding words in the list relating to 'access' under s. 6. However, it *cannot be agreed* that the genus of 'viewing, reading, examining, inspecting' is purely that of actions which 'do not tamper with or alter the state of the documents'. These preceding words are actions which neither alter, tamper with, nor remove information from records in any other way that in the mind of the reader. Where confidentiality is of such great importance to all parties concerned to allow copies to be taken, from which subsequent copies could be taken, would defeat the doctrine of doctor/patient confidentiality. Further, this view is reinforced by the express provision under s. 4(2)(b); that where a correction is made to a health record or medical report by the holder at the request of a patient, the holder is required to 'supply the applicant with a copy of the correction or note'. The rule of *inclusio unius, exclusio alterius* may be applied to this; that is, had Parliament meant 'access' to include 'copying' it would have expressly provided for it as is the case under s. 4(2)(b).

At this point it is intended to look more closely at Forceps J's reason in item (ii).

To state that the court cannot look beyond the strict wording of the Act is to deny the history and purpose of this legislation. We must, therefore, look to *common law prior* to this Act to understand the motives of Parliament in its introduction.

The first problem which presents itself to the individual seeking access to his medical records is one of ownership. Generally, the common law with regard to property allowed no cause of action (save in the very unusual circumstances of a private patient/doctor contract which expressly provided that records were the property of the doctor). There were some exceptions made to his general doctrine one of which, *C v C* (1946), allowed patients access to medical records pending litigation. This case was not, however, concerned with a situation where a doctor held records pertaining to the condition of the patient's health when the doctor had contributed to that condition and, therefore, did little to improve the common law status. The intending litigant was also then to be afforded the discretion of the court in ordering disclosure of medical records prior to litigation under ss. 33 and 34 of the Supreme Court Act 1981. So what then was the technical legal difficulty Parliament intended to remedy by the enactment of the statute in question here, in 1989?

Sir John Donaldson, MR, in *Lee v South West Thames Regional Health Authority* (1985) looked at the anomaly created by our common law; that whilst a doctor would be bound to answer his patient's questions as to intended treatment the doctor was under no obligation to inform his patient of the treatment which had actually taken place. Again, in *Naylor v Preston Area Health Authority* (1987), the Master of the Rolls, *obiter*, entirely repudiated the view that a doctor should only be obliged to disclose information held on a patient where there existed a contractual obligation to do so.

Obviously, laws which only allow access in this contractual situation are of little use to the majority of patients in this country who are treated under the National Health Service and hence have no such contractual right.

Therefore it would appear that Parliament intended to make provision for an individual, not intending litigation, to gain access to, and have corrected if necessary, his own medical records so that if, for example, a notational error or medical misjudgment became part of a patient's medical records he could, firstly, become aware of it and, secondly, have it corrected.

However, one of the very cornerstones of medical ethics is that of the doctor/patient confidentiality and one which must surely have had a significant effect upon the drafting of this Act, upon the attempt to find a balance between a right of access and the expectation of confidentiality.

In view of this latter expectation it must surely then be considered whether Mrs Fitzherbert, had she been alive, would have consented to a waiver of her rights of confidentiality under such circumstances. The answer to this question would undoubtedly be in the negative and therefore whilst not expressly stated as a condition under s. 1(1)(e) it must surely be implied that ' . . . a claim arising out of the patient's death' is conditional upon whether it is likely that the patient would have consented to such a course of action had she been alive to do so, in order not to entirely undermine the patient's right to confidentiality which every patient sees as a fundamental right within their relationship with their doctor.

In conclusion, therefore, it is contended that, for any or all of the above reasons, the court should uphold Glanvil's appeal against the decision of Forceps J thereby denying Bracton access to the late Mrs Fitzherbert's records.

Length: 1935 words

Index